Albert Legault

OIL
GAS
and other energies

A PRIMER

Translation by :
Barbara Chunn
Betsy McFarlane

2008

Éditions TECHNIP, 25 rue Ginoux, 75737 PARIS Cedex 15, FRANCE

FROM THE SAME PUBLISHER

• Oil and Gas Exploration and Production
  Reserves, costs, contracts
  CENTRE FOR ECONOMICS AND MANAGEMENT (IFP-SCHOOL)

• Petroleum Economics
  J. MASSERON

• Refinery Operation and Management
  Vol.5 Petroleum Refining
  J.P. FAVENNEC

• Maritime and Pipeline Transportation of Oil and Gas
  Problems and Outlook
  A. POIRIER, G. ZACCOUR

• Manual of Process Economic Evaluation
  A. CHAUVEL, G. FOURNIER, C. RAIMBAULT

This book is a translation by Mrs Barbara Chunn and Betsy McFarlane of « Pétrole, gaz et les autres énergies – Le petit traité », Albert Legault, © 2007, Éditions Technip, Paris.

© Éditions Technip, Paris, 2008
ISBN : 978-2-7108-0905-0

Preface

In early 1999, the price of a barrel of oil was below $10 and OPEC faced serious financial difficulties. Meanwhile, buoyed by the success of the new economy, North Americans and Europeans continued to drive large gas-guzzling automobiles. The Western world showed little concern about the threat of global warming and the possibility of oil shortages.

This portrayal of the late 1990s stands in stark contrast to the situation existing in 2007, when Albert Legault produced this book, which is a veritable compendium of knowledge on global energy issues. In the spring of 2007, the price of a barrel of oil was fluctuating between $60 and $70, and world markets were anxiously awaiting the hurricane season in the Gulf of Mexico. At the G8 Summit in Germany, world leaders spoke out for the first time about the impacts of global warming, although George Bush, the President of the United States, continued to express opposition to any kind of binding emission targets. Large energy companies flush with oil revenues sought opportunities to diversify, triggering bidding wars for oil companies and uranium processing plants. In the United States, the race to produce ethanol pushed corn prices to unprecedented levels. And several geopolitical events sent shock waves through the energy market: the Russian Kremlin consolidated its control over oil and natural gas supplies when state-run Gazprom acquired a stake in its bankrupt rival Yukos; Venezuela's President, Hugo Chavez, nationalized the oil companies of the Orinoco basin. China, with its desperate need to secure energy supplies, has continued to acquire oil interests in Sudan, seeming to lend credence to the current government and its involvement in the civil war in the Darfur region. Meanwhile, gas prices at the pump continue to rise in the United States and Europe.

It is definitely time to take stock of the global energy situation and not just from an economic standpoint. That is precisely what Albert Legault has achieved with this new book. For readers who know little about geomorphology and geology, this book provides a valuable overview of the field extending well beyond the usual topics related to fossil fuels. It also delves into climate change issues and covers renewable energies. With respect to oil and gas, various scenarios are examined that help to shed light on the new strategies that Russia, China and the United States are pursuing in the energy market.

Some theorists have been too quick to call the 20th century the end of the oil era. The third oil shock (2004?) showed that although black gold has lost some of its destructive influence on the world economy, oil continues to inspire ambition and inflame passions, playing a central role in conflicts.

While most of the energy-related topics of concern in the 21st century are discussed in this book, one specific Issue deserves greater emphasis: the impact that oil and gas have on the producing countries themselves. This phenomenon, called *Dutch Disease* because of the economic problems experienced by the Netherlands following the discovery of natural gas in the North Sea, can be characterized more broadly as the evils of petroleum.

Many of the hopes born in the 1970s have been cruelly dashed, and problems of corruption and poverty have plagued areas of the world ranging from Nigeria to Algeria and Venezuela to the Persian Gulf.

In today's world, skyrocketing oil prices still have the ability to bolster the most backwards dictatorships and the least enlightened theocracies as well as to foster the renaissance of totalitarian regimes. With his expert knowledge of world conflicts, Albert Legault is well aware that the rich resources beneath the subsurface can drive industrial revolutions, but also spur human folly. May this book help readers gain a better understanding of the forces at play.

Philippe Chalmin
Professor at the Université Paris-Dauphine
President of Cyclope

Table of Contents

Chapter 8

Chapter 9

Chapter 10

Note to Readers

Unless otherwise specified, all the figures in this book are in U.S. dollars. Conversion tables of commonly used units are provided to help readers go between the International System of Units, administered by the Bureau international des poids et mesures (BIPM), and the Imperial System. All the statistics are up-to-date as of July 2007.

Acknowledgments

I wish to express my heartfelt thanks to the Canada Research Chairs Secretariat for awarding me a Canada Research Chair in International Relations (CRCIR), which has given me the opportunity to devote all my efforts to research. I am deeply grateful to UQAM (Université du Québec à Montréal), and particularly to Jacques Lévesque, former Dean of the Faculty of Political Science and Law, as well as to Jean-Pierre Beaud and Jean-Guy Prévost, who have successively headed up the Department of Political Science at UQAM. Without their support, I could not have written this book. The author is also grateful and indebted to Norman J. Hyne, whose book Nontechnical Guide to Petroleum, Exploration, Drilling, and Production was extremely helpful in drafting parts of Chapters 1, 2 and 5.

My thanks also go to Célia DeLalandre, who helped me research and write Chapter 9, which deals with liquefied natural gas (LNG). And to Marilou Grégoire-Blais who carefully reviewed every part of the manuscript. Minor updates have been incorporated into the English edition, published after the original French version of the book. While every effort has been made to ensure the accuracy of the information in this book, the author accepts responsibility for any errors.

Unit Conversions and Abbreviations

Common Units for Oil and Natural Gas

Oil		Natural Gas	
Unit		Unit	
		cf or cu. ft.	cubic feet
Bbl	barrel	m³	cubic metre
b/d	barrels per day	Bcf	billion cubic feet
Mb/d	thousand barrels per day	Bcm	billion cubic metres
m³	cubic metre	Tcf	trillion cubic feet
MMbbl	million barrels	Tcm	trillion cubic metres
MMb/d	million barrels per day	Bcf/d	billion per cubic feet per day

Prefixes, Equivalents and Conversions

Prefix		Equivalent	Common Conversions		
			From	To	Multiply By
k	(kilo)	10^3	(m) metres	feet	3.048
M	(mega)	10^6	(km) kilometres	miles	0.621
G	(giga)	10^9	(m³) cubic metres	barrels (oil or LNG)	6.292
T	(tera)	10^{12}	(m³) cubic metres	cubic feet of natural gas	35.301

Prefix		Equivalent	Common Conversions		
			From	To	Multiply By
P	(peta)	10^{15}	(L) litres	US gallons	0.265
E	(exa)	10^{18}	(L) litres	Imperial gallons	0.220
Electricity			(bbl) barrels	US gallons	42.0
gigawatt hour (GWh)		10^6 kWh	(bbl) barrels	Imperial gallons	34.972
kilowatt hour (kWh)		10^3 Wh	(t) metric tonne	(lb) pounds	2204.6
gigawatt hour (MWh)		10^6 Wh	kilometres/litre	miles/gallon	2.825
Energy			Gigajoules (GJ)	million British thermal units (BTU)	0.95
gigajoule (GJ)	10^9 joules	0.95 million BTU 0.165 barrels of oil 0.28 megawatt hours of electricity	(m) metres	feet	3.048

Source: National Energy Board (Canada),
at http://www.neb.gc.ca/Statistics/EnergyConversions_e.htm

Main Chemical Symbols for Greenhouse Gases (GHG)	
CH_4 methane	CF_4 carbon tetrafluoride
C_2H_6 ethane	HFC hydrofluorocarbon
C_3H_8 propane	H_2S hydrogen sulphide
C_4H_{10} butane	N_2O nitrous oxide
$CaCO_3$ calcium carbonate	NO_x nitrogen oxide
Greenhouse gas (GHG)	O_3 ozone (troposphere)
CO_2 carbon dioxide	PFC perfluourocarbon
CFC chlorofluorocarbon	SF_6 sulphur hexafluoride
HCFC hydrochlorofluorocarbon	SO_2 sulphur dioxide

Abbreviations and Acronyms

AAPG	American Association of Petroleum Geologists
AAU	Assigned Amount Units
ADB	Asian Development Bank
ADEME	Agence de l'environnement et de la maîtrise de l'énergie (France)
ADNOC	Abu Dhabi National Oil Company
AEIETS	Association européenne de l'industrie électrique thermosolaire
AFP	Agence France Presse
APERC	Asia Pacific Energy Research Centre
BBOE	Barrel of oil equivalent (also abbreviated as BOE)
BGMR	Bureau of Geological and Mining Research (U.S.)
BRGM	Bureau de recherches géologiques et minières (France)
BTU	British thermal unit (also abbreviated as Btu)
CDM	Clean Development Mechanism
CDMO	Centre de Droit Maritime et Océanique (France)
CEA	Commissariat à l'Énergie Atomique (France)
CEC	California Energy Commission
CCEE	Countries of Central and Eastern Europe
CEE	Center for Energy Economics
CERU	Certified Emission Reduction Units (see ERU)
CIS	Commonwealth of Independent States
CMOL	Centre for Maritime and Oceanic Law
COP	Conference of the Parties
CRS	Congressional Research Service
DOE	Department of Energy (U.S.)
EDC	Export Development Canada
EERE	Energy Efficiency and Renewable Energy (U.S.)
EIA	Energy Information Administration (U.S.)
EITI	Extractive Industries Transparency Initiative
EPA	Environmental Protection Agency (U.S.)
EPAC	Energy Policy Act (U.S.)

EPAC	Petroleum Industry Research Associates
EPICA	European Project for Ice Coring in Antarctica
EPRI	Electric Power Research Institute (U.S.)
EREC	European Renewable Energy Council
ERU	Emission Reduction Units (see CERU)
ESTIF	European Solar Thermal Industry Forum
ET	Emissions Trading
ETS	Emissions Trading Scheme
EUDO	European Union Data Office (see Eurostat)
EUROSTAT	Statistical Office of the European Communities
FDI	Foreign Direct Investment
FERC	Federal Energy Regulatory Commission (U.S.)
GtC	Gigatonne of carbon
GTR	Gross Registered Tonnage
GWEC	Global Wind Energy Council
HHV	Higher heating value
IAEA	International Atomic Energy Agency (Vienna)
IAEE	International Association for Energy Economics
IAGS	Institute for the Analysis of Global Security
IEA	International Energy Agency (Paris)
IEEJ	Institute of Energy Economics, Japan
IEFS	International Energy Forum Secretariat
IEPF	Institut de l'énergie et de l'environnement de la Francophonie
IETA	International Emissions Trading Association
IFHVP	Institut Français des Huiles Végétales Pures (France)
IFP	Institut français du pétrole (France)
IFREMER	Institut Français de Recherche pour l'Exploitation de la Mer
IGA	International Geothermal Association
IGCC	Integrated Gasification Coal Combined Cycle
IHHI	Ishikawajima-Harima Heavy Industries
IMF	International Monetary Fund
IMO	International Maritime Organization
INOGATE	Interstate Oil and Gas Transport to Europe
IOC	International Oil Companies
IPCC	International Panel on Climate Change
IQPC	International Quality and Productivity Center (U.S.)
ISPS	International Ship and Port Facility Security Code
ITL	International Transaction Log (see JTI)
IUPA	International Union of Pure and Applied Chemistry
JBIC	Japan Bank for International Cooperation
JEC	Joint Economic Committee

JODI	Joint Oil Data Initiative
JI	Joint Implementation
LAEO	Latin American Energy Organization
LEGG	Laboratory of World Production and Globalization Economics
LHV	Lower heating value
MCL	Marine Current Turbines Ltd
MENA	Middle East and North Africa
MICEX	Moscow Interbank Currency Exchange
MMS	Mineral Management Service (U.S.)
NASA	National Aeronautics and Space Administration
NBP	National Balancing Point (U.K.)
NEB	National Energy Board (Canada)
NEMS	National Energy Modeling System (U.S.)
NGO	Non-governmental organization
NGX	Natural Gas Exchange (Canada)
NOC	National oil company
NRC	Natural Resources Canada
NRTEE	National Round Table on the Environment and the Economy (Canada)
NREL	National Renewable Energy Laboratory
NYMEX	New York Mercantile Exchange
ODAC	Oil Depletion Analysis Center
ODS	Ozone-depleting substance
OECD	Organisation for Economic Co-operation and Development
OEE	Office of Energy Efficiency (Canada)
OGEL	Oil, Gas & Energy Law Intelligence (London)
OPEC	Organization of the Petroleum Exporting Countries
ORNL	Oak Ridge National Laboratory
OSC	Ocean Shipping Consultants
PEL	Petroleum Economics Limited
PEMEX	Petroleos Mexicano
PIA	Petroleum Industry Research Associates
PONARS	Program on New Approaches to Russian Security
ppb	parts per billion
ppm	parts per million
REN21	Renewable Energy Policy Network for the 21st Century
RGGI	Regional Greenhouse Gas Initiative (U.S.)
RFE	Russian Far East
RTS	Russian Trade System
SCO	Shanghai Cooperation Organisation
SEC	Securities and Exchange Commission (U.S.)
SOLAS	International Convention for the Safety of Life at Sea

SRV	Shuttle and regasification vessel
STL	System turret loading
TCD	Trinity College, Dublin University
TCE	Tonne of coal equivalent
TOE	Tonne of oil equivalent
TNC	Transnational companies
UFIP	Union Française des industries pétrolières (France)
UKOOA	United Kingdom Offshore Operators Association
UNCTAD	United Nations Conference on Trade and Development
UNDP	United Nations Development Programme
UNEP	United Nations Environment Programme
UNFCCC	United Nations Framework Convention on Climate Change
UNSD	United Nations Statistics Division
UQAM	Université du Québec à Montréal
USGS	United States Geological Survey
WB	World Bank
WEC	World Energy Council
WLNGIG	World LNG Importers Group
WMO	World Meteorological Organization
WTO	World Trade Organization

Oil and Gas Pipelines

BPS	Baltic Pipeline System
BTC	Baku–Tbilisi–Ceyhan pipeline
CPC	Caspian Pipeline Consortium
ESPO	East Siberia/Pacific Ocean pipeline
IPI	Iran–Pakistan–India (pipeline)
NEG	see NEGP
NEGP	North European Gas Pipeline (or NEG)
SCP	South Caspian Pipeline
SEEGR	South-East European Gas Ring
SEEL	South East European Line (pipeline)
SOOP	East Siberia/Pacific Ocean (pipeline)
TEN	TransEuropean Network

Principal Publications

AEO	Annual Energy Outlook (Washington)
ASB	Annual Statistical Bulletin (OPEC)
BP	BP Statistical Review of World Energy (London)
IEO	International Energy Outlook (Washington)
IFP	Panorama (annual publication of the IFP)

IPE	International Petroleum Encyclopedia
O&GJ	Oil and Gas Journal (U.S.)
PIW	Petroleum Intelligence Weekly
WEO	World Energy Outlook (IEA/OECD)
WIR	World Investment Report (UNCTAD)

Principal Petroleum Companies

BP	British Petroleum
CNOOC	China National Offshore Oil Corporation
CNPC	China National Petroleum Corporation
COP	ConoccoPhilips
CNQ	Canadian Natural Resources Ltd
CFP	Compagnie française des pétroles (now called Total)
CVX	Chevron Texaco
ECA	EnCana (Canada)
LUK	Lukoil (a vertically integrated Russian oil company)
ONGC	Oil and Natural Gas Corporation (India)
PEMEX	Petroleos Mexicanos
Petrobras	Petróleo Brasileiro S.A.
PTR	PetroChina
RAO	Rosneft Oil Corporation
RDS	Royal Dutch Shell
SINOPEC	China Petroleum & Chemical Corporation
XOM	ExxonMobil Corporation

1

The Extraordinary History of the Earth

The earth is the only planet in the solar system with an atmosphere that can sustain life, thanks to its unique combination of constituents –nitrogen, oxygen, carbon dioxide and water vapour. It is also the only planet that harbours an incredibly rich diversity of life forms.

Several times during the earth's history, all life on the planet has come close to being extinguished.[1] About 65 million years (Ma) ago, a comet or a meteorite struck the planet full force, at a speed of 160,000 km/h. The cataclysm triggered by this event is reflected in the abnormally high levels of iridium-121 (Ir^{121}) that have been identified

---

[1] Cataclysmic events occurred 440, 365, 250, 200 and 65 million years ago. "The fourth great extinction, when three quarters of all life forms disappeared, is probably contemporary with the Manicouagan crater in northern Canada. The impact, which occurred 200 million years ago, created a circular depression 70 km across and triggered a global firestorm followed by an impact winter caused by the dust released into the atmosphere." See *Pour la Science*, November 2004, p. 23. "During the first cataclysmic event at the end of the Ordovician, or 440 million years ago, 60% of plant and animal species became extinct, including 85% of marine species. The second event occurred at the end of the Devonian (365 million years ago), with effects stretching over seven million years, and saw the extinction of 60% of the planet's species. The event that followed was the most devastating, with 90% of marine species disappearing in just one million years as well as two thirds of reptile and amphibian families and 30% of insect orders. This event occurred during the transition between the Permian and the Triassic (250 million years ago), in a degraded environment characterized by extremely low sea levels, huge volcanic eruptions, particularly in what is now South China, and very low levels of atmospheric oxygen. The result was a profound transformation of biodiversity. The fourth event eliminated 20% of all life forms, including reptiles, gastropods and bivalves." See "Extinction et apparition des espèces" at http://ase.ouvaton.org/evolgenextinc.htm. According to a recent study, the greatest wave of extinctions probably occurred 250 million years ago after a meteor strike in Antarctica. The resulting crater, now hidden roughly 1.6 km under the Antarctic ice shelf, was about 483 km across. See "Un météore tombé en Antarctique a failli tuer toute vie", *Agence France-Presse*, June 3-4, 2006. Other hypotheses have been advanced to explain the end of the Permian 251 million years ago. According to Peter Ward, this was likely caused by a severe greenhouse effect and toxic gases rather than by an asteroid strike. See his very convincing study, "Impact from the Deep", *Scientific American*, October 2006, pp. 64-71.

1

in the thin clay stratum separating the Mesozoic (formerly called the Secondary) era from the Cenozoic (Tertiary) era all over the world. This rare radioactive element is found primarily in meteorites. The clay stratum is thickest in the Caribbean, near a small fishing village called Chicxulub, in Mexico's Yucatan Peninsula. The impact crater, measuring 208 km across, lies one thousand metres under the sea. Its age corresponds to the end of the Mesozoic era, which marks the sudden and complete extinction of the dinosaurs as well as 75% of all plant and animal species.[2]

From time to time in the earth's history, the continents have come together to form a single supercontinent (see "Continental Drift" below) and then broken apart again, most recently to form the smaller continents familiar to us under the names of Asia, Europe, America, Australia, Antarctica, and so on. Sometime in the future, all these continents will join together again.

Several times in the past, lithospheric plates bearing slices of oceanic crust and continents have faced off in epic combats, with several possible outcomes: slabs of seafloor are thrust downwards into the earth's mantle; continents collide, causing their basement rocks to be thrust upwards and overturned; or the two plates simply slide slowly past each other. If we could turn back geological time like we can turn back our clocks, the history of humanity would likely be very different from how we know it today. As René Thom, the originator of catastrophe theory, said, history is made up of discontinuities, multiple singularities, or even unforeseeable catastrophes. Catastrophe theory seeks to describe how an abrupt change can arise spontaneously from gradually changing circumstances.

Many researchers agree that the cut-off between the Tertiary and the Quaternary occurred at the Pleistocene–Pliocene boundary, or roughly 2.5 million years ago according to the 1991 Beijing Congress of the International Union for Quaternary Research (INQUA). The advent of the Quaternary corresponds to what some studies describe as the beginning of the "anthropogenic era." By convention, the International Commission on Stratigraphy has set the beginning of the Quaternary at 1.64 Ma.[3]

Going Back in Time

Travelling back in time is now possible thanks to radiometric dating, combined with advances in seismology, geology, satellite surveys, paleontology, petrology,

[2]   See Norman J. Hyne, *Nontechnical Guide to Petroleum Geology, Exploration, Drilling, and Production* (second edition), Tulsa, Oklahoma, PennWell Corporation, 2001, p. 47. Hereafter cited as Hyne.

[3]   See the lengthy discussion under "Vivons-nous à l'ère tertiaire ?" at www.geog.umontreal.ca/ donnees/geo3132/Texte%20DANS%20QUELLE%20ERE%20.doc.

biostratigraphy and other fields. The geologic time scale shown in Figure 1[4] is divided into eras and periods, but excludes the shortest intervals, epochs or ages, which are numerous and often continent-specific, and the longest intervals, eons.

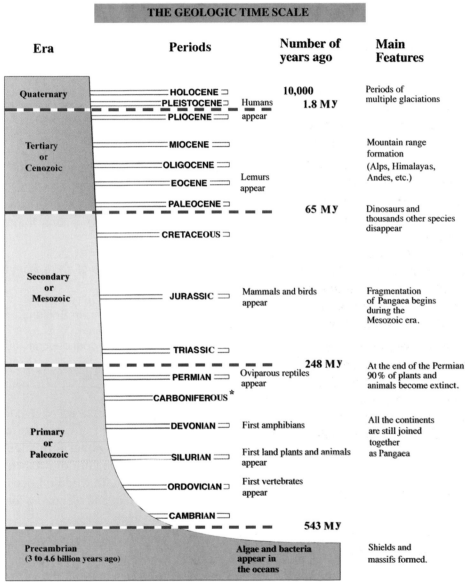

Figure 1: The geologic time scale

---

[4]   This is a vertical, non-linear scale.

Table 1: Etymology of the divisions of geologic time

Eons From the Greek *aion*, eternity	Hadean From Hades, God of the underworld	Archean From the Greek *archeos*, ancient	Proterozoic From the Greek *proteros*, first, and *zoon*, life or animal	Phanerozoic From the Greek *phaneros*, visible or apparent, and *zoon*, life or animal
	4.6 – 3.96 billion years ago	3.9 – 2.5 billion years ago	From 2.5 billion years to about 540 million years ago	Encompasses the Paleozoic, Mesozoic and Cenozoic eras (which brings us to the present)

Eras
Paleozoic (from *paleo*, ancient), **Mesozoic** (from *mesos*, middle or median) and **Cenozoic** (from *koinos*, common) are of Greek origin.

Periods
Periods often are named for the region in which the formations were first described or based on some distinguishing characteristic. According to the Musée national français d'histoire naturelle (www.mnhn.fr/mnhn/geo/periodespal.html):

Cambrian (540 – 500 Ma) comes from the Latin *Cambria*, the name of a Pre-Roman tribe from Wales
Ordovician (500 – 435 Ma) comes from *Ordovices*, a Pre-Roman Celtic tribe
Silurian (435 – 408 Ma) comes from *Silures*, a Pre-Roman people from England
Devonian (408 – 355 Ma) comes from the English region Devonshire
Carboniferous (355 – 295 Ma) comes from the name of the major coal deposits of Central Europe
Permian (295 – 250 Ma) comes from Perm, the city and region in Russia

Since the main focus of this book is oil and gas, it is important to ask where these resources come from and how they are formed, questions that are covered in greater detail in Chapter 2. For example, if oil is discovered in Devonian formations in Algeria, in Upper Jurassic to Late Pleistocene formations in the Gulf of Mexico,[5] in Proterozoic or Lower Paleozoic formations in eastern Siberia, in Middle Eocene or Lower Paleocene formations in the Black Sea, or in Devonian and Cenozoic formations in Canada, does this mean that the oil or gas has an age?

Although the question is valid, the initial hypotheses are false. This is because the seafloor and the earth's crust have undergone innumerable transformations over the ages, as deformational and intrusive events have occurred, resulting in the intrusion,

---

[5] *Atlas of Gulf of Mexico Gas and Oil Sands*, OCS Report, MMS (Minerals Management Service) 2001-086, U.S. Department of the Interior, New Orleans, September 2001, available at www.mms.gov/itd/abstracts/2001-086a.pdf.

displacement or alteration of existing geological strata. Although a great deal of the earth's oil was formed during the Devonian and the Upper Jurassic (see Figure 9, Chapter 2), the age of the oil or gas does not necessarily correspond to the inferred age of the rock layers in which the resource is discovered.

Geological formations may be dated using absolute or relative dating methods. Absolute dating is based on the half-life of specific isotopes like uranium-238 (U^{238}), uranium-235 (U^{235}), rubidium-87 (Rb^{87}) and potassium-40 (K^{40}), which have half-lives ranging from one to several billion years.[6] Although carbon-14 dating is used widely in archaeology, it is not as useful in geology because its half-life, some 5,710 years, is too short. **Radiometric dating** is useful for igneous and metamorphic rocks[7] but much less so for sedimentary rocks. Although the age of the grains making up sedimentary rock can be accurately determined, those grains can come from a variety of pre-existing rocks and they therefore do not tell us when the sediment was formed or laid down. By contrast, the age of an igneous intrusion located within sedimentary strata can be estimated, as can the age of a lava flow. A lava flow overlying a sedimentary rock layer will always be older than the under-lying sedimentary rocks, just as an igneous intrusion will always be younger than the sedimentary rocks that it cuts.

Enormous progress has been made in relative dating –which is based on the order in which a series of events occurred– thanks to the insights of paleontologists, who have succeeded in working out the ages of most known fossils. Fossils are the remains or traces of living beings that have been preserved in rocks. Although a major drilling operation will likely damage most of the fossils in the drilled mate-rial, it will still be possible to view the microfossils under a microscope. Foraminifera, radiolaria, coccoliths and diatoms are good indicators of the age of drilled sedimentary layers[8] and, in general, fossils are excellent indicators of evolution over geologic time.

During its first billion years, our planet was probably just an immense incandes-cent ball.[9] No life forms have been found from the early Precambrian. About 3.5 billion years ago, the first bacteria appeared, followed a little later by algae in the oceans. The explosion of life on earth did not occur until the Paleozoic era. The

---

[6] For example, uranium-238 decays into lead-206 and potassium-40, into argon. Each of these atoms has a specific half-life that provides information about the absolute age of the observed natural decay. Rubidium has a very long half-life: 4.7×10^{10} years.

[7] These are the two most common types of rocks; sedimentary rocks are the third type.

[8] Hyne, *op. cit.,* p. 43.

[9] Recent studies seem to indicate that the earth's crust formed more quickly than previously thought, perhaps only a few dozen million years after the planet's birth. See *Science & Vie*, January 2006, p. 30. Ancient rocks have been found in Australia that date back 4.2-4.4 billion years. In addition, complex bacterial ecosystems probably existed 3.4 billion years ago. See *Le Monde*, June 9, 2006.

first vertebrates arrived on the scene during the Ordovician; tetrapods (limbed fishes), during the Devonian; and mammals, dinosaurs and birds (including the winged dinosaur *Archaeopteryx*), during the Triassic and the Jurassic. Although mammals diversified greatly during the Eocene, humans did not emerge until 1.8 to 2 million years ago. By compressing geologic time into a single year, we get the following:

> The oldest rocks on earth date from mid-March. The first organisms appeared in the oceans in May. Land plants and animals emerged in late November and the swamps that eventually formed large coal deposits were only around for four days in early December. Dinosaurs were dominant in mid-December but disappeared on December 26 (the same day that the Rocky Mountains in the U.S. began to be pushed upwards). Animals similar to humans appeared on New Year's Eve, the night of December 31. The last ice sheets in North America and northern Europe began to retreat one minute and 15 seconds before midnight the same day. Rome dominated Europe for 5 seconds from 23:59:45 to 23:59:50. Christopher Columbus discovered America 3 seconds before midnight and the science of geology was born a second before midnight as the year ended.[10]

We will revisit the major cataclysmic events marking the earth's history in a later chapter on climate change, glaciation and deglaciation episodes and greenhouse gas (GHG) emissions caused by the burning of fossil fuels.

Inside the Earth

The earth's interior is made up of three layers –the core, the mantle and the crust– representing roughly 17%, 81% and less than 2% of the planet's volume respectively. Our planet is often compared to an egg, with the shell representing the crust; the egg white, the mantle; and the yolk, the core.

The Core

The core is divided into an inner core and an outer core. The inner core is solid and consists mainly of iron and nickel, hence the term "nife" (Ni/Fe) formerly used to designate it. The inner core floats within a liquid outer core composed of molten iron, in which powerful convection movements occur. Such movements, coupled with the earth's rotation on its axis, create a dynamo effect, producing the earth's magnetic field.

---

[10]   See "Temps géologique", Cours de géologie 019, chapitre 13, Université Libre de Bruxelles.

No direct observations have ever been made of the core. The most widely accepted hypothesis is that the inner core is solid, which seems to be confirmed by seismic surveys. The inner core is subject to enormous pressures, 3.6 million times as great as the pressures on the planet's surface, and it may be as hot as the surface of the Sun, with temperatures of 5,500°C or even 6,000°C. Other hypotheses have been advanced to explain the exact nature of the core.[11] For example, according to some geologists, rather than being a ball of iron in a sea of molten metal, the inner core is a "black hole" in which heavy elements like iron are compressed under the enormous pressures found deep inside the earth.

The Mantle

The mantle is made up of two distinct parts: the lower mantle (formerly called the mesosphere) and the upper mantle, which in turn can be divided into two components, the lithosphere (literally "rocky sphere") and the asthenosphere (from the Greek *asthenes*, or weak). The lithosphere is more solid but less dense than the asthenosphere, which is more fluid or ductile. This is an important characteristic since major geological events are triggered in part by movements in the asthenosphere, which sometimes penetrates the lithosphere. The mantle is defined by two discontinuities, or boundaries between layers that are characterized by a change in density.[12]

As in the case of the core, the internal structure of the mantle has never been directly studied. Instead, scientific conclusions about the mantle have been reached strictly through the study of seismic waves. Based on the refraction times for primary (P) waves and secondary (S) waves (also called pressure and shear waves, respectively), which differ according to the nature and composition of the medium through which they travel, scientists can obtain a kind of ultrasound of the earth bit by bit.

The Crust

The crust is the outermost part of the earth, extending from the surface (0 km) to a depth of roughly 100 km. Zero depth corresponds to the mid-ocean ridges, where new crust is being created. Continental crust is thicker than oceanic crust, because the seabed is underlain by a stratum of basalt, which is on average only eight km

---

[11] Some have described the inner core as a "georeactor", a natural, 8-km-diametre reactor that creates a chain of fission reactions, while others believe it is made up of an alloy of iron and potassium-40 (K^{40}). A small percentage of potassium-40 would be enough to explain the sizeable amount of heat given off by the earth. See Kheira Bettayeb, Isabelle Cuchet, Fabienne Lemarchand and Xavier Müller, "Mais que cache le Centre de la Terre ?" *Science & Vie*, No. 1042, July 2004, pp. 36-43.

[12] The Mohorovicic discontinuity, named after the seismologist Andrieja Mohorovicic (1857-1936) who discovered it in 1909, is the boundary between the crust and the upper mantle. A few years later, in 1914, another seismologist, Beno Gutenberg (1889-1960), discovered the discontinuity between the lower mantle and the outer core. There is a third discontinuity, between the outer and inner core, called the Lehman discontinuity after its discoverer Inge Lehman.

(five miles) thick. The continents, on the other hand, sit on a basement of granite that is 27 km (17 miles) thick on average, which in turn overlies a layer of basalt.[13] On average, oceanic crust ranges in thickness from 5 km to 15 km and continental crust, from 30 km to 65 km.

The following table summarizes the earth's main layers, which can be differentiated by their density as well as their solid, liquid or plastic state. Readers should note two things: density increases with depth (from the crust to the inner core) and the state of the successive layers varies depending on the layers overlying them. These variations are particularly important in the case of the lithosphere and the asthenosphere, since the asthenosphere harbours strong convection currents (**convection** is the transfer of heat through the movement of matter), which allow the lithosphere to slide on top of it. We are now witnessing a new set of dynamics: plate tectonics.

Table 2: The structure of the earth

Layer	Subdivisions	Thickness	Density of Rock
Crust	**Continental crust** Granite in composition	30 – 65 km	2.7 – 3 g/cm³
	Oceanic crust Basalt in composition	5 – 15 km	3.2 g/cm³
Mantle	**Lithosphere** Solid, rigid	100 km under the oceans and < 300 km under the continents	3.3 g/cm³
	Asthenosphere More plastic portion Semi-fluid	From 100 – 200 km to 700 km	3 – 4.5 g/cm³
	Lower mantle (mesosphere) Solid, deformable	2,100 – 2,885 km	4.5 – 6 g/cm³
Core	**Outer core** Liquid	2,885 – 5,155 km (2,270 km)	10 g/cm³
	Inner core (Iron and nickel) Solid	5,155 – 6,371 km (1,216 km)	13 g/cm³

Source: From André Bourque, *Planète Terre*, Web site and other sources

---

13 Norman J. Hyne, *op. cit.*, p. 136.

Continental Drift

The publication of *Die Entstehung der Kontinente und Ozeane*[14] in 1912 by the physicist and meteorologist Alfred Wegener was met by a hue and cry in the scientific community. According to Wegener's hypothesis, all of the continents were once assembled together in a supercontinent, Pangaea (from the Greek for "all lands"), that began to break apart some 200 million years ago (or perhaps even in the late Permian), giving rise to two continents: Laurasia in the north and Gondwanaland in the south. These two landmasses subsequently split into smaller and smaller pieces to form the continents as we know them today. Many scientists called Wegener's hypothesis into question, because at the time it offered no explanation of how the continents could plough through the seafloor and move to the positions they occupy today.

Today there is a great deal of evidence supporting Wegener's hypotheses. We will discuss just a small part of it. The most obvious piece of evidence is the great similarity in the indentations and fit of the coasts of South America and Africa: their identical outlines suggest that the two continents once were joined. Similarities have also been observed in the rock formations and geological structures on the west coast of Africa and the east coast of South America. It is difficult to see this simply as the result of random chance. There are other obvious indications, such as the presence of similar fossils of Paleozoic plants and animals on the coasts of both continents. It is highly improbable that animals could swim or that plants could be transported by the wind over such great distances. Another piece of evidence relates to the fact that many parts of Gondwanaland were covered by an ice sheet about 250 million years ago, particularly portions of South Africa, India and Australia (see Figure 3).

In addition, North America and Eurasia were much closer to the paleoequator than they are today. Furthermore, some continents formerly covered by a thick ice sheet have drifted to more clement skies—India, for example, wandered extensively before colliding with the Tibetan Plateau.

To demonstrate his continental drift theory, Wegener only had the 300 Ma or so that he could visualize or imagine at the time. Were there, in fact, earlier Pangaeas? Will the world move towards "a new continent of all lands" in the future? According to the paleogeographer Christopher R. Scotese, a long-standing scientific advisor to *National Geographic*, over 1,000 Ma ago there was likely a supercontinent, called Rodinia,[15] which was "centered over the Equator and

---

[14] *The Origin of Continents and Oceans.* The expression "continental drift" comes from Wegener's "shifting of the continents", in German, *Die Verschiebung der Kontinente.*

[15] From the Russian word for motherland.

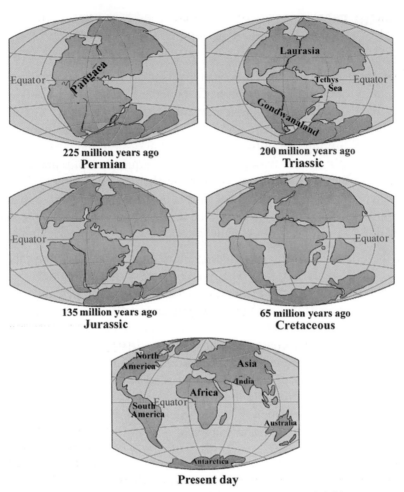

225 million years ago
Permian

200 million years ago
Triassic

135 million years ago
Jurassic

65 million years ago
Cretaceous

Present day

Figure 2: Wegener's theory of continental drift
Source: United States Geological Survey (USGS)

extended from latitudes 60°N to 60°S".[16] In addition, another supercontinent, Pannotia, is postulated to have formed in the late Precambrian, roughly 550 million years ago.[17] Relatively short-lived (65 million years), Pannotia gave birth to the continents Laurentia, Baltica (northern Europe), Siberia and Gondwana[18] (Africa,

---

[16] Centre national de la recherche scientifique, press release, March 17, 2004, "La Terre : boule de neige, avis de grand froid il y a 750 millions d'années", available at http://www.insu.cnrs.fr/web/article/art.php?art=674. Rodinia began to break up around 800 or 750 million years ago.

[17] W. D. Dalziel, the first to describe it, named this supercontinent in 1997.

[18] The term appears to come from the "Gondwana beds", geological formations in central India. The Austrian geologist Edward Suess popularized this term by giving the name Gondwanaland to a hypothetical continent made up of the present-day southern continents based on the shared geological features of their rock formations. See http://www.palaeos.com/Earth/Geography/Gondwana.htm.

southern Europe, India, Australia, South America and Antarctica). These four continents would go on to merge, forming the supercontinent Pangaea. We've now come full circle.

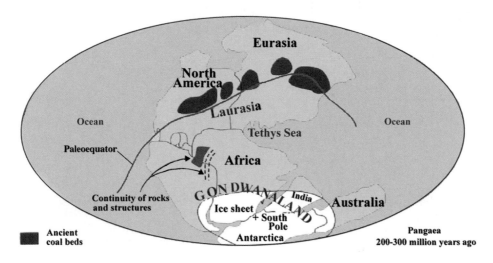

Figure 3: Wegener's ideas in 1912
Source: From Pinet et al., 1998

What does the future have in store for us? Some paleogeographers believe that a supercontinent cycle (Wilson cycle) occurs every 300-500 Ma, during which the continents merge into a supercontinent and then separate again.[19] Do we really want to think about the earth's distant future? Christopher R. Scotese has already done so and produced a map showing what the world might look like in 50 Ma.[20] According to Scotese, the African and Eurasian continents will join, resulting in the disappearance of the Mediterranean Sea and the creation of a major mountain chain; Australia will drift inexorably towards Southeast Asia as Baja California slides toward the Alaskan coast. The entire North American continent will turn slightly counterclockwise, while Eurasia moves clockwise, bringing Siberia closer to hotter, more tropical, climes.

---

[19] This cycle is said to take from 300 Ma to 500 Ma. Canadian geologist Tuzo Wilson was the first to define the overall process, hence the term "Wilson cycle." See http://www.ulg.ac.be/geolsed/geol_gen/geol_gen.htm#LE%20MOUVEMENT%20DES%20PLAQUES.

[20] Scotese has some stunning maps on his Web site and he even provides a rough sketch of the next Pangaea in 250 Ma.

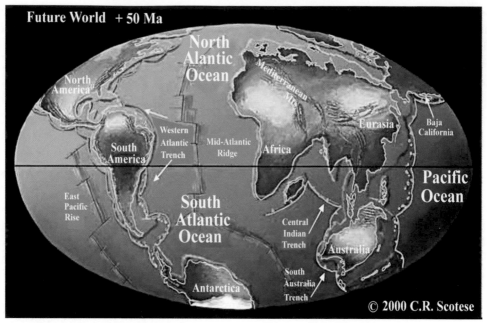

Figure 4: The earth as it might look in 50 Ma
Source: "Plate Tectonic Maps and Continental Drift Animations",
C. R. Scotese, PALEOMAP Project (www.scotese.com)

In short, our planet is subject to recurring major transformations but one element is still missing from the picture. How do continents and the ocean floor move?

Seafloor Spreading and Continental Drift

Many scientific discoveries have been made since the physicist and meteorologist Alfred Wegener came up with his continental drift theory. In fact, as Université de Laval geologist Pierre-André Bourque once commented, even if Wegener demonstrated fairly convincingly that all the continents were once assembled together, he was never able to explain how they had been drifting around for the last 200 Ma.[21] A new theory put forward in the 1960s would clarify and complete Wegener's hypotheses, which were essentially intuitive. This is the seafloor spreading theory, which quickly achieved prominence through the work of Harry Hammond Hess,[22] who postulated that the seafloor separates along rifts and that new seafloor forms there and spreads laterally. This would explain how Pangaea broke up into several continents and how they subsequently drifted apart. The theo-

---

[21] See his "Planète Terre" site (in French only), Université de Laval, Geology Department: www.ggl.ulaval.ca/personnel/bourque/intro.pt/planete_terre.html

[22] His ideas were first published in 1962 in a paper entitled "History of Ocean Basins".

ries of continental drift and seafloor spreading are thus reconciled based on a single explanation: continents drift, but so does the seafloor. In other words, all oceans and all continents float on a huge mass of viscous rock now known as the asthenosphere.

The theory can be summarized as follows. Powerful convection currents keep the interior of the earth in perpetual motion. Although these currents are not strong enough to pierce the earth's crust, they cause it to blister or bulge out and eventually open up, allowing molten material from the asthenosphere to flow onto either side. These flows spread at right angles from either side of the resulting ocean ridge. As the process continues, the seafloor spreads laterally, with the portions farthest away from the ridge being cooler than those closer to it. The oldest oceanic crust is displaced farther and farther away on either side of the mid-ocean ridge as new seafloor is created along the rift; the oldest portion of seafloor eventually disappears by plunging under another lithospheric plate (see part B of Figure 5). Every ocean has a ridge, the best-known being the Mid-Atlantic Ridge, which is 80,000 km long.[23] This is the only mid-ocean ridge that has two areas above sea level that are of great interest to scientists as well as tourists: Iceland and the Azores.

As Lavoisier once said: nothing is lost; nothing is created; everything is transformed. This principle also holds true for lithospheric plates. Oceanic crust is constantly being recycled, with new crust being created and old crust being destroyed simultaneously, a little like a conveyor belt. This explains why fossils older than 180 Ma[24] or sediments older than 150 Ma are rarely found in the seafloor, and yet the earth itself is several billion years old.

The two diagrams (A and B) at the bottom of Figure 5 summarize what has previously been discussed in this chapter. Readers should note, however, that the thickness of the asthenosphere is greater under oceanic crust than under continental crust (Part A of Figure 5). The central portion of the figure (C, D and E) shows what happens when two lithospheric plates converge, while the upper part (F) illustrates several phenomena related to the movement and interaction of lithospheric plates.

Convergent Plates

When two oceanic plates originating from different ridges collide along a convergent boundary (see C in Figure 5), the denser one is subducted, or thrust under the other one. The process of subduction results in the formation of a long, narrow depression called an ocean trench. The farther the plate is thrust downwards towards the earth's interior, the greater its temperature. Once the subducted plate becomes hot enough, melting occurs and the lightest molten rocks rise to the

---

[23] Hyne, *op. cit.,* p. 35. The ridge runs northward between Europe and North America and southward between South America and Africa, before meeting up with the East Pacific Rise.

[24] According to Hyne, *op. cit.,* p. 136. The oldest sediments in ocean basins date back to the Jurassic, or roughly 150 Ma.

surface, forming a chain of volcanoes next to the ocean trench. The chain of volcanoes produced on the seafloor by the two converging oceanic plates (for example, the Aleutian Islands) is called an **island arc.**

A **continental arc** (such as the Andes) is created when a continental plate and an oceanic plate collide (E in Figure 5). Here, too, it is always the oceanic plate that is subducted because it is less dense. Lastly, in the case of two converging continental plates (D in Figure 5), neither is subducted because both are composed of granite and are therefore too dense. Instead, the margins of both continents become compressed and multiple folding and faulting events occur, giving rise to mountains. The Himalayan Mountains, for example, are the result of a collision between the Indo-Australian and Eurasian plates, and the Alps and the Appalachians were formed in the same way. The intensity of the tectonic forces at work is illustrated by the composition of the summit of Mount Everest: it consists of marine limestone.[25] As J. Scoates said, "the rock that makes up the summit of the highest mountain on the earth's surface was formed under the ocean on the continental shelf in relatively shallow waters", well before the continental plates collided.

Two plates can also slide horizontally past each other at what is called a transform plate boundary. This phenomenon is shown in the middle of F in Figure 5 where there is a transform fault offsetting the oceanic ridge. This explains the different speeds at which the plates are moving relative to one another.

Divergent Boundaries and Hot Spots

Divergent boundaries exist solely at a mid-ocean ridge where plates are separating and oceanic crust is being created. The underlying mechanism was explained earlier and is shown in B in Figure 5, as well as in the middle of F.

Some volcanic chains do not seem to readily fit into the plate-tectonics model. The concept of hot spots was therefore introduced, postulating the existence of magma conduits fixed in the mantle that produce rising jets of molten material, creating stationary hot spots. Since the lithospheric plates carrying continents and the seafloor drift slowly but surely, a string of volcanoes forms as the plates move over these conduits. Such conduits are believed to be responsible for hot spots or mantle plumes. The Hawaiian-Emperor seamount chain in the Northwest Pacific and the Galapagos Islands are examples of volcanic chains created by hot spots. Hot spots are not linked to the creation of island arcs or mid-ocean ridges, but rather to intraplate volcanism. Recent findings confirm, however, that there are mobile hot spots, which really complicates things since a hot spot, when it stops being a fixed point, can no longer serve as a marker for tracking plate motions.[26]

---

[25] See "Tectonique des plaques", Cours de géologie 019, chapitre 10, Université Libre de Bruxelles.

[26] See "L'histoire de la Terre n'est pas celle que l'on imaginait", *Science & Vie*, November 2003, p. 11. Born off Kamchatka (Russia) 80 million years ago, the hot spot responsible for the Emperor seamount chain moved to its current location 45 million years ago.

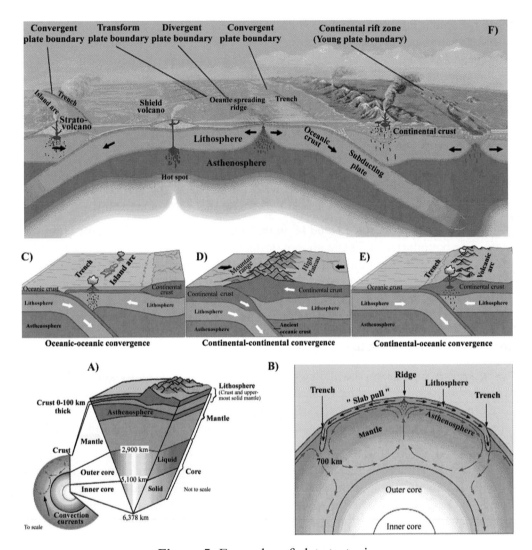

Figure 5: Examples of plate tectonics
Source: USGS, Smithsonian Institution and the U.S. Naval
Research Laboratory (F is by José F. Vigil)

Creation of a Rift Valley: Birth of a New Ocean?

Rifting involves a thinning of the earth's crust, resulting in a depression bounded on either side by faults. A rift can be used to describe an elongated depression in either continental or oceanic crust. Rifts are always accompanied by episodic volcanism. On land, rifts correspond to a fracture zone in the earth's crust, which, once it has collapsed, forms a deep valley. Part F of Figure 5 shows a rift being formed. A careful look at the illustration shows that the movements of the lithosphere are similar to those that occur during the formation of a mid-ocean ridge. A rift may therefore give birth to an ocean. For the past several million years, the Afar Depression has been rifting apart as part of a process that could lead to the creation of a new ocean owing to its location at the junction of the Ethiopian, Gulf of Aden and Red Sea rift systems.[27] In twenty or thirty thousand years, rifting similar to that occurring in the Red Sea region could occur in the Great Rift Valley, splitting Africa apart again.[28]

Plate Boundaries

Obviously, friction and tension are greatest along the plate boundaries. For example, the **Pacific Ring of Fire** is one of the areas in the world most prone to earthquakes and volcanic eruptions. But where do plates begin and end?

No matter where we are on land or on the sea, we are literally sitting on a moving plate. The boundaries of a plate are not defined by terrestrial or marine topography –for example, a chain of mountains is not generally a place where two plates meet. Instead the three types of plate boundaries (divergent, convergent and transform) are characterized by the seismic expression of the interaction between the plates. In other words, the motions of the plates relative to one another are determined by these processes. Plate boundaries are therefore defined by a rift (mid-ocean ridge), a subduction zone or a collision zone.

Figure 6 below shows the main tectonic plates that are currently known. The red arrows show primary instances of divergence and the blue arrows, examples of convergence; if all movements of convergence (colliding plates), divergence (spreading plates) and transform faulting were shown, the map would be almost impossible to read.

The North American Plate begins at the foot of the Mid-Atlantic Ridge and extends westward to the Eurasian Plate. The Juan de Fuca and Cocos plates are being subducted underneath the southwestern part of the North American Plate and, one day, will completely disappear. The Pacific Plate is moving in a northwesterly direction against the North American Plate, with a major convergence zone around the Aleutian Islands. Farther south, the collision of the same two plates has produced the famous San Andreas Fault and Mount St. Helens. Antarctica is a continent on its own, unlike the Arctic, which is part of the North American Plate. The Antarctic Plate is one of the largest plates in the world.

---

[27]　See http://www.infoscience.fr/breves/breves.php3?niv=1&Ref=1877

[28]　Hyne, *op. cit.*, p. 141. Unless it is the failed arm (aulocogen) of a three-branched rift (triple junction) formed from a crustal dome at the onset of continental rifting. We will come back to this later.

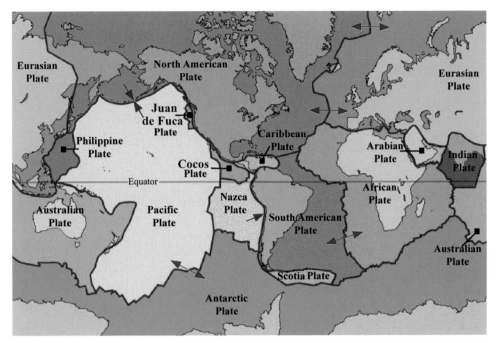

Figure 6: Main tectonic plates
Source: From USGS and Hyne, *op. cit.*

The rate at which the plates are moving is also variable. The North American Plate is drifting westward at a rate of 2.5 cm per year (or 25 km per million years), while the European continent is moving eastward at the same speed. The Nazca Plate is separating from the Pacific Plate at a speed of 16 cm annually, while the Cocos Plate is being subducted beneath the North American Plate at an average speed of 5 cm a year. According to Hyne, the plates are moving at rates of between 1 cm and 17 cm annually.[29]

In short, seafloor spreading is the result rather than the cause of continental drift.

---

[29] Hyne, *op. cit.,* p. 141.

2

The Formation of Oil and Gas

Just as humans go through a cycle of birth, growth and death, nature, too, is characterized by cycles. Natural cycles discussed here include the rock cycle, the carbon cycle, the cycle of sea-level changes and the cycles that affect the global climate.

The Three Main Classes of Rocks

There are three main classes of rocks: igneous rocks, metamorphic rocks and sedimentary rocks.

Igneous (from the Latin *ignis*, meaning fire or produced by the action of fire) rocks are formed through the cooling and solidification (recrystallization) of molten material from the asthenosphere: granite and basalt are prime examples. Metamorphic rocks, such as gneiss and marble, are rocks that have been transformed under the influence of high pressures and temperatures.[1] Sedimentary rocks, as their name implies, are produced from sediments deposited on land or on the bottom of a body of water, such as a lake, lagoon, delta, sea or ocean. Some precipitated salts can also form sediments (**evaporites**).

In varying proportions, sandstone, clay and limestone account for 99 percent of the sedimentary rocks in the earth's crust.[2] In spite of their prevalence, sedimentary rocks "represent only 1/20th of the total volume of the continental crust's upper layer, which is 16 km thick."[3] Nevertheless, it is sedimentary rocks that are of primary interest to us, since they are the source of oil and gas.

---

[1] Note that igneous rock can also undergo direct metamorphism, such as when oceanic basalts are entrained into a subduction zone.

[2] Norman J. Hyne, *Nontechnical Guide to Petroleum Geology, Exploration, Drilling, and Production*, (2nd edition), Tulsa, Oklahoma, PennWell Corporation, 2001, p. 33. Hereafter cited as Hyne.

[3] "Une introduction aux processus sédimentaires", Département de géologie, Université de Liège, Belgium, available online at http://www.ulg.ac.be/geolsed/processus/processus.htm.

Sediments can be classified on the basis of particle size, ranging from boulders through cobbles, pebbles, sand and silt to clay, which is characterized by microscopic particles (< 0.005 mm).[4] Particle size classification can be used to determine the depositional environment of sediments and therefore their origin (e.g., glacial, lacustrine, continental or marine). Figure 1, taken from J. Mirabaud's *Lexique de géologie*, uses a ternary diagram to illustrate the composition of typical sedimentary rock. The three apexes of the triangle correspond to sandy sediments (sandstone), calcareous sediments (limestone) and clay sediments (shale). Mudstones, which are related to shales, have a particle size smaller than 1/16 mm. Each side of the triangle therefore expresses a dual relationship. For example, a sediment can have a composition that is more calcareous than sandy, more sandy than clayey or more clayey than calcareous, or vice versa, if we reverse the relationships in a clockwise direction. Marl is a sedimentary rock made up of a mixture of limestone and clay. It can therefore be either a silt or a clay.[5]

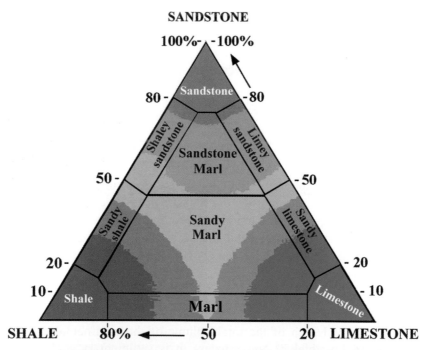

Figure 1: Composition of typical sedimentary rock
Source: Lexique de géologie by J. Mirabaud

---

4   See "Processus de sédimentation et de métamorphisme", Cour de géologie 019, chapitre 8, available online at http://homepage.ulb.ac.be/~jscoates/teach/GEOL019_chap8.html. Hereafter cited as GEOL019.

5   "Clay-based marls are 5-35% calcium carbonate; marls are 35-65% calcium carbonate; and limestone marls 65-95%. When heated, clay-based marl yields lime, marl produces hydraulic lime and limestone marl yields cement." See *Lexique de géologie, op. cit.*, under the entry for "marne".

These distinctions can help to provide a better understanding of the composition of the layers of sedimentary rock that are likely to be encountered when an oil well is drilled. Since, as sediments accumulate, the older underlying materials become buried deeper and deeper, a drill core cross-section should normally reveal the following vertical sequence: sandstones at the top, then shales and finally limestones at the bottom. During the sedimentation process, the heaviest particles settle first, while lighter particles take longer to be deposited.

The Rock Cycle

Rocks undergo a geological cycle, which is illustrated in the simplified diagram in Figure 2.

This cycle is dual in nature, consisting of mantle and terrestrial processes. In the mantle cycle, rocks at the earth's surface are transported toward its interior during the subduction of lithospheric plates. The resultant melting generates new flows of magma and, if crustal uplift occurs, igneous rocks will be formed. The terrestrial, or surface, cycle is based essentially on solar energy, which drives the major changes that occur in the atmosphere and the hydrosphere. Erosion, rain, wind, hurricanes and other natural processes can play a role in the transport and deposition of sediment. Sediments are minerals that have been deposited by water, wind or glaciers, whereas sedimentary rocks are formed from sediments at or near their site of deposition. The particles or debris constituting sediment are derived from igneous, metamorphic or sedimentary rocks. The accumulation of sediment is the result of transport rather than chemical alteration. Sediment is therefore mineralized material containing a small percentage of organic matter.

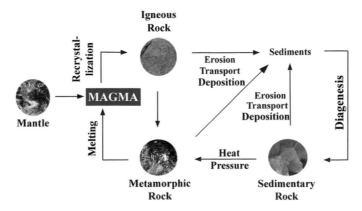

Figure 2: The rock cycle
Source: "Une introduction aux processus sédimentaires", *op. cit.*

There are roughly 600 sedimentary basins in the world; of the basins that have been developed, 40% are considered productive. Approximately 90% of the world's oil reserves occur in just 30 of these basins.[6] In some locations, the continental crust is not overlain by sediments and the basement rocks are exposed at the surface. Such **shield** areas, which are found on every continent, do not contain oil or gas. For example, all the Saudi Arabian oil fields are located in sedimentary strata in the northeastern part of the Arabian Peninsula, rather than in the southwestern part, which is on the Arabian Shield.

Before we talk about diagenesis, it is important to review the key elements of the carbon cycle.

The Carbon Cycle

In Chapter 8, we will revisit the complex interactions that occur among the planet's four environmental **compartments**: the lithosphere, the hydrosphere, the biosphere and the atmosphere. It is the fluxes that take place between these four **compartments** that control the carbon cycle.

During a period of some 10,000 years, the carbon dioxide released into the atmosphere through respiration by living beings and through the decomposition of organic matter, was counterbalanced (see Figure 3) by the CO_2 absorbed by forests and other types of vegetation through photosynthesis.[7] According to the Canadian Department of Agriculture and Agri-Food, the atmospheric CO_2 concentration stood at about 270 parts per million by volume (ppmv) during that period,[8] in contrast with the present-day level of 380 ppmv. This average level varies with the seasons and from region to region.[9] The equilibrium that once existed is no longer a given. The carbon balance is threatened by a large number of factors, including deforestation, industrial development and the growing use of fossil fuels for transportation. We will come back to this topic in a later chapter.

Obviously, the atmosphere is not the planet's largest reservoir of carbon –sediments and sedimentary rocks are. Since CO_2 is highly soluble in water, especially cold water, an enormous quantity of carbon is also present in the oceans in the form of precipitated carbonates such as calcites. On the subject of carbon reservoirs,

---

[6] Hyne, *op. cit.*, p. 26.

[7] The Oak Ridge National Laboratory (ORNL) has estimated that 110-120 billion tonnes of CO_2 per year is recycled through the process of photosynthesis. Respiration accounts for 40-60 billion tonnes and the decomposition of organic matter, 50-60 billion tonnes. See "The Global Carbon Cycle", at http://www.esd.ornl.gov/lab/lab2-2.htm.

[8] See "The global carbon cycle", at http://res2.agr.gc.ca/publications/ha/2da_e.htm.

[9] See *Science & Vie*, No. 1061, February 2006, p. 65.

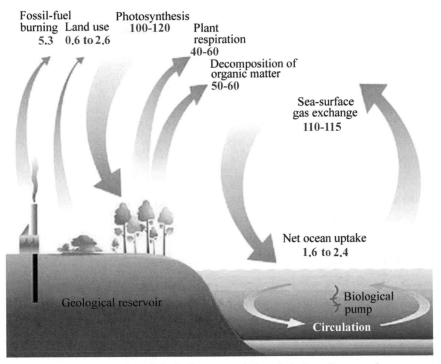

Figure 3: Simplified diagram of the global carbon cycle
(in gigatonnes of carbon: GtC)
Source: Oak Ridge National Laboratory

Pierre-André Bourque of Université Laval has estimated that 760 gigatonnes (GtC) is stored in the atmosphere; 610 GtC, in organic matter (plants and animals); 39,000 GtC is dissolved in the deep ocean and 50 million GtC[10] is stored in sedimentary rocks. Fossil fuels alone represent an estimated 5,000 GtC of carbon. The earth is not likely to run short of carbon any time soon!

All living organisms are composed primarily of carbon, hydrogen, nitrogen and oxygen, as well as proteins and lipids (essential constituents of animal fat and plant oils). Trees and other plants contain lignin –the non-cellulose part of the woody tissues of plants. When living organisms die, how quickly they decompose is determined by their location. All dead organisms are rapidly oxidized in free air, that is, in an **aerobic** environment. The same is true for plankton, algae and other marine organisms. However, when sedimentation occurs in an **anoxic** environment (with

---

[10] See Pierre-André Bourque, "Planète Terre", section 3.4.2 (Le cycle du carbone), at www.ggl.ulaval.ca/personnel/bourque/intro.pt/planete_terre.html. Hereafter cited as Bourque.

no free oxygen), lipids and lignins become incorporated in the sediments and are therefore protected during burial. Under the influence of heat in particular, lipids produce oil, and lignins give rise to coal, including lignite, a form of coal intermediate between peat and anthracite.[11] Until the early 20th century, the process by which fossil fuels formed remained a mystery, although it was known that oil and gas are usually found in the vicinity of coal deposits.[12] What we know today is that coal originates from plant material, while oil originates from marine sediments.

The Kerogen Story

Kerogen[13] is the organic material found in **source rock,** which can be converted to oil through **pyrolysis** given favourable temperature and pressure conditions.[14] There are several types of kerogen, with the three most common being Type I, Type II and Type III. Type I kerogens are derived from lacustrine sediments; Type II, from marine sediments of planktonic origin; and Type III, from continental sediments, including humic coal. Kerogens are generally classified on the basis of two markers: the atomic hydrogen-carbon (H/C) ratio and the oxygen-carbon (O/C) ratio.[15] Type I kerogens are rich in hydrogen but poor in oxygen; Type III kerogens are poor in hydrogen but rich in oxygen. Peat is a kerogen that is rich in oxygen, but less so than wood, which is why it is so difficult to put out peat fires. Type II kerogens have an H/C ratio lower than that found in Type I, but a slightly higher O/C ratio.[16]

A **source rock** is usually a dark-coloured, clay-based or carbonate sedimentary rock that is rich in organic material and that was transformed by heat and pressure during burial, giving rise to hydrocarbons. In other words, a small amount of organic material is captured within the original sediment matrix. The transformation process is aptly summarized below:

---

[11] See "Hydrocarbons", Geology for Engineers, Trinity College, University of Dublin (TCD), available at www.tcd.ie/Geology/Main-Page/CE3A8/oil.pdf.

[12] See Bernard Durand, "A History of Organic Geochemistry", *Oil & Gas Science and Technology, Rev. IFP*, Vol. 58 (2003), No. 2, p. 205 (203-231). This article is available on the Internet.

[13] Kerogen: from the Greek word *keros*, meaning wax.

[14] Kerogen can also be defined on the basis of chemical reactions. It is the fraction of organic matter that is insoluble in solvents, in contrast with bitumen, which is soluble in solvents. See http://eaps.mit.edu/geobiology/biomarkers/kerogen.html. Pyrolysis is a process of chemical decomposition that occurs in response to heat.

[15] This classification is based on a van Krevelen diagram, named after the Dane who created it to gain insight into the properties of coal.

[16] See Earth, Atmospheric and Planetary Sciences, Massachusetts Institute of Technology, at the address http://eaps.mit.edu/geobiology/biomarkers/kerogen.html.

Oil forms within the earth as a result of the decomposition of marine organisms. Several million years ago, many plants, microorganisms and plankton species lived in the oceans. As successive generations of these organisms died, their remains were deposited on the sea bottom. Over the course of millions of years, these remains accumulated and became mixed with mud and silt, forming organic-rich layers of sediment, which are called kerogen.

As sediments keep accumulating, these layers of organic material become buried deeper and deeper and, through compression, they are transformed into rocks that become oil reservoirs. The rocks containing the raw materials of oil are called source rocks. As the sedimentary layers build up, the temperature increases, causing the organic material to be transformed into simpler substances, hydrocarbons, which are composed of carbon and hydrogen. The result is oil.[17]

Of disarming simplicity, these definitions do not describe the entire complexity of the processes involved. **Diagenesis** can be defined as all the physical, chemical and biological processes that are involved in the transformation of sediment into rock. These changes occur in three stages: compaction, cementation and recrystallization. The weight of accumulated layers of sediment results in **compaction** and a concomitant reduction in the pore volume of the sediment grains (i.e., the space between the particles), because of the water that is expelled. The interstitial water can also cause calcium carbonate ($CaCO_3$) or silica (SiO_2) to precipitate out and form a sort of glue or cement between the grains.[18] This process is called **cementation**. Lastly, **recrystallization** results from the transformation of certain less stable minerals into more stable forms. This is the common process by which accumulations of calcium carbonate are incorporated into coral reefs. These three processes can be subsumed under the term **lithification**.

Maturation of Kerogen

The definitions provided so far shed little light on the fundamental question of how oil and gas form. We need to take a closer look at the decomposition of kerogen to gain a better understanding. At shallow depths, an initial biochemical transformation occurs (reduction of oxygen and nitrogen atoms) through the decomposition action of anaerobic bacteria –bacteria capable of exploiting the oxygen contained in molecules of organic matter in an anoxic environment. At

---

[17] See http://marquant.free.fr/petrole/composition.htm.
[18] GEOL019, chapitre 8.

this stage, the organic matter (**CHON**) is converted to carbon and hydrogen (**CH**) as a result of the removal of nitrogen and oxygen molecules. This process is called oxidation–reduction. In the first 1,000 metres of burial depth, bacteria are always the active agents.[19] Below the first 1,000 metres, thermal degradation takes place (**catagenesis**). As burial depth and temperatures increase, transformations occur that initiate the process of oil generation. Temperatures increase by about 30°C per km on average; however, every sedimentary basin has its own thermal history. At a burial depth of 2,000 metres, part of the kerogen is transformed into oil, and a smaller portion into gas (see Figure 4). Professor Pierre-André Bourque summarizes the process as follows:

> It is at a depth of between 2,000 m and 3,000 m that oil generation from kerogen is greatest. Below 3,000 m, insignificant amounts of oil are produced. Beginning at a depth of 2,500 m, however, gas generation increases and becomes significant such that, by 3,500 m, no further oil is generated but a great deal of gas is. Thermal degradation gradually leads to carbonization processes, which convert any remaining kerogens –those not already transformed into oil or gas– to carbon residues. At burial depths beyond 4,000 m, the intense heat destroys everything, including the oil and gas.[20]

The values in this diagram are provided solely for illustrative purposes, since the actual parameters vary depending on the type of kerogen involved. This is especially true if the goal is to measure the degree of kerogen maturation based on the total percentage of carbon generated. As a rule, lacustrine sediments produce the most gas and oil. The range of depths at which oil forms is called the **oil window**, in contrast with the **gas window**, which is where gas forms.[21] The area characterized by conditions conducive to the formation of oil and gas is referred to as the hydrocarbon kitchen or the source kitchen. This brings us to an important question: how does oil become trapped and when and where is it found?

---

[19] "It should be noted that one fifth of natural gas reserves result from the decomposition of organic matter by bacteria rather than from the pyrolysis of kerogen. This gas is called biogenic gas in opposition to thermogenic gas". See http://culturesciences.chimie.ens.fr/dossiers-dossierstransversaux-EEDD-Combustibles_Fossiles_Demirdjian.html#d0e116.

[20] Bourque, *op. cit.*, section 3.3.2 (Les combustibles fossiles).

[21] *Ibid.*

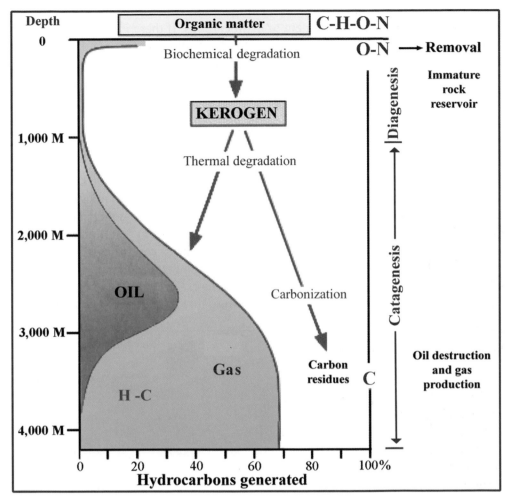

Figure 4: Transformation of kerogen into oil and gas
Source: From P.-A. Bourque, "Planète Terre", Les combustibles fossiles

Migration and Trapping

Source rock has evolved in the earth's crust for millions of years. Organic matter, as we have seen, is present in very small amounts in mineralized sediments. Only a microscopic amount of kerogen is contained in a grain of sand or sandstone (see illustration in Figure 5). The kerogen has to escape from the matrix in which it is held. Given the enormous pressures and extreme temperatures to which the buried material is subjected, the kerogen eventually finds an escape route out of the source rock.[22] This marks the stage of **primary migration**, which is characterized by the concentration and gradual movement of hydrocarbons. If there is nothing to impede them, the hydrocarbons will either rise to the earth's surface or solidify into bitumen, losing their volatile constituents in the process.

Secondary migration refers to the movement of hydrocarbons from the source rock to geological zones where they become trapped and concentrated in **reservoir rock**, or more specifically, in the fissures of such rock. Here, the hydrocarbons occupy microscopic spaces between the rock crystals, somewhat like "water stored in a sponge or wet chalk".[23]

Hydrocarbon migration is a lengthy process primarily because water moves very slowly at great depths in the subsurface. Since the hydrocarbons migrate with the water contained in the rock formations, they are subject to the geological characteristics of the region in which they travel. It is often difficult to determine the provenance of hydrocarbons following their discovery in a **reservoir rock**. This is because hydrocarbons can travel distances of several dozen kilometres or more by moving along faults or other geological structures. Eventually, they encounter impermeable structures that keep them from migrating any farther, called **traps**.

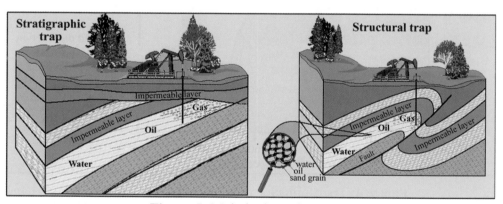

Figure 5: Main hydrocarbon traps
Source: From *Calgary Geoscape,* Natural Resources Canada

---

[22] The expulsion of hydrocarbons from source rock long remained a mystery until Philippe Ungerer of the Institut français du pétrole (petroleum institute in France) developed a dual-flux model to explain it. How can hydrocarbons escape given the enormous capillary forces holding the water and oil in place? It is actually the water that is expelled first, permitting the incipient generation of hydrocarbons in the source rock. At maturity, these hydrocarbons are able to escape from the source rock. See Bernard Durand, *op. cit.,* Section 3.6 (The Mysteries of Primary Oil Migration).

[23] "For example, 1 m^3 of impregnated rock contains less than 150 litres of oil, and with current oil extraction techniques, barely 40 litres will reach the wellhead when the deposit is brought on stream". See http://www.industrie.gouv.fr/energie/comprendre/q-r-pet-pdt.htm.

There are two main types of traps: **structural** and **stratigraphic**. Structural traps are related to faults or folds which enable hydrocarbons to accumulate in reservoir rock (right-hand portion of Figure 5). All structural traps result from the deformation of the reservoir rock associated with plate tectonic processes. The most effective traps are dome-shaped ones (anticlines). The fluids within traps are organized according to density, with water in the lowest part of the trap, oil overlying it and gas in the upper part.

The phenomenon of fluid concentration is the same in stratigraphic traps. Their origin is more complex, however, than structural traps and beyond the scope of our analysis,[24] particularly since some geological formations have the properties of both structural and stratigraphic traps. The basic principle is the same. The movement of the fluids is blocked when they encounter an impervious layer of rock. Salt domes (diapirs) are excellent **cap rocks** –the name given to the impermeable layers of rock that overlie reservoir rock– because they prevent subsequent migration of the hydrocarbons. The U.S. Strategic Petroleum Reserve, currently composed of about 700 million barrels of crude oil, is stored in underground salt caverns along the coast of Louisiana.[25]

Model of a Petroleum System

A number of conditions must be present in order for oil and gas to form. All of these interrelated conditions can be referred to collectively as a "petroleum system". Since a system is made up of interacting constituent parts, improper functioning of just one component can cause the whole system to break down. Figure 6 shows a model of a petroleum system.[26]

In short, the existence of a petroleum system implies that sediment deposition is occurring, that the sediments are buried rapidly under thermal conditions that promote the maturation of organic matter, and that primary and secondary migration

---

[24] A study by Schlumberger is especially informative. See "Exploring for Stratigraphic Traps", at www.slb.com/media/services/resources/oilfieldreview/ors97/win97/traps.pdf. According to this study, 40% of world oil discoveries are made in stratigraphic traps. These traps consist of pinchouts, unconformities or impermeable barriers created by coral reefs.

[25] The stocks are stored in about 60 cylindrical salt caverns that have a diameter of up to 200 feet (61 m) and a height of 2,000 feet (610 m). The largest cavern is so huge it could accommodate the entire Sears Tower (Chicago) with 170 feet (52 m) to spare. For more information, go to http:// fossil.energy.gov/programs/reserves/spr/spr-sites.html.

[26] Arthur R. Green, "Global Energy: The Next Decade and Beyond", AAPG Distinguished Lecture, 2004-2005, at www.searchanddiscovery.com/ documents/2005/green/index.htm.

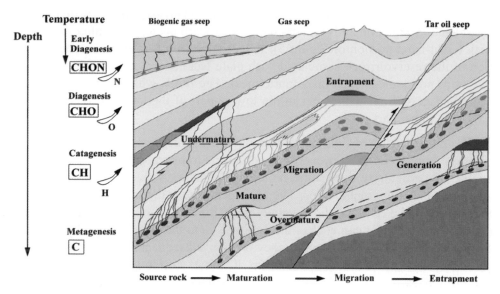

Figure 6: Model of a petroleum system
Source: From Arthur R. Green, "Global Energy" (see footnote)

processes occur under conditions conducive to the trapping of oil and gas in structures that lend themselves to exploitation.[27]

Once Upon a Time in Calgary

Figure 7, which illustrates the geology of the site of present-day Calgary several million years ago, summarizes most of the situations described above. Readers will be surprised to learn that, several million years ago, the site was covered by the sea. In geology, what we see today is not necessarily what existed in the past. However, the present does provide useful clues to the past.

During the Paleozoic era, several hundred million years ago, sediments were deposited on the shield that extended across much of North America.[28] This sedimentation process resulted from the eastward extension of an ancient Pacific Ocean. Some time later –in the Mesozoic– the sedimentary rocks were pushed upward and eastward after a major faulting event occurred on the west coast of Canada. The Rocky Mountains were created 65 million years ago during the later stages of the break-up of

---

[27] See Bernard Durand, *op. cit.*, Section 4.1 (Petroleum Systems and Basin Simulators).
[28] This description is based on the findings of Godfrey Nowlan and Terry Poulton of the Geologic Survey of Canada.

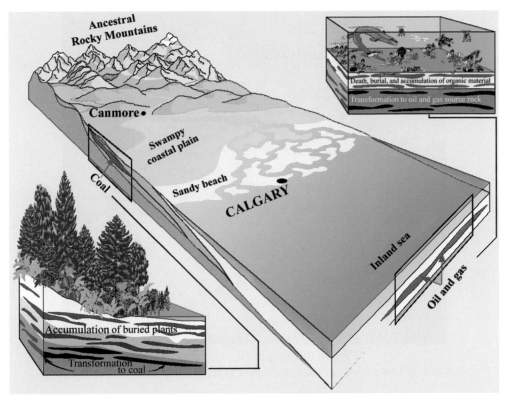

Figure 7: Calgary, millions of years ago
Source: From *Calgary Geoscape*, Natural Resources Canada

Pangaea. The Parks Canada Agency provides a romanticized description of the region before orogeny:

> "Seventy-five million years ago, what is now eastern Alberta was a low-lying coastal plain at the edge of a large shallow sea. The climate was subtropical, similar to that characterizing northern Florida today. Countless creatures flourished there –fish, amphibians, reptiles, birds, primitive mammals and about 35 species of dinosaurs. When some of these animals died, their remains ended up in river channels and mudflats and their bones became buried in fresh layers of sand and mud".[29]

Cut to 18,000 years ago, however, and life in what is now Canada was anything but romantic: it was covered almost entirely by a thick ice sheet (see Figure 8). Only Newfoundland, warmed by the Gulf Stream, appears to have been spared this period of glaciation.

---

[29] http://www.pc.gc.ca/progs/spm-whs/itm2-/site3_e.asp.

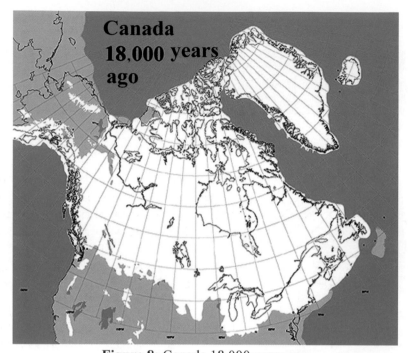

Figure 8: Canada 18,000 years ago
Source: A. S. Dyke, A. Moore and L. Robertson, *Geological Survey of Canada*, File 1574

We are providing these details not only to show the importance of the major geological changes that have occurred over time, but also to emphasize the role played by another natural cycle which we have not yet explored: the cycle of sea-level changes.

The Cycle of Sea-Level Changes

This cycle is controlled by the alternating periods of glaciation and deglaciation that have affected our planet. Global warming and cooling periods alternate on a cycle of 100,000 years.[30] This cycle, named the Milankovitch cycle after Serbian geophysicist Milutin Milankovitch, is caused primarily by changes in the shape of

---

[30] The Milankovitch cycle is actually much more complex. "The alternation between glacial and interglacial ages has been explained in terms of astronomical cycles of 100,000 years, 40,000 years and 20,000 years, which correspond to the variation in the eccentricity of the Earth's orbit, the angle of tilt of Earth's rotation axis (nutation) and the precession (Earth's rotation about its axis), respectively". See François Ploye, *Effet de serre, Science ou religion du xxí^e siècle ?*, Edition Naturellement, 2001. See http://www.planetecologie.org/menus/Fr_rubriquemois.html.

the Earth's orbit round the Sun (between a circular orbit and an elliptical orbit), which occur on a cycle of 100,000 or 125,000 years. This process modifies the distance between the Earth and the Sun and hence the insolation, or the amount of solar energy received. It is estimated that, during the most recent major glaciation event, which occurred 18,000 years ago, temperatures were about four degrees colder than they are today.

During the planet's first 1.6 billion years, temperatures were too hot for glaciation to occur. According to some studies, however, the earth's climate was not as hot at this time as previously thought.[31] During the Cenozoic, a gradual cooling trend occurred which culminated in the Pleistocene glaciations. Although it is not as cold today as it was during the Pleistocene epoch, another ice age is expected to occur sometime in the future. For millions of years the planet underwent global warming, notably during the Cretaceous period. There were no polar ice caps, and living conditions were probably very good, even in Greenland. Other mechanisms controlling climatic variations must be found, because a number of transformation processes seem to be involved. We will come back to these issues in a later chapter.

For now, let us simply keep in mind that sea and ocean levels drop during periods of **transgression**, and rise during periods of **regression**. In other words, the less ice there is on the continents, the more water there is in the oceans, and vice versa. Sea levels are estimated to have dropped 130 metres during the maximum extent of the most recent glaciation.[32] This phenomenon is significant in the formation of oil and gas, as "once upon a time in Calgary" clearly shows.

Bernard Durand has aptly summarized this phenomenon. During major transgressions, when the oceans spread farther over the land than before, "closed seas formed, providing conditions favourable for the creation of Type I or II source rocks, which are the most productive for oil generation. By contrast, during major regressions, which were marked by the permanent retreat of the sea from land areas, detrital sediments were dominant; they are more conducive to the formation of coal".

Distribution of Source Rocks Over Geological Time

This appears to be a geological oddity, since there is no evidence of a source rock production cycle. Did fossil fuels disappear during certain periods of geological time, only to reappear during other periods? Or did the cycle of sea-level

---

[31] See John Valley, "A Cool Early Earth", *Scientific American*, October 2005, 8 pages.

[32] See R. van Woesik, "Geology, Geomorphology and Reef Growth", at http://my.fit.edu/~rvw/ Lectures/Geol.htm. See also B. P. Tissot, "Effects on Prolific Petroleum Source Rocks and Major Coal Deposits caused by Sea-Level Changes", *Nature*, Vol. 277, pp. 463-465.

changes affect their distribution over time? Does some other explanation need to be found for this anomaly?

More than 90% of the world's reserves of gas and oil were generated from source rocks deposited during the following six stratigraphic intervals:

– Silurian (9% of world reserves)
– Upper Devonian/Tournaisian (8% world reserves)
– Pennsylvanian/Lower Permian: (8% of world reserves)
– Upper Jurassic: (25% of world reserves)
– Middle Cretaceous (29% of world reserves)
– Oligocene/Miocene (12.5% of world reserves)

This finding by authors Klemme and Ulmishek is reported in an article published in 1999.[33] Klemme helped to prepare the United States Geological Survey (USGS) 2000 report on world petroleum reserves.

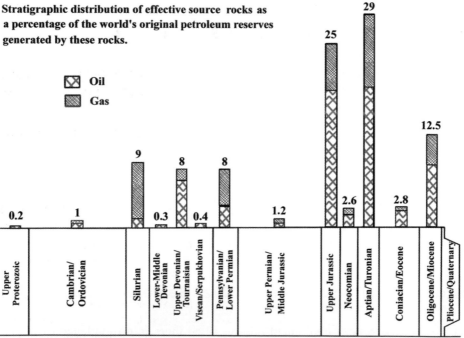

Figure 9. Production of source rocks over geological time
Source: H. D. Klemme and G. F. Ulmishek, *AAPG*, Vol. 75, 1991

[33] See H.D. Klemme and G. F. Ulmishek, "Effective Petroleum Source Rocks of the World: Stratigraphic Distribution and Controlling Depositional Factors", *AAPG Bulletin*, December 1991, Vol. 75, No. 12, pp. 1809-1851.

Readers should note that, in this study, the figures were normalized to 100% (the sum of the percentages is 100) for all the stratigraphic periods. Figure 9 is self-explanatory. First, it illustrates the very unequal distribution of source rock generation over time: in other words, several different cycles of source rock production occurred rather than just one cycle. Second, the accumulation phase took place mainly during the Mesozoic Era. Third, more than 70% of the source rocks were generated during glacial **transgression** phases (Silurian, Upper Devonian, Upper Jurassic and Middle Cretaceous),[34] while 20% of the source rocks were deposited during **regression** phases (Pennsylvanian/Permian and Oligocene/Miocene).

The authors note, however, that kerogen types have evolved significantly over the ages. During the Paleozoic, for example, source rocks were composed exclusively of organic matter of marine origin, whereas in the Tertiary, source rocks were mainly of terrestrial sedimentary origin. They conclude that **biological evolution** played a key role in the process of deposition of source rocks.[35]

How Does Oil Form in a Marine Environment?

The answer is simple: the same way as it forms in the earth. Although the dynamics of the transformations and the topography differ, the processes of hydrocarbon maturation, burial and trapping are identical.

Offshore oil is important, since it accounted for 40% of the increase in world oil reserves during the period 2000-2006.

Shallow Water

Continental shelves (see Figure 10) are part of the continents to which they are attached. The width of continental shelves can vary by a factor of 1,000, ranging from 0.8 km to 800 km, with an average of 80 km.[36] When continental shelves are taken into account, the percentage of the earth's surface that is occupied by seas and oceans

---

[34] These figures are consistent with the findings of Bois, Bouche and Pelet, who concluded in 1982 that 69% of the world's hydrocarbon reserves were deposited in the basins of the ancient Tethys Sea (Cenozoic). See C. Bois, P. Bouche and R. Pelet, "Global Geologic History and Distribution of Hydrocarbon Reserves", *AAPG Bulletin,* September 1982, Vol. 66, No. 9; pp. 1248-1270.

[35] "We suggest that biologic evolution played an important role in the history of source rock deposition. Different groups of producers evolved and colonized new ecologic niches that expanded areas of bioproduction. Source rocks with terrestrial organic matter appeared. However, the contemporaneous evolution of consumers and decomposers resulted in the decrease of variety of conditions suitable for the preservation of organic matter with Type II kerogen". Klemme and Ulmishek, *op. cit.*

[36] Hyne, *op.cit.,* p.129.

amounts to only 60% rather than 70% or 71%. Pierre-André Bourque defines the main components of the continental shelf:

The **continental shelf**, which is the margin of the continental crust, is characterized by very shallow water depths, ranging from zero metres to less than 200 metres, compared with the great depths characterizing the oceans. Continental shelves have a very gentle slope, only 0.7° on average. On the seaward side of the continental shelf, there is a pronounced change in gradient called the **shelf break**. The shelf break occurs at a water depth of 132 metres on average. Below this break is the **continental slope**, which has a gradient of about 4°. Although this slope is not very steep, it is typically represented as a sharp drop-off in illustrations. At the foot of the slope, there is a gently sloping plain called the **continental rise**. The entire area, from the shoreline to the base of the continental rise, is known as the **continental margin**.[37]

Continental shelves are the site of intense prospecting and development activities because they usually contain thick sequences of sedimentary rocks. These areas are also the first to be affected by sea-level changes.

The almost universal gradient of continental slopes is attributable to the tides, which affect sea level but also "create powerful horizontal flows of water on the sea floor". [38] Continental slopes are shaped by "internal tides", which "provide the best explanation for the gentle incline of the slope". The continental slope marks the geological boundary of the continents.

A number of structures that begin onshore or along beaches also extend *offshore* and conversely, some folds and faults that begin under the sea extend onto the continents. For example, the San Andreas Fault, after cutting across a broad swath of California, extends offshore onto the continental shelf in the northern part of the state.

Submarine canyons which can extend for hundreds of kilometres are incised into the continental shelf and rise. They are formed by major turbidity currents (water masses carrying a load of suspended sediment) caused by a sudden slump of sediment, or a submarine landslide, on the continental shelf and slope. Less powerful turbidity currents scour, sweep and erode the submarine canyons. The left portion of Figure 11 shows a computer-generated 3D reconstruction of the Zaire Canyon. The right-hand side illustrates the turbidity current that occurred on the Grand Banks in 1929.[39]

---

[37] Bourque, *op. cit.*, 3.2.1, (Le relief des fonds océaniques).

[38] See David Cacchione and Lincoln Pratson, "Les marées des profondeurs", *Pour la Science*, January 2006, pp. 76-82.

[39] The left portion of Figure 9 is taken from IFREMER at http://www.ifremer.fr/ drogm_uk/rap-activ2001/Zaiango1.htm and the right-hand portion from http://www.fredshark.net/ Historique/vie7.htm.

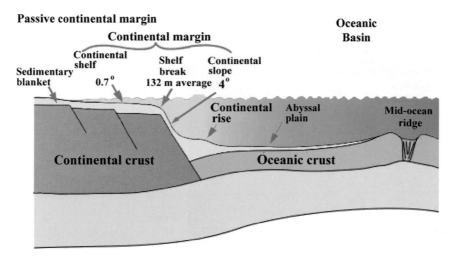

Figure 10: Cross-section of a continental shelf
Source: From P.-A. Bourque, *Planète Terre*

The water depth in the left-hand part of Figure 11 is 2,000 m; the canyon is 700 m deep and 7-10 km wide. The arrows represent the turbidity currents. The terraces act as confined levees.[40] The right-hand side illustrates a turbidity current triggered by an earthquake whose epicentre was located on the continental slope south of Newfoundland. Tonnes of sediment were displaced and spread over a distance of more than 800 km on the Sohm Abyssal Plain. All of the undersea telegraph cables were severed by the submarine landslide that occurred on the Grand Banks in 1929.

There are some extensive submarine canyons in the Pacific Ocean off California, but canyons also occur off rivers such as the Mississippi, the Amazon, the Ganges, the Niger and the Nile. Rivers can even bring about the downstream formation of *offshore* canyons. The sediment that accumulates at the base of the canyons creates what is called a submarine **fan** or cone. The coarsest sediments are deposited at the head of the fan, while the lightest particles are carried to the outer edges. The result is a graded bed with each layer exhibiting a progressive change in particle size as the sediments were deposited, usually with the fine materials at the top. The main channel cut by the turbidity currents branches into smaller channels as the sandy flows spread out and sediment is deposited in the fan lobes.

---

[40] See A. Gervais and T. Mulder, "Construction des levées bordant le canyon de l'éventail profond du Zaïre par débordement des courants de turbidité", at http://www.epoc.u-bordeaux.fr/fr/themee/me6a4. htm.

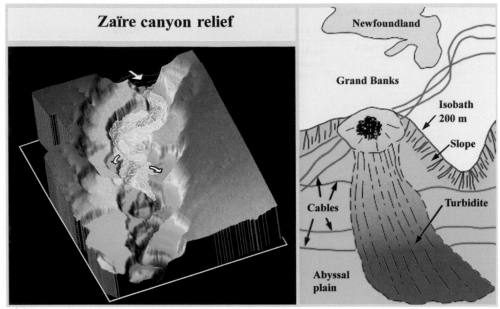

Figure 11: Submarine canyons and turbidity currents
Source: IFREMER (left portion); see note about the right-hand portion.

The sediment deposits (turbidites) created by turbidity currents are excellent hydrocarbon reservoirs. Deepwater oil production, particularly from what has been called the Deepwater Golden Triangle (West Africa, Gulf of Mexico and Brazil) targets sediment deposits created by turbidity currents in submarine canyons and in adjacent channels. The deposits are relatively young and not buried excessively deep.[41]

One of the largest gas-producing *offshore* basins is the Frigg field, which is located in the United Kingdom and Norwegian sectors of the North Sea. The data indicate that this basin was formed from a submarine canyon and fan. The basin is of Paleocene age and has a maximum depth of about 1,800 m. There is an inverse relationship between river deltas and submarine canyons. When sea levels are relatively high, sediments accumulate in the deltas, and the submarine canyons and fans cease to be active. The opposite situation is seen when sea levels are relatively low: sediment deposition occurs mainly in the submarine canyons and fans, with little accumulation in deltas.[42]

---

[41] Hyne, *op. cit.*, p. 131.
[42] *Ibid.*, p. 134.

Deepwater

In deepwater zones, the situation is quite different. The average thickness of sediment layers on the ocean bottom is only 0.8 km.[43] The reasons for this were explained in the previous chapter. Early in the break-up of continents, **triple junctions** form from two rifting arms joined in a Y shape. In most cases, the two arms continue to rift, eventually giving rise to an ocean, whereas the third arm becomes a **failed arm**. A failed arm is a **graben**, defined as a "trough fault between two normal *faults*, which can represent an early stage of continental *plate* separation".[44] Grabens become excellent sediment reservoirs and many of them are conducive to gas and oil production.

During the Mesozoic, when the break-up of Pangaea occurred, a number of triple junctions formed. When North America separated from Europe, two arms joined to form the Atlantic Ocean, while a third arm became the Central Graben that cuts across the depths of the central part of the North Sea. It is characterized by a thick accumulation of sediments, ranging in thickness from 900 metres to 1,800 metres. This layer is much thicker than the adjacent sedimentary rocks on the bottom of the North Sea.[45] Similarly, when South America separated from Africa, two arms joined to form the southern Atlantic Ocean, whereas the third arm failed. The failed arm is now located under Nigeria. The bulk of Nigerian oil production comes from deposits that accumulated in the Niger River Delta fed by the Benue Trough.[46]

The distinction between deepwater and shallow water environments is of little significance nowadays, given major advances in technology. Drilling can be done almost anywhere in the oceans provided that there is sufficient potential for the discovery of oil. In September 2001, deepwater hydrocarbon reserves were estimated at 57 billion barrels of oil equivalent (BBOE). Only 25% of these reserves have been exploited by drilling wells in deepwater zones, defined as ocean depths of 500 metres or more.[47] Today, there is an increasing focus on ultra-deepwater zones (> 1,500 metres), and drilling could reach a depth of 2,000 metres in 2010.[48] We are not talking about actual drilling depth but rather the depth of water reached before the drill head touches the ocean floor.

---

[43] *Ibid.*, p. 144.

[44] Lexique J. Mirabaud, *op. cit.*

[45] Hyne, *op. cit.,* p. 146.

[46] Hyne, *op. cit.,* p. 147.

[47] Roger M. Slatt, "Deepwater Turbidite Deposits and their Economic Significance", *Touch Oil and Gas*, at http://www.touchoilandgas.com/deepwater-turbidite-deposits-their-a100-1.html.

[48] "Deepwater Expenditures to reach $20 billion/year by 2010", *Offshore*, Vol. 65, December 2005, p. 29.

Carbonate Platforms

Sandstones and limestones constitute excellent reservoir rocks, but not all of these zones are productive. It depends on the environment and the conditions in which the rocks were formed. Paradoxically, in the case of rivers, deltas and the sands of coastal beaches, reservoir rocks are often sandstones. Conversely, many limestone platforms are found in the subsurface, indicating that they derive from ancient marine environments.

Ancient coral reefs and even atolls can form prolific hydrocarbon reservoirs, with those in North America being a prime example. A substantial portion of Canadian oil production comes from ancient coral reefs or atolls that formed in the Devonian. An example is the Leduc field discovered in 1947 and the Redwater field discovered a year later.[49] The Redwater oil field is an ancient buried atoll that extends over a distance of 24 km. Production from this field is expected to reach 850 million barrels or 135 cubic metres of oil.[50]

During the Permian, a large part of the eastern and central United States lay underwater. The last area to be flooded consisted of western Texas, New Mexico and Mexico. Today, this region is home to several large basins of Permian age: the Midland, Marfa and Delaware basins. In the Silurian period, a coral reef built up along the northern boundary of the Michigan Basin. More than 1,200 wells have been drilled in this region, with 900 of them being productive.

In the Middle East, most of the large producing basins are of karstic origin –limestone altered by carbonic acid. These reservoir rocks are highly permeable and porous. Similarly, many of the oil fields in western Canada are located in dolomitized reservoir rocks.[51] They are ten times more permeable than reservoir rocks formed from reefs of limestone origin.

---

[49] The Redwater field is located northeast of Edmonton.

[50] Hyne, *op. cit.*, p. 97.

[51] Dolomite is named after French minerologist Dolomieu, who was the first to describe the rock; it is an altered form of calcite in which the calcite ions have been replaced by magnesium ions [$CaMg(CO_3)_2$].

3

Energy, Past and Present

The word energy comes from the Greek *energeia*, meaning "activity", itself derived from the Greek *ergon*, which means "work." The concept of energy pervades all aspects of life, which should make it familiar to all of us. As a technical concept, though, energy is very complex.

A Few Essential Definitions

Early humans tamed first fire, then wind, then water –all of which are now considered renewable energies. In some respects, our ancestors were more modern than we might think, and we would do well to imitate them.

A distinction can be made between three different levels of energy use. **Primary energy** can be defined as the energy available in nature. These natural, unconverted forms of energy have long been used for human survival and comfort. Primary energy can be divided into **non-renewable** (gas, coal, oil and uranium) and **renewable** (hydro, solar, wind, geothermal and tidal power and biomass) sources. Renewable forms of energy will be discussed in the next chapter.

Secondary energy consists of energy resulting from the conversion of primary energy sources. The main energy converters are electric utilities, the oil and gas industry and other industries (for process steam). Conversion processes include the storage and transport of energy, refining and, perhaps, in the future, hydrogen production (if hydrogen joins electricity as a major secondary energy vector).[1]

The third level is **final energy**, or energy that is actually consumed. France's Commissariat de l'énergie atomique (CEA) divides this into three categories:

---

[1] See "Chaînes et systèmes énergétiques", CEA (Commissariat à l'énergie atomique), available at: www.cea.fr/fr/Publications/clefs44/fr-clefs44/clefs4412.htm. Readers will also find a highly instructive diagram on energy systems.

mechanical energy (industrial and household motors and transport), **thermal energy** (heating and air conditioning, and metallurgical processes) and **radiant energy** (lighting, telecommunications, radar and medical imaging). A related notion is **useful energy,** the portion of final energy that is actually available after final conversion, distribution and losses from such things as malfunctioning automobile ignition systems, defective electric appliances and poorly insulated dwellings. According to the CEA, useful energy amounts to a little over a third of primary energy, with about 63% of primary energy being lost. This loss of 63%, which is substantial, can be broken down into 24.5% conversion losses, 4.4% distribution losses and 34.4% losses in final use.[2]

Two Key Types of Energy

The term that no doubt best describes the state of the universe, including the earth itself, is energy. Even before Albert Einstein proposed the equivalence of mass and energy in his famous equation $e = mc^2$, energy was defined as anything that can be converted into work or into another form of energy. Although energy may be changed from one form to another, the same basic principle always applies: the total amount of energy in an isolated system remains constant. This is the principle of the **conservation of energy**. In other words, the energy in the universe is neither created nor destroyed; however, any conversion of energy from one form to another results in a decrease in energy quality. Our Sun is a good example of the conversion of matter to energy. The Sun consumes its own hydrogen, converting it into helium through fusion and releasing huge quantities of energy in the process (minus a small mass loss associated with the fusion reactions).

Although energy comes in many forms, there are two key types, which together make up mechanical energy: **kinetic energy** (from the Greek *kinetos,* or moving), the energy associated with movement, and **potential energy**, the energy associated with the position of an object. The sum of the two remains constant and is another piece of evidence supporting the principle of conservation of energy. For example, when a flowerpot falls from a 10th floor balcony, its kinetic energy increases with its speed, while its potential energy decreases with its altitude. The example of a swinging pendulum is even clearer.

---

[2]   *Ibid.*

"When a pendulum is swinging in a gravitational field, at the middle point of the swing, the maximum kinetic energy is attained; this is offset by the minimum potential energy attained, since the bob is at its lowest point. Similarly, at the end of the swing, the kinetic energy is zero (since the speed is zero), while the potential energy is at its maximum because the bob is at its highest point. Between these two extremes, the pendulum's energy is at a constantly changing balance of kinetic and potential energy, but the sum of the two (the system's mechanical energy) always remains constant."[3]

Similarly, "an object attached to a stretched spring has potential energy that can be converted into kinetic energy as soon as the spring is released."[4] The principle of the conservation of energy can be summed up in three equations: the total energy of a body is equal to the sum of its kinetic energy and potential energy; the potential energy of a body is equal to its total energy minus its kinetic energy; and the kinetic energy of a body is equal to its total energy minus its potential energy. These three equations are identical. The term "stored energy" is also used to refer to a body's potential energy, but this is not totally accurate since potential energy designates a reserve of energy rather than a stored quantity.

The Different Forms of Energy

The different forms of energy and their main uses include:

Mechanical energy:[5] movement, force, pressure, speed, deformation
Electrical energy:[6] batteries, light bulbs, heaters, motors
Thermal energy:[7] temperature variations, combustion, geothermal energy
Nuclear energy:[8] energy released by nuclear reactions (fission or fusion)
Radiant energy:[9] microwaves; ultraviolet, alpha, beta and gamma rays
Chemical energy:[10] energy contained in chemical bonds, e.g., fossil fuels

---

[3]   Cited in http://fr.encarta.msn.com/ text_761566038___3/énergie.html
[4]   Jean Olbregts, "La notion d'énergie: un peu d'histoire…", Chimie physique moléculaire, Université Libre de Belgique, available at www.ulb.ac.be/sciences/intra/inforscc_archives/nrj/carati.htm
[5]   Can only be defined as the sum of its kinetic and potential energy.
[6]   Comes from the movement of electrons in the conducting medium, and thus from their kinetic energy. Can be transformed into movement or work in motors and electrical devices.
[7]   Consists of the disorganized movement of molecules and atoms, called thermal agitation.
[8]   Derives its energy from the fission of heavy atoms or the fusion of light atoms under confinement at high temperatures.
[9]   Designates the process of energy emission or transmission in the form of electromagnetic waves or particles or acoustic waves. The sun's radiant energy is key to the phenomenon of photosynthesis.
[10] Chemical energy encompasses all the processes related to the association and dissociation of chemical bonds between atoms, with the attendant release of energy. The electrolysis of water produces chemical energy in the form of hydrogen and oxygen. In a car battery, energy is also present in chemical form.

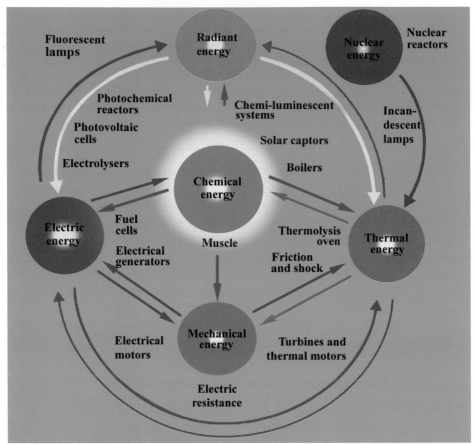

Figure 1: Conversion of the six main forms of energy
and a few examples of energy converters[11]
Source: From CEA/DSE/SEE, Clefs CEA No. 44, Winter 2000-2001

Although there is agreement in the international community concerning these six forms of energy, there are a few problems with this scheme. For example, electrical energy is not a source of energy per se. Even though electric power plants are energy carriers or vectors, they do not produce energy. All they do is release the potential energy of water stored in a dam to convert it to kinetic energy, which is used to turn the turbines, which drive the alternators that generate electricity. Power plants are therefore not a primary energy source (although they could be some day if we succeed in taming lightning, or so-called natural electricity).[12]

---

[11] A similar diagram can be found at http://www.climat.be/fr/definition.html
[12] "Some 2,000 to 5,000 thunderstorms occur on the earth at any given time, producing a hundred or so lightning strikes per second. [...] Temperatures in a lightning bolt can reach 30,000°C. A bolt can last from 2/100th of a second to 2 seconds, and flashes up to 100 times." *Science & Vie*, July 2004, p. 99.

Although coal, gas and oil are commonly thought of as fossil fuels, they are actually fossilized solar energy. Wind and waves are considered kinetic or mechanical energy, but when we exploit them, we are indirectly using solar energy. Wind, waves, biomass and even hydroelectricity exist only because of the solar energy produced by fusion reactions in the sun. Renewable energies are aptly named, but they are dependent on the sun.

Chemical and nuclear energy must be correctly differentiated. Chemical energy results from the strength of the bonds between atoms. When subjected to a heat source, carbon and oxygen bind to form carbon dioxide, releasing energy in the form of heat. In turn, this heat drives the reaction further, and it continues as long as both ingredients are present. Chemical energy, interactions between atoms and the formation of molecules all result solely from **processes of interaction between electrons**; the nuclei of the atoms (and their protons and neutrons) do not play any role. All chemical reactions, from the combustion of gasoline to the explosion of TNT (trinitrotoluene), occur in the same way.

Nuclear energy, on the other hand, comes from the energy of the protons and neutrons in the nucleus. The nucleus is always positively charged, while the electrons that orbit around it are negatively charged. An atom's stability results from the very strong forces of attraction between the positive nucleus and the negative electrons. To disrupt this stability, a source of neutrons is needed that can penetrate the nucleus and create fission.

Uranium-235 fission causes the nucleus to split into two atoms of average weight and eject several neutrons (either two or three), producing an enormous amount of energy. The ratios for the conversion of mass to energy from nuclear fission are difficult to compare with conversion ratios for other types of energy. When coal burns in the presence of air, for example, only 1×10^{-10} of its mass is transformed into energy, whereas during the fission of uranium-235, 1×10^{-3} of the total mass is converted into energy.[13] The fission of a gram of uranium-235 releases more energy than the combustion of two and a half tonnes of coal, which itself requires close to 35 tonnes of air.

Although we have succeeded in harnessing fission to produce energy in nuclear reactors, this is not yet true of fusion, a reaction in which the nuclei of lightweight atoms, such as hydrogen and its isotopes (deuterium and tritium), fuse to form heavier atoms, giving off an enormous amount of energy. At present, the only nuclear fusion applications are thermonuclear bombs (H-bombs), which require a fission bomb to trigger the fusion process. This creates, within a vessel containing light elements, the temperatures of over several million degrees that are required to

---

[13] For more details on chemical and nuclear reactions, see Albert Legault and George Lindsey, *Le feu nucléaire*, Paris, Seuil, 1973, pp.13-32.

fuse the nuclei. Today, a great deal of hope centres in the International Thermonu-clear Experimental Reactor (ITER), which is to be constructed at Cadarache, France, despite protests from environmentalists and a number of well-known scientists. All the major powers, including the United States, Russia, China and even Japan (which had hoped to land this international project) are participating in this major program.

The History of Energy

The first energy converters used by humans were biological. Muscles burn glucose and thus produce movement. *Homo erectus* likely discovered all the benefits of fire very early on. Human use of fire dates back to 400,000 or 500,000 years before Jesus Christ, and probably even older fire pits have been found.[14] The use of wind in the form of sail power can be traced back to 3,000 BC. The Persians built the first windmills around 200 BC, although the technology did not make its way to Europe until some 1,000 years later, in the 12th century; Holland's famous landscape of windmills did not appear until the 14th century.[15] After fire and wind came water: the Pharaoh Menes built the first dam in Egypt in 2,900 BC for irrigation.[16]

Scientific and social advances, changing lifestyles and social organization, and even the way society calculates things have influenced the history of energy. Although the onset of the industrial revolution in Great Britain is usually associated with the invention of the steam engine by James Watt in 1775, a host of other technological innovations had already occurred. The first steam locomotive, invented by the Cornish engineer Richard Trevithick, travelled at a speed of 20 km/h when empty and 8 km/h when fully loaded (6 tonnes)[17]. In 1879, the first electric locomotive was built for the Berlin Exhibition. A decade later, the first electric rail line, *The Giant's Causeway Tramway,* was constructed in Ireland. From the early 19th century to the Second World War, two successive combinations of technologies drove advances in science and technology: "the coke-smelting-steam system during the first three quarters of the 19th century and the steel-electricity-chemicals-motor system after 1875."[18] Over the centuries, the use of wood as a fuel was superseded

---

[14] In Israel, China and maybe even the Czech Republic (Prezletice site). See http://www.hominides.com/html/dossiers/feu_domestication.htm

[15] See Total's Planète-Énergies site at http://www.planete-energies.com/contenu/energie/definition-energies/histoire-source-energies.html

[16] *Ibid.*

[17] See "Chronologie du chemin de fer", at http://hypo.ge.ch/www/cliotexte/html/chemin.de.fer.html

[18] Institut Jules-Destrée, "Histoire économique et sociale", available at http://www.wallonie-en-ligne.net/1995_Wallonie_Atouts-References/1995_ch09-3_Halleux-R_Bernes-A-C_Etienne-L.htm

by coal and then petroleum. The use of petroleum ushered humanity into a new industrial era. Coal still has a good future ahead of it, since it is the only abundant fossil fuel and, in many countries, it is the main source of primary energy for generating electricity, much like wood is used as a fuel for heating and cooking in resource-poor countries.

The Measurement of Energy

Every body has its own heating value. Long before heat was understood to be a form of energy, heat transfer studies led to the adoption of the unit of heat called the **calorie,** defined as the amount of heat required to raise the temperature of a gram of water by 1°C.[19] Today, the calorie, which is too small to provide a useful basis of comparison, has been relegated to the field of nutrition, where it occurs in the form of the kilocalorie (or food Calorie).[20] In other fields, the calorie has been replaced by the **joule**[21] (symbol **J**), the unit of heat used in the International System of Units (SI) since its adoption by the General Conference on Weights and Measures. The British have always remained fiercely attached to their pounds and feet and have therefore selected their own heat unit –the British Thermal Unit (BTU), defined as the quantity of energy required to raise the temperature of a pound of water (a mass of 0.4535924 kg) by 1°F. One BTU is equivalent to 1,055 joules, 252 calories or 0.293 Wh (see below).[22] BTUs are still commonly used to express the total amount of primary energy that countries consume –generally in quadrillions (1×10^{15}) of BTUs, or "quads."

Energy transfers are characterized not only by the quantity of energy transferred but also by the duration of the process. Power, or the amount of energy consumed or produced per unit of time, is expressed in **watts** (W); a watt, by definition, corresponds to the transfer of one joule of energy per second. One watt-hour (**Wh**) is equal to 3,600 J, and one kilowatt-hour (**kWh**) to 3,600,000 J. Note that joules are not much better than calories as units for measuring common energy transfers. Once a relationship has been established between mechanical energy and heat, it is easy to establish a correspondence between energy types. One kilowatt-hour (kWh) represents the energy produced by a device with a power output of 1,000 W in one hour (one hour = 3,600 seconds; = 3600 × 1000 J = 3,600,000 J). In practice, the energy

---

[19] At normal atmospheric pressure and an initial water temperature of 15⁰C.

[20] A calorie is equal to 4.186 joules. Therefore, 4,186 joules are required to increase the temperature of 1 kg of water at 15°C by one degree.

[21] Despite his French-sounding surname, James Prescott Joule was an English physicist.

[22] In actual fact, an international agreement on weights and measures signed in 1956 was required to reconcile the BTU with the joule, making one BTU equal to 1,055.056 joules.

generated by hydroelectric stations is calculated in megawatts (MW = one million watts or 1×10^6) and, as a general rule, the electricity produced by a country is calculated in terawatts (one thousand billion watts = **TW** or 1×10^{12}).

The notion of work and the measurement of secondary (converted) energy have always reflected their social and scientific context. Today, no one would think of using the outmoded unit of horsepower (1 HP = 735.5 W) except in the automotive field.[23] Similarly, the 1962 edition (in ten volumes) of the *Grand Larousse encyclopédique* contains the following curiosities:[24]

- White coal = energy obtained from falling water
- Blue coal = energy obtained from tides
- Colourless coal = energy obtained from the wind
- Gold coal = energy obtained from solar radiation
- Red coal = energy obtained from the heat in the deep layers of the earth (geothermal energy)
- Green coal = energy obtained from hydroelectric plants

As one can see, coal was much more important back then. Such old-fashioned definitions are amusing today, though the currently popular expressions "blue gold" (tidal power) and "green gold" (biomass) are not much different. In any event, oil has taken over as the unit of comparison for energy. A **TOE** (tonne of oil equivalent), which has replaced the formerly used TEC (tonne of coal equivalent), corresponds to the energy produced by the combustion of one tonne of oil. Each TOE represents 42 gigajoules (GJ: 1×10^9 J).[25]

Every body has a specific heating value, and consequently a combustion constant. The combustion of one kilogram of wood provides 14.6-15.5 MJ, compared to 56 MJ for one kilogram of natural gas (methane) and 120 MJ for one kilogram of hydrogen. Oil provides 42 MJ. A TOE therefore is equivalent to 1,000 kg $\times$ 42 MJ = 42 GJ.

Table 1 is a very useful tool for comparing different types of energy, and will be referred to in subsequent chapters. However, some of the definitions used in the table are problematic, particularly for electricity production. As a rule, world energy consumption is calculated based on **primary energy consumption**. Primary energy

---

[23] The Scot James Watt was responsible for advancing the notion of horsepower, defining it as equal to 745.7 W. For more information on differences in interpreting these units of measure, see Gérard P. Michon, "Measurements and Units" at http://home.att.net/~numericana/answer/units.htm

[24] Bituminous coal is one of the non-anthracite mineral coals. The previous chapter contained a discussion on the degree of maturation of sediments of plant origin. The sequence is as follows: peat (50% C), lignite (72% C), bituminous coal (85% C) and anthracite (93% C). See Pierre-André Bourque, Planète-Terre, "Les combustibles fossiles" at http://www.ggl.ulaval.ca/personnel/bourque/intro.pt/ planete_terre.html

[25] This figure is rounded off; the actual TOE value is 41.6 GJ.

Table 1: Energy conversion coefficients

ENERGY	Unit	In gigajoules GJ (LHV)	In TOE (LHV)* (ratio GJ/42, except for electricity, nuclear power and geothermal power)
COAL	1 tonne		
Bituminous coal	1 tonne	26	0.619
Coke (from bituminous coal)	1 tonne	28	0.667
Lignite agglomerates and briquettes	1 tonne	32	0.762
Lignite and by-products	1 tonne	17	0.405
PETROLEUM			
Crude oil, diesel/ domestic fuel oil	**1 tonne**	**42**	**1**
LPG	1 tonne	46	1.095
Gasoline and aviation fuel	1 tonne	44	1.048
Heavy fuel oil	1 tonne	40	0.952
Petroleum coke	1 tonne	32	0.762
ELECTRICITY			
From nuclear power	1 MWh	3.6	0.086/0.33 = 0.2606
From geothermal power	1 MWh	3.6	0.86/0.10 = 0.86
Other types of production (imports and exports), consumption	1 MWh	3.6	0.086
WOOD	1 stere (=1 m³)	6.17	0.147
NATURAL AND INDUSTRIAL GAS	1 MWh	3.24	0.077

Note: The LHV (lower heating value) as opposed to the HHV (high heating value). For more details, see definitions at http://www.industrie.gouv.fr/energie/statisti/methodef.htm

Source: See www.industrie.gouv.fr/energie/comprendre/q-r.htm

consists of all sources of raw energy (wood, coal, oil or gas at the well head[26]), which Jean-Marie Martin of the Institut d'économie et de politique de l'énergie de Grenoble describes as energy that exists "before physical processing (oil refining or

---

[26] For gas, Canada uses consumption at the burner tip rather than the wellhead –in other words, where the gas is being consumed.

gas liquefaction) takes place and before conversion into electricity in a conventional generating station."[27] In Table 1, the coefficients for nuclear and geothermal energy are calculated at the plant outlet and take account of existing facilities' energy efficiency ratios.[28] This has the effect of considerably minimizing the role of electricity production in France's primary energy consumption.

World Primary Energy Consumption (1800-2005)

Figure 2 shows the evolution of primary energy consumption for coal, oil and gas over several centuries (1800-2005), a time span that makes the exercise a statistically interesting one. Consumption is expressed in millions of TOE.[29]

Note the break in the scale for 2005. The original table stops at 2000; the figures for 2005 were taken from the *BP Statistical Review of World Energy 2005*. In addition, the paper by J.-M. Martin includes biomass (firewood) and provides statistics on world electricity consumption for the time period in question, while, here, we show only the three fossil fuels for the entire period of 1800-2005. This was done to make the graph more readable and to illustrate certain elements that we emphasized earlier.

Several key points can be made here. Oil consumption really started to take off in the 1930s: world oil consumption rose from 207 MTOE (million tonnes of oil equivalent) in 1930 to 3,767 MTOE in 2005. The spectacular rise in coal consumption dates back to the last few decades of the nineteenth century, and consumption of this fuel has grown steadily ever since. In 2005, world coal consumption reached

---

[27] Jean-Marie Martin, "La consommation des sources d'énergie : utilisations finales, efficacité et productivité" available at web.upmf-grenoble.fr/iepe/Equipe/martin/ martinPubli.html. Hereafter cited as J.-M. Martin.

[28] The actual figure is 33% for nuclear power plants –the rest is dissipated in the form of heat or is used to heat the buildings– and 10% for geothermal plants, which explains why in Table 1 the equivalence coefficients are reduced by a ratio that takes account of energy efficiency. This explains the huge differences in the coefficients for electrical energy from abroad (the international standard for calculations) and TOE equivalents for nuclear or geothermal energy. In short, everything depends on what is being measured: what the consumer pays for or uses or what a country produces in the form of primary energy. If energy sources are to be replaced by the kWh that they supply, measured at the power plant outlet, "one speaks of primary electricity as opposed to secondary energy, which is produced from the combustion of fossil fuels or biomass." See J.-M. Martin, *Ibid*.

[29] Many people have problems with oil-gas equivalents. The conversion factor is fairly simple: 6,000 cubic feet of gas is equivalent to a barrel of oil. This convention is used in oil companies' annual reports although, a few years ago, when natural gas prices were low, some firms used 10,000 cubic feet of gas as the equivalent of a barrel of oil.

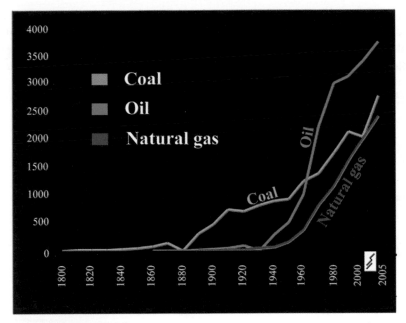

Figure 2: World energy consumption (1800-2005) (in millions of TOE)
Source: Adapted from Appendix 1 of the text by J.-M. Martin, *op. cit.*

2,778 MTOE, or around two thirds of the figure for oil. This is something we –and environmentalists in particular– tend to forget (see Chapter 8 on climate change).

Although steam-powered ships played a primary role in the First World War, oil came into its own during the Second World War, when the Allies' control of oil supplies gave them a decisive advantage over Germany. In the early 1960s, oil took over from coal as the most heavily used primary energy source. Natural gas, whose prices have paralleled those for oil more often than not, still remains behind coal, but the gap between the two is expected to narrow in the future. The use of natural gas, which is relatively non-polluting, is expanding quickly at present, particularly liquefied natural gas (LNG); however, it will be another 20 years before it catches up to or surpasses coal as a world source of primary energy. This is due to both high gas production costs and the fact that the gas market has not yet been completely globalized (see chapter on liquefied natural gas). Figure 3 shows world primary energy consumption during the period 1980-2030, expressed in quadrillions of BTUs (quads). What stands out is the predominance of oil –which made up 38% of the world's primary energy basket in 2003– but also the parallel progression of coal and natural gas. According to projections, these two types of energy will remain very competitive with respect to one another until 2030, when they will be practically neck and neck. The recent rise in oil prices explains the renewed strength of coal during the period in question. World consumption of natural gas, which stood at 95 quadrillion cubic feet in 2003, is expected to reach 134 and 182 quadrillion cubic feet in 2015 and 2030, respectively. Nuclear energy will grow slightly, but renewable energies are steadily gaining ground. The world faces a serious problem: the absolute predominance of fossil fuels in world energy consumption.

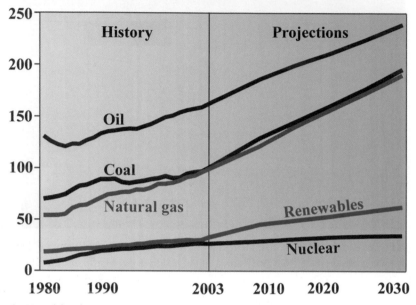

Figure 3: World primary energy consumption, 1980-2030 (in quadrillions of BTUs)
Source: EIA, International Energy Outlook 2006 (IEO 2006)

According to the Energy Information Administration's (EIA) reference case scenario, world energy consumption (all fuels combined) should grow from 421 quads in 2003 to 722 quads in 2030.[30] This is an increase of 71% in only 27 years. Two thirds of this growth is expected to come from developing countries.

Primary Energy Consumption in the United States in 2006

In 2006, primary energy consumption in the United States stood at 99.9 quads. The most important sources of energy (in descending order) were oil, natural gas, coal, electricity and renewable resources. The heaviest energy consumers were the electric power, transportation, industrial and residential and commercial sectors.

As Figure 4 shows, the transportation sector depends on petroleum for 69% of its energy needs. Natural gas fulfills 35% of requirements in the industrial sector and

---

[30]   *International Energy Outlook 2006* (IEO 2006), DOE, EIA, June 2006, p. 7.

33% in the residential sector; the electric power sector also relies on natural gas to a large degree (29%). Coal is also an important energy source. It accounts for 22.6 quads of BTUs (or nearly 23%) of the United States' total primary energy production; 91% of this output is used by the electric power sector.

Every country has its own primary energy budget. For example, in 2003, petroleum represented 19% of primary energy production in Russia, compared with 40% in the United States. On the other hand, natural gas made up 53% of Russia's primary energy production, compared with 23% in the United States. Coal represented 16% of Russia's primary energy production, compared with 23% in the United States and 65% in China. Many factors affect a country's energy basket, making strategic choices difficult.

Economic Development and Energy Intensity and Efficiency

Owing to the complexity of processing and conversion chains, the strategic choices that countries face are difficult ones. In the case of the United States, Figure 4 provides a good illustration of the thorny technological decisions required. From the original energy source to final use, there are many steps in the energy supply chain: resource extraction, physical and chemical processing, transportation and distribution, final conversion and final energy.[31] Any conversion of energy results in losses and any substitution of one type of energy for another entails expenses and investments on the part of the energy services producer. It is understandable that producers and consumers view energy choices very differently.

Links Between Economics and Energy

Figure 5 shows the relationship between per capita energy use and income for selected countries. In the graph, the y-axis represents per capita total energy consumption in gigajoules (GJ), while the x-axis shows per capita income in thousands of dollars of **purchasing power parity** (PPP), expressed in 1997 U.S. dollars.[32]

The graph demonstrates that a country's per capita growth in energy consumption is closely linked to its economic development, a relation that appears to be

---

[31] Energy that is actually consumed; depends in particular on conversion efficiency coefficients. The electric power sector is especially inefficient owing to transmission losses.

[32] This diagram is taken from British Petroleum's "Exploring the Future, Energy Needs, Choices and Possibilities, Scenarios to 2050."

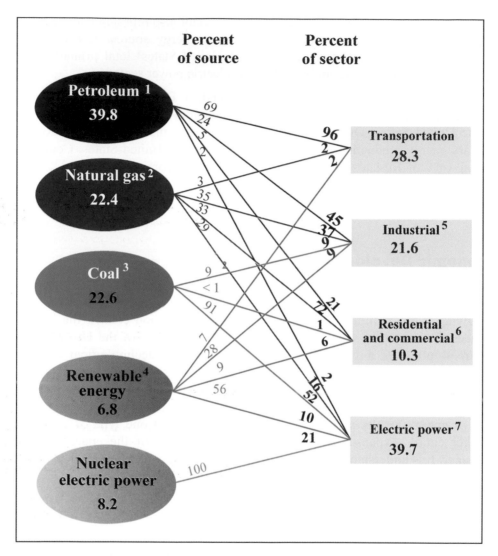

1. Excludes 0.5 quadrillion Btu of ethanol, which is included in "Renewable Energy".
2. Excludes supplemental gaseous fuels.
3. Includes 0.1 quadrillion Btu of coal coke net imports.
4. Conventional hydroelectric power, geothermal, solar/PV, wind, and biomass.
5. Includes industrial combined-heat-and-power (CHP) and industrial electricity-only plants.
6. Includes commercial combined-heat-and-power (CHP) and commercial electricity-only plants.
7. Electricity-only and combined-heat-and-power (CHP) plants whose primary business is to sell electricity, or electricity and heat, to the public.

Figure 4: Primary energy consumption in the United States in 2006 (in quadrillions of BTUs)

Source: From EIA, *Annual Energy Review 2007*

stable across time and space.[33] In other words, there is a strong association between per capita income and per capita energy consumption. When per capita income reaches roughly $15,000, a levelling off can be seen which continues until a saturation point is reached at $25,000. At this point, economic growth continues without an increase in energy consumption.

In the real world, the actual relationship is not as uniform as Figure 5 would suggest, however. According to Leif Magne Meling, Vice-President of the Norwegian firm Statoil, average per capita petroleum consumption in the world is 4.6 barrels, compared with 25 barrels in the United States and between 10 and 18 barrels in Europe and other developed nations. Per capita consumption is only 2 barrels in China and 0.9 in India.[34] China rightly maintains that it is not the only country responsible for the growth in world oil demand. In 2020, per capita annual income in China should reach $3,000 and Chinese oil consumption should then equal what the U.S. consumption was in 2006.[35]

Figure 5 provides a grossly oversimplified picture, particularly because it conceals a multitude of secret variables no doubt familiar to the IMF and BP. We are exaggerating, of course, because the problem in itself is complex, a fact of which economists are only too aware. There are three general assumptions underlying this diagram.

The first assumption involves the definition of the benchmark. Many economists have observed that using exchange rates when making country-to-country comparisons introduces too much distortion.[36] Economists and international economic organizations agree that per capita income should be calculated based on **purchasing power parity** (PPP). Although PPP is not perfect, it does take account of differences in living standards from country to country. If a litre of milk costs one dollar in one country and five dollars in another, this means that, in terms of purchasing power parity, the currency of the first country is worth five times more than that of the second. A smaller PPP coefficient will therefore be applied to the second country's currency.

---

[33] Except for the periods 1973-75 and 1979-82, J.-M. Bourdaire notes that, in general, primary energy demand increases by roughly 2.5% per year when the GDP increases by 3%. See J.-M. Bourdaire, "Le lien entre consommation d'énergie et développement économique." Bourdaire, a former department head at the International Energy Agency (IEA) who has now joined TotalFinaElf, has uncovered the links between development and energy. See www.worldenergy. org/wec-geis/global/lists/bourdaire.asp

[34] See Leif Magne Meling, "The Origin of Challenge: Oil Supply and Demand", Part 1, *Middle East Economic Survey,* Vol. XLIX, No. 24, June 12, 2006. The original study is no doubt a few years older. Available at www.polyteknisk.no/.../download/1732/5869/file/Meling.pdf?eZSES SIDpolytekn=cf907ef41c7d34b94fd4dd25d3d722a4

[35] *Ibid,* based on an annual economic growth rate of roughly 7%.

[36] May range from 1 to 3 according to J.-M. Bourdaire, *op. cit.*

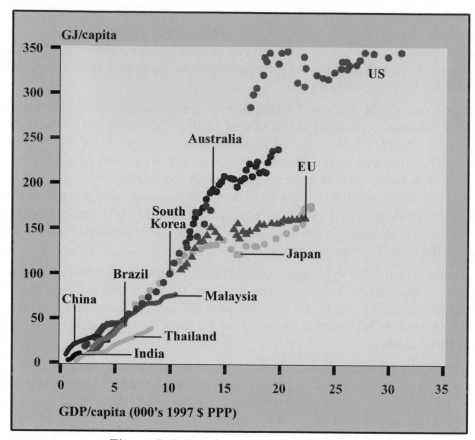

Figure 5: Per capita energy use and income
Source: IMF and BP, "Exploring the Future, Scenarios to 2050", 2001.

The second assumption relates to **energy intensity,** defined as the quantity of energy consumed per unit of gross domestic product (GDP): in other words, the amount of energy required to add a dollar (here, considered as a unit) of wealth to a country's production. What is measured here is only part of the picture since the GDP includes exports –and therefore domestically produced goods– but not imports. Furthermore, should we distinguish between developed countries based on the structure of their production economy? What has been termed the "dematerialization" of the GDP is an extremely important phenomenon, since highly advanced economies are increasingly service-oriented (banking, insurance, finance, information technologies) and service industries are not heavy consumers of energy as manufacturing is. This variable expresses the degree of saturation observed in the ascending scale of energy use (Figure 5). J.-M. Bourdaire points out that, "in a global economy characterized by the removal of tariff protections, the rise in energy prices following oil shocks has revealed, or even provided the impetus for, the delocalization of industries that are heavy energy consumers."[37]

The third and last assumption deals with the very notion of primary energy consumption. The general approach is to include all fossil energies, along with renewable energies and nuclear power, in primary energy consumption. As explained earlier, there is no problem with converting the various forms of energy based on a tonne of oil equivalent (TOE) or the work supplied in gigajoules. However, electricity and hydrogen are final energies that do not exist in nature. They are termed secondary energies because they must be produced.

Should the focus be on final energy demand rather than on the primary energy content of the GDP? This is an important choice. For example, just after the beginning of the new millennium, France modified its method of calculating energy produced from electricity.[38] This caused nuclear power to drop from 30% of energy consumption in 2000 to about 16% in 2001.[39] This assumption can be defended on the grounds that if nuclear power has to be replaced by other forms of energy some day, we will have to use fossil fuels (wood, coal, gas, oil) or renewable energies. Therefore, it all depends on what we want to measure. The U.S. Department of Energy defines **primary energy** as the amount of energy delivered to the final consumer, minus losses associated with the generation, transmission and distribution of energy. **Final energy**, on the other hand, is based on the assumption that the energy from a **unit of production output** is the energy delivered to the final consumer, excluding losses associated with generation, transmission and distribution. Therefore, final energy is the quantity of energy delivered to the consumer. It all boils down to deciding what we want to measure.

---

[37] J.-M. Bourdaire, *op. cit.*

[38] Jean Laherrère does not sugar-coat things. He believes that this approach reflects the fact that scientists have given up in the face of a complex reality. "Most countries use IEA conventions (nuclear power equivalent to a conventional power plant with 33% efficiency and geothermal, to one with 10% efficiency). In 2001, France went from a system that was compatible with the IEA's to its own system –the IEA's wasn't much better but was more widely used. As a result, primary energy consumption went from 257 MTOE to 269 MTOE and petroleum, from 31% to 39% and tidal, wind and solar power from 6.9% to 2.5%. Final energy consumption went from 232 MTOE to 175 MTOE, petroleum from 40% to 51% and renewable thermal from 4.6% to 6.1%. Although the media viewed this significant change as political manipulation, it was more a matter of scientists giving up when faced with a complex problem." See "Énergie et agriculture: tout a un pic" at www.hubbertpeak.com/laherrere/Strasbourg.pdf. Sharp criticism of France's decision to go it alone energy-wise can be found in Yves Lenoir, "Les illusoires progrès de l'indépendance énergétique française : trucage des données électriques, statut national de l'uranium importé", available at www.unige.ch/sebes/textes/1995/95YLillusoire.html.

[39] See Jean-Marc Jancovici, "Quelle part de l'électricité dans la consommation française d'énergie ?" at www.manicore.com.

Energy Intensity and Energy Efficiency

The above-mentioned concepts are fundamental in distinguishing the notions of **energy intensity** and **energy efficiency**. Despite the interpretation problems that we have just outlined, energy intensity is a ratio describing a simple quantitative economic dimension: the amount of energy that goes into producing something. Calculating the various inputs is far from child's play, however. Energy efficiency, on the other hand, is generally more qualitative. Although it is sometimes associated with the notion of intensity, it operates by subtraction. In 2005, Canada's Office of Energy Efficiency (OEE) reported the following results:

> Energy consumption increased between 1990 and 2002. If energy efficiency had not improved, the increase would have been 31% due to activities, meteorological conditions and the structure and level of services. However, thanks to the 13% improvement in energy efficiency, actual energy consumption only increased by 18%.[40]

This would be hard to understand if we did not know how the results were obtained: Canada uses factor analysis, a method also adopted by the International Energy Agency and several other countries. This method of determining energy efficiency takes several fundamental variables into account, such as energy consumption by sector,[41] structural changes,[42] temperature anomalies[43] and the extent to which auxiliary heating and air conditioning equipment are being used in institutional buildings. The importance of each variable is analyzed, while other variables remain constant. Relative changes in energy consumption can be measured on a yearly basis, but the question of energy intensity per se is not taken into account.[44] According to the U.S. Department of Energy, there are four basic methods for determining a country's energy efficiency, including factorial decomposition, which is used in Canada.[45]

---

[40] *The State of Energy Efficiency in Canada*, Report 2005, Office of Energy Efficiency, Ottawa, Natural Resources Canada. Hereafter cited as NRC, 2005 Report.

[41] Residential, commercial, institutional, industrial, agricultural, etc.

[42] For example, the replacement of one type of fuel by another or an increase in the productivity of one industry relative to another.

[43] The figures are standardized to take account of variations from the norm.

[44] The report provides more details on what improved energy efficiency represents. During 2002 alone, Canadians reduced their energy bill by $11.6 billion and, according to the most recent statistics, there was a drop of $13.4 billion in 2003. This amount is significant since it is approximately equal to the annual budget of the Department of National Defence.

[45] The other approaches are the market-basket approach, the comprehensive approach and the divisia index approach. The DOE refers readers to the basic texts used to develop the different indicators and the associated analysis methods. See http://www.eia.doe.gov/emeu/efficiency/measure_discussion.htm.

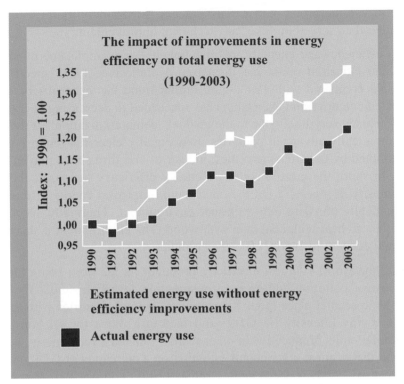

Figure 6: Energy efficiency and consumption
Source: From OEE's 2005 report and *Energy Efficiency Trends*, 2005

Energy efficiency can be defined as any process that, for a given level of energy service, either reduces energy use (inputs) while maintaining a comparable performance or improves performance while using the same quantity of energy.[46] In the first case, all inefficient or poorly performing devices must be eliminated from the market and manufacturers must be encouraged to produce energy-efficient devices. The second case is a little more complex. It involves doing more with less energy input, i.e., producing more while reducing energy consumption (for example, fewer kilowatts used per tonne of copper produced). However, using "the minimum amount of energy theoretically needed to perform a task"[47] may require improvements in organization and management rather than technology changes. This is why

---

[46] The definition in the U.S. Department of Energy's glossary is as follows: "increases in energy efficiency take place when either energy inputs are reduced for a given level of service or there are increased or enhanced services for a given amount of energy inputs."

[47] Cited in "Ecological Fiscal Reform (EFR) and Energy", National Round Table on the Environment and the Economy at http://www.nrtee-trnee.ca/eng/programs/Current_Programs/EFR-Energy/ Case_Studies/200406_Energy-Efficiency-CS/200406_Energy-Efficiency-CS_Contents_E.htm. Hereafter cited as Round Table.

we chose to use the broad phrase "any process" in the definition of energy efficiency, rather than something like "any technical improvement."

Energy efficiency and intensity are often linked. For example, energy intensity in the Canadian industrial sector has decreased overall since 1990, specifically "by 27% in 2002 compared with 1990."[48] A similar trend has been observed in most industrialized countries and even China has succeeded in decreasing energy input in its GDP.[49] This is very likely due to the gradual "dematerialization" of the GDPs of large, economically advanced countries. It is equally clear that energy efficiency policies adopted by governments, cities, industries and firms have played a significant part. In short, the more a country's energy efficiency increases, the more its energy intensity decreases.[50] On the other hand, improved energy efficiency does not automatically translate into a cleaner environment. Thermally speaking, it is more efficient to heat with coal than with wood. The environment is therefore also an important concern in energy efficiency policies.

Canada, the world's largest electricity producer, is far from being the country with the lowest pollution and energy consumption levels. In 2002, for example, Canada was in second place (after Luxembourg) among countries with the highest per capita energy intensity (in GJ),[51] and in fourth place for GJ consumed per $1,000 of GDP units produced.[52] In other words, Canada's total energy intensity is greater than that of most other countries, either on a per capita or GDP unit basis.[53] This is because Canada is also a major producer of oil and gas and other raw materials. Furthermore, Canada has a huge landmass and is subject to particularly severe climatic variations in winter. We will return in a later chapter to the question of

---

[48] *Ibid.*

[49] According to the French agency Agence de l'Environnement et de la Maîtrise de l'Energie (ADEME), China, "which had the highest energy intensity levels in 1980, saw these levels decrease four times faster than in the rest of the world, and they are now near the international average."

[50] Everything else being equal. Obviously, this relation can be distorted if a country decides to massively focus on the development of heavy industry, which is a huge consumer of energy.

[51] NRC, 2005 Report, *op. cit.*

[52] *Ibid.*

[53] It depends also on the unit of measurement chosen and the phenomenon to be measured. As EDC Senior Vice-President and Chief Economist Stephen S. Poloz said in October 2004, "the U.S. economy consumes 0.75 barrels of oil per US$1,000 of GDP, compared with 1.27 barrels in 1980. The major European economies and Japan consume much less oil, roughly 0.40 barrels per US$1,000 of GDP, also roughly 30-40% less than in 1980. Canada is a relative glutton, given our harsh climate, since we consume 0.99 barrels of oil per US$1,000 of GDP, which still represents a 40% decrease over 1980. The developing countries' dependence on oil is much greater. China and India, for example, consume 1.50 to 1.60 barrels of oil to produce US$1,000 of GDP, and the figures are similar for Mexico, Indonesia, Malaysia and Thailand. Russia consumes 1.75 barrels; and Turkey, South Africa and South Korea, 1.10 to 1.15 barrels." See Stephen S. Poloz, Export Development Canada (EDC), "Economic Reports", *Weekly Commentary*, Ottawa, October 20, 2004.

increased greenhouse gas (GHG) emissions from the burning of fossil fuels. It should be kept in mind that primary energy sources, rather than secondary ones, are used to calculate carbon dioxide emissions, although adjustments (energy equivalents) take account of this second level of energy.[54]

The topic merits further exploration. Energy efficiency means consuming energy more wisely, whereas energy intensity is measured by the amount of energy that goes into the accumulation of national wealth (GDP growth). Does wiser consumption mean consuming less energy? The Canadian statistics on this are revealing. "Between 1995 and 2001, the activity share of less energy intensive industries has increased while the share represented by more energy intensive industries has decreased, leading to a decline in total energy use of 11.5% relative to 1995."[55] In short, the two are one and the same. Either energy efficiency is a measurement of more effective energy use, and is obviously linked to energy intensity, or we are measuring the evidence –in other words, any growth in the GDP is not caused solely by energy efficiency, but can be attributed more to structural macroeconomic factors linked to energy consumption as well as to the transformation of production factors in advanced economies. We have come full circle to the questions we had concerning Figure 5. There is a great deal to reflect on.

Resource Concentration and Vulnerabilities

One of the most important risk factors that oil-consuming nations have had to grapple with is the concentration of oil and gas reserves in the Middle East. During the 1973 Arab-Israeli War, Arab nations did not hesitate to slap a major oil embargo on the West. This move did have some positive impacts, however, such as the creation of the International Energy Agency (IEA) in Paris and member countries' establishment of large oil reserves,[56] which they could tap in another crisis to soften the most severe blows. The United States created a major strategic reserve of 700 million barrels. Beyond these preventive measures, how can the risk related to this geopolitical variable be defined?

First, let us define **energy insecurity**. In technical terms, the greatest threat would come from a **major breakdown in the energy system**, like the immense blackout that occurred in the United States over several days in August 2003. In the space of a few minutes, the country lost 61,800 MW of electricity, and 50 million

---

[54] At least in Canada.

[55] Round Table, *op. cit.*

[56] This occurred largely because of the desire to have "an emergency energy distribution system in case of a disruption in energy supplies." The IEA currently has 26 member countries.

customers were plunged into darkness. There was a cascade of events that the authorities were powerless to stop. Whether the error was human or technical is completely irrelevant. The fact is that even the best systems are not immune to major technical problems. The only possible response to this risk is to increase the reliability of systems and facilities. A great deal of effort has gone into securing facilities, and this has nearly been achieved in the case of nuclear reactors. Energy security is also affected by **natural disasters** such as Hurricane Katrina, whose effects lasted for many months. These two phenomena can be subsumed under what insurance companies call fortuitous events or an act of God. Security concerns are omnipresent and we live with them, but we cannot really assign the responsibility for a cascade of events to a particular individual, system or organization and, even if we could, this would not solve the problem. All we can do is prepare better for the future and better manage risks to mitigate impacts, but there will always be some unforeseeable events.

A third form of insecurity has military or police implications –the perceived threat of **acts of terrorism** directed against so-called critical national infrastructures (energy facilities, nuclear power plants, hydroelectric dams, airports, communications infrastructures, banking systems and the like). Such threats are a reality, but the police and security forces or the military are the ones responsible for countering them. Therefore, they are not included among the factors contributing to countries' strategic vulnerability.

A country's **geopolitical vulnerability** can be divided into three components: its structural dependence on foreign energy supplies, the structural composition of its primary energy mix and its structural capacity to replace an increasing percentage of its energy imports with domestic production.

Domestic Substitution

We will begin with the third element, which is the easiest to explain. If all countries were energy self-sufficient, dependence on foreign supplies would not be a problem. For example, the United States was self-sufficient at least in terms of petroleum demand until the late 1950s. As soon as a country's energy production no longer meets domestic demand, however, it must turn to foreign sources to cover its energy deficit. The more dependent a country is on a given region, the more vulnerable it is. In such a situation, any domestic substitution, such as the greater use of renewable energies, is a valuable asset in decreasing a country's vulnerability.

A parallel can be seen in the situation 30 or 40 years ago when some Latin American countries wanted to adopt an import substitution policy to counter the United States' economic supremacy. This raises interesting economic issues that also involve strategic political considerations: how to mitigate the risks of increased foreign dependence. Economics cannot be separated from politics.

The Energy Mix

A country is also more vulnerable if its primary energy mix tips dangerously toward a single resource. If a country relies on oil and gas for its economic development, for example, and the resource is in short supply, its economic prospects will be seriously threatened. Conversely, the more diversified a country's energy basket, the greater its economic flexibility. A good example is electricity production in the United States. This is admittedly secondary energy, but it illustrates very well the increased choices that countries with a diversified energy portfolio have. The United States' portfolio has evolved over the years and coal is now used to generate over 50% of the country's electricity.

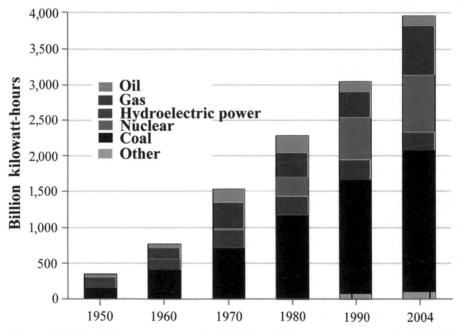

Figure 7: Electricity generation in the United States, by source (1950-2004)
Source: Annual Energy Review 2004, Table 8.2a

In addition, the role of oil and gas in electricity generation began decreasing in the 1990s, while the contribution of nuclear energy increased. In 2003, for example, oil and gas accounted for no more than 3% of electricity production in the United States.[57] The most important element is obviously the growing role of natural gas-fired power plants. The situation has changed considerably over the years, owing to

---

[57] See *Energy: Useful Facts and Numbers*, CRS Report for Congress, January 10, 2006, p. 19.

factors such as Washington's shifting energy policies. After the 1973 oil crisis, an attempt was made to increase the use of natural gas in electricity production, but the continent's trade in natural gas was still regulated and gas-fired power plants were reserved for the use of other economic sectors under the Fuel Use Act of 1978. Much of the 1978 act was subsequently repealed and in 2000, 16% of electricity generated in the U.S. came from natural gas-fired power plants.[58]

We have presented these figures to illustrate an important phenomenon: a country's domestic energy mix reflects not only economic considerations but also the important role that governments can play in ensuring energy self-sufficiency. The wider the mix, the greater the country's flexibility. The more economically powerful the country, the greater its influence and margin of manoeuvre, allowing it to influence price setting. This structural variable partly depends on the degree to which the country has succeeded in diminishing its dependence on foreign energy supplies. It also depends on price differentials between energies, and is therefore more circumstantial than the issue of dependence on foreign supplies. This phenomenon is all the more important in that, on one hand, the United States is a rich country and a voracious energy consumer and, on the other, that its energy policy has a potentially global impact. For example, the global expansion of the liquefied natural gas (LNG) market is no doubt occurring because of the increased worldwide demand for this resource. However, if the United States makes LNG the cornerstone of its clean energy campaign, it will be forced to directly compete with Europe for firm supply contracts, both over the short and long terms.

Structural Dependence on Imports

A simple principle is involved: a country should not put all its eggs in one basket and should instead diversify its foreign sources of supply. We will return to these geopolitical considerations in a later chapter. The problem is all the more acute since projections for 2025 and 2030 (see Chapter 7) suggest that, just as in 1973, the industrial world will depend on the Middle East and Gulf states for over 50% of its oil and gas supplies. The question is: have we made any real progress?

In December 2004, the IEA published an interesting study by William Blyth and Nicolas Lefèvre on the structural vulnerability of countries and the main risk factors involved.[59] The risks of vulnerability to resource concentration can be quantified, just like the ripple effects that renewable energies can have on a country's energy mix. Despite the fundamental importance of oil and gas in industrial nations' energy baskets, countries still have a little time to react politically to the issue of resource

---

[58] *Ibid.*

[59] *Energy Security and Climate Change Policy Interactions: An Assessment Framework*, Paris, IEA Information Paper, December 2004.

concentration, although currently they seem to be refusing to face this problem due to laziness, inertia, recklessness or simple ignorance.

As we will see in Chapter 6, a country's energy dependence can be measured by a simple ratio: the ratio of imports to consumption. This is the only measure that is currently accepted by the community of energy specialists. Obviously, the real situation cannot be conveyed by such a simple formula. Oil prices respond first and foremost to the laws of supply and demand, but many other factors also come into play. There are some people who still claim that the best way to conserve our resources for future generations is to keep hydrocarbon prices high. In actual fact, if oil prices were expressed in real, constant dollars, oil would not cost more than in the early 1980s. It is all a matter of perspective, investments and the price consumers are willing to pay to get around and develop economically. Up to now, our economies have supported high energy costs without too much harm, simply because they have improved their energy efficiency and decreased their energy intensity. We are far from the day when, according to some of the U.S. Department of Energy's best economists, a country's GDP growth will drop by half a percentage for each $5 increase in the price of a barrel of oil. That being said, cheap energy is a thing of the past and we will have to get used to it.

4

Renewable Energies

All renewable energies (RE or renewables, for short) have become increasingly popular given skyrocketing oil and gas prices on one hand and legitimate concerns over rising levels of CO_2 in the atmosphere on the other. Some renewables are already well established while others are marginally competitive; some are on the way to becoming cost effective while, for others, this is still a long way off. According to the *Renewables 2005: Global Status Report*, renewables account for 14-17% of the world's primary energy production.[1] The renewables market was worth no less than US$38 billion in 2005 alone.[2] Since it is impossible to cover all renewable energies in depth in a single chapter, we will limit ourselves to the essentials: biofuels, wind, solar, geothermal, ocean (tidal and wave power) and hydrogen fuel cells. In addition, we will touch briefly on current research into the production of electricity from nuclear fusion.[3]

But before we begin, let us spend a little time on terminology. Although electricity can be considered a renewable form of energy, such as when it is produced from renewable sources such as biomass, it is often generated from nonrenewable resources such as coal. Therefore, it is important to differentiate between the energy sources used to generate electricity.

---

[1] We will return to this report on the status of renewables later in the chapter. The figure of 17% can be reduced to 13% or 14% depending on whether small hydro (here, defined as plants with a capacity below 10 MW) is included or not in the total production from renewables. Renewable energies are defined as "new" renewables, i.e., small hydro, biomass, wind, solar, geothermal and biofuels. See *Renewables 2005: Global Status Report*, 2005, at the Renewable Energy Policy Network for the 21st century (REN21) site: www.ren21.net/Globalstatusreport/re2005_global_status_report.pdf. According to ABS Energy Research, in 2006, renewables accounted for 14% of primary energy production. See *Renewable Energy Report 2006*, at http://www.marketresearch.com/product. Renewables supplied 18.2% of world electricity production in 2004.

[2] Compared to US$30 billion in 2004.

[3] Nuclear power from fission is considered to be a nonrenewable form of energy because the reactors are powered by fossil fuels produced from a nonrenewable resource, uranium.

Figure 1: Winds of change?
Source: Science & Décision, May 2005

A large percentage of the world's electricity is produced from fossil fuels such as coal and natural gas, and from nuclear power; hydropower represents only 16% of world production (see Table 1). On the other hand, hydropower makes up the lion's share of renewable resources (90%) used for electricity generation, followed by biomass; contributions from other renewable energy sources are very small.

Table 1: Structure of world electricity production and world electricity production from renewables in 2005 (renewables are shown in bold)

	Percentage of 2005 world electricity production (%)	Percentage of 2005 world electricity production from renewables (%)
Hydro	**16.2**	**89.5**
Biomass	**1.0**	**5.6**
Wind	**0.5**	**3.0**
Solar	**...**	**0.1**
Geothermal	**0.3**	**1.7**
Nuclear	15.2	
Fossil	66.4	

Source: La production d'électricité d'origine renouvelable dans le monde, Huitième inventaire, Édition 2006. http://www.energies-renouvelables.org/observ-er/html/Chapitre01FR.pdf

To distinguish among the various contributions to electricity production, different units of measurement are used. The power produced by photovoltaic (PV), or solar, cells is measured in peak watts (W_p)[4], while power produced by solar thermal power plants and geothermal facilities is measured in thermal watts (W_{th} or W_t).

Biomass

Biomass, together with hydropower, are the most heavily used renewable energy sources in the world.[5] In 2005, biomass[6] accounted for 50% of energy production from renewables in the United States, compared with 41% for hydropower, 1% for solar, 3% for wind and 5% for geothermal. It should be noted, however, that renewables made up only 7% of the country's total energy production.[7] With respect to biomass use, the industrialized world is abuzz over **biofuels,** which the Institut français des huiles végétales pures (IFHVP) has defined as any fuel resulting from biosynthesis, as opposed to fossil fuels, which are produced from oil, gas or coal. According to a European Community (EC) directive, biofuels consist of ten products:[8]

- bioethanol[9]
- biodiesel[10]
- biogas[11]
- biomethanol
- biodimethylether
- bioETBE
- bioMTBE
- synthetic biofuels
- biohydrogen
- pure vegetable oil (PVO)

---

[4]   Peak watts are measured under the following conditions: solar irradiance (insolation) of 1,000 W/m^2 under optimum load and a cell temperature of 25°C. In other words, 1 W_p delivers electric power of 1 W using 1,000 W/m^2 of sunlight.

[5]   The U.S. Department of Energy's (DOE) Energy Information Administration (EIA) estimates that these two resources accounted for 7.8% of world energy consumption in 2002. This percentage is expected to decrease slightly to 7.5% in 2025. See Table A8 in the *International Energy Outlook 2005*.

[6]   Biomass is not used solely to produce biofuels. The recovery and reprocessing of wood and wood residues (woodchips) and Municipal Solid Wastes (MWS) accounts for the vast majority of energy derived from biomass in the United States and most other countries.

[7]   EIA, "Renewable Energy Trends, 2005 Edition."

[8]   European Directive 2003/30/EC.

[9]   Bioethanol is derived from the fermentation of plants such as potatoes, sugar beets, grain and sugar cane.

[10] Biodiesel (such as Diester in Europe) is produced by extracting the oil from oilseed crops.

[11] Biogas is obtained from the bacterial fermentation of waste (manure, wastewater treatment sludge, fermentable waste, plant residues). See *Science & Vie*, December 2005, p. 56.

Today, additives or oxygenates are added to some fuels to improve performance (octane and cetane, cold properties) and reduce toxicity and other potential environmental impacts. Gasoline additives include mainly alcohol, ethers and esters (see Table 2). Biofuels fall into two distinct categories: **sugar- (and starch-) based** (potatoes, sugar beets, corn) **forms** used to produce ethanol, which can be blended directly with gasoline or diesel in differing proportions, and **oil-based forms** obtained from oilseed crops.[12] The latter, once filtered, can be used directly as fuel or transformed into biodiesel. **Sugar-based** biofuels are designed for gasoline engines, while **oils** (rapeseed, sunflower, palm) are for diesel engines.[13]

Bioethanol production reached 21.5 million tonnes in 2004. Brazil and the United States together produce 75% of the world's ethanol fuel. According to the *Washington Post*, U.S. ethanol production is heavily subsidized, to the tune of $3 billion a year. A total of 34 corn ethanol processing plants are to be constructed in the United States.[14] Ethanol production is expected to increase everywhere, and in several U.S. states, ethanol is gradually replacing methyl tertiary butyl ether (MTBE), which has been found to be harmful for the environment.[15] In 2004, biofuels only satisfied 1.2% of energy needs in the transport sector.[16] In Europe, the plan is to blend conventional fossil fuels (gasoline and diesel) with up to 5.75% oil esters or ethanol by 2010.

In general, the use of biofuels can decrease greenhouse gas emissions from fossil fuel combustion by 60-70%. "The impact of the use of ethanol on greenhouse gas emissions is roughly 2.5 times less than that of gasoline", comments Étienne Poitrat of France's Agence de l'environnement et de la maîtrise de l'énergie (ADEME), who adds that the impact of Diester is 3.5 times less than that of diesel[17]. However, crops grown for this purpose compete with the agri-food industry for land use. At

---

[12] Sugar-based biofuels are produced through fermentation, and oil-based ones through esterification. Biodiesel is a third type, produced through the gasification of cellulose.

[13] "Les biocarburants : une fausse-bonne idée ?" *Le Monde*, June 8, 2006.

[14] Justin Blum, "Fuel for Growth", *The Washington Post*, February 18, 2006.

[15] An April 2005 joint study sponsored by the USDA and the DOE suggests that by 2030, 30% of current petroleum consumption will be replaced by biofuels. See *Biomass as Feedstock for a Bioenergy and Bioproducts Industry: The Technical Feasibility of a Billion-Ton Annual Supply* at http://feedstockreview.ornl.gov/pdf/ billion_ton_vision.pdf. Although some proposals are obviously a thinly veiled attempt to come to the aid of the ailing U.S. agri-food industry, this report is nonetheless based on important economic considerations. For a more in-depth analysis, see L.L. Wright, M.A. Walsh, M.E. Downing, L.A. Kszos, J.H. Cushman, G.A. Tuskan, S.B. McLaughlin, V.R. Tolbert, J. Scurlock, J. and A.R. Ehrenshaft, *Biomass Feedstock Research and Development for Multiple Products in the United States*, Bioenergy Feedstock Development Program, Oak Ridge National Laboratory, Tennessee, at http://bioenergy.ornl.gov/papers/ bioam2000/bfdp_research2000.html

[16] See *Science & Vie*, December 2005, p. 57.

[17] La France à petits pas, *op. cit.*

Table 2: Main additives and biofuels

Additives or oxygenates comprise:	BIOFUELS	
	Biogasolines	Biodiesels
• *Alcohols*: methanol, ethanol • *Ethers* like MTBE (methyl tertiary butyl ether) • *ETBE* (ethyl tertiary butyl ether) • *TAME* (tertiary amyl methyl ether) • *esters*: rapeseed, dimethylester, etc. • *chemical compounds*: tetraethyl (TEL) and tetramethyl (TML) leads and detergents	• *Bioethanol*: ethanol produced from biomass and/or the biodegradable fraction of waste • *Biomethanol*: methanol produced from biomass and/or the biodegradable fraction of waste • *BioETBE*: ethyl tertiary butyl ether produced from bioethanol (the percentage by volume of bioETBE that is calculated as biofuel is 47%) • *BioMTBE*: methyl tertiary butyl ether produced from biomethanol (the percentage by volume of bioMTBE that is calculated as biofuel is 36%)	• *Biodiesel*: diesel-quality methylester produced from vegetable or animal oil • *Biodimethylether*: dimethylether produced from biomass • *Fischer-Tropsch biofuel*: synthetic Fischer-Tropsch diesel produced from biomass • *Cold-pressed bio-oils*: oil produced from oilseed through mechanical processing only • All other *liquid biofuels* that are **added to, blended with or used straight** as transport diesel

Source: International Energy Agency annual questionnaire for petroleum companies.
See http://www.iea.org/Textbase/stats/questionnaire/Oileng.pdf.

present, biofuel production costs are greater than those for fossil fuels, but they could become competitive in the future should the price of a barrel of oil reach $80, according to Stéphane His of the Institut français du pétrole (IFP[18]).

Wind Energy

Wind turbines are a direct descendant of the old-time windmill, which turned a dozen times a minute and was used mainly for milling grain. Today, strictly speaking, the term "wind turbine" refers to a device that converts the kinetic energy of the wind into mechanical energy, while wind generators convert the mechanical energy to electricity and windmills use the mechanical energy to directly drive machinery. We will adopt the more general meaning of wind turbine here.

---

[18] *Ibid.*

Harnessing the wind as an energy source is dangerous and difficult, but enormous progress has been made in the last quarter century. Wind turbines exploit the kinetic energy present in moving air. The ratio between the energy of the wind and the mechanical energy recovered by the rotor depends on several factors, the primary ones being air density, the area swept by the rotor and wind speed.[19] The power provided by the turbine is directly proportional to the square of the radius of the rotor and the cube of wind speed.[20] In other words, when you double the length of the blades, you quadruple the power. At the largest wind farms in Germany (Brunsbüttel), designers went from 15-m diameter blades in 1980 to 124-m diameter blades in 2005. Since the wind is generally stronger offshore than onshore, some countries like Denmark have also begun to build wind farms at sea, and France, Canada, Germany and Great Britain may soon follow suit.[21]

Wind turbines need a minimum wind speed (the cut-in speed) to begin turning, generally at least 20 km/h.[22] At 30 km/h, things start to get interesting and, at 55 km/h, the turbine is running at full speed. At 90 km/h or more, the blades are beginning to turn too fast and, at 115 km/h, the turbine has to be shut down to prevent serious damage.[23] When siting wind farms, it is advisable to consult a wind map.

This is the main weakness of wind power. As everyone knows, winds are notoriously variable and can gust, change direction or die off altogether, which is a disadvantage if the goal is to produce electricity on a continuous basis. To make up for this, wind turbines are often connected to the conventional electrical grid.[24] Wind's

---

[19] The Danish Wind Industry Association provides a scientific summary of how a wind turbine works. See http://www.windpower.org/en/tour/wtrb/comp/index.htm

[20] See *Science & Vie*, June 2005, p. 96. The power available in wind moving perpendicularly over a circular surface (the rotor) is given by: $P = \frac{1}{2}\, r.v^3..r^2$, where P = power in watts (W); r = (rho) = mass density of air in kilograms per cubic metre at sea level and at a temperature of 15°C; v = velocity of the wind in metres per second; = 3,1416... and r = radius of the rotor in metres. See http://www.windpower.org/en/tour/wtrb/comp/index.htm. Concerning the cube of wind speed, this means that if wind speed drops by one half, the power delivered is divided by eight. See Jean-Luc Wingert, *La vie après le pétrole*, Paris, Éditions Autrement, 2005, p. 152.

[21] In terms of the offshore market, calls for tenders have been issued for wind power projects totalling 400 MW in Denmark, 500 MW in France and over 8,200 MW in the UK, according to EurObserv'ER's "2005 European Barometer of Renewable Energies."

[22] The site http://www.awstruewind.com provides online wind maps for all regions of the globe.

[23] These figures vary depending on the capacity of the wind turbine installed. See "Le vent tourne", *Science & Vie*, September 2001, pp. 127-130.

[24] "In 2002, the production of wind power decreased by 500 MW in 15 minutes when the wind suddenly died. The German network was close to dragging the Belgian network down in its wake. An equivalent amount of power, that can be brought on stream fast, must be permanently available." See presentation to the Académie des technologies by Bernard Tardieu, "L'énergie hydroélectrique et l'énergie éolienne", November 2005, at http://www.academie-technologies.fr/V2/ecrit05/energieEnvironnement/EnergieHydrauliqueEolienne%20Nov2005.pdf. Hereafter cited as Tardieu, op. cit.

strong points are the clean energy it produces, its relative quietness (except inside the nacelle, which contains the gear box and generator) and the fact that "each megawatt-hour of electricity that is generated by wind energy helps to bring about a reduction of 0.8 to 0.9 tonnes in the greenhouse gas emissions that are produced by coal or diesel fuel generation each year."[25]

Table 3: Total world installed wind power capacity (2004-2006)

Ten top-ranking countries	2004 installed capacity (MW)	2004 installed capacity (as a % of total)	2006 installed capacity (MW)	2006 installed capacity (as a % of total)
Germany	16,629	35.1	2,233	14.7%
Spain	8,263	17.5	1,587	10.4%
United States	6,740	14.2	2,454	16.1%
Denmark	3,117	6.6	(not in top ten in 2006)	?
India	3,000	6.3	1,840	12.1%
Portugal	(not in top ten in 2004)		694	4.6%
Italy	1,125	2.4	417	2.7%
Netherlands	1,078	2.3	(not in top ten in 2006)	
Great Britain	888	1.9	634	4.2%
Japan	874	1.8	(Not in top ten in 2006)	
China	764	1.6	1,347	8.9%
France	(not in top ten in 2004)		810	5.3%
Canada	(not in top ten in 2004)		776	5.1%
Total for top 10 countries	**42,478**	**89.8**	**12,792**	**84.2%**
Rest of the world	4,839	10.2	2,405	15.8%
Total for world	**47,317**	**100**	**15,197**	**100**

Source: Global Wind Energy Council (GWEC): www.gwec.net
Global Wind Report 2006

---

[25] Natural Resources Canada (NRCan), "About Wind Energy." Available at http://www.canren. gc.ca/tech_appl/index.asp?CaId=6&PgId=232

Although wind turbine performance has a theoretical limit of 59%,[26] the best performance achieved today is around 50%. The load factor (which is roughly equivalent to the time during which energy is produced) rose from 18% to 27% in one decade. Production costs have decreased substantially, making the per-kWh cost competitive with that of conventional hydropower. Although a few major difficulties –particularly regulatory ones[27]– remain with connecting wind farms to existing distribution networks, wind technology is very useful in remote regions that are off the grid.

In December 2006, total worldwide installed wind power capacity came close to 75,000 MW[28], with a generating capacity of roughly 100 TWh. In 1999, the comparative figure was only 10,000 MW. This increase is a little or a lot, depending on your point of view. In 2004, the wind sector grew by 20% and figures were similar for 2005 (24%) and even better for 2006 (32%). In Europe, the leaders in wind energy are Germany and Spain. Worldwide, the United States ranks third in installed capacity (see Table 3), but the massive increase in its installed capacity in 2005 and expected growth in 2006 (an additional 3,000 MW) put it in a good position to make second place. Nonetheless, Europe is currently in the forefront of wind energy use, which demonstrates its desire to reduce its energy dependence and the importance it places on the environment. In 2006, Europe had roughly 65% of world installed capacity. In keeping with the objectives established by the European Commission for 2010, the EU plans to increase its installed capacity to 40,000 MW, 10,000 MW of which will come from offshore wind farms.

The *Wind Force 12* project put forward by the Global Wind Energy Council (GWEC) and Greenpeace recommends that 12% of the total electricity generated worldwide be supplied by wind by the year 2020, an economically feasible goal in their view.[29] Under this proposal, installed wind power capacity would rise to 1,200 GW, generating 2 million jobs and reducing CO_2 emissions by 10.7 billion tonnes in the process, with the proviso that all countries must join in the effort and international regulations must be strengthened and harmonized.

---

[26] According to the law formulated in 1919 by the German physicist Albert Betz. See *Science & Vie*, June 2005, *op. cit.*

[27] Regulations are often insufficient or contradictory and some utilities refuse to allow small wind turbines to be connected to their grid.

[28] According to the *Renewables Global Status Report 2006 Update*, world installed wind power capacity was 59 GW at the end of 2005.

[29] "Wind Force 12: A Blueprint to Achieve 12% of the World's Electricity from Wind Power by 2020", Global World Energy Council (GWEC) and Greenpeace, May 2004, available on the GWEC web site.

Solar Energy

Solar energy is essential not only to our existence but to the very existence of our planet. Current technology provides three ways of harnessing the sun's energy. The first is **photovoltaics** (from photon and volt –or PV for short). A photon is a "grain of light" which has its own kinetic energy, but no mass or electrical charge, and demonstrates both particle and wave properties.[30] The energy of a photon is proportional to its frequency –and that means wavelength. These characteristics are important in the design of efficient **photovoltaic (PV) cells**. There are three types of PV cells: **monocrystalline, polycrystalline** and **amorphous**.[31] Crystalline (mono and poly) cells make up the vast majority of PV cells sold in the United States and elsewhere.[32] PV modules (also called solar panels) consist of a group of PV cells connected in series; the power provided by PV cells is expressed in peak watts (W_p).[33]

A PV cell is simply a **solar battery** in which the energy from electromagnetic radiation is converted directly into electricity. This technology quickly became widespread when the United States launched satellites that required an independent energy source in order to operate in space. Three scientists from Bell Laboratories discovered the principles of the PV cell.[34] Since PV cells are made from silicon, this led to the ascendancy of Silicon Valley and the reign of semi-conductors.[35]

---

[30] We are entering here into the field of quantum physics. How do you explain that a particle without mass can have kinetic energy? The explanation requires a broader discussion of the theory of relativity, which clearly exceeds the scope of our analysis.

[31] For an in-depth description of these cells and their performance, see www.outilossolaires.com. Amorphous cells are composed of non-crystalline silicon (i.e., in which the atoms are unorganized and form a continuous random network), and are used in manufacturing thin-film solar cells.

[32] Over 85%. See DOE, EIA, "Solar Thermal and Photovoltaic Collector Manufacturing Activities 2004", Figure H4.

[33] See footnote 4.

[34] Daryl Chapin, Gerald Pearson and Calvin Fuller in 1954. It was Antoine Becquerel (1788-1878) –rather than the Edmond Becquerel cited in many web sites– who discovered the photovoltaic effect in 1839 (conversion of light to electricity), 57 years before his grandson Henri discovered radioactivity. Henri Becquerel gave his name to the becquerel (Bq), a unit of measurement for radioactive decay equal to one disintegration per second.

[35] PV cells contain two layers of silicon, an upper layer of silicon doped with impurities that conduct electrons better. Since the outer shell of each silicon atom tends to share electrons with four of its neighbouring silicon atoms, thus forming bonds, to increase the semiconductor's "free charge", we dope the top layer of the cell with an atom containing five electrons (phosphorous, for example), This is the positive layer or p-layer. Conversely, the lower layer can be doped with atoms containing only three electrons in the outer orbit (such as boron) so that it is missing one electron (these atoms are called holes). The lower layer is called negative or n-layer. The two layers are bonded to each other, creating a so-called p-n junction (a potential barrier, which is the basic principle behind a diode). The result is a constant flow of pairs of electrons and holes called electron-hole pairs, creating a continuous internal electrical field. All you have to do is put resistance between the two terminals to harness the difference in potential.

There are two other ways of recovering solar energy: **concentrated (thermodynamic) systems** and **nonconcentrated (thermal) systems**. In the concentrated systems used in solar power plants, collectors are used that concentrate the sun's rays to warm a heat transfer fluid, with the resulting thermal energy being converted into energy in the form of electricity. This is no different from a conventional thermal power plant, except that the sun rather than coal or natural gas is used as the heat source. In nonconcentrated systems, which are used for applications such as water and space heating, the principle is the same except that the fluid is brought to the boiling point and is used directly for heating, thus saving the conversion step.

According to legend, the ancient Greek scientist Archimedes of Syracuse employed giant mirrors that used the sun to set afire Roman warships that were coming to attack his home city. Harnessing the energy from the rays of the sun and converting it into heat is the basic principle behind solar thermal power plants. These plants consist of a collector to concentrate the light, a receiver, and a heat conversion system (air, water, other fluids, molten salt) to create steam that drives a turbine and ultimately a generator. The diagram below (Figure 2) shows the basic elements of these systems.

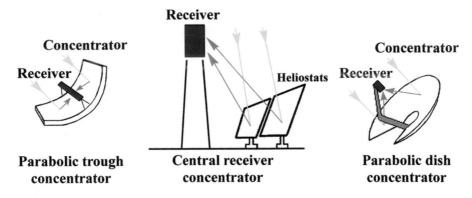

Figure 2: Operating principles of solar power plants
Source: www.powerfromthesun.net/chapter1/Chapter1.htm
Courtesy of web site authors William Stine and Michael Geyer

The three main collector designs are parabolic trough, central receiver (power tower) and parabolic dish.[36] Parabolic-trough collectors concentrate the sun's rays on a tube-shaped receiver along the focal line of the trough (Figure 2). In the case of central receivers, also known as power towers, the tower is the focal point, with light reflected on the receiver at the top of the tower from the mirrors (heliostats) installed on the ground, which are computer controlled to track the sun throughout

---

[36] Hundreds of photos of these collectors can be found at the National Renewable Energy Laboratory (NREL) web site (U.S. Department of Energy).

the day. Several experimental power plants using this type of design have been built in the United States, particularly *Solar I* and its successor *Solar II* (now dismantled), which had a capacity of 10 MW$_e$ (megawatt electrical). These experimental designs have been used as a basis for Spain's *Solar Tres* and have led to improved versions (operating with hot air) in such places as Australia. The hope is to build heliostat-based systems with a capacity of 200 MW$_e$ in the future. The temperatures generated at the receivers of these systems often exceed 1000°C. Parabolic-dish based systems, on the other hand, use a Stirling engine in the focal point of the dish, which transforms the heat into kinetic energy that turns a turbine.

Figure 3: The three main types of solar power plants
Source: Solar II (Barstow) with heliostats, TREC (left); EUROdish, CIEMAT (centre);
DOE, courtesy of SunLabs (right)

Just as wind turbines are subject to the caprices of the wind, solar power is dependent on meteorological conditions. If there is no sun, there is no energy. In addition, the amount of sunlight available varies from location to location on the Earth and areas with the best exposure are obviously the best sites for installing solar panels.

The solar energy industry is rapidly expanding. In 2004, to get a clearer picture of the evolving market and particularly to better compare statistics on different sources of electricity production (gas, coal, solar energy, etc.), the United States, the International Energy Agency (IEA), the European Solar Thermal Industry Forum (ESTIF) and other members of the solar community agreed to calculate solar energy production in thermal watts (W$_{th}$ and, by extension, kW$_{th}$, MW$_{th}$ and GW$_{th}$). In addition, the solar industry and solar experts agreed to apply a conversion factor of 0.7 kW$_{th}$/m^2 to the collector area in square metres. Based on the surface area of the collectors, this allows the capacity of solar farms or solar power facilities to be measured in kW$_{th}$ or MW$_{th}$, thus providing a common unit of measure and allowing country-to-country comparisons. As a result, international statistics on solar energy –which are still scarce although specialists are increasingly focusing on this area– can be better interpreted.

The progress made has not, however, prevented the United States from continuing to provide statistics on solar energy in square feet. In 2005, installed collector

area in the United States was 16 million square feet,[37] compared with 1.5 million m²
in Europe.[38] Total world installed capacity in 2004 was roughly 13 million m².
Much of this came from China: 10 million m², which the country wishes to expand
to 52 million m² in 2015.[39] Germany (39%) and Japan (30%) were tops in the world
in their share of total solar MW installed in 2004.[40] The rest of Europe had 8%, the
United States, 9%, and other countries, 14%. In terms of existing installed capacity
in Europe, three countries dominate: Germany (47%), Greece (14%) and Austria
(12%), followed by Spain and Italy, while France is sixth.

With respect to installed collector area, in 2006, the European Union (EU) broke
the 2.6-million m² mark (this corresponds to roughly 1,894 MW_{th} of power.)[41] In
the same year, the European solar market increased by 44% over the previous year
(2005).

Another way of evaluating the relative importance of solar power is to calculate
solar thermal capacity in operation per capita (expressed as kW_{th}/1,000 or kW_{th} per
1,000 inhabitants).

Cyprus, where 93% of households have solar collectors, is in an enviable
position since it has 450 kW_{th}/1,000 capacity, twice as much as Austria and Greece,
which have 225 kW_{th}/1,000 capita and roughly 190 kW_{th}/1,000 capita capacity
respectively, all as of 2005[42]. Other leaders include (in descending order) Germany,
Denmark, Slovenia and Switzerland. The mean for EU countries was 26 kW_{th}/1,000
in 2005. Outside Europe, countries like Japan and Israel have a much higher per
capita installed capacity.

Internationally, the Solar Thermal Power 2020 project (2004) sponsored by the
European Solar Thermal Power Industry Association (ESTIA) and Greenpeace
recommended that photovoltaic generation capacity (from solar power plants) be
increased to 5,000 MW by 2015; 21,540 MW by 2020; and 36,000 MW by 2025. If
these optimistic goals are reached, the report's authors estimate that by 2040, 5% of
the world demand for electricity can be met by solar power[43].

---

[37] The conversion factor used is 1 sq. ft. = 1 × 0.0929 m. Source: EIA, DOE, "Solar Thermal and
Photovoltaic Collector Manufacturing Activities 2004", Figure H1.

[38] The August 2005 "Solar Thermal Barometer" cites an installed collector area of 1,693,004 m² and
total power of 1,185 MW_{th}. *Systèmes solaires,* No. 168, July-August 2006

[39] European Solar Thermal Industry Forum (ESTIF), *Solar Thermal Markets in Europe,* June 2005.
Available at http://www.estif.org/9.0.html. This corresponds to 7 GW_{th} of power.

[40] See *Marketbuzz 2005*, "2004 World PV Market Report Highlights."

[41] See "Solar Thermal Barometer", *Systèmes solaires*, No. 175, October 2006. 2004 collector area
was 1.7 million m² or a nominal capacity of 1,182 MW_{th}.

[42] See ESTIF, *Solar Thermal Markets in Europe*, June 2006, p. 6 and Table 3.

[43] See www.ruralserv.com/Solar-thermal-energy.php.

Geothermal Energy

Vulcan was the Roman god of fire and metalwork, both of which originate in the earth. The ancients were not so far off the mark when it comes to the vocations they assigned their gods, some of which are very relevant in today's technology-driven world. Energy transfer through heat occurs in *three ways: **conductive**, **convective** and **radiogenic** fluxes.* The latter flux is caused by the natural decay of isotopes in radioactive materials such as uranium, thorium and potassium. Contrary to popular misconceptions, geothermal energy does not come from the earth's core, but rather chiefly from the mantle, the site of convection currents so powerful they are thought to move the earth's lithospheric plates (see Chapter 1). The crust is the second most important source, followed by the core, which represents less than 2%.

Geothermal energy specialists have borrowed from the petroleum industry the notions of proven, probable and possible reserves (see Chapter 6), except that the word "resources" rather than "reserves" is used.[44] Similarly, they speak of economically recoverable resources, which, like hydrocarbon reserves, must meet two basic criteria to receive this designation: they must be available (or accessible) and it must be economically feasible to exploit them. The latter criterion is often based on depth below the surface, and Mary H. Dickson and Mario Fanelli use the term "subeconomic zones" to refer to heat sources located below a depth of three kilometres. However, such considerations have not prevented Iceland from pursuing its experimental Deep Drilling Project, which will reach depths of 5,000 metres, where the reservoir temperature is expected to reach 450-600°C. France has a similar project underway at Soultz-sous-Forêts in the Alsace region, with drillholes also reaching 5,000 metres.[45] The successful use of this technology could open the door in the future to the economically feasible exploitation of heat sources deep in the earth.

Geothermal systems are made up of three elements: a heat source, a reservoir and fluids that transfer the thermal energy. The quality of the **heat source** varies depending on its location. Heat is obviously greater near volcanic areas, which facilitates its widespread distribution. Iceland is a good example: 88% of the country's residences are heated with geothermal power. **Reservoirs** are simply areas with a high volume of permeable hot rocks, generally overlain by a layer of impermeable rock, which traps the heat or reduces its dissipation by diffusion, very much like the petroleum traps described in Chapter 2. In some cases, reservoirs can be artificially created by hydraulic fracturing, a technique used by the oil and gas industry to

---

[44] A text for general readers has been published by the International Geothermic Association (IGA). See Mary H. Dickson and Mario Fanelli, "What is Geothermal Energy?" February 2004, at http://iga.igg.cnr.it/geo/geoenergy.php.

[45] For details on this project, see "Géothermie profonde en Alsace", Fiche de synthèse scientifique, No. 6, March 2004, in *Les enjeux des géosciences*, available on the Web.

maximize extraction. **The fluid** acts as a carrier that transfers the heat through convection. Sometimes steam is used to turn a turbine that drives a generator; in other cases, boiling water is used to bring another fluid (called the working fluid) from the liquid to the gaseous state, which then drives the turbine.[46]

Both reservoirs and fluids can be artificially created. Geothermal energy is not always an inexhaustible resource. The overexploitation of geysers in Los Alamos, New Mexico, resulted in the almost total disappearance of water from the local water table. Overexploitation sometimes results in operators having to pump water from towns forty or so kilometres from the geothermal source. Similarly, by using hydraulic fracturing techniques (water injected under pressure) or even explosives, dry hot rocks can be fractured, which allows more heat to be recovered each time water is reinjected. This system, called the hot dry rock (HDR) system, has been used in the United States since the 1970s.[47] The Soultz project in the Alsace is based on the same principle.[48]

Although an absolute consensus has yet to be reached on how to classify geothermal energy sources,[49] three categories are currently recognized:[50]

- High-temperature geothermal ($\geq 150°C$)
- Medium- and low-temperature geothermal ($\geq 90°C$, $< 150°C$)
- Very-low-temperature geothermal ($< 90°C$)

---

[46] DOE, National Renewable Energy Laboratory (NREL), "Geothermal Energy Basics" at http://www.nrel.gov/learning/re_geothermal.html.

[47] See Dickson and Fanelli, *op. cit.*, who provide a complete diagram of this system.

[48] See "Ruée vers l'eau chaude à Soultz-sous-Forêts", *Science & Vie*, No. 1065, June 2006, pp. 113-118.

[49] The head of the International Geothermal Association (IGA), Ruggero Bertani, discusses in the organization's newsletter *News*, No. 53, various estimates made by specialists in the field. See "What is Geothermal Potential?" at iga.igg.cnr.it/documenti/IGA/potential.pdf.

[50] The site of the Bureau de Recherches Géologiques et Minières (BRGM) (France) provides the following definitions of various types of geothermal energy. Deep geothermal: captures heat from rocks located 3-5 km below the earth's surface to produce steam to fuel power plants. High energy or high enthalpy geothermal: fluids in reservoirs 1,500-3,000 m below the earth's surface at temperatures over 150°C are tapped in the form of steam to produce electricity. Medium energy or medium enthalpy geothermal: hot water or wet steam at 90-150°C is tapped from sedimentary basins at depths of 2,000-4,000 m. Low energy or low enthalpy geothermal: extraction of water at temperatures below 90°C in deposits located 1,500-2,500 m below the surface for heating and some industrial applications. Very low energy geothermal: heat pumps are used to exploit shallow aquifers at temperatures below 30°C for heating and air conditioning. See *Fiche de synthèse scientifique*, No. 10, April 2005.

Table 4: A portrait of geothermal energy in 2004

Type of application	World installed capacity*	Comments
Electricity generation (high-temperature geothermal)	8,910 MW$_e$ including 822.1 MW$_e$ in the EU (9.2%)	Installed geothermal capacity represents 0.3% of world electricity production.
Heating (medium- and low-temperature geothermal)	12,103 MW$_{th}$ including 2,059 MW$_{th}$ in the EU (17%)	Energy obtained equivalent to 4.2 MTOE
Very-low-temperature applications (heat pumps*)	13,815 MW$_{th}$ including 4,531 MW$_{th}$ in the EU (33%)	1.15 million units (averaging 12 kW$_{th}$) Energy obtained equivalent to 1.45 MTOE
* Capacity is the thermal capacity that geothermal heat pumps can deliver rather than the thermal capacity that they are able to extract from the ground. Heat pumps require electricity to operate; the figures represent the energy delivered minus the electricity consumed by the pumps.			

Source: From "Baromètre Géothermie", December 2005

Only high-temperature geothermal energy is used to generate electricity and, among renewables, geothermal is the fourth most common means of electricity generation after hydro, biomass and wind.[51] World installed geothermal capacity in 2005 was 9.3 GW, according to the *Renewables 2005: Global Status Report.*[52] The major players in this sector are basically the United States and the Philippines, which together account for 50% of the electricity produced from high-temperature geothermal energy.[53] Other countries are fairly large producers, including Italy, Indonesia, Japan and, more recently, Mexico,[54] which has stepped up its efforts. California, a model geothermal state, generated 21.5% of its total electricity in 2003 from geothermal energy.

Geothermal heating is produced using **geothermal heat pumps** (GHP), which need electricity to operate. Their coefficient of performance (COP) depends on the ratio between electricity input (in kWh) divided by thermal energy output (in kWh).[55] These pumps generally operate as a closed-loop system, in which a production well pumps the hot water from the reservoir to the heat exchanger and the reinjection well

---

[51] "Baromètre géothermie", December 2005.

[52] Geothermal only posted 3% growth in 2005. See *Renewables Global Status Report 2006 Update*, Table N3, at www.ren21.net.

[53] United States (29%) and the Philippines (21.7%). The figures for 2004 were taken from "Baromètre Géothermie", December 2005.

[54] The IGA site provides detailed production figures by country for 2000.

[55] For each kWh consumed by the pump compressor, 3 kWh is obtained as output in the form of heat; the COP is 3.

returns the cooled geothermal water to the reservoir.[56] The process resembles a closed-system pump and is reversible: depending on the type of equipment used, the process can be tailored to provide air conditioning in summer or heating in winter. The most common applications are (in descending order) pools and public baths (including thermal baths), space heating for buildings and greenhouses, and aquaculture (see Figure 4).

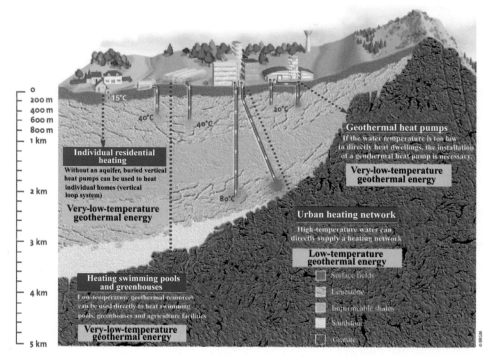

Figure 4: Applications of geothermal energy
Source: BRGM, *Fiche de synthèse*, No. 10, April 2005

The use of geothermal energy has been growing steadily for a number of years now, but its share of overall heat generation has remained stagnant due to the addition of kWh from new hydropower plants around the world. In Europe, Sweden is way ahead of the pack in terms of geothermal heat pump use. In 2004, over 70 countries were involved in renewable geothermal, compared with only 28 in 1995. The future of geothermal energy lies in hybrid systems and cogeneration (heat and electricity) or other complementary systems. The best example is the new Berlin Reichstag building which combines geothermal, heat pumps and biodiesel-based

---

[56] For the Soultz project, two reinjection wells instead of one are planned.

cogeneration.[57] The popularity of geothermal heat pumps in new houses and government incentives for geothermal in the form of tax credits, tax reductions for individuals and industry assistance will no doubt encourage the move to geothermal for heating or as a back-up to existing systems. However, it is predicted that, in 2015, geothermal kWh (0.08) will no longer be very competitive with other systems: nuclear (0.03), gas (0.04), coal (0.045) and wind (0.04).[58]

By the end of 2006, installed geothermal (electricity generation) capacity in EU countries was 854.6 MW$_e$ and thermal capacity was 9,564.6 MW$_{th}$, including 7,228 MW$_{th}$ from heat pumps.

Ocean Energy

After extolling the earth and its inexhaustible resources, we should not neglect the oceans. Up to now, the oceans have revealed some intriguing possibilities, but not much real usable energy. Is there actually something there or is this merely wishful thinking?

As early as the Middle Ages, dams were built in Brittany to trap the high tide and, then, when the tide receded, the sluice gates were opened and the water let out to turn a millwheel. Of course, technology has advanced since then. We are now able to harness the energy in ocean swells, tidal currents, ocean currents, osmotic pressure (exploiting the salinity gradients in marine currents to generate electricity) and ocean thermal gradients.[59]

Currently, the most commonly exploited forms of ocean energy are tides and waves. Tides are the result of the combined gravitational forces of the Earth, Sun and Moon.[60] Tides can be predicted over centuries, compared with only a few days for waves. Ocean waves (swells, breaking waves, etc.) have been defined as "surface water undulations that are propagated towards the coast but only move water masses a

---

[57] Fiche de synthèse, April 2005, *op. cit.*

[58] BRGM, *Fiche de synthèse scientifique*, No. 6, March 2004.

[59] Observatoire des énergies renouvelables (EurObserv'ER), "Thalasso energy", *Le baromètre européen 2005 des énergies renouvelables – 2005 European Barometer of Renewable Energies*, 5ᵉ bilan/5th report.

[60] The most comprehensive French-language text on the subject, although it deals with the Seine estuary, is by Pierre Le Hir and Ricardo Silva Jacinto, "Courants, vagues et marées : les mouvements de l'eau", available at seine-aval.crihan.fr/_commun/_documents/fascicules?lfr_Seine_aval_02.pdf. For an explanation of tides, see "D'où viennent les marées", *Science & Vie*, July 2002, pp. 120-123.

little."[61] Ocean waves travel for hundreds or thousands of kilometres. Although tidal power has been exploited for some time, only recently have people begun to get interested in harnessing wave energy and there are many projects still at the experimental stage.

Up to now, efforts to harness tidal energy have produced mixed results. The energy generated by a tidal power plant is proportional to the area of the lagoon or basin and the square of the amplitude of the tide.[62] In 1966, France commissioned the largest tidal power plant in the world on La Rance River (240 MW). A few other countries have followed suit, albeit at a smaller scale, including Canada (Annapolis Tidal Generation Station in Nova Scotia with a capacity of 20 MW), China (5 MW) and Russia (Kislogubsk near Murmansk with a capacity of 0.4 MW). According to the Observatoire des énergies renouvables, the constraints inherent in this type of facility, especially having to construct a dam across a stretch of sea, have led to projects being abandoned.[63] At La Rance, dam construction profoundly modified the estuary and caused the silting of the marine Rance ecosystem. However, Europe continues to be interested in developing tidal potential, agreeing to partly fund the Land Installed Marine Power Energy Transformer (LIMPET) project in Scotland. According to Natural Resources Canada, tidal energy still has a future: "estimates for world capacity range from a conservative 100 GW to as much as 1000 GW."[64]

Technically speaking, tidal energy is based on the same principles as conventional hydropower: accumulation of water, exploiting the difference in height between the water and the turbines (head) and generation of electricity. Although electricity cannot be stored, the water's potential energy can be exploited by using excess generation capacity to pump the water from a lower basin to an upper basin during times of low electrical demand; during peak demand, water is then released back into the lower reservoir through the turbines. Since each of these operations results in a loss, this type of system, also known as a pumped storage facility, has additional costs that can be recouped since electricity rates are higher during peak hours. The accumulation of water in the basin depends on many other natural phenomena such as dry or rainy season, snowfall in winter and rain in summer. Therefore the potential of the water (head) can decrease or increase in volume.

---

[61] Observatoire des énergies renouvables (EurObserv'ER), "Thalasso energy", *Le baromètre européen 2005 des énergies renouvelables – 2005 European Barometer of Renewable Energies,* 5e bilan/5th report.

[62] Presentation to the Académie des technologies by Bernard Tardieu, member of the Académie, November 2005, available at www.academie-technologies.fr/ecrit05/energieEnvironnement/EnergieHydrauliqueEolienne%20Nov2005.pdf.

[63] *Baromètre européen des énergies renouvelables. Ibid.*

[64] *Renewable Energy in Canada: Status Report 2002,* available at http://www2.nrcan.gc.ca/es/oerd/CMFiles/renewables-eng228LAU-05012004-337935IFB-2172006-1326.pdf

Substantial energy can also be derived from ocean waves: this energy is permanent and has yet to be exploited commercially to any great degree. The World Energy Council estimates that wave power could eventually meet 10% of world electricity needs. For example, in the United States, in 2003, 270 TWh/year in hydropower was generated; in comparison, harnessing wave power along the coasts (including Alaska and Hawaii) could provide an estimated 2,300 TWh/year, or close to ten times the power generated by conventional hydropower in 2003, according to the Electric Power Research Institute (EPRI). The United States is in the enviable position of having the goose with the golden egg, it just has to get the goose to lay the egg. In Europe, wave power potential has been estimated at 740 TWh/year.[65]

The physical appearance and layout of ocean power plants varies depending on the type of facility. The vast majority of tidal power plants are located along the shore, although in the future, some may be moored to the ocean bottom to harness the energy of tidal currents. Devices to capture the energy of waves or currents vary in design. Some are very conspicuous, to the great displeasure of some United States Senators who do not like to see their seascapes spoiled. Others are more discrete and invisible, since they are submerged at depths that do not hinder shipping. Still others, like the **Pelamis** system, are floating (semi-submerged) but moored to a land-based structure designed to collect the electricity. Figure 5 provides a few examples of configurations. On the lower right is the **LIMPET** (Land Installed Marine Power Energy Transformer) facility, which runs on tidal power[66], while in the lower middle is the French **Hydrohélix**[67] project, which is anchored on the sea bottom so as not to hinder shipping. On the lower left is the **Pelamis** "sea snake." On the upper left is the **Archimedes Wave Swing** (AWS) system, which is totally submerged, while on the right is an illustration of the partly submerged, partly above-water marine current turbine system (SeaGen), a prototype developed by the British firm Marine Current Turbines Ltd (MCL).

---

[65] *Systèmes solaires*, No. 84/85.

[66] In this system, the counter-rotating turbine is activated in both directions: first by air compressed by the surging waves and then by air decompressed (or sucked back) by the receding waves. The system has been connected to the UK's national electricity grid since 2000.

[67] Hydrohélix is a firm in Quimper, France, specializing in recovering kinetic energy from marine currents. It has proposed three sites for ocean energy facilities off the tip of Brittany (see photo of submerged turbines in Figure 5).

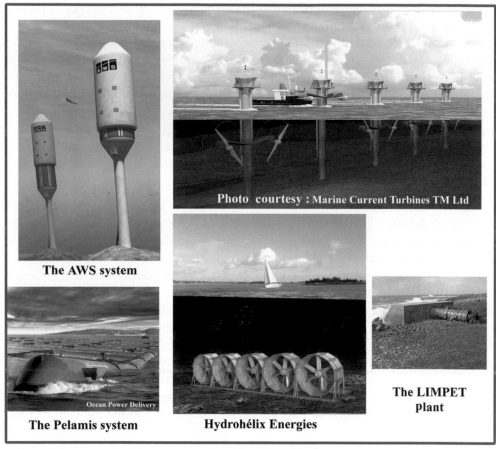

The AWS system

Photo courtesy : Marine Current Turbines TM Ltd

The Pelamis system Hydrohélix Energies The LIMPET plant

Figure 5: Examples of ocean energy technologies

Sources: (from upper left to lower right): Archimedes Wave Swing Machines/Marine Current Turbines TM Ltd./Ocean Power Delivery/Marénergy Project, Hydrohélix Energies (1 MW facility or 5 × 200 kW)/LIMPET Wave Energy Device, courtesy Wavegen

Ocean energy is still at the exploratory stage. The most promising projects have sci-fi names reminiscent of Jules Verne: sea snakes, underwater hot-air balloons, underwater wind turbines, whales' tails and floating swimming pools, just to name a few.[68] *Science & Vie* gives a good description of some of the systems currently under study:[69]

---

[68] Including the "Salter duck", named after its inventor Professor Stephen Salter, the "Clam" and other systems using oscillating water column generators.

[69] Emmanuel Julien, "La ruée vers l'or bleu a commencé", *Science & Vie*, October 2002, pp. 74-79. For a more in-depth scientific analysis of these systems, see S. Petroncini and R. W. Yemm, "Introducing wave energy into the renewable energy marketplace", at www.oceanpd.com/PDFS/SimonaPetrocini-Paper.pdf.

Sea snakes: always facing into the waves, these amphibious steel snakes, called **Pelamis**, peacefully undulate with the waves. Each consists of four or five sections linked by hydraulic cylinders. In response to the wave action, each structure bends and folds, activating the cylinders, which compress the oil inside and drive a hydraulic motor connected to a continuously operating electrical generator. Anticipated capacity: 2 MW.

Underwater hot-air balloons: in these cylindrical shaped buoys, moored to the seabed, the waves move an air-filled casing (the floater) up and down against a lower fixed cylinder at a rate of seven metres every ten seconds. This powers a linear motor-generator set that operates intermittently. The commercial version of the **AWS** (Archimedes Wave Swing) will generate 6 MW per unit.

Underwater wind turbines: Marine currents drive underwater turbines much like wind does a wind turbine but at much slower speeds (17 rpm). These turbines generate significantly more energy for their size than their wind-powered counterparts. Commercial versions should generate 1.5 MW.

Whales' tails: Driven by the currents, the wings (tails) oscillate up and down, setting in motion a moveable arm to which they are connected. This activates the cylinders, which drive a hydraulic motor and an electric generator operating intermittently (anticipated capacity: 500 kW).

Floating swimming pools: Raised three metres above sea level, the pool fills up and empties out constantly. Two fixed parabolic arms focus the waves towards the reservoir of the **Wave Dragon**, where the water accumulates and then is let out through a number of turbines which operate continuously. Anticipated capacity: 4 MW.

Bernard Tardieu aptly distinguishes wave energy from tidal energy:

The energy from waves (roughly 1 W/m² or 50 kW per m of coastline) is very diluted. Several facilities in Great Britain harness the power of swells: each wave goes up a slanted ramp perpendicular to the wave movement and fills a reservoir, and the water is then let out through traditional turbines.

The energy of marine currents has potential, particularly near the coast in areas with high tides [...] where the speed of the current is several metres per second. The blades are very large and resemble underwater wind turbines.[70]

The properties of waves and tides are obviously very different. Of all renewable energies (solar, wind, ocean), waves have the greatest power density.[71] However, wave power parks operate in a hostile environment with high operating and maintenance costs, particularly in the case of submerged facilities, which must withstand

---

[70]   Tardieu, *op. cit.*
[71]   Measured according to the height and frequency of the wave. In addition, the density of water is 800 times greater than that of wind.

salt corrosion and violent currents. Access can be dangerous even for teams of highly experienced divers. Other facilities have underwater jacks to bring the turbines above the surface for maintenance (in photo on the upper right in Figure 5, which shows the MCL system, a maintenance crew in a ship is visiting the facility). According to a 2005 report by the Electric Power Research Institute (EPRI), nearly 80% of the total operating costs of underwater systems fall into three categories of expenditures: power conversion modules (28%), reinforced anchoring and attachment structures (11%) and operating and maintenance costs (40%).[72]

The EPRI, after examining a dozen or so systems, defined three stages of development for marine systems: complete; almost complete; and in progress (involving lab testing and simulations). At the time, only one system was in an advanced stage of development, Ocean Power Delivery's **Pelamis** (named after the pelamid, or bonito tuna), and four other systems were about to reach this stage.[73] There is a growing interest in such technologies.[74]

The U.S. Energy Policy Act,[75] approved by President George W. Bush in August 2005, was good news for the U.S. industry, providing personal and corporate tax credits for renewable energies. The U.S. ocean power industry is now on its way. However, before massively investing in ocean energy, the industry will no doubt demand that the current two-year tax credit arrangement be extended for a longer time period.

Nuclear Fusion

In 2005, nuclear power accounted for 16% of total world electricity production, with 441 reactors in 30 or so countries generating 368 GW_e in all. In addition, in the same year, a total of 27 reactors were under construction, 16 of them in Asia.[76] The year 2004 was the 50th anniversary of civil nuclear power. Nuclear's share in elec-

---

[72] Roger Bedard, "Final Summary Report, Global Energy Partners", *Report E21 EPRI Global, WP 009 –US Rev 1*, p. 22, available on EPRI Web site.

[73] The WaveSwing system developed by AWS (Netherlands), oscillating water columns developed by Energetechs (Australia), the WaveDragon system (Denmark) and PowerBuoy, a system of floating buoys developed by Ocean Power Technologies. See EPRI, *op. cit.*, p. 14.

[74] Canada's National Round Table on the Environment and the Economy (NRTEE), which has focussed on the issue over the years, concludes: "It is estimated that wave technologies are more than 15 years behind wind and are five years behind even tidal power, indicating that widespread wave energy use before 2020 is unlikely." http://www.nrtee-trnee.ca/eng/publications/renewable-power-grid-electricity/renewable-grid-power-eng.pdf

[75] Section 206(d) of the *Energy Policy Act* (EPACT 2005), signed into law on August 8, 2005.

[76] See International Atomic Energy Agency (IAEA), *Nuclear Technology Review 2006—Report by the Director General*, GC(50)/INF/3, available at IAEA web site. Hereafter cited as *NTR 2006*.

tricity production has remained relatively stable over the past 19 years. Much of the increased capacity comes, not from the construction of new facilities, but rather from the "increased availability of existing ones, a change directly linked to security improvements around the world."[77]

As of December 31, 2005, six countries obtained a large proportion of their electricity from nuclear power: France (78.5%), Lithuania (69.6%), Slovakia (56.1%), Belgium (55.6%), Ukraine (48.5%) and Sweden (46.7%).[78] The United States was 19th (19.3%) and Canada, 21st (14.6%). In its 2005 annual report, the International Atomic Energy Agency (IAEA) estimated that world installed capacity would reach 640 GW$_e$ and 418 GW$_e$, in 2030, respectively in best- and worse-case scenarios. The U.S. Department of Energy (DOE) estimates that demand for nuclear power will increase beginning in the 2020s owing to the gradual depletion of fossil fuels (aside from uranium, of course).[79] In addition, China and India are considering increasing their nuclear capacity. In 2005, nuclear represented only 2.8% of India's total power production but the country hopes to increase this share to 25% by 2050.[80] China would like to double its installed nuclear capacity by 2020, from 2.0% to 4-5%.[81]

At present, nuclear power is produced exclusively from fissile fuels inserted in the reactor core. In its energy plan (Plan de prévision énergétique), Belgium includes a very instructive table on the evolution of nuclear power technology.[82]

    – **First generation reactors** correspond to systems commissioned before the 1970s, most often with the mission of facilitating the production of weapons-grade plutonium.

    – The purpose of the **second generation** of reactors, commissioned in the 1970s, was to reduce dependency on oil and gas. This generation currently accounts for most of the world's capacity. In some countries like France, this has been supplemented by an intensive policy to reprocess spent fuel. Belgium's nuclear power facilities consist entirely of second generation reactors.

---

[77] *Annual Report 2005*, IAEA, Vienna.

[78] See IAEA, *Nuclear Power Reactors in the World*, April 2006.

[79] The DOE presents two scenarios for the development of nuclear power for 2025. Under the lower projection, the world installed capacity will be 296 GW, compared with 570 MW under the most optimistic scenario. See *International Energy Outlook 2005*, Tables F2 and F3.

[80] NTR 2005, *op. cit.*, p. 6.

[81] *Ibid.*

[82] See www.plan.fgov.be/fr/pub/pp/PP095/PP095fr.pdf.

– The purpose of **third generation reactors,** designed after the accidents at Three Mile Island (1979) and Chernobyl (1986), was to improve safety by incorporating passive safety systems. This did not involve any new design features and did not resolve the issue of managing nuclear waste or eliminate the danger of nuclear proliferation. The French-German EPR project and, in the U.S., Westinghouse's AP1000 and AP600 reactors are in this category and are described as advanced design reactors.

– In **fourth generation** reactors, unlike the preceding ones, the generation system (reactor, fuel, treatment system) is completely redesigned to achieve more cost-effective, safe systems that produce less waste, optimize fuel use and stand up to the threats of terrorism and nuclear proliferation. This generation of reactors will have other applications besides electricity generation (hydrogen production, seawater desalination). Generation IV reactors, also known as revolutionary reactors, will not be available on a commercial scale until 2025-2040.

A great deal of technological progress is required before fourth-generation reactors see the day.[83] The same is true for using nuclear fusion to provide power –the time frame is mid-century if not much later. To make the fusion of hydrogen (or its isotopes) or Li_6 possible, at least three conditions must be met: the number of fast neutrons produced must be greater than the number of lost neutrons, temperatures must reach tens of millions of degrees and longer confinement times must be automatically maintained. Currently, the JET (Joint European Torus) tokamak[84] reactor has only been able to do this for a few seconds, while the Tore-Supra tokamak (Cadarache, France) managed it for a few minutes (four minutes, 25 seconds, to be exact, in September 2002); a much greater confinement time is hoped for the International Thermonuclear Experimental Reactor (ITER), which will be the largest tokamak reactor in the world.[85]

To obtain controlled fusion, the most common solution is to use an intense magnetic field to confine plasma (the fourth state of matter, in which nuclei and electrons are freed to form a hot gas) in a doughnut-shaped vessel (see Tore-Supra vacuum vessel and cross-section of ITER in Figure 6). This limits the plasma to a small portion of the vessel and prevents it from coming into contact with the vessel

---

[83] For a more in-depth scientific analysis, see the report *Les filières nucléaires aujourd'hui et demain,* Académie des Technologies, Commission énergie & environnement, August 2003. For fourth-generation systems being developed in the United States, see U.S. Department of Energy, Office of Nuclear Energy, Science and Technology, "U.S. Generation IV Priorities." As in many other countries, the two favoured systems are very high temperature reactors (with a thermal neutron spectrum) and fast-neutron reactors.

[84] Russian acronym for *To*roidalnaya *Ka*mera ee *Ma*gnitnaya *K*atushka (variously transcribed), or roughly, toroidal chamber and magnetic coil.

[85] For the origins of the project see the previous chapter.

**JET
(Joint European
Torus)**

Tore-Supra

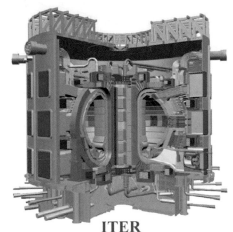

ITER
(International Thermonuclear Experimental Reactor)

Figure 6: The three main types of experimental fusion reactors
Sources (from top): EFDA-JET/P, Fiet-CEA (2001)/ITER published with permission of ITER

walls. In addition, the magnetic confinement of plasma favours collisions between light nuclei, increasing the probability of fusion. In the ITER design, a plasma volume of roughly 800 m^3 should be achievable, which is considerable compared with previous tokamak designs. What remains to be seen is how long the ignition point can be maintained (i.e., when the fusion reaction becomes self-maintaining).

The ITER's target fusion power is 500 MW for 400 seconds typically. The external diameter of the plasma ring will be 16.4 metres. With a little luck, the ITER should be operational in a dozen years, the time expected for its construction. Since it works with hydrogen, this reactor is considered a fourth-generation system. The hydrogen in seawater could theoretically meet all our planet's energy needs.[86] Harnessing hydrogen could usher in the new age of the *Hydrogen Economy*, as described in a book by Jeremy Rifkin.[87]

Fuel cells

Of the nearly one dozen fuel cells in existence,[88] which are basically batteries, hydrogen fuel cells have generated the most excitement.[89] Not only do they fit in with a zero-emissions vision of the future, but they also promise to herald in a fourth industrial revolution (following on the heels of the first two industrial revolutions in the eighteenth and nineteenth centuries and the third one, the information technologies revolution, of the twentieth century). According to Rifkin:

A decentralized, hydrogen energy regime offers the hope, at least, of connecting the unconnected and empowering[90] the powerless. When that happens, we could entertain the very real possibility of "reglobalization", this time from the bottom up, and with everyone participating in the process.[91]

---

[86] The problem is elsewhere. "The reality is that, currently, hydrogen production is 6.5 exajoules (exa = 10^{18}), compared with world primary energy demand of 400 exajoules. This means that current hydrogen production would only cover 1.5% of world energy needs." See http://www.rfi.fr/fichiers/MFI/ScienceTechnologie/845.asp.

[87] Published by Polity Press, Cambridge (U.K.), 2002, 304 pp. Hereafter cited as Rifkin.

[88] The nomenclature is vast. There is basic agreement over seven main types: (1) alkaline fuel cells (AFC); (2) polymer exchange membrane fuel cells (PEMFC); (3) direct methanol fuel cells (DMFC); (4) phosphoric acid fuel cells (PAFC); (5) molten carbonate fuel cells (MCFC); (6) intermediate solid oxide fuel cells (ITSOFC); and (7) solid oxide fuel cells (SOFC). For a good description of the processes involved, see Benchrifa Rachid, Zejli Driss, Bennouna Abdelaziz and Zaki Khalida, "Piles à combustible, mode efficace et propre de production d'électricité", at http://www.cnr.ac.ma/teer/indexe. Useful information on systems currently under development can be found on the CANMET Energy Technology Centre (CTEC) web site (Natural Resources Canada).

[89] "Fuel cells –unlike conventional batteries, which wear out as electrochemical reagents generate a current– generate electricity by using the reaction between constantly renewed hydrogen and oxygen in the air, producing water and freeing electrons." http://www.rfi.fr/fichiers/MFI/ScienceTechnologie/845.asp.

[90] A pun; *empower* here means both emancipate politically and provide access to energy

[91] Rifkin, *op. cit.*, p. 18.

These observations should be tempered by comments made by Bernard Tardieu:

Low-level power supplied to rural communities provides the vital minimum for people to live, termed *first level* (pumping water, refrigeration in health clinics, lighting of common rooms), and access to a better standard of living, termed *second level* (lighting in schools, radio, television, communications). However, these levels do not provide for sufficient economic development (the so-called *third level*) to stem rural depopulation.[92]

This argument is important, since it applies to all renewable energies and brings up the issue of key strategic choices. We will come back to it later.

There is no miracle technology for producing hydrogen.[93] Options include using fossil fuels[94] –for coal gasification, for example, or natural gas reforming (see Chapter 5)– or very high temperature (1,000-1,200°C) nuclear reactors for thermo-chemical water splitting. Another possibility in the more distant future is high-temperature solar power plants. All these processes involve very high heat and very large amounts of energy. The other option is water electrolysis, which requires an electrical current, but the energy yield of water is not very high. Other processes exist, such as the production of synthetic gas through the gasification of fermentable waste or the use of **photolysis**, now being studied experimentally, which employs photoelectrochemical processes (solar energy and electrolysis).[95] Whatever the technology used, hydrogen is expensive to produce. The energy required to liquefy hydrogen represents 40% of the energy that would be obtained in the final product."[96]

Nevertheless, Natural Resources Canada (NRCan) estimates that, in 2011, the world market for hydrogen technologies will be worth $46 billion. The train has already left the station, so to speak. The Canadian government has announced its plans for a hydrogen highway, the first section of which will be built between

---

[92] Tardieu, *op. cit.*

[93] Several government web sites (CEA in France, NRCan in Canada, DOE in the United States) provide excellent documents explaining how a hydrogen fuel cell works (for example, for the DOE, see http://www1.eere.energy.gov/hydrogenandfuelcells/fuelcells/basics.html).

[94] Currently used in over 90% of hydrogen production.

[95] See Total's web site: http://www.planete-energies.com/contenu/energies-renouvelables/voie-du-futur/pile-a-combustible/fabrication-hydrogene.html.

[96] According to the HFC (Hydrogen Fuel Cell) Consulting Group, "given the current state of technological advancement, in the hydrogen economy, upstream operations would consume 69% of the energy produced, only delivering 29% to the end user." See http://www.pile-a-combustible.com/ecoh.html.

Vancouver and Whistler, BC. Jeremy Rifkin invites us to consider the hydrogen energy web, from which all consumers can obtain power according to their needs or sell the excess capacity to someone else.[97] Therefore, for many, hydrogen is the ideal candidate to replace oil and gas (the same thing was said about nuclear power in the 1950s). However, scientists and non-scientists alike can occasionally deceive themselves. With time and money, everything is possible.

What Does the Future Hold in Store for Renewable Energies?

Does this question really need to be asked? Since all countries are seeking to reduce their dependence on fossil fuels, clearly each step towards adopting renewables, no matter how tiny, constitutes progress in diversifying energy sources and ensuring if not a healthy environment, at least one that can be passed down to future generations. Both excessive optimism and excessive pessimism are unfounded. It is impossible to know what ExxonMobil executives had in mind when they published their forecasts for the period 1980-2030 (see Figure 7). The chart is instructive, however, showing forecasts for various categories of energy demand for 2000-2030 based on an average growth rate. The mean predicted growth in petroleum demand is 1.4% compared with 1.6% for all energy sources together; therefore renewables are expected to gain ground. Even though the scale is different, the same holds true for the middle portion of the graph. The demand for wind and solar power will grow by 11.1% on average, compared with a mean growth rate of 2% for biomass, hydropower and nuclear. With yet a different scale, demand for wind power will grow by a steep 12.4%, compared with 9.6% for solar.

This is very good news, indeed. However, things can also be viewed from the opposite angle. According to these scenarios, wind and solar power will only supply the equivalent of roughly 3 million MBDOE (millions of barrels per day of oil equivalent) in 2030, which is very low. Let's go back another step. Wind farms and solar power plants will only represent a negligible amount compared with total energy production from other renewables. Our only consolation is that solid municipal wastes and biomass will reign supreme among renewables, which we already knew.

---

[97] "The worldwide hydrogen energy web (HEW) will be the next great technological, commercial and social revolution in history. It will follow on the heels of the development of the worldwide communications web in the 1990s and, like the former, will bring with it a new culture of engagement." Rifkin, *op. cit.*, p. 9.

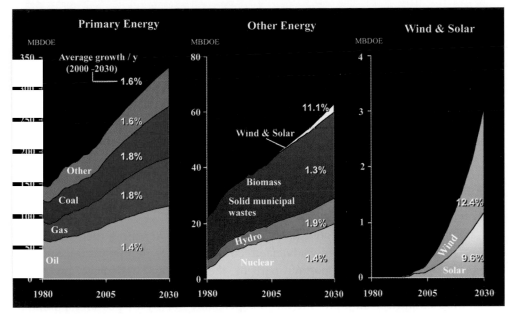

Figure 7: Evolution of energy demand by energy source (2000-2030)
Source: ExxonMobil, *The Outlook for Energy*, A 2030 View

What legitimate conclusions can be drawn from this analysis? The first and most obvious is that renewables are in great demand despite their marginal role in total energy production. Changing people's minds is often the most difficult part; this has been achieved and the great majority of people are aware of the problem. What remains is the cost that each and everyone is ready to pay to go green, blue or white. Let us not forget that when the automobile industry was starting to take off, oil cost more than coal.

Secondly, renewables are mainly a first-world phenomenon. Europe is the clear frontrunner, with an installed capacity at least twice as great as that of the United States. World installed capacity is close to 160,000 MW and is increasing at a yearly rate of 25 GW.[98] In the United States alone, total installed wind power capacity is expected to increase from 9,700 MW to 35,000 MW during the period 2005-2015, while installed solar power capacity will reach 250 MW in 2006, with over 80% of this on grid. According to the *Renewables 2005: Global Status Report* cited at the beginning of the chapter, phenomenal growth occurred in installed capacity and technologies in 2000-2004: for wind, 28%; biodiesel, 25%; solar space

---

[98] *State of Renewable Energy 2006*, US Energy Association, January 17, 2006 (paper by Michael Eckhart), available at American Council On Renewable Energy web site: www.acore.org.

and water heating, 17%; off-grid solar, 17%; installed geothermal capacity, 13%; and ethanol, 11%.

A proviso must be added, however, to these general observations. For renewables, technology and markets are not always in synch. Some technologies are still being developed, others are not yet accessible (nuclear fusion) and for others, adequate infrastructures have yet to be developed. The important thing is that renewables complement existing networks and do not threaten the security of the former.[99] The European Renewable Energy Council (EREC) remains optimistic on this front. With adequate policies, the EREC believes that, by 2040, the world will be able to produce nearly 50% of all its energy from renewables.[100] Such a scenario must be viewed with caution: it assumes that, ocean energy will exceed even solar thermal (excluding photovoltaics).

Lastly, all industrialized countries are very interested in selling their renewable energy technologies. For some advanced countries like Germany and Sweden, renewables make up an important part of their foreign assistance programs. Although renewables are peripheral in many industrialized countries, in many developing countries, they provide an indispensable supply of power for populations unable to access local or national networks. This of course raises all sorts of issues over sustainable development and technology transfer. Meanwhile, renewables are all the more popular in the industrialized world given that the price of a barrel of oil reached unequalled levels in 2005 and has continued to climb ever since and people are increasingly concerned with the future of our planet.

---

[99] A good example of this is provided in footnote 24.
[100] See the fascinating report by the EREC, *Renewable Energy Scenario to 2040*, at: www.erec-renewables.org/ publications/EREC_publications.htm.

5

The Essence of Oil and Gas

Before we can discuss the different types of oil and gas and the products derived from them, it is important to have a basic understanding of the chemical composition of these conventional forms of energy.

Chemical Composition of Natural Gas and Oil

All hydrocarbon-based fuels (gas, oil and coal) are composed of carbon (C) atoms and hydrogen (H) atoms. Whereas crude oil contains more carbon atoms than natural gas, some gases contain proportionally more hydrogen atoms than oil does. The essential difference between oil and natural gas is the size of their constituent hydrocarbon molecules. All hydrocarbons that have five or more carbon atoms occur in liquid form. However, at surface temperatures and pressures, hydrocarbon molecules with one to four carbon atoms linked to one or more hydrogen atoms occur in gaseous form. These molecules –methane (CH_4), ethane (C_2H_6), propane (C_3H_8) and butane (C_4H_{10})– are the main constituents of natural gas (see Table 2). Natural gas, specifically methane, is the simplest and lightest gaseous hydrocarbon associated with crude oil. Crude oil also occurs in semi-solid and solid forms, which are primarily bitumens.

Table 1 gives the mean percentages of the chemical elements that make up crude oil and natural gas. In addition to carbon and hydrogen, oil and gas contain toxic substances such as sulphur and nitrogen. Crude oil also contains highly toxic aromatics like benzene, toluene and xylene. Since toxicity tends to increase with molecule size and since the heaviest, most toxic hydrocarbon molecules are the last to evaporate, it is important to clean up an oil spill as fast as possible. Sulphur, which exists as an impurity in crude oil and natural gas, is very corrosive and must be removed to prevent damage to pipeline walls and processing equipment. Further- more, when oil and gas burn, the sulphur found in them can form sulphur dioxide, which is the primary cause of acid rain. For these reasons, sulphur is usually removed either at the wellhead or the refinery. The sulphur that is recovered can be sold for use in the manufacture of fertilizers.

Table 1: Typical chemical composition of natural gas and crude oil

	Crude Oil	Natural Gas
	In percentage	In percentage
Carbon	84-87	65-80
Hydrogen	11-14	1-25
Sulphur	0.06-2	0-0.2
Nitrogen	0.1-2	1-15
Oxygen	0.1-2	0

Source: Norman J. Hyne, 2001, *op. cit.*, p. 1

Four different hydrocarbon molecules, called hydrocarbon series, determine the chemical composition of crude oil. The four hydrocarbon series are as follows: the alkanes or **paraffins;** the cycloalkanes or **naphthenes** (sometimes called cycloparaffins); the aromatics or **benzenes;** and the **asphaltics**, heavy molecules with 40 to more than 60 carbon atoms.[1] Since crude oils differ in the relative percentage of each hydrocarbon series they contain, and this characteristic controls their physical and chemical behaviour, this is an important consideration for refineries in choosing among crude oils. Asphalt-based crude oil, which has a very low paraffin content, can be refined to produce high-grade gasoline and asphalt.[2] This type of crude is usually black.[3] By contrast, paraffin-based crude oil contains little or no asphalt, and when refined, it yields kerosene and high-quality lubricants. A mixed-base crude oil is a mixture of these two types of crude.

In the right-hand column of Table 2, the different hydrocarbon series found in crude oil are listed along with their percentage by molecular weight. Naphthenes represent the primary series, accounting for almost 50% of the composition of crude oil. Crude oil with a high naphthene content is not as economically valuable as

---

[1] Hydrocarbons whose carbon atoms are linked by a single bond are said to be "saturated", whereas those linked by one or more double bonds are termed "unsaturated." Alkanes (paraffins) are saturated hydrocarbons. They have the formula C_nH_{2n+2}, where n is a whole number. Naphthenes have five or more carbon atoms linked by saturated bonds; they have the formula C_nH_{2n}. Aromatic molecules contain at least one benzene ring (a closed 6-carbon ring); some of the bonds are unsaturated. The general formula is C_nH_{2n-6}.

[2] "Paraffin-based crude oils are characterized by bitumens, whose adhesive properties and waterproofing qualities are lower than those of asphalt-based crudes." See "Choix des composants d'enrobés selon l'usage", Vol. 10, No. 4, April 2005, at www1.mtq.gouv.qc.ca/fr/publications/reseau/infodlc/2005/05-04.pdf.

[3] Paraffin-based crude oils are generally greenish.

paraffin-based crude. Crude oil containing a high percentage of aromatics is highly prized by the industry, and refineries are often willing to pay a premium for aromatic-rich crude oil, since it yields very high octane gasoline and a valuable feedstock for the petrochemical industry. Although crude containing asphaltics is also popular with the refining industry, asphaltics are problematic since they represent the organic matter portion of petroleum which is insoluble in pentane and heptanes.[4] Furthermore, the asphaltic hydrocarbon series contains a larger number of nitrogen, sulphur and oxygen (NSO) molecules, which must be removed or reduced during the refining process because of their harmful effects. In summary, all of the different crude oils present various challenges for refineries.

Table 2: Main constituents of natural gas and crude oil

Components of natural gas		Hydrocarbon series in crude oil	
	Percentage by molecular weight		Percentage by molecular weight
Methane	70-98%	Paraffins	30%
Ethane	1-10%	Naphthenes	49%
Propane	Negligible to 5%	Aromatics	15%
Butane	Negligible to 2%	Asphaltics	6%

Source: Norman J. Hyne, 2001, *op. cit.*, p. 4 and 10.

Natural gas is composed of paraffin-type hydrocarbon molecules. Methane is a gas with one carbon atom in the hydrocarbon molecule; ethane has two carbon atoms; propane has three; and butane has four. Table 2 shows the average percentage of these different types of gas that are found in natural gas fields. Although the percentages vary between gas fields, methane is always the dominant gas. Methane is transported by pipeline and used for domestic heating as well as in a range of industrial processes. The natural gas found in Canada is almost identical to that in the United States. The average composition of natural gas in both countries is 93.9% methane, 3.2% ethane and 0.7% propane.[5]

---

[4] Experts are divided on how to define asphaltics. Oil from the Athabaska deposit in Alberta and that from the Boscan oil field in Venezuela has an asphaltic content greater than 15% by weight.

[5] William E. Liss and David M. Rue, "Natural Gas Composition and Quality", Gas Technology Institute, February 2005, available at www.energy.ca.gov/.../2005-02-17+18_workshop/comments/R0401025_Comments_Occidental_of_Elk_Hills.pdf.

Classification of the Main Gases

The International Union of Pure and Applied Chemistry (IUPAC) uses the suffix "ane" to designate saturated hydrocarbons, that is, hydrocarbons with only single bonds between the carbon atoms. In this book, the gases that interest us –methane, ethane, propane, butane and pentane– contain from one to five atoms of saturated carbon.[6] Table 3 describes the molecular structure of these gases, and Figure 1 is a schematic representation of the industrial classification used for them.

Table 3: Chemical formula of certain gases

Condensed structural formula	Number of carbon atoms	Common name and molecular formula	
CH_4	1	Methane	CH_4
CH_3CH_3	2	Ethane	C_2H_6
$CH_3CH_2CH_3$	3	Propane	C_3H_8
$CH_3CH_2CH_2CH_3$	4	Butane	C_4H_{10}
$CH_3CH_2CH_2CH_2CH_3$	5	Pentane	C_5H_{12}

Gas treatment plants and refineries are the primary producers of liquefied petroleum gas (LPG). Natural gas liquids (NGLs) are produced mainly at gas plants, as is the case for liquefied natural gas (LNG). The diagram below (Figure 1) illustrates the close relationships between the different gases.

In Canada, according to the National Energy Board (NEB), "Crude oil prices help set the price ceilings for propane and butane because they compete with oil-based products (in particular, naphtha, heating oil and gasoil) in major markets."[7] Whereas propane is used primarily for domestic heating, the bulk of ethane production is destined for the petrochemical industry. Ethane has the highest extraction costs of all the natural gas liquids.

Whereas about 60% of global LPG production comes from gas treatment plants, in Europe, LPG is produced mainly at refineries.

Natural gas can be compressed and cooled to $-167°C$ to produce a liquid called liquefied natural gas (LNG). LNG occupies about 1/645th the volume of natural gas at standard temperature and pressure, making it more practical to transport by ship.

---

[6] The 5 saturated hydrocarbons containing 6 to 10 carbon atoms are hexane, heptane, octane, nonane and decane, in that order. The first 10 alkanes are saturated hydrocarbons containing 1 to 10 carbon atoms.

[7] See http://www.neb-one.gc.ca/energy/energypricing/howmarketswork/ngl_e.htm.

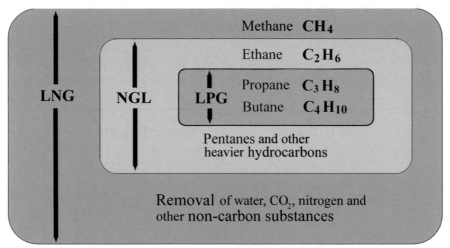

Figure 1: Classification of the principal gases (LNG, NGL and LPG)
Source: Memonline.free.fr/05_a_30.pdf

API Gravity, Sulphur Content and Benchmark Crudes

The chemical composition of natural gas and crude oil depends on their place of origin. There are roughly one hundred different types of crude oil, or nearly as many as there are oil and gas deposits. Crude oils are classified based mainly on their API gravity –a standard established by the American Petroleum Institute– and their sulphur content. API gravity (°API) is calculated using the formula below:

°API = 141.5/(density or specific gravity at 15°C or 60°F) − 131.5, where the specific gravity is the ratio of the density of oil to the density of water at 10°C.

In the metric system, oil density is expressed in kilograms per cubic metre (kg/m³): 900 kg/m³ is equal to 25.7 °API.[8] This is the threshold value that separates heavy crude from light crude. Figure 2 illustrates the relationship between density and grade. The higher the °API, the lighter the oil; the lower the °API, the heavier or more viscous the oil. Crude oils have an API gravity between 5 and 55, with most of them falling in the

---

8   Or 25.63 °API, more precisely. See the Chevron conversion table, "Fuel and Marine Marketing", at www.fammllc.com/famm/fuel_conversion_chart.asp. This is the value used by the Canadian government to define the cut-off between heavy crude and light crude. By contrast, the industry uses the API gravity scale (see Figure 2).

range of 25 to 35. Light oils range from 35 to 45. Heavy crude oils have an °API lower than 25.[9] In the industry, crude oil is divided into four types: extra-heavy (bitumens) with an °API less than 10; heavy with an °API below 22.3; medium density with an °API between 22.3 and 31.1; and light with an °API greater than 31.1.[10] Some crude oils from the Lloydminster region in Alberta have an °API between 9 and 18.

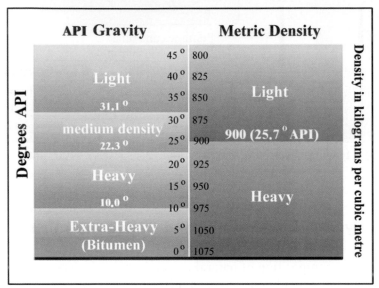

Figure 2: The different types of crude oil
Source: Canadian Centre for Energy Information

The sulphur content of crude oils varies from region to region. Kuwaiti crude has a sulphur content of 2.5%; Arabian light, 1.8%; and Iranian light, 1.4%. Oil from Alaska's North Slope contains 1.04% sulphur, but Nigerian crude and North Sea crude (Ekofisk deposit in Norway) have an even lower sulphur content, or less than 0.2%. Nigerian and North Sea crude oils are called **sweet crudes** because they contain less than 1% sulphur, in contrast with crude oils containing more than 1% sulphur, which are termed **sour crudes**.

The fact that crude oil characteristics like API gravity and sulphur content are economically significant is illustrated by the gasoline crisis that occurred in the United States in the wake of Hurricane Katrina. During 2000-2005, non-OPEC countries began producing increasingly heavy oils with a higher and higher sulphur

---

[9]   Norman J. Hyne, *op. cit.*, p. 4.
[10]   http://www.centreforenergy.com

content.[11] Some refineries decided to process only light crudes while others shut down, and the growing imbalance in demand and supply of the various types of crude oil plunged the United States into a crisis after Katrina. It took about a year for supply and demand to restabilize. A number of refineries are currently being built at a cost of several billion dollars.

Benchmark Crude Oils

Certain types of crude oil are used as **benchmarks** in setting market prices. In the United States, the most commonly used benchmark is West Texas Intermediate (WTI). WTI is a light crude, with an API gravity between 38 and 40°API; it is a sweet crude, containing less than 0.3% sulphur. U.S. refineries usually base their crude purchases on the WTI index price. Another benchmark used in the United States is West Texas Sour (WTS), which is slightly heavier than WTI and has a higher sulphur content (1.6%). In Europe, Brent crude (from the North Sea) is the key benchmark; its properties are almost identical to those of WTI. In the Middle East, Dubai crude is the benchmark used in the pricing of oil from the region.

Crude Oil and Petroleum-Based Products

Whatever its origin, crude oil has little value until it is refined, that is, until the impurities have been removed and the oil has been distilled into various fractions. The refining process yields, on average, 46% gasoline, 27% heating oil, 10% jet fuel, 5% coke, 4% liquefied gas, 3% petrochemical feedstocks, 3% asphalt and 1% each of kerosene and lubricants.[12] Petrochemical feedstocks are some of the most important refinery products, since they are sold to petrochemical plants, which reform the molecules and make a large variety of products, including plastics, synthetic fibres, fertilizers, medications, solvents, polystyrene, explosives and synthetic rubber.

---

[11] From 2000 to 2005, the mean API gravity decreased from around 33.2 °API to below 31.4 °API, while the sulphur content increased from 0.89% to over 1.04%. See "Sweet and Sour Crude", August 21, 2005, at http://www.econbrowser.com/archives/2005/08/sweet_and_sour.html.

[12] Data provided by the American Petroleum Institute and cited in Norman H. Hyne, *op. cit.*, p. 9.

Refinery Operations

Refineries use of a range of technologies and processes depending on the products they are manufacturing. These processes include distillation, thermal cracking, catalytic cracking and hydrocracking, which involves the use of hydrogen gas, not water as one might assume.

Distillation: At the refinery, crude oil is first heated at very high temperatures until the hydrocarbon molecules vaporize (change from a liquid to a gas); the vapour is then fed into a distillation tower (see Figure 3). The heavier the hydrocarbon molecule, the higher the temperature needed to vaporize it. The vapours rise in the tower through a series of distillation stages: the heavier components (viscous liquids) collect at the bottom of the tower, but the lightest, most volatile components (gases) reach the top. As the vapours rise in the tower, the decreasing temperature causes them to condense, and the resulting liquids are drawn off in collector trays as separate components, called fractions or cuts. The different hydrocarbon fractions that are obtained represent distillate (product) streams with a similar boiling point. In order of cooling temperatures, the fractions obtained are heavy gas oil, light gas oil, kerosene and naphtha, and, at the top of the column, **straight run gasoline**. Vacuum distillation, using lower pressures and therefore lower boiling temperatures, is performed on the residual bottoms to separate out more fractions. The bottom product from each distillation tower becomes the feedstream for the next tower. Distillation, the process used to achieve the separation of crude oil components, is central to the whole refining process.

Thermal cracking: Cracking is a process that splits the longer, heavier hydrocarbon molecules to form shorter, lighter ones. In thermal cracking, heavier oil distillation fractions, called residuals or residues, are heated at elevated temperatures and pressures in cracking towers. Cracking operations can be performed in several stages. The longest hydrocarbon molecules are fed into a succession of cracking towers, which fractionate the remaining heavy molecules, ultimately producing gasoline and gasoil. Thermal cracking is an industrial process that has been in use since the 1930s and is carried out to add value to the outputs of the initial distillations.

Catalytic cracking: This process, invented in the late 1940s, involves the use of catalysts –substances that accelerate or initiate chemical reactions– in combination with high temperatures (up to 500C)[13]. Rapid circulation of the catalyst in the catalytic cracking unit is an essential characteristic of the process. The objective is to split heavy hydrocarbon fractions into lighter ones to obtain liquefied petroleum gas (LPG), gasoline, gasoil and other products. Cracking is often used to blend performance-

---

[13] Catalytic cracking can also be performed in chemical reactors using much higher temperatures.

enhancing additives into gasoline. Refineries also supply the petrochemical industry with many products derived through catalytic reforming and alkylation.[14]

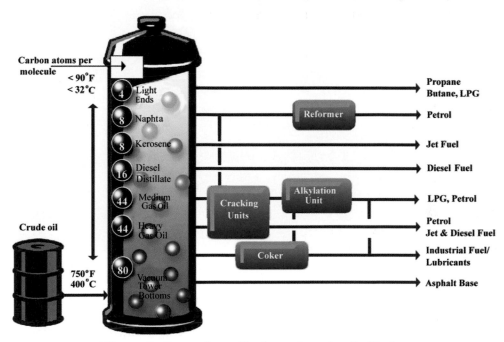

Figure 3: Separation of hydrocarbons by distillation

Source: ExxonMobil, "A Simple Guide to Oil Refining", at http://www.exxonmobil.com/Australia-English/PA/Files/ publication_2006_Simple_Guide_Refining.pdf

Figure 4 shows the principal production chains for jet fuel (thick pink lines) and for premium-grade gasolines (heavy green, blue and yellow lines). Hydrodesulphurization (HDS) must be performed at almost every stage of the refining process.

Hydrocracking: Hydrocracking is based on the same principles as catalytic cracking; however, the cracking takes place at lower temperatures and higher pressures, in the presence of hydrogen, and different catalysts are used, typically powders. Hydrocracking is carried out to produce jet fuel and high-grade lubricants (see Figure 4).

---

[14] "An alkylation unit is a refining process for chemically combining isobutane with olefin hydrocarbons. The product, alkylate, an isoparaffin, is blended with motor and aviation gasoline to improve the antiknock value." See *Glossary*, National Energy Board (NEB), in *Short-term Outlook for Natural Gas and Natural Gas Liquids*, Ottawa, October 2005.

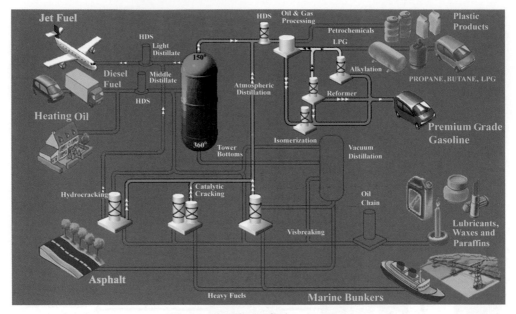

Figure 4: The refining process
Source: Panorama pétrolier, Union Française des Industries Pétrolières (UFIP).

Oil contains alkanes, but no alkenes (olefins).[15] However, alkenes like ethene (ethylene) or propene (propylene) are essential ingredients in the production of plastics. Steam cracking is the main industrial process used to produce the lighter alkenes.

Steam cracking: This process, which involves the use of steam but no catalysts, is carried out at a reaction temperature of about 800°C and pressure of about one bar."[16] A variety of products can be obtained depending on the composition of the feed and the reaction conditions.

Gas-to-Liquids (GTL) and Coal-to-Liquids (CTL) Technologies

A number of synthetic fuels can be derived from gas, coal or even biomass (Biomass-to-Liquids, or BTL). These fuels are termed "synthetic" because they are produced from synthesis gases composed almost entirely of hydrogen and carbon

---

[15] "Alkenes have boiling temperatures slightly lower than those of the corresponding alkanes. A double bond occupies more space than a single bond and it takes less energy to break them; the boiling temperatures are therefore lower." Source: http://fr.wikipedia.org/wiki/Alc%C3%A8ne.

[16] See "Craquage catalytique et vapocraquage", at http://marquant.free.fr/petrole/craquage.htm.

monoxide. The manufacturing process for synthetic fuels bypasses the traditional refining approach.[17] Once the synthesis gas (syngas) has been produced through reforming of natural gas, the Fischer-Tropsch process[18] (developed by the Germans and the Japanese during the Second World War) can be used to convert the syngas into liquid fuels. The industry can produce a range of liquid fuels that can go directly to market: naphtha, lubricants, kerosene, diesel, dimethyl ether and ultra-pure diesel[19].

Annual Energy Outlook 2006 (*AEO 2006*) predicts that, by 2030, global production of liquid fuels produced using coal-to-liquids (CTL) technologies will be between 1.7 and 2.3 million barrels per day (MMb/d).[20] The figures are similar for gas-to-liquids (GTL) production –between 1.1 and 2.6 MMb/d. At present, Malaysia and South Africa are the only countries producing GTL on an industrial scale; however, they will soon be joined by other countries such as Russia, Qatar,[21] Algeria, Australia, Egypt, Iran and Nigeria. The industry aims to reduce GTL capital costs to below $20,000 per barrel, which compares with a cost of $15,000 per barrel for a conventional petroleum refinery.[22] Nevertheless, GTL production remains expensive and energy intensive: it takes 10,000 cf of gas to obtain a single barrel of liquid fuel using the Fischer-Tropsch process.[23]

Although long left by the wayside, these processes are now attracting the interest of large international corporations such as Shell, Sasol and Exxon, as well as major research laboratories like Rentech and Syntroleum. Skyrocketing oil prices and the

---

[17] See the Energy Information Administration's schematic diagram of the processes in the Issues in Focus section of *Annual Energy Outlook 2006*.

[18] Named after the German inventors Franz Fischer and Hans Tropsch, the Fischer-Tropsch process is used to convert syngas to paraffin wax, which then undergoes hydrocracking. For a technical overview of synthetic fuels, see the presentation by Colin Baudouin of the Institut français du pétrole (IFP), "Coal to Liquids," at www.ifp.fr/IFP/fr/fichiers/ifp/IFP_LiquefactionDuCharbon_ColinBaudoin_EPFL-AISEN_021105.pdf; also "Nouvelles filières énergétiques", at the IFP web site: http://www.ifp.fr/IFP/fr/ifp/fb04_02.htm

[19] Less than 5 parts per million of sulphur. The fuel obtained is more energy efficient and less polluting.

[20] *AEO 2006*, p. 55. According to Daniel Yergin of Cambridge Energy Research Associates (CERA), China is projecting that by 2015 it will produce 60 million tonnes of fuels derived from coal; this production is predicated on the construction of 12 facilities, each capable of producing 5 million tonnes per year. See Daniel Yergin (CERA), *The Oil Industry's Growth Challenge: Expanding Capacity from the Wellhead to the Consumer*, The International Energy Forum, Riyadh, November 19, 2005, p. 21.

[21] Qatar Petroleum and Shell Gas have already demonstrated the use of GTL fuel in a turbo diesel car. See *OPEC Bulletin*, May-June 2006, p. 42.

[22] *AEO 2006*, p. 55.

[23] John Malone, "The Economics of Gas-To-Liquids", *Industry Insights*, August 10, 2006, John S. Herold, Inc.

progressive depletion of oil reserves, combined with the push to develop cleaner, more efficient technologies, are all factors that have contributed to the renewed interest in deriving liquid fuels from coal and gas.[24]

Natural Gas (NG) and Natural Gas Liquids (NGL)

Natural gas can be recovered from a gas well, an oil well or a condensate well.[25] The gas from a gas well or condensate well is referred to as "non-associated" gas, which means that it is free natural gas not in contact with crude oil. By contrast, the gas found in an oil well is called "associated gas" or "dissolved gas." Regardless of origin, raw natural gas does not meet the quality requirements for pipeline transport. It contains several types of gas and many impurities, including water vapour, hydrogen sulphide $-H_2S$,[26] carbon dioxide, helium, nitrogen and other trace substances.

The owners of a gas or liquid hydrocarbon pool do not necessarily carry out the drilling operations. Strict definitions are required in order to avert litigation between owners and operators. As a general rule, a well is defined as an oil well if it produces more than one barrel of crude oil for every 100,000 cf of gas recovered. Conversely, a gas well produces more than 100,000 cf of gas for every barrel of oil produced.[27] Alberta uses a similar definition in its *Mines and Minerals Act*, as does OPEC.[28]

Natural gas liquids (NGLs) include ethane, propane, butane, isobutane[29] and natural gasoline. NGLs are initially extracted from natural gas at field plants located in natural gas producing regions. Some of these facilities even straddle strategic

---

[24] See Volume 4 of *Oil in Fifteen Volumes*, Center for Global Energy Studies, 2006, pp. 188-199 and pp. 270-285.

[25] Specifically, a natural gas well that contains liquid hydrocarbons (pentanes) and heavier hydrocarbons.

[26] The industry considers natural gas as sour when it contains more than 5.7 milligrams of hydrogen sulphide per m^3.

[27] See "Hydrocarbon Liquid Phase Definition, Determination and Allocation in Two-Phase Hydrocarbon Reservoirs", Society of Petroleum Engineers (International), SPE 78363, 2002, p. 1. The authors are A.N. Hamoodi, S.A.W. Babajan and A.H. Desouki, all members of the Abu Dhabi National Oil Company (ADNOC), and V. Ruffier-Meray and A. Pina of the Institut Français du Pétrole (IFP). The proposed definition corresponds to directive 79 of the State of Texas.

[28] *Ibid.*

[29] Similar to butane but with a lower boiling point.

points on gas pipelines, hence the name straddling plants.[30] The clean or marketable natural gas that is produced can be delivered to storage units or directly to points of use.

Natural gas treatment generally comprises four stages: oil and condensate removal, water removal, separation of natural gas liquids and sulphur and carbon dioxide removal.[31] The first operation is often carried out at the wellhead, because the lower pressures present at the surface enable the gas to escape from the oil/condensate. Removing water entails the use of dehydration agents such as glycol, which has a strong affinity for water.[32] Separation of NGLs is achieved either by absorption, which involves bringing the natural gas into contact with absorbing oils in absorption towers, or through cryogenic processes, which involve cooling the gas to $-48.8°C$ ($-120°F$). One of the most effective cryogenic methods (turbo expansion) uses a turbine to rapidly expand the chilled gases, causing a sharp drop of temperature. Ethane and other hydrocarbons in the gas stream are condensed, whereas the methane remains in a gaseous state. This allows the recovery of more than 90% of the ethane. Sulphur extraction is usually achieved in absorption towers by using amine solutions, such as monoethanolamine (MEA) or diethanolamine (DEA), which have an affinity for sulphur. Following sulphur extraction, the solutions can be recycled for use in the absorption process.

Gas treatment plants play an important role in recovering products that have significant commercial value, in the same way that oil refineries recover NGLs such as LPG. When natural gas production drops off, so does the quantity of NGLs produced. According to the *Oil & Gas Journal*, in 2005, 38% of global NGL production came from North American gas treatment plants, compared to 52% in 2001.[33] The United States and Canada still hold the lead in NGL production, although Saudi Arabia and Kuwait are not far behind.[34]

---

[30] Canada's National Energy Board (NEB) defines a straddling plant as follows: "A reprocessing plant located on a gas pipeline that extracts natural gas liquids from previously processed gas before such gas leaves or is consumed within the province." See NEB's report *Short-term Outlook for Natural Gas and Natural Gas Liquids*, October 2005, p. 55.

[31] See www.naturalgas.org.

[32] Glycol dehydration is usually performed using diethylene glycol (DEG) or triethylene glycol (TEG). Since the boiling point of glycol is almost twice that of water, it is easy to remove the water from the glycol solution. The solution can be reused in the dehydration process. For details, go to www.naturalgas.org.

[33] See "Storms Help Tip Balance of Gas Processing from Historic Centers", *Oil & Gas Journal*, June 26, 2006, p. 55.

[34] *Ibid.*, p. 58. In 2005, Canada accounted for 9.6% of world production, Saudi Arabia for 9.4% and Kuwait for 6.2%.

Demand for liquefied petroleum gas (LPG), which was estimated at just under 220 million tonnes in 2005, is expected to reach 228 million tonnes in 2006 and 258 million tonnes in 2010. In view of the large number of countries producing LPG, supply could exceed demand in the future.[35] At the refinery, LPG is extracted either during distillation operations, or during the cracking or reforming of heavy hydrocarbons.

Although NGLs make up a small percentage of world gas production, they represent an important and lucrative market. In 2005, the United States and Canada accounted for 33% of worldwide NGL production,[36] compared with 42% in 2002. Decisions over the future of the NGL supply system basically revolve around the question of whether NGLs should be extracted when the natural gas is liquefied or when the liquefied natural gas (LNG) is delivered to its final destination. The *Oil & Gas Journal* summarizes the issue as follows:

> Many projects that primarily supply LNG to consumers in the Far East, specifically Japan and Korea, do not extract NGLs from the gas. Conversely, LNG that contains relatively large amounts of NGLs is essentially incompatible with markets in both Europe and North America.[37]

Industry stakeholders will need to make key strategic decisions by taking into account regional and local gas requirements in a complex environment that is also shaped by the evolution of global demand for the various oil and gas resources. Depending on the source of the LNG, its ethane content can vary between 3% and 10%, by volume.[38] Economic choices related to LNG supplies therefore depend on the end use for the gas. We will return to these issues in Chapter 9, which deals with liquefied natural gas. The outlook for oil and natural gas resources is illustrated in Figure 5.

---

[35] See "World LPG Production May Outpace Demand", *Oil & Gas Journal*, June 26, 2006, pp. 60-69.

[36] *Oil & Gas Journal*, June 26, 2006, p. 54.

[37] *Ibid.*, p. 65

[38] LNG typically contains less than 1% butane or isobutane and 0.1-3% propane by volume. See "Extracting NGL from LNG: No Easy Decision", *Oil & Gas Journal*, June 26, 2006, p. 65.

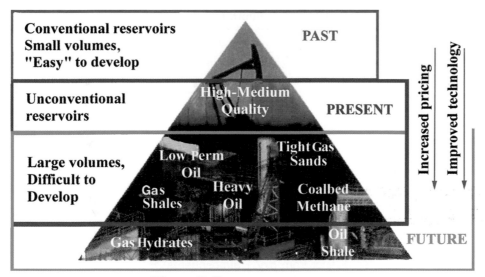

Figure 5: Future energy sources
Source: Drilling Contractors, November-December, 2004.
http://www.iadc.org/dcpi/dc-novdec04/dcpi.html

Primer on Conventional and Unconventional Gases

We will have the opportunity to revisit much of the terminology discussed in this chapter later in the book. The diversity of concepts related to oil and gas has generated a very rich vocabulary that can be difficult to assimilate. Tables 4 and 5 provide a summary of conventional and unconventional gases that should help readers better understand the differences between the various types of natural gas.

The term "unconventional" simply denotes that the natural gas is not located in conventional reservoir rock; instead, these resources are recovered from formations that are more difficult to exploit. There are no major differences in the properties of conventional and unconventional gases, however, and they are used for the same purposes. Table 5 presents the key characteristics of unconventional gases, specifically natural gas from coal (NGC), tight gas, shale gas and gas hydrates.

Table 4: Conventional gases

Condensate	Liquefied petroleum gas or LPG
Hydrocarbons with 5-7 carbon atoms that occur in gaseous form under reservoir conditions but condense to a liquid at surface temperatures and pressures. Condensate, commonly referred to as **casinghead gasoline**, is recovered with oil at the wellhead. Regulatory agencies classify condensates as crude oil when they are extracted from a reservoir. Condensate can be added to crude oil to lower the API gravity (**spiking**) and increase the volume of oil produced. Natural gas that contains condensate is known as **wet gas**, as distinct from **dry gas**, which consists of almost pure methane.	Mixture of light hydrocarbons that are gaseous at normal atmospheric temperatures and pressures. Mixes of LPG are maintained as liquids in pressurized containers, facilitating storage, transport and handling. Liquefied petroleum gas consists essentially of propane, butane or mixtures thereof.[39] It is produced at gas treatment plants and refineries. LPG is easily liquefied at normal temperatures and low pressures (4-18 atmospheres).[40]
Natural gas liquids or NGL	**Associated or dissolved gas**
The hydrocarbons (condensate and butane, propane and ethane) that can be separated from natural gas as liquids are referred to as natural gas liquids. They are similar to LPG but lighter.	These gases are either dissolved in the crude oil or occur in contact with the crude oil in an overlying space trapped within the reservoir. The gas cannot exist as free gas separate from the oil in the subsurface.

---

[39] See URSA Chevron glossary at http://www.texacoursa.com/glossary/index.html. LPG is a mixture of light hydrocarbons containing three or four carbon atoms, that is, propane, propylene, n-butane, isobutene and butylene, in varying proportions. See www.motorlegend.com/new/technique/gpl.

[40] As opposed to uncondensable gases, such as methane, ethane and ethylene, which can only be brought to a liquid state at room temperature under extremely high pressures. See *Ibid.*

Table 5: Unconventional gases

Natural gas from coal (NGC)	Shale gas
NGCs are also known as **coalbed methane** (CBM). As the coal has a very low porosity, the gas is chemically adsorbed in coal seams, where it remains trapped. These deposits date back to the Carboniferous period. The permeability of the reservoirs varies with location. If the permeability is too low, the deposits will be uneconomic; if the coal is too permeable, dehydration and desorption may be hindered along with methane recovery. The richest deposits in the United States are the Powder River Basin (Montana and Wyoming) and the San Juan Basin (Colorado and New Mexico), as well as deposits in Alaska and in the Appalachians. In 2005, NGC accounted for about 8% of U.S. natural gas production, compared with 2% in Canada.	According to the Canadian Centre for Energy Information, shale gas is "produced from reservoirs predominantly composed of shale with lesser amounts of other fine grained rocks." Very similar to clay, shales are rich in organic matter (1.5-20%). They are found in regions of low-grade metamorphism and correspond to type III kerogens. The main shale gas deposits in the United States, in order of importance, are Ohio, Antrim, Barnett, Lewis and New Albany. They account for 8% of U.S. natural gas production. The North American Energy Working Group predicts that U.S. production of shale gas will increase from 1.6 Bcf/d in 2002 to 2.8 Bcf/d in 2015 and then to 3.1 Bcf/d in 2025.
Tight gas	**Gas hydrates****
This gas is found in reservoirs that have low permeability and low porosity (7-12%)* owing to the fine-grained nature of the sediments, hence the name *tight* gas. The natural gas is not easy to produce economically, as the low pressure contributes to low flow rates. Tight gas can be recovered by injecting water in order to fracture the reservoirs, or by drilling horizontal wells. Advances have been achieved through enhanced simulation methods. In the U.S., tight gas is the main source of production of unconventional gas.	Gas hydrates are solid mixtures of water and natural gas that form under intense pressure at temperatures below 0°C. When melted, one cubic centimetre (cc) of this ice-like substance produces more than 160 cc of methane (CH_4). So far, no method has been found to produce gas economically from gas hydrates, although pilot tests have been carried out in a number of countries. Conventional mining methods cannot be used since the methane would simply escape into the atmosphere following the release of pressure. Drilling techniques that could help melt the hydrates are under study; however, it has not yet been determined whether the energy required to recover the gas hydrates would be less than the energy contained in them.

* *The permeability of reservoir rock is measured in units of darcies, which relate to the ease with which a fluid can flow within a reservoir rock. By contrast, porosity is the percentage of rock (by volume) that is not occupied by solid matter. Porosity is a measure of a reservoir rock's fluid storage capacity. Tight formations are often estimated to have permeability levels of less than 0.1 millidarcy.*

** *Hydrates are abundant under the sea floor in water depths exceeding 500 metres and under the permafrost in Russia, in the Arctic and elsewhere. Some view the production of hydrates as an impossible dream while others see this resource as a solution to the world's energy problems.*

6

Geography of Oil and Gas

The geopolitics of oil and gas are tied to the concentration of hydrocarbon resources in certain regions of the world and the resulting supply vulnerabilities in others.

Different Heartlands

To borrow a well-known idea put forward by the British geographer Halford J. Mackinder (1861-1947), we can talk about a heartland of oil –the Middle East– which is home to 62% of the world's proved oil reserves. It is important to point out, however, that this "geopolitical" conception is based solely on the "physical" concentration of petroleum resources. The world's oil and gas reserves are not static, however, since they are based on estimates and these estimates can vary depending on the methods used to calculate them. For example, if unconventional oil reserves, such as the tar sands in Canada or Venezuela, are added to proved conventional oil reserves, Canada moves from twelfth place to second place, right after Saudi Arabia, on the list of countries with the largest oil reserves. Technology is another important variable that needs to be considered in examining global reserves, since technological advances can pave the way for developing previously inaccessible offshore oil resources as well as permit enhanced recovery from oil wells.

If we look at natural gas, we see that the heartland for this resource differs from that of oil, because proved natural gas reserves are largely concentrated within the Russian Federation, which has 26.6% of world reserves, and within Iran, which has 14.9%. These two states alone account for nearly 42% of the world's natural gas reserves and thus represent a second heartland in the geography of oil and gas. The natural gas market is greatly dependent on complex infrastructure and facilities, such as gas pipelines, that are costly to build and maintain and often located in fairly inaccessible regions. By contrast, the liquefied natural gas (LNG) market, which is expanding rapidly, is tied to marine transportation capacities and liquefaction and regasification facilities.

Security of Supply

Regardless of how the issues of concentration of resources and vulnerability are defined, **security of supply** is the primary concern of all stakeholders, given the need to ensure that oil and gas can be obtained for reasonable prices within a relatively near future. It follows that market conditions play a decisive role in shaping supply and demand.

Demographic and Economic Growth

Unlike previous crises –the 1973 Arab oil embargo, the Iranian Revolution in 1979 and the Iran-Iraq War (1980-1988)– the present crisis, which was exacerbated by the severe 2005 hurricane season, stems largely from pressures created by demand exceeding supply. China and India, with their rapid economic growth, are now exerting very strong pressure on supply. Demographic growth combined with economic growth, especially per capita growth in GDP, are two factors that are strongly correlated with oil prices.[1] It is therefore expected that the pressure associated with the imbalance in supply and demand will persist over the coming years, in spite of China's efforts to contain its growth and keep its economy from overheating.

The Issue of Reserves

Before we can talk about reserves, we need to provide some background information on this concept. In Canada, a set of regulations setting out standards of disclosure for oil and gas activities (National Instrument 51-101) has been in effect since March 2004. These disclosure standards are based on what is called the probabilistic method, which differs from the deterministic method used by the U.S. Securities and Exchange Commission (SEC) headquartered in Washington, D.C. Both approaches have their advantages and disadvantages. The main characteristics of these methods are described in Table 1.

---

[1] See Chapter 3 for details on this topic. See also Patrick Criqui and Pierre Noël, "Marchés énergétiques et géopolitiques pétrolières, 1990-2030", *Institut d'Économie et de Politique de l'Énergie*, Grenoble, September 1998 (available online).

Table 1: Categories of reserves: deterministic and probabilistic methods

Deterministic Method Securities and Exchange Commission (SEC)		
Category of reserves	**Degree of confidence**	**Risk level**
Proved reserves (1P)	Conservative (reasonable certainty)	Low risk
Proved reserves and probable reserves (2P)	Single best estimate (more likely than not)	Moderate risk
Proved reserves + Probable reserves + Possible reserves (3P)	Optimistic (less likely than probable)	High risk
Probabilistic Method Canadian Standard 51-101		
Proved reserves (1P)	Probability of at least 90%	Lower than or equal to 10%
Proved reserves + Probable reserves (2P)	Probability of at least 50%	50/50
Proved reserves + Probable reserves + Possible reserves (3P)	Probability of at least 10%	Higher than or equal to 90%

Some experts have criticized the SEC for restricting companies to publishing proved reserves, thereby creating a situation in which it is almost impossible for actual reserves to be less than the reported reserves.[2] Furthermore, not disclosing probable reserves means that information that could be useful for government decision makers, bankers and investors will be lost. The SEC rules are fairly outdated since, in order for oil companies to be able to report proved reserves, they have to carry out drilling, which is very expensive in the case of offshore oil. The large U.S. multinational companies that operate in the Gulf of Mexico therefore want to be exempted from the "proved" criterion –and the SEC has taken this step– given that the new 3D seismic imaging technology along with 4D techniques (3D surveys repeated over time) provide them with equally credible results.

Under Canadian regulations, oil companies are required to disclose their reserves according to three categories of probability of recovery:

– Proved reserves P90
– Proved reserves and probable reserves P50
– Proved reserves, probable reserves and possible reserves P10

---

[2]   See Jean Laherrère, "Technologie et reserves", *Bulletin de l'Association française des techniciens et professionnels du pétrole*, No. 406, January-February 1997, pp. 10-28. Available at http://www.oilcrisis.com/laherrere/tecres.htm.

The first category (proved reserves) means that there is at least a 90% probability of recovery, because drilling, tests and measurements have been carried out, indicating that the oil or gas is producible using current technology at current prices.[3] By contrast, probable reserves have been tested, but they are not in production, and they have a probability of recovery of at least 50% at current market prices. Possible reserves have a probability of recovery of at least 10%.[4] Figure 1 provides a schematic representation of the three categories of reserves.

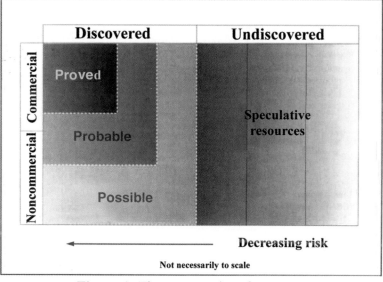

Figure 1: Three categories of reserves
Source: Alberta Securities Commission
(Working Group, 2000)

While at first glance these criteria seem simple, the methodology used is not straightforward and it has important implications for the financial health and management of oil and gas companies.[5] First, there are about as many sets of disclosure rules as there are countries engaged in oil production. In addition, recent studies have shown that, in the case of large oil companies, combining the proved

---

3   An important debate has arisen with regard to the method that should used for the reporting of reserves. Should the average price for the year be used, or the price as at December 31 of the year in which they are reported. Oil companies want to use the average price, but the SEC only allows reporting of the value of reserves as of December 31 or the last day of the fiscal year.

4   See Albert Legault, "Pétrole et transparence : De la nécessité d'améliorer le système de divulgation des réserves pétrolières", *Diplomatie*, No. 11, November-December 2004, pp. 81-85.

5   The probabalistic method should not be confused with the deterministic method, in which 2P means proved reserves + probable reserves. See the criticism of Jean Laherrère, "Hydrocarbon Reserves: Abundance or Scarcity", www.hubbertpeak.com/laherrere/Comm-OAPEC-IFP2005.pdf.

and probable reserve categories gives a probability of recovery of about 65%, compared with probabilities of 90% and 50%, respectively, when only proved or probable reserves are considered.[6]

The SEC's disclosure rules nevertheless serve as a sort of common denominator for the oil and gas industry. Foreign companies are not allowed to list their shares on the New York Stock Exchange unless they have previously complied with the SEC's rules of disclosure. And that is the crux of the problem since the SEC restricts disclosure to proved reserves. In early 2004, the Royal Dutch/Shell Group announced that it was re-categorizing some of its proved reserves, which amounted to restating them downwards significantly. This announcement took a heavy toll on the company's share price and its international reputation and sent a shock wave through the financial community. Although the upward or downward revision of companies' proved reserves is nothing new, the scope of the recent restatements of reserves is worrisome.

Towards Greater Transparency

Bankers, investors and shareholders are calling for greater transparency in the disclosure of oil and gas data, the adoption of a more credible universal disclosure system and mandatory auditing of reported reserves by independent experts. The recommendation about auditing entails the establishment of a professional certification system for geologists, geophysicists and engineers as well as a procedure for "decertifying" these experts in cases where their evaluations are found to be inaccurate or erroneous. The United States appears to be moving towards more stringent disclosure controls for oil companies in the wake of the Sarbanes-Oxley Act of 2002 (named after its two sponsors), which was passed in order to ensure respect for minimum standards of professional conduct in corporate governance. On the international level, seven different international organizations[7] have joined forces in implementing the Joint Oil Data Initiative (JODI).[8] The aim is to increase the transparency and reliability of oil data and the timeliness of reporting, particularly with respect to oil reserves and production. This initiative will enhance oversight of the oil market. At present, the International Energy Agency (IEA) does not have a

---

6 See J. H. Laherrère, "The Evolution of the World's Hydrocarbon Reserves." 1998, available at http://dieoff.org/page178.htm.

7 The Asia Pacific Energy Research Centre (APERC), the Statistical Office of the European Commission, (EUROSTAT), the International Energy Agency and the Organisation for Economic Co-operation and Development (IEA/OECD), the International Energy Forum Secretariat (IEFS), the Latin American Energy Organization (OLADE), the Organization of the Petroleum Exporting Countries (OPEC) and the Energy and Industry Statistics Section of the United Nations Statistics Division (UNSD). For more information on JODI, go to www.jodidata.org

8 An approach similar to the Extractive Industries Transparency Initiative (EITI).

mandate to verify the accuracy of data on oil reserves. This means that when producing its long-term production estimates, it has to rely on other organizations.

No disclosure system is perfect. As a columnist writing in the *International Herald Tribune* humorously stated: "In general, reserves estimates can vary for three major reasons. Or maybe five reasons. Although it might be four. Or even six. Everything depends on how you count."[9] This description ties in with the somewhat ironic analogy made by the Alberta Securities Commission, which compared oil reserves to fish:

"**Proved developed reserves**: The fish is in the boat. You have weighted him. You can smell him and you will eat him. **Proved undeveloped reserves**: The fish is on your hook, in the water, by the boat and you are ready to net him. You can tell how big it looks (of course they always look bigger in the water!). **Probable reserves**: There is fish in the lake. You caught some yesterday. You may be able to see them but you haven't caught any today. **Possible reserves**: There is water in the lake. Someone told you there are fish in the water. You have the boat on the trailer and are ready to go fishing but you may go golfing instead."[10]

There will always be some gray areas, but unless the entire system is governed by uniform rules of conduct, it will be difficult to have a clear picture of reserves. A good example of this is the reserves of OPEC countries, in particular, the many uncertainties related to the situation of Saudi Arabia, which has always refused to participate in this type of exercise.[11] As is often underscored in the *British Petroleum Statistical Review of World Energy*, these countries' reserves have barely changed over the past 20 years. How is it that the production of the past 20 years has not affected the countries' reserves? There is an obvious reason for this. Each OPEC countries' production quota is dependent on the size of its reserves. Resolving this issue will take some time and require the co-operation of all oil producing countries.[12]

---

[9] Ken Belson, *International Herald Tribune*, March 12, 2004.

[10] See http://www.oilpatchupdates.com/encyc.asp?view=1.

[11] For example, the former executive vice-president of Saudi Aramco, Sadad Al Husseini, stated that the company's proven reserves stood at 130 billion barrels, and yet Saudi Aramco is still reporting that is has reserves of almost 257 billion barrels. See Adam Porter, "The Elusive Truth about Oil Reserve Figures", *Economy News*, Aljazeera, August 12, 2004. Many articles have been written on the topic, notably in the *Oil & Gas Journal*. The work that gives the most alarming picture, predicting a peak in Saudi production in 2010, is the book by Matthew R. Simmons, entitled *Twilight in the Desert: The Coming Saudi Oil Shock and the World Economy*, John Wiley & Sons, 2005, 422 p.

[12] See Ali Hussain, "Market Gives Opportunity to Improve Oil Reserves Data", in *Oil & Gas Journal*, June 27, 2005, pp. 20-22.

Where Do We Stand in 2006?

Oil companies are required to prepare their financial and "physical" reports on an annual basis. The issue of reserves is therefore central in terms of the strengths they want to emphasize or the weaknesses they want to mask. Unfortunately, reserves are not a reliable indicator of future production. Some oil reservoirs or fields turn out to be a lot smaller than previously estimated, necessitating a drastic downward revision; some do not produce as much as expected; and some produce more than expected. So how do we make sense of all this?

Proved World Reserves

Figure 2 provides a schematic representation of the proved world reserves of oil and gas for the two ten-year periods 1986-1996 and 1996-2006 based on the *BP Statistical Review of World Energy 2007.*

Although the BP (British Petroleum) figures are comparable to those found in the *Oil & Gas Journal* and the data published by ExxonMobil in 2003, there can be appreciable differences among the different information sources[13].

When we look at Figure 2, two things stand out. First, gas reserves increased much more rapidly than oil reserves. The majority (60%) of mergers and acquisitions that occurred during the period 1997-2003, both in North America and worldwide, involved assets or gas reserves held by private companies.[14] Second, the absolute growth rates for the period 1996-2006 are much lower than those of the previous ten-year period, 1986-1996, which suggests that things are not going as well as we were led to believe, given that world demand for oil and gas has expanded in the meantime. During the period 1996-2006, the mean annual increase in natural gas consumption was 2.4%, compared to 1.6% for oil. During the same period, gas reserves rose 2.1% per annum and oil reserves, 1.4%.[15] This means that we are consuming natural gas faster than new resources are being discovered, or, to put it simply, we are using up our hydrocarbon heritage.[16]

---

[13] See "A Look Back at a Look Ahead", ExxonMobil, 2003, available at www.exxonmobil.com. In 2003, ExxonMobil estimated the planet's proven reserves of hydrocarbons at a little over 1.2 trillion barrels. On the variations in evaluations, see Jean Laherrère, "Abundance or Scarcity", *op. cit.* As of January 1, 2006, the *International Energy Outlook 2006* estimated the world's proved oil reserves at 1,293 billion barrels (The difference is only in the last two decimals) . See *IEO 2006*, p. 27. For natural gas, the same publication estimated the proved reserves at 6,112 Bcf, or 171.1 Bcm. *Ibid*, p. 38.

[14] See by the same author "Les fusions-acquisitions en matière de gaz et de pétrole : Le cas de l'Amérique du Nord", *Études internationales*, vol. 35, n° 3, September 2004, pp. 435-469.

[15] The growth rates were calculated based on the statistical data in the *BP Statistical Review of World Energy 2006*.

[16] According to John S. Herold, Inc., in 2004 alone world reserves grew 2% and production, 2.8%. See John S. Herold, Inc., *"2005 Global Upstream Performance Review"*, p. 11.

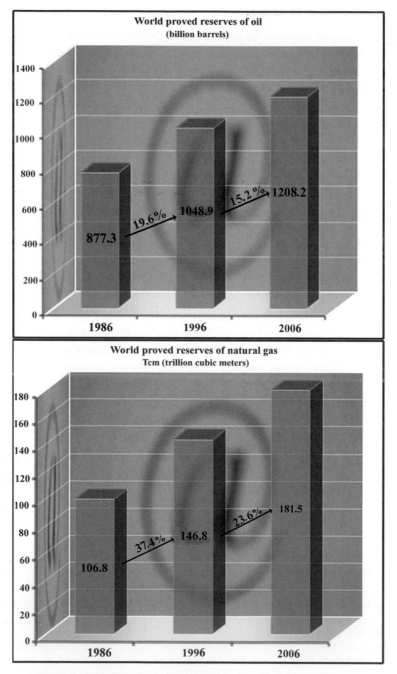

Figure 2: Proved world reserves of oil and natural gas
Source: British Petroleum Statistical Review of World Energy 2007

The Peak-Oil Theorists Versus the Technology Optimists

The above statement about using up our hydrocarbon heritage has significance for the heated debate between peak oil theorists (also called depletionists) and technology optimists. On July 14, 2003, the *Oil & Gas Journal* devoted a special issue to the depletion of oil and gas reserves worldwide. In recent years, the discussion between geologists and energy economists has heated up, with geologists emphasizing that oil and gas reserves are finite resources and that reasonably priced supplies will soon be a thing of the past, and with energy economists arguing that oil still has a promising future, provided that adequate investments and technological advances are made. The peak oil group is represented by the Association for the Study of Peak Oil & Gas (ASPO), headquartered in Sweden, whose founder is the well-known geologist Colin Campbell, assisted by his colleague Jean Laherrère, formerly of TotalFinaElf, who now heads a consulting firm in Geneva. There is also an Oil Depletion Analysis Centre in London, directed by Roger Bentley. In a nutshell, the "peak oil" theory contends that the end of the age of oil is imminent. Jeremy Rifkin, author of *The Hydrogen Economy,*[17] is a proponent of this school of thought, which is based on the premise that oil production will peak a lot sooner than many experts are predicting, and that when the oil dries up, production will plummet, oil prices will skyrocket and a global recession is likely to ensue. Clearly, the debate has huge implications and is captivating oil companies, investors and consumers alike.[18]

The "Peak Oil" School

Figure 3, originally from *Le Monde*, eloquently illustrates the depletionists' line of reasoning. Oil production from a reservoir can be represented by a bell curve, with a fairly steady rise in growth followed by a peak in production and finally a period of gradual decline. This pattern has been described as the law of diminishing returns. If this general law –developed by the American geologist M. King Hubbert– is applied to all oil deposits, there will be a point at which 50% of the reserves have been consumed. This will be followed by a drop in production and a rise in costs.

The value of this diagram is purely pedagogical, since the whole issue centres on determining the point at which oil production will peak. If the bell curve is shifted to the right or to the left along the abscissa, a whole new perspective emerges. The London-based company Douglas-Westwood Ltd. has forecast that oil production

---

[17] Polity Press, Cambridge (U.K.), 2002, 304 p.

[18] See the article by the editor Bob Williams, "Debate Over Peak-Oil Issue Boiling Over, with Major Implications for Industry, Society", *Oil & Gas Journal*, July 14, 2003, pp. 18-29.

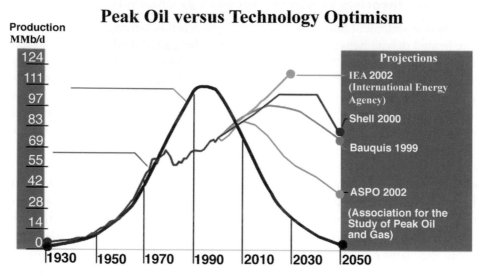

Figure 3: Theoretical curve of reserve depletion before the oil shock of 1973
Source: Infographie, Le Monde.fr

will peak around 2016 (see Figure 4) at roughly 90 million barrels a day (MMb/d). These forecasts are not very far from those of Jean Laherrère and Colin Campbell, who predicted that production will peak as early as 2010, likewise at around 90 MMb/d.[19] Jean Laherrère says that our grandchildren will have to make do with little oil and gas. The golden age of petroleum disappeared with the arrival of the new millennium. We are entering the age of gas, but it won't last long. The oil and gas reserves that built up over a period of more than 500 million years will be used up in just two centuries, which is just a very short time in the history of human-kind."[20]

At present, neither the International Energy Agency (IEA), the U.S. Department of Energy (DOE) nor the major oil companies are overly concerned about the industry's current capacity to meet world demand until at least 2030. But what about after 2030? Meanwhile, exploration and development costs continue to rise,[21] and it is becoming more and more difficult to find huge reservoirs that will permit high production rates using a single recovery infrastructure. Non-OPEC oil

---

[19] See *Oil & Gas Journal*, July 14, 2003, p. 20.

[20] Jean Laherrère, "Vers un déclin de la production pétrolière?", Institut supérieur industriel de Bruxelles, October 11, 2000, p. 19. Available at this site: www.hubbertpeak.com/laherrere/isib.

[21] According to John S. Herold, Inc., discovery and development costs increased by almost 75% over the preceding five years. See "*2005 Global Upstream Performance Review.*"

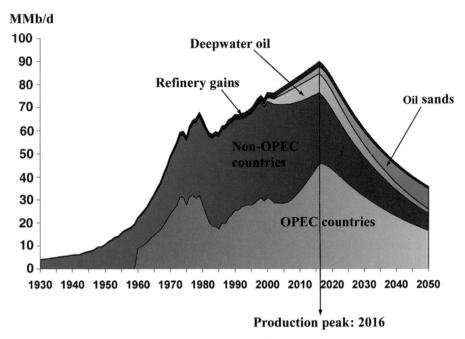

Figure 4: A century of oil production
Source: Douglas-Westwood Ltd., 2004, www.dw-1.com.

producing countries are expected to show a levelling off of production between 2010 and 2015, and it is forecast that the average increase in their oil production will be limited to 300,000-400,000 barrels per day during the years 2006-2010.[22]

Studies carried out by PFC Energy, based in Washington, D.C., are not at all reassuring.[23] Table 2, from PFC Energy, identifies 8 countries that have already reached or gone beyond their production plateau, along with 18 other countries whose production is declining. The formula developed by PFC Energy is interesting, since it rightfully takes into account the change in production divided by the change in reserves and relates it to total production.

---

[22] *Oil & Gas Journal*, November 14, 2005, p. 31.
[23] PFC or Petroleum Finance Corporation is the former name of the company.

Table 2: Oil producing countries
whose production has reached a plateau, is declining or has increased

Non-OPEC countries whose production has reached a plateau or begun to decline	Mexico, Brunei, Malaysia, China, India, Denmark, Canada, Yemen
Countries whose production is believed to be in decline	(Since 2002) Pakistan, Congo, Oman and Norway; Australia (since 2001); Columbia (since 2000); Great Britain (since 2000); Argentina and Gabon (since 1999); New Zealand (since 1998); Syria (since 1997); Democratic Republic of Congo (since 1996); Papua New Guinea and Egypt (since 1995); Cameroon (since 1990); Peru, Tunisia and the United States (since 1995).
Non-OPEC countries whose production is likely to increase in the future	Mauritania, Chad, Ivory Coast, Thailand, Sudan, Equatorial Guinea, Brazil, Angola, Vietnam, Ecuador (Of all the former countries of the Commonwealth of Independent States (CIS), Russia, Azerbaijan and Kazakhstan should also post an increase in production in the coming years)

According to *PFC Energy*, "Global Crude Oil and Natural Gas Liquids, Supply Forecast", September 2004, pp. 11, 12 and 17.

If the premises on which this analysis are based are borne out, it will become difficult to meet the requirements associated with world economic growth.

The Technology Optimism School

Technology optimists have also put forward some solid arguments, emphasizing that, in the past, only a third of reservoir capacity was tapped, and that the new technologies available today can increase recovery yields. Some have even forecast a recovery rate of 65%. In 1980, the average oil recovery rate for actively exploited fields worldwide stood at 22%, which compares with a rate of 35% today.[24] For others, including Jean Laherrère, recovery depends essentially on the geology of the reservoir. "The Intisar reef in Libya has the highest oil recovery factor, 80%, but the rate of decline is very rapid, 30% per year, whereas the rate for a fractured reservoir is about 3%."[25] The difference here is enormous. It is estimated that an increase of 1% in hydrocarbon recovery worldwide would supply the equivalent of two years of global consumption.[26] According to the IEA, increasing the worldwide average

---

[24] See Leonardo Maugeri, "Time to Debunk Mythical Links Between Oil and Politics", *Oil & Gas Journal*, December 15, 2003, p. 20

[25] Jean Laherrère, "Vers un déclin de la production pétrolière ?", Institut supérieur industriel de Bruxelles, October 11, 2000, p. 15.

[26] *Oil & Gas Journal*, August 4, 2002, p. 21.

recovery rate to 45% in existing fields would bring forth new oil reserves larger than those of Saudi Arabia.[27] Finally, 3D and 4D technologies can be used to prevent unnecessary drilling and can reduce the risk of inadvertently reducing the pressure in reservoirs that are under production, thereby helping to increase yields.

A number of studies have been carried out that bring grist to the mill of the technology optimists. The 20 or so studies cited in the *Oil & Gas Journal* article of July 14, 2003 give estimates that place the ultimately recoverable oil reserves worldwide in the range of 1.7-2.2 trillion barrels. The most optimistic forecasts are those of the U.S. Geological Survey (USGS).[28] The USGS study was used by the IEA in a comprehensive report on oil and gas reserves and resources in 2005.[29] According to its estimate, the planet has reserves of 20 trillion barrels of oil equivalent (BOE), with nearly half of this amount consisting of conventional oil. Of this total, only 5-10 trillion BOE are technically recoverable; the recoverable proved reserves are estimated to be some 2.2 trillion barrels. For the most part, the figures of the IEA and the USGS are in agreement, and they also agree with those of the *International Energy Outlook 2005* (*IEO 2005*). For the period 1995-2025, global proved oil reserves are projected to be 1,227.7 billion barrels, and these reserves are expected to increase by 730.2 billion barrels. This indicates that the planet has proved reserves totalling 2 trillion barrels.

A final argument invoked by the technology optimists is the contribution that non-OPEC countries are making to world production, given that they have boosted their output year after year. During the period 1993-2002, for example, non-OPEC countries produced 9 MMb/d, supplementing OPEC's production. However, this argument does not go far, since, in order to satisfy world oil demand between now and 2025, non-OPEC countries would have to produce 16.8 MMb/d, and OPEC countries would have to deliver 24 MMb/d. Non-OPEC production could only partly cover the needs associated with world growth. According to the *IEO 2005*, OPEC member countries will cover 59% of these requirements, compared to 41% for non-OPEC countries.[30] *Oil Outlook to 2025*, published by the OPEC Secretariat, provides a more modest outlook, predicting that in 2025 oil demand will stand at 115 MMb/d, and OPEC's share of production will be 50.9%.[31]

---

[27] IEA, "Resources to Reserves: Oil & Gas Technologies for the Energy Markets of the Future", Paris, 2005.

[28] They vary with the probabilities. For example, there is a 95% probability of extracting 2.2 trillion barrels, an average probability of reaching 3 trillion barrels, and a 5% probability of attaining a production of 3.9 trillion barrels. See *Oil & Gas Journal*, July 14, 2003, p. 28.

[29] See "Resources to Reserves: Oil & Gas Technologies for the Energy Markets of the Future", Paris, 2005, *op. cit.*

[30] See *IEO 2005*, p. 29. These statistics do not appear to take account of unconventional oil production.

[31] See Table 4 in *Oil Outlook to 2025*, OPEC Review Paper, 2004, p. 12.

The voracious oil appetite of our industrialized planet is undeniable. In a 2000 presentation on world oil and gas resources, the USGS estimated that, of the world's original oil resources, 539 billion barrels have been extracted (see footnote), excluding the United States.[32] The IEA estimates previous world oil production at 1,000 billion barrels, a figure that includes U.S. production; it puts previous world gas production at 450 BOE.[33] As at January 1, 2005, global oil consumption was roughly 30 billion barrels per year.[34] Taking into account the increase in consumption, there is only a half-century to go before global proved oil reserves are depleted. The days of oil are numbered.

There is a general consensus about the gradual depletion of hydrocarbon resources. The real issues are three in number. The first concerns the likely timing of peak production. There will probably not be just one peak in production. Instead of peaking all at once, production will reach a plateau for a number of years, with the production curve showing a saw-tooth pattern. The second area of uncertainty relates to technological progress. Technologies such as 3D seismic imaging, lateral drilling and gravity-assisted hydrocarbon recovery, among others, may help to slow the rapid decline of exploitable resources. Lastly, the planet still has its coal reserves, which will last for a few more centuries. For a number of years, pilot projects have been carried out with the hope of extracting oil, distillates or naphtha from coal (e.g., the Gas-to-Liquids and Coal-to-Liquids approaches described in Chapter 5). In spite of all the remaining uncertainty, one thing is sure: producing hydrocarbons during a period when these resources are in short supply will be costly, not to mention the additional energy requirements associated with generating alternative energy or renewable energy.

Gas and Oil: Different Markets

With regard to oil consumption, Asia Pacific follows close on the heels of North America. Figure 5 gives an idea of the difference between these two regions. Asia Pacific imports most of its oil from the Middle East, with smaller amounts coming from other regions. It is more dependent on the Middle East than North America.

---

[32] See the report by the team director, Thomas Ahlbrandt, "Future Oil and Gas Resources of the World –Unresolved Issues", USGS, 2000, available at http://www.netl.doe.gov/otiic/ World_Oil_Issues/Ahlbrandt_NREL_Talk.pdf. In reality, the oil endowment outside the United States is estimated at 2,659 billion barrels worldwide, from which previous production amounting to 539 billion barrels must be subtracted. The remaining volume is therefore 2,120 billion barrels.

[33] See Doris Leblond, "IEA Underscores Technology's Contribution to Future Oil Supply", (Figure 3), *Oil & Gas Journal*, October 17, 2005, p. 19.

[34] According to the figures published by the *BP Statistical Review 2005*, specifically 81 MMb/d, multiplied by 365 days.

The United States' strategy can be summarized as making sure that it does not put all its eggs in one basket. It imports from the Middle East, but it also obtains supplies from its neighbours, Canada and Mexico, from all of Latin America, from Europe and from Africa. Much of the sense of security that the United States has regarding its supplies –whether or not this belief is well founded– comes from its constant efforts to diversify its sources of supply.

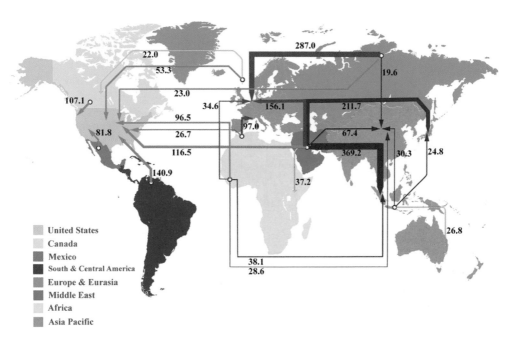

Figure 5: Main oil flows to the United States and Asia Pacific (in millions of tonnes)
Source: BP Statistical Review of World Energy, 2006

As Figure 6 shows, the prevailing inflows and outflows for natural gas are very different. Two regions, North America and Europe, depend mainly on regional sources of supply: Canada is the source of supply for North America, and Russia holds this position for Europe. We can also see the emergence of a significant liquefied natural gas (LNG) market for Asia Pacific. The thickness of the arrows in Figure 6 is proportional to the volume of gas exported, with red denoting natural gas and blue, LNG.

The markets for oil and natural gas are very different. In the case of gas, the production and consumption curves are essentially identical, with production and consumption exhibiting parallel trends (see Figure 7). This situation is linked to the local or regional nature of gas markets, which are still dependent on the existing infrastructure. The global oil market, on the other hand, is fully integrated. This market is often likened to a shared pool that all participants can draw from while remaining subject to the laws of supply and demand. The gas market is becoming increasingly integrated as well.

Natural gas is the fossil fuel that will experience the strongest growth in demand between now and 2025. The projected mean growth rate is 2.3% per year compared to 1.9% for oil, and 2% for coal.[35]

The United States has long depended on Canada for the bulk of its gas imports, with Canadian gas making up 15-17% of its total imports depending on the year. However, Canadian resources are declining and Washington is turning increasingly towards liquefied natural gas (LNG) markets. Trinidad and Tobago is an important new source of LNG for the United States (see Figure 6). Figure 6 illustrates the dominant characteristics of the natural gas market in 2005, as described in the *BP Statistical Review of World Energy 2006*.

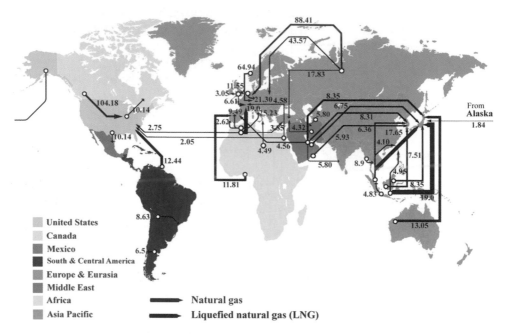

Figure 6: Main gas flows to the United States,
Europe and Asia Pacific (in billions of cubic metres, or Bcm)
Source: BP Statistical Review of World Energy, 2006

The estimate of U.S. demand for LNG given in the *Annual Energy Outlook 2006* (*AEO 2006*) for the period 2004-2025 is lower than that reported by the Energy Information Administration (EIA) a year earlier (see Chapter 9). This decrease in the projections is due to the increased demand for LNG from other regions, but also to the increase in crude oil prices, which influence LNG prices. The United States' interest in LNG can be expected to lessen if LNG prices rise as predicted.

---

[35]   *IEO 2006.*

"International trade in natural gas continued to grow robustly in 2005, rising by 6.4%, close to the 10-year average. Pipeline shipments also rose by 6.4%. While a large number of producers increased pipeline shipments, the largest increments were recorded by Norway, Algeria, Libya and Russia. Liquefied natural gas (LNG) shipments rebounded in 2005, rising by 6.4%. Egypt became an LNG exporter in 2005 and shipments from Qatar, Australia and Malaysia increased significantly. US LNG imports declined slightly, while European LNG imports rose by 19%. Asian LNG consumption continued to increase, with the ramp-up of Indian imports the key driver."[36]

LNG has a long history and its development is essentially linked to goals of energy security. A number of Asian countries have almost no gas resources or they are not connected to regional pipeline facilities. Japan, South Korea and Taiwan are good examples.[37] It is not surprising, therefore, that the main LNG shipbuilders are Japanese and South Korean companies, with Daewoo, Samsung and Hyundai being the leading suppliers of huge LNG carriers.[38] LNG prices have historically been higher in the Pacific Basin than in the Atlantic Basin, but this situation could change over the long term with the globalization of markets. The list of producing countries is growing. The dozen or so major producers that exist at present will be joined by about ten other countries, and meanwhile the number of facilities is growing rapidly in Asia, Western Europe and Africa. These three regions together account for more than 70% of the projected total spending on LNG facilities and associated investments during the period 2003-2007.[39]

In 2002, 49% of total LNG production, that is, 55 million tonnes out of global production of 113 million tonnes, came from Pacific countries, with Indonesia, Malaysia and Australia being the main exporters. In 2004, Asian production rose to 88 million tonnes.[40] It is projected that in 2015, LNG imports from Asia will amount to about 156 million tonnes; Japan is still the leading consumer in the region (64 million tonnes in 2015). In terms of absolute volume, in 2025 Asia Pacific will still be the primary consumer of natural gas thanks to the appetites of China and India.

Some observers are predicting that between now and 2025, global natural gas exports could exceed oil sales on a tonne of oil equivalent (TOE) basis.[41] LNG trade alone could

---

[36] *BP Statistical Review of World Energy 2006*, p. 4.

[37] A proposal for a pipeline between Sakhalin Island and Japan is under study, however.

[38] See "The World LNG & GTL Report 2003-2007", Douglas-Westwood Ltd., brochure, 2003.

[39] *Ibid.* Asia (43.1%), Western Europe (14.9%), Africa (13.7%). The total projected expenses amount to $39 billion, which includes the cost of terminals, tankers and liquefaction plants.

[40] Allison Ball, "Asia-Pacific LNG Market", *Australian Commodities*, Vol. 12, No. 2, June 2005.

[41] See the statement by Charles Watson, director of Shell Gas & Power, as reported in the article by Bob Tippee, "Worldwide Gas, LNG Demand Poised to Surpass Oil", *Oil & Gas Journal*, September 22, 2003, p. 28. Royal Dutch/Shell have made similar statements.

represent 500 million tonnes in 2030.[42] The traditional markets of Europe, Asia and North America will account for 60% of the demand growth over the next 20 years.[43] According to Cedigaz, the share of LNG in worldwide natural gas production will be 30% in 2010 and 32% in 2020.[44] Since it is unlikely that a single market price will be set in the short term, price differentials will undoubtedly persist between the three dominant markets –Asia Pacific, continental Europe and the U.S./U.K. market– especially as there will be continued competition between the two main modes of transport, pipelines and ships.[45] Depending on the change in U.S. demand, there could even be tight competition between LNG destined for Asia Pacific and that destined for North American markets or Europe. We will come back to these issues in the chapter on LNG.

Energy Dependency Relationships by Region

As we have seen, when it comes to energy resources, some regions of the world are better off than others.[46] There are several ways to calculate the level of dependence of a country or a region. The simplest formula consists in dividing total imports by total consumption. Let us take the hypothetical example of U.S. oil demand of 30 MMb/d. If the United States' domestic production amounts to only 10 MMb/d, the shortfall will be 20 MMb/d. Dividing the shortfall by total demand (20/30), we get a level of dependence of 66%.

In the following paragraphs, we will use a similar method, which looks at the percentage of oil and gas consumption in relation to production. Dependence is defined here as the ratio of production to consumption. Although dividing a percentage by a percentage is admittedly unorthodox, this approach has the advantage of being simple and providing an overview of the situation over the long term.

---

[42] According to the *International Petroleum Encyclopedia, 2003* (*IPE 2003*), Penwell, 2003, p. 179.

[43] See Bob Tippee, *op. cit.*

[44] See Panorama 2004, "The Dynamics of the World Gas Trade", available at www.ifp.fr/IFP/en/ files/cinfo/ IFP-Panorama04_03-CommerceVA.pdf. Douglas Westwood projected that LNG's share in the natural gas market will be about 27% in 2025. See Steve Robertson, "Trends and Developments in the LNG Sector", May 2004, at www.dw-1.com.

[45] According to Andy Flower, Andy Flower LNG Associates, cited in "The Global Liquefied Natural Gas Market: Status & Outlook", DOE, EIA, 2003, p. 4, "the economic crossover –the point at which transporting LNG via tanker is cheaper than transporting natural gas via pipelines– occurs at a distance of around 2,000 km for offshore pipelines and around 3,800 km for onshore pipelines."

[46] Readers can go back to the *BP Annual Statistical Review* to find out which countries are included in each region. The only problematic region is Europe/Eurasia, which encompasses the countries of Eastern and Western Europe, as well as the Russian Federation, and the countries of Central Asia, such as Turkmenistan, Kazakhstan and Uzbekistan. Asia Pacific includes China, India, Australia and the countries of Southeast Asia, whereas North America includes the U.S., Canada and Mexico.

The biggest oil producing regions are the Middle East, Europe/Eurasia[47] and North America, followed by Africa, Asia Pacific and South and Central America (in 2006). As Figure 7 shows, North America dropped from second place to third place during the period of study (1994-2006), when it was surpassed by Europe/Eurasia whose share of production in the world market reached almost 22%. This situation is due essentially to the arrival of Russian oil exports on the global market. Despite the drop in the Middle East's production in 2001 and 2002, its market position has been relatively stable, since other regions have taken up the slack, namely Europe/Eurasia and Africa. Africa's share has increased by 1.7% in 12 years, during which time the share of Europe/Eurasia rose 1.3%. In all the graphs, the left-hand scale indicates production and consumption in millions of barrels per day (MMb/d), but the start and end of the curves for 1994 and 2006 define the regions' share of world production and consumption.

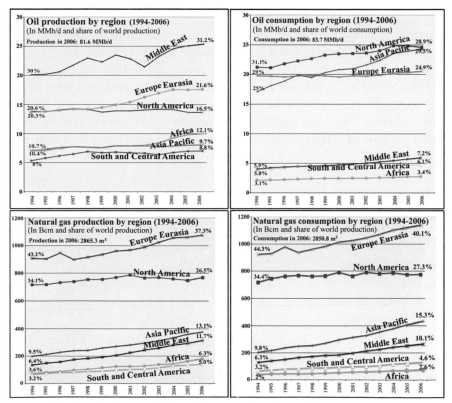

Figure 7: Regions' share of oil and gas production and consumption, 1994-2006
Source: BP Statistical Review of World Energy, 2006 and 2007

---

[47] Europe/Eurasia takes in all European countries and the countries that made up the former Soviet Union.

The biggest oil consuming regions are North America, whose share of the world market declined from 31.1% to 28.9%, Asia Pacific, whose share rose from 25% to 29.5%, and Europe/Eurasia, whose share fell from 29% to 24.9%. The three lowest ranking regions were stable, except for the Middle East, whose share of consumption increased by 1.3% in 12 years, undoubtedly because of its population growth and its rising energy needs (including hydroelectricity).

With respect to natural gas, one region stands out from all the rest –Europe/ Eurasia– which accounts for more than 37% of world production (21.6% by Russia and about 10% by the five main European producers: Great Britain, Norway, Netherlands, Germany and Italy, with Denmark not far behind). North America ranks second, but its share of production decreased from 34.1% in 1994 to 26.5% in 2006. All the other regions have experienced rapid growth, with the Middle East posting a gain of 5.3% in its share of world production over 12 years.

In terms of consumption of natural gas, Europe/Eurasia still has the lead, although its share of the pie fell 4.2% relative to the 1994 level. The 25 countries of the EU consume some 53% of the gas produced within the Europe/Eurasia region. This share has remained fairly constant over the past 10 years. Consumption in North America is also in sharp decline, with a decrease of over 7% in 12 years, whereas the other regions' consumption has grown rapidly, with the exception perhaps of Africa, which gained only a sixth of a per cent over a period of 12 years.

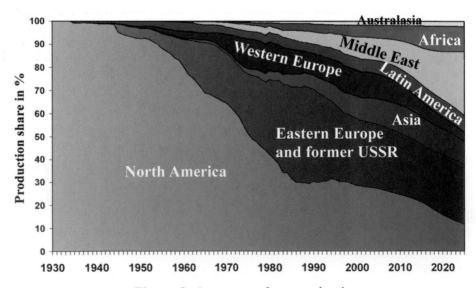

Figure 8: A century of gas production
Source: From Douglas-Westwood Ltd., 2004, www.dw-1.com.

Table 3: Regions' dependency ratios (1994 and 2004)

Oil	2006 Region's share of world production	2006 Region's share of world consumption	2006 Prod./cons. ratio	1994 Prod./cons. Ratio	1994 Region's share of world consumption	1994 Region's share of world production
North America	16.5%	28.9%	0.57	0.66	31.1%	20.6%
South and Central America	8.8%	6.1%	1.44	0.94	5.8%	8%
Europe/ Eurasia	21.6%	24.9%	0.87	0.7	29%	20.3%
Middle East	31.2%	7.2%	4.33	5.08	5.9%	30%
Africa	12.1%	3.4%	3.56	3.35	3.15%	10.4%
Asia Pacific	9.7%	29.5%	0.33	0.43	25%	10.7%

Natural gas	2006 Region's share of world production	2006 Region's share of world consumption	2006 Prod./cons. ratio	1994 Prod./cons. Ratio	1994 Region's share of world consumption	1994 Region's share of world production
North America	26.5%	27.3%	0.97	0.99	34.4%	34.1%
South and Central America	5.0%	4.6%	1.08	1	3.2%	3.2%
Europe/ Eurasia	37.3%	40.1%	0.93	0.98	44.3%	43.2%
Middle East	11.7%	10.1%	1.16	1.02	6.3%	6.4%
Africa	6.3%	2.6%	2.42	1.8	2%	3.6%
Asia Pacific	13.1%	15.3%	0.86	0.97	9.8%	9.5%

Source: Table compiled using data
from the *BP Statistical Review of World Energy 2006* and *2007*.

Figure 8 links the past and the future and provides a broader overview. Although North America dominated gas production for a half-century, the 1970s saw a gradual decline in its output. Meanwhile, the share of the countries in the former Soviet Union was gradually increasing. Beginning in 2010, the Middle East and Africa will increase their production, whereas most other regions, except Russia, will experience a marked drop in production.

Table 3 provides a more detailed look at the relationships of dependency between regions that are oil or natural gas consumers or producers. The production/consumption ratios are for the years 1994 and 2006. With respect to oil, the Middle East eclipses all the other regions, with a ratio of 4.33. The production/consumption ratios are also highly favourable for Africa, and South and Central America. Relative to 1994, three exporting regions have successfully increased their ratio of production/consumption: Africa, South and Central America and Europe/Eurasia, but not the Middle East.

The three oil exporting regions obviously correspond to the natural gas exporting regions, but the relative ranking of the regions differs. Africa occupies first place with a favourable ratio of 2.4, whereas the Middle East is vying for second place, with South and Central America hot on its heels. All the other regions are natural gas importers, with Asia Pacific seeing its position deteriorate faster than that of North America.

These ratios show that dependency is less marked for natural gas than for oil. Overall, and in 2006, Asia Pacific and North America show strong dependence on oil imports, with ratios of 0.33 and 0.57, respectively. But their reliance on natural gas imports is lower, as evidenced by ratios of 0.86 for Asia Pacific and 0.97 for North America.

Table 4: Oil dependency of Russia, China and the United States (1994 and 2006)

Oil	2006 Share of three countries in world production	2006 Share of three countries in world consumption	**2006 Prod./cons. ratio**	**1994 Prod./cons. ratio**	1994 Share of three countries in world consumption	1994 Share of three countries in world production
Russian Federation	12.0%	3.3%	**3.64**	**2**	4.8%	9.6%
United States	8.4%	24.6%	**0.34**	**0.48**	26%	12.5%
China	4.5%	8.9%	**0.51**	**0.96**	4.6%	4.4%

If we compare the three major countries, Russia, China and the United States, Russia stands out for its high oil production (see Table 4), a position that grew much stronger between 1994 and 2006. Also noteworthy is the growing dependence of the United States in relation to oil, although it shows a smaller difference in its ratio compared to China, whose ratio nearly doubled, from 0.96 to 0.51, over a 12-year period.

Projected Investment Requirements for the Oil and Gas Sectors

In fall 2005, the IEA published a major report, *World Energy Outlook 2004* (*WEO 2004*), which looked at investment requirements in the energy sector. This report was updated in the *WEO 2006*. The figures speak for themselves. About US$20.2 trillion (2005 dollars) will be required to meet the needs of world energy growth between now and 2030.[48] Of this sum, $11.3 trillion will need to be allocated to the modernization and development of the electricity sector. Already in an earlier report (*WEO 2003*), the IEA said that the sum of $3.5 trillion was needed to develop electricity generation infrastructure in Asian countries. Given its outdated facilities, North America will also need to invest huge sums ($1.979 trillion) to update its electricity generation facilities.

As Figure 9 shows, capital investments required in the gas and oil sectors are as follows: about $3.9 trillion for the gas sector and $4.3 trillion for the oil sector. Of these amounts, 37% is needed for gas transport, distribution and storage networks, and 73% for oil exploration and development activities. In other words, for the two sectors, a capital investment of more than $300 million is required annually. The *WEO 2006* estimates that the cumulative investment required for China from now until 2030 is $3.7 trillion, or 18% of the projected total world investment. The lion's share of this amount (81%) should go to the electricity sector, 9% to the oil sector and 3% to the gas sector.[49] A total of $7.3 trillion will be required to develop the energy sector in OECD countries, compared with $10.5 trillion for developing countries. It should be noted that the priorities differ for OECD countries and developing countries. In both cases, the electricity sector is the main priority, but the order is reversed for the gas and oil sectors. OECD countries will need to invest more in the gas sector than in the oil sector by a factor of 1.5, whereas the reverse is true for developing countries.[50]

---

[48] Compared with $16.0 trillion in the report for the previous year. The figures were revised mainly because of the depreciation of the U.S. dollar and the fact that the 2005 dollar was adopted as the basis for calculating investments.

[49] *World Energy Outlook 2006*, IEA, Paris, 2006, p. 77. Hereafter cited as *WEO 2006*.

[50] For OECD countries, $1.744 trillion will go to the gas sector and $1.149 trillion to the oil sector; in the case of developing countries, $2.223 trillion will go to the oil sector and $1.516 trillion to the gas sector. See *WEO 2006, op. cit.*, p. 77.

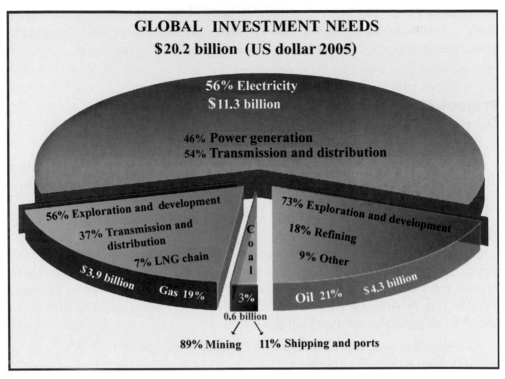

Figure 9: Projected investment requirements by sector, 2005-2030
Source: IEA, *World Energy Outlook 2006*, p. 78.

Projected Investment Requirements by Region

Capital requirements obviously vary from one region to another. The *WEO 2004* predicts that only 9% of all global investments, or about $1.5 trillion should go to the Middle East and North Africa (MENA).[51] Of this total, 41% would go toward developing the oil resources of countries in the region,[52] 30% toward modernizing their electricity infrastructure[53] and 29% toward supporting their gas production.[54]

---

[51] The IEA includes the following countries in the MENA: Iran, Iraq, Kuwait, Qatar, Saudi Arabia and the United Arab Emirates (U.A.E.); and for the region of North Africa: Algeria, Egypt and Libya.

[52] The first three countries are Saudi Arabia, Iran and Kuwait, with Iraq close behind. See *WEO 2005*, p. 561.

[53] The first three countries are Saudi Arabia, Iran and the United Arab Emirates, with Egypt not far behind. *Ibid.*

[54] The first 3 countries are Qatar, Iran and Kuwait. *Ibid.*

In the *WEO 2006*, the Middle East takes a larger share, that is, 14%, of the total capital investments required for energy infrastructure.

Figure 10 shows the enormous investment requirements in the electricity sector, with the most pressing needs being felt in Asia Pacific and China, followed by the United States and Europe. In the case of oil, the needs centre in the major production zones, in particular, the Middle East, Russia and Africa. The ranking of the regions varies somewhat for natural gas. The United States ranks first, given its needs related to infrastructure for receiving liquefied natural gas (LNG). A similar situation exists for the OECD (Europe), which is on an almost equal footing with Africa and Russia.[55] In terms of aggregate investments for the period 2005-2030, Asia Pacific (China and Asia/others in Figure 10) comes first, mainly because of the energy demand from China and India, whereas North America is a close second, and Europe comes in third.

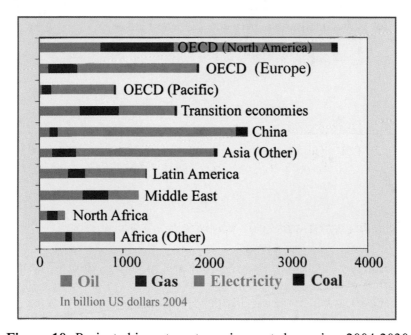

Figure 10: Projected investment requirements by region, 2004-2030
Source: IEA, *World Energy Outlook 2005*

While the total sum of $20.2 trillion may seem exorbitant, it is not far from reality. According to the statistics published by John S. Herold, Inc.,[56] the major oil

---

[55] According to the *WEO 2006, op. cit.,* p. 77, the investment requirements for the gas sector are as follows for Europe, Africa and Russia respectively: $417 billion, $485 billion and $478 billion.

[56] The statistics compiled by John S. Herold, Inc. encompass more than 200 oil and natural gas companies.

companies' acquisition, exploration and development investments totalled $211 billion and $276 billion in 2004 and 2005, respectively.[57] Admittedly, however, 2004 and 2005 were special years, given the spike in the price of oil during that period. Royal Dutch Shell and ExxonMobil made investments of $10.6 and $10.5 billion, respectively, in the upstream sector. There appears to be no shortage of capital for investing in oil and gas, especially since in 2004 the oil companies' cash flows were higher in most cases than the amount of capital invested on a regional basis, except in the United States and Canada. In addition, oil companies used their capital to buy back their own shares. In absolute terms, money spent on share redemption exceeded exploration spending by 20%.[58]

Overall, the average investment required in the energy sector during the period considered is equal to about 1% of world GNP.[59] However, Russia, Africa, countries whose economies are in transition, and the Middle East will need to allocate more than 3% of their GDP to energy development, whereas the corresponding proportion for China and India is between 2.2% and 2.5%.

---

[57] John S. Herold, Inc., "Global Upstream Performance Review", *2005* and *2006*, pp. 14-15.
[58] *Ibid.*, pp.7 and 12.
[59] See *World Energy Investment Outlook, 2005*, IEA, Paris, 2005.

7

The Outlook for Petroleum Prices and Demand Until 2030

This chapter will focus on the demand for oil and competing fuels (natural gas demand will be examined in greater depth in Chapter 9, which deals with liquefied natural gas). In his book, *Les grandes batailles de l'énergie*, Jean-Marie Chevalier distinguishes between key energy trends and energy uncertainties.[1] Here we will discuss two such trends: demographic growth and economic development.

Demographic Pressure on Resources

According to Population Action International (PAI), a major international non-governmental organization (NGO), the world population was 6.5 billion in 2005. For 2025, it is projected that the global population will be between 7.5 and 8.3 billion[2]; of this total, PAI estimates that 2.75 billion people will be living less than 100 km from the coasts and 57%, in cities.[3] By mid-century, the population should reach between 7.9 billion and 10.9 billion. Similar projections have been made by the Population Division of the United Nations' Department of Economic and Social Affairs: 7.2 billion in 2015, 8.19 billion in 2020 and 9.1 billion in 2050.[4]

---

[1] Key trends according to the author are the inertia and rigidity of energy systems, the inertia of transportation systems, globalization, increased consumption in non-OECD countries, the renewed popularity of nuclear power and the trend toward lower energy intensity. Uncertainties include the effects of climate change, technological changes, new balances of power, unforeseen events and investments. See Jean-Marie Chevalier, *Les grandes batailles de l'énergie*, Paris, Gallimard (Collection Folio), 2004, p. 30.

[2] See http://www.populationaction.org/resources/publications/mappingthefuture/index.htm.

[3] See "Actualités, Planète Terre", *Science & Vie*, October 2006, pp. 28-29.

[4] See *World Population Prospects: The 2004 Revision Volume III Analytical Report*, UN, Population Division of the Department of Economic and Social Affairs at http://www.un.org/esa/population/publications/WPP2004/WPP2004_Volume3.htm.

The growing world population means more mouths to feed and, in general, a greater drain on all the earth's biological and physical resources, from fresh water, forests and land for growing food to the products of the sea.[5] Declining fertility rates in the last 40 years –from an average of five children per woman to fewer than three– provide a small glimmer of hope, however.[6] Better policies for controlling population growth could no doubt ease some of the pressures on the planet's resources.

In terms of energy demand, according to Colin Baudouin of the Institut français du pétrole (IFP), based on International Energy Agency (IEA) statistics, per capita primary energy demand increased by 11% between 1970 and 2000 and should increase again by 27% between 2000 and 2030.[7] As Table 1 shows, total primary energy demand (TPED) is expected to triple in 60 years, while the population will roughly double.[8]

Table 1: Projected per capita primary energy demand
(in TOE = tonne of oil equivalent)

World population World consumption	3.7 billion 5 billion TOE	6 billion 9.2 billion TOE	8.2 billion 15.3 billion TOE
	1970	**2000**	**2030**
Per capita consumption	1.35 TOE per capita	1.5 TOE per capita **(+11%)**	1.9 TOE per capita **(+27%)**

Source: Colin Baudouin, IFP (see[7])

Per capita energy consumption obviously varies from country to country, ranging from 2.4 barrels of oil equivalent (BOE) per capita annually in India, to 6.6 BOE in China and 60 BOE in the United States.[9] In Canada, the average is 69 BOE

---

[5] On this issue, see Robert Engelman, Richard P. Cincotta, Bonnie Dye, Tom Gardner-Outlaw and Jennifer Wisnewski, *People in the Balance: Population and Natural Resources at the Turn of the Millennium,* Washington, D.C., Population Action International, 2000. A report by the World Wildlife Fund (WWF) (now the World Wide Fund for Nature), *Living Planet Report 2006,* says that humanity is consuming more biological resources than the planet produces. See also "Les États-Unis, l'Europe et la Chine puisent à l'excès dans les réserves biologiques", *Le Monde,* October 23, 2006.

[6] Population Action International, *op. cit.*

[7] Colin Baudouin, "Coal To Liquids", presentation to EPFL-AISEN conference, École polytechnique de Lausanne, November 2, 2005, at www.ifp.fr/IFP/fr/fichiers/ifp/IFP_Liquefaction DuCharbon_ColinBaudoin_EPFL-AISEN_021105.pdf.

[8] In primary energy, a TOE is equal to 7.4 barrels of oil (or 7.8 barrels in terms of useful energy consumed). See http://www.solcomhouse.com/Energy.htm.

[9] These figures come from a presentation by Simons & Company International, "Energy Prices and Energy Fundamentals: Is there a Link?" (p. 12), given at a symposium organized in July 2004 by the London-based Centre for Global Energy Studies. It places energy use in Canada at 69 barrels per capita.

per capita. According to the *Annual Energy Outlook 2006* (*AEO 2006*), per capita energy consumption in the U.S. in the transportation sector, which is a heavy consumer, will increase by 15% during the period 2003-2030.[10]

Global population growth and the attendant increase in energy demand will of course have a direct impact on greenhouse gas (GHS) emissions. Organisation for Economic Co-operation and Development (OECD) countries alone produced 12.9 gigatonnes (GT) of carbon dioxide (CO_2) emissions in 2004, 32.4% from coal and 44% from oil and gas.[11] Globally, CO_2 emissions are expected to increase from 25 GT in 2003 to 43.7 GT in 2030.[12] On a per capita basis, the Stern report on the economics of climate change gives the following figures: 2.7 metric tonnes (t) in China, 1.2 t in India, 9 t in Europe and 20 t in the United States. France, thanks to its reliance on nuclear power, has managed to decrease its per capita emissions to 6.2 t.[13]

Scenarios for Economic Growth and Primary Energy Demand

Most international institutions like the World Bank (WB) and the International Monetary Fund (IMF) publish data and projections on economic development. In the field of energy, the International Energy Agency (IEA) is the world authority,[14] while, in the United States, the Energy Information Administration (EIA) of the Department of Energy (DOE) is the main source of analyses and information. In the case of petroleum producing companies, the Organization of the Petroleum Exporting Countries (OPEC) plays a lead role in providing such information. Major international oil companies like British Petroleum (BP) and ExxonMobil also publish useful energy outlook statistics and reports.

To spare our readers, we will not provide an exhaustive account of all these sources, but rather an overview of forecasts of primary energy needs. We will then take a brief look at the projected demand for oil and gas until 2025 or 2030 since both of these components are directly linked to economic growth.

---

[10] See *Annual Energy Outlook 2006*, DOE, EIA, p. 74. Hereafter cited as *AEO 2006*.

[11] In 1971, CO_2 emissions stood at 14 GT. See Sunil Malla, "Cobenefits of Energy Related Climate Change Policies in Selected Developing Asian Countries", at www.epa.gov/ies/documents/ Workshops/ Malla.pdf.

[12] According to the *International Energy Outlook 2006*, DOE, EIA (hereafter cited as *IEO 2006*), p. 4 and p. 93. See also *Oil Information* (2006 edition), IEA, p. II-8.

[13] See the report by the economist Sir Nicholas Stern. The data are taken from the article in *Le Monde* of November 3, 2006, "Les États approuvent le rapport Stern, sans être prêts à amplifier leur action."

[14] Which publishes the annual *World Energy Outlook* (*WEO*).

Projected Global Energy Demand and Growth Rates for the Main Fuels

Table 2 illustrates the expected growth in energy demand for the period 2003-2030 in terms of total primary energy demand and the specific demand for oil, natural gas and coal. Since growth rates can vary considerably over time, the table shows the average for the entire period examined. Readers should particularly note the high growth in demand expected for natural gas (2.4% per year on average) and the growth rate for coal (2.5% per year on average). These rates are much higher than the projected growth rate for oil, which is 1.4% per year.

The greatest disparity in energy demand is that between developed and developing nations. For OECD nations as a whole, energy demand is expected to grow by only 1% per year, compared with 3% for non-OECD nations. In other words, developing countries will take an ever-larger share of the energy pie, representing over two thirds of the projected increase in demand. The fundamental differences between developing and developed countries relate to the developed world's greater energy efficiency, the dematerialization of the economies of industrialized countries (a phenomenon discussed in Chapter 3) and also the fact that most major oil and gas as well as mining development projects, which consume large amounts of energy, are in developing nations.

The World Energy Council's publication *World Energy in 2006* correctly states that these kinds of forecasts illustrate the reversal in demand patterns that is occurring between industrialized and developing countries. Whereas the industrialized world accounted for 62% of global energy demand in 1971, its share was only 51% in 2003, and the projections show a continuing downtrend, reaching 42% in 2030. In addition, the major oil consuming countries will have to accommodate the combined demand from China and India, estimated at 18.9 million barrels a day (MMb/d). These changes could result in diverging geopolitical interests, not to mention political tension.[15]

Projections of primary energy demand vary depending on the source consulted. For example, the U.S. Energy Information Administration (EIA), in Appendix H to its *International Energy Outlook 2006* (*IEO 2006*), compares the projections by the International Energy Agency (IEA), Petroleum Industry Research Associates (PIRA) and Petroleum Economics, Ltd. (PEL) with its own forecasts for the period 2002-2010. During this period, the EIA's *IEO 2006* reference case projects a 2.7% growth in primary energy demand, compared with 2.2% for the IEA, 2.7% for PIRA and 2.4% for PEL. The differences are all the more significant (0.5% between the highest and lowest projections) given that this is a macroeconomic measurement for the entire world. The differences between the projections in the *IEO 2006* (Table 2) and those in the IEA's *World Energy Outlook 2006* (*WEO 2006*) are very small.

---

[15]   World Energy Council, *World Energy in 2006*, p. 13.

Table 2: Global energy demand and growth rates for selected fuels (2003-2030)

	2003	2015	2030	Expected growth rate for 2003-2030
Total global energy demand	421 quadrillion BTUs	563 quadrillion BTUs	722 quadrillion BTUs (71% increase over 2003)	Non-OECD nations (including China and India): 3% Non-OECD nations (Asia): 3.7% Central and South America: 2.8% Africa 2.6%; Middle East: 2.4% Non-OECD nations in Europe and Eurasia: 1.8% OECD: 1%
Global oil demand	80 million barrels a day (MMb/d)	98 MMb/d	118 MMb/d (see **Note 1**)	1.4% per year The transportation sector accounts for over 50% of projected growth and industry for another 39%.
Global gas demand	95 billion cubic feet (2.6 Bcm)		182 billion cubic feet (5.1 Bcm) (92% increase over 2003)	2.4% per year Demand is driven by the electricity sector (2.9% per year) and industry (2.8%).
Global coal demand	5.4 billion tons (2,000 lb.)		10.6 billion tons (96% increase over 2003)	On average, 3% a year between 2003 and 2015; decreasing to 2.0% **after** 2015; 2.5% per year for the period 2003-2030 China and India account for 70% of the growth in world demand.

Note 1: This is 38 MMb/d more than in 2003. To respond to the growth in demand, OPEC countries will have to increase production by 14.6 MMb/d. The strong demand for oil will also stimulate efforts to develop unconventional oil resources. Assessed at 1.8 MMb/d in 2003, the latter could reach 11.5 MMb/d in 2030, or 10% of projected world oil production.

Source: International Energy Outlook 2006 (IEO 2006), DOE, EIA, June 2006.

Annual growth in global oil demand is projected to be 1.4% according to the *IEO 2006*, compared with 1.3% according to the *WEO 2006*.[16] The IEA predicts that this demand will reach 99 MMb/d in 2015 and 116 MMb/d in 2030.

---

[16]   See *WEO 2006, op. cit.*, p. 85.

Forecasts of Global Economic Growth

Similar differences are found in projections of global economic growth. According to the EIA's *IEO 2006,* which covers the period 2003-2030, the world gross domestic product (GDP) will grow by 3.8% annually on average.[17] The IEA in Paris, on the other hand, has projected annual world GDP growth of 3.4% for the period 2004-2030.[18] OPEC estimates that the annual growth in the world gross national product (GNP) will be 3.5% for 2006-2025 (see Table 3). According to ExxonMobil, the world GDP will grow at an annual rate of 2.7% during the period 2000-2030.[19] These differences are substantial, since a difference of 1% in either direction has major implications for world oil consumption. Although it is to OPEC's advantage to provide high growth figures, if only to better allocate world demand among its members, it must also strive to guarantee stable supplies over the long term, which means that it has to make the right decisions at the right time, particularly regarding investments.

Table 3: OPEC projections: average annual increase in GNP
(as a percentage)

	2006-2010	2011-2015	2016-2020	2021-2025	2006-2025
OECD	2.4	2.3	2.2	2.2	2.3
Developing countries	5.5	4.8	4.6	4.4	4.8
Transition economies	4.4	3.4	3.2	3.0	3.5
World	3.8	3.3	3.4	3.3	3.5

Source: OPEC, "Oil Outlook to 2025", *OPEC Review*, September 2004. Available at: www.opec.org/ library/OPEC%20Review/OWEM04.pdf. Hereafter referred to as *Oil Outlook to 2025.*

Table 3, which presents the GNP growth rate projections produced by the OPEC Secretariat, illustrates what we have already emphasized: that growth rates among OECD nations and developing nations are asymmetrical. In addition, although there are a few differences between five-year periods, the projections seem to decline over

---

[17] *IEO 2006, op. cit.,* p. 86. This decreases to 2.6% for OECD nations and to 3.1% for North America, but climbs to 6% for China and 5.4% for India. All calculations were made in 2000 dollars.

[18] *WEO 2006, op. cit.,* p. 53.

[19] See "The Outlook for Energy: A View To 2030", April 2006, p. 3, available at http:// www.exxonmobil.com/Corporate/Citizenship/Imports/EnergyOutlook05/index.html. Readers should note that these calculations are based on the gross domestic product (GDP), which excludes imports, rather than the gross national product (GNP).

the long term, except for the period 2016-2020. Beginning in 2016, the GNP growth curve for OECD nations either remains relatively stable or declines. For the entire period 2006-2030, there is a difference of 1.2% in the annual GNP growth rate of OECD countries and that of non-OECD (developing) countries, which is significant.

OPEC's Dilemma

The scenarios produced by the different organizations are of critical importance to firms and countries that rely on such projections in making key long-term investments. In addition, the greater the discrepancy between the two extremes of the range, the greater the caution required (or the greater the opportunity for risk-takers). For example, the natural gas market has seen a number of ups and downs, mainly because of price volatility on the U.S. market.[20] Oil has also faced a series of crises, the most drastic ones being the Iranian Revolution and the Iran-Iraq War (see section on oil crises and oil price shocks). In general, observers agree that high demand is here to stay, along with relatively high oil prices.

Table 4 shows OPEC's projections for oil demand under a low economic growth scenario. Under this scenario, OPEC projects a 1% annual decrease in demand, compared with an expected increase of 1.7% under its "dynamics as usual" (reference case) scenario. In the event of sluggish world economic growth, non-OPEC production would be relatively stagnant beginning in 2010, but OPEC production would start to show sustained growth at this time. According to OPEC, since the 1990s, OPEC countries' capacity utilization rates have remained in the range of 80-90%.[21] Under the low economic growth scenario, this rate would drop to 66%, the level seen in 1986-87.

Table 4: World oil supply and demand under a low economic growth scenario (millions of barrels per day)

	2005	2010	2015	2020	2025
World demand	79.9	84.2	88.8	93.2	97.4
Non-OPEC production	51.3	54.5	56.3	56.6	55.9
OPEC production	28.6	29.7	32.5	36.6	41.5

Source: From OPEC, *Oil Outlook to 2025*, p. 41.

---

[20] On this subject, see the article by Robert J. Michaels, "Natural Gas Regulation" in *The Concise Encyclopedia of Economics,* available at http://www.econlib.org/library/ENC/NaturalGasRegulation.html.

[21] OPEC, "Oil Outlook to 2025", *OPEC Review*, September 2004, p. 41. Available at www.opec.org/library/OPEC%20Review/OWEM04.pdf. Hereafter referred to as *Oil Outlook to 2025.*

Although this scenario is obviously extreme and highly unlikely, under it, a significant drop in demand would occur: 4.5 MMb/d in 2010 and 17.3 MMb/d in 2025 (see Figures 1 and 2). Regions with sharply reduced imports would include North America and Western Europe in 2010, and South Asia, North America, China and Western Europe in 2025. The OPEC Secretariat has been quite blunt in emphasizing the seriousness of the dilemma that would result under such a scenario. OPEC countries would either have to delay investments to avoid excess production or accept a considerable reduction in oil prices. Either option would run the risk of introducing destabilizing mechanisms that would be harmful for prices, markets and investments. In its study on the world oil outlook to 2025, OPEC emphasizes that some investment decisions could have an impact on capacity within months, while others could have effects that would not be felt for several years. How then, can the right decisions be made in such an uncertain climate?[22] The acting OPEC Secretary General stated in September 2006 that the wide range in potential demand, when translated into actual investments required (somewhere between $230 billion and $470 billion), "takes on a very worrying look."[23]

At this point, we need to use other analysis methods to assess the impact of energy demand on oil production forecasts.

Effects of Oil Prices on Economic Growth

As previously discussed, economic growth and demographics are two of the basic parameters used to assess demand and associated production requirements. In a global free-market economy, the price of a barrel of oil is of paramount importance. OPEC's mission, as stated on the organization's web site, is "to coordinate and unify the petroleum policies of Member Countries and ensure the stabilization of oil prices in order to secure an efficient, economic and regular supply of petroleum to consumers, a steady income to producers and a fair return on capital to those investing in the petroleum industry." What this means in practical terms is that there should be a more open and transparent dialogue between producers and consumers, with both groups putting forth arguments to support their own interests.

In the global economy, the important role that oil prices play in economic growth has not escaped the keen eye of World Trade Organization (WTO) economists. According to the WTO's *World Trade Report 2006,* "the negative impact of the oil

---

[22] *Oil Outlook to 2025, op. cit.,* p. 43.

[23] Speech delivered by Mr. Mohammed S. Bardinko, Acting OPEC Secretary General, at the 3rd OPEC International Seminar, Vienna, Austria, September 12-13, available on OPEC web site at http://www.opec.org/opecna/Speeches/2006/BarkindoSeminar.htm

price hike on world economic growth has so far been less far-reaching than observed in the past and predicted by most model simulations. Four explanations can be offered for this more benign outcome: first, the recent oil price hikes originate from the strength of oil demand and not from a disruption of oil supplies,

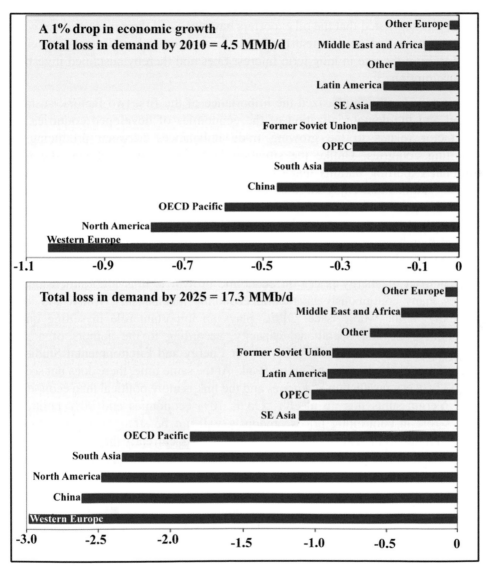

Figures 1 and 2: Decrease in OPEC production in 2010 and 2025
in response to a 1% drop in economic growth
MMb/d (millions of barrels per day)
Source: OPEC, *Oil Outlook to 2025*, figures 17 and 18, page 42.

which is considered to be less damaging to economic activity. A second factor is the reduced oil intensity of GDP growth in OECD countries caused by efficiency improvements in energy use and a shift in output towards services, which are less energy intensive than other sectors. This was not fully taken into account in the simulations. The third proposition is that the oil exporters spend their increased export earnings faster on imports of goods and services than in previous oil crises. Finally, it is suggested that the oil exporters have invested their increased net wealth in US corporate and government bonds, and not in more liquid assets, which has helped to limit the rise in long-term interest rates and thereby sustained investment and consumption."[24]

We have already emphasized the importance of the first two factors: sustained demand and the dematerialization of the economies of developed countries. The third factor relates to the growing trade imbalances between producing and consuming countries. Unlike the situation in the past, when it was the major traditional exporting nations that had a trade surplus, today it is the petroleum exporting nations that enjoy large trade surpluses.[25] The WTO report goes further: "It is striking to see how closely the peak of the real oil prices in 1974, 1990 and 2005 match closely the peak levels of the share of both the Middle East and Africa in world merchandise exports. The trough levels of oil prices in 1978, 1988 and 1998 coincide also with those in these regions' export shares."

The impact of energy prices on economic growth is thus multidimensional. It involves many continuously interacting economic mechanisms, which add to the complexity of the whole issue. OPEC plays an important role in setting quotas, production levels and operational capacity, according to the authors of a study published by Boston University's Center for Energy and Environmental Studies, in cooperation with the European Central Bank. At the same time, there does not seem to be a link between production and prices and the link is more political than economic.[26] Daniel Yergin sums this up nicely: "Oil is 10% economics and 90% politics."[27] OPEC's role in controlling prices obviously will not be strengthened by Russia's triumphal return to the global oil market. Saudi Arabia, currently the only country able to influence OPEC's decisions one way or the other, is keeping an eye out for trouble.

---

[24] WTO, *World Trade Report 2006*, p. 3.

[25] The WTO report explains: "The largest net importers of fuels are the European Union (25), Japan, the United States, the Republic of Korea and China. All these economies recorded a larger deficit or a reduced surplus in their current account as the value of their imports rose faster than exports, with the notable exception of China."

[26] The authors note a negative correlation between the two variables of price and production. See Robert K. Kaufmann (Boston University) and Stephane Dees, Pavlos Karadeloglou and Marcelo Sanchez (European Central Bank), "Does OPEC Matter? An Econometric Analysis of Oil Prices", *The Energy Journal,* Vol. 25, No. 4, 2004, pp. 67-90.

[27] Cited in Éric Laurent, *La face cachée du pétrole*, Paris, Plon, 2006, p. 174.

The IEA's Latest Estimates

World Energy Outlook 2006 (*WEO 2006*) devotes an entire chapter to the issue of oil prices.[28] In it, the International Energy Agency reconfirms its previous analyses and presents three forceful arguments. First, oil prices and the economic health of the global economy are linked. Without the oil price increases that have occurred since 2002, world GDP would have increased by an average of 0.3% annually.[29] Secondly, all the economic effects of higher oil prices have not worked their way through the economic system. There are growing signs of inflationary pressures, leading to higher interest rates, under which debtor nations will suffer the most.[30] Thirdly, although high oil prices are beginning to slow demand, since demand from the transportation sector is relatively price-inelastic compared with other sectors, it is the other growth sectors that are maintaining pressure on the demand for fossil fuels (oil, gas, coal and electricity).[31]

WEO 2006 asks what would have happened if oil prices had not risen since 2002. The answer is clear: demand for the fuel would have increased by 4.1% a year for two years (until 2004) and this would have translated into additional global economic growth of 0.1%.[32] The report then asks: "why has the adverse macroeconomic impact been so obscure?" The following factors are cited in response:

– Relatively strong underlying economic growth;[33]
– The higher oil prices have affected other exports, mitigating the impact of the price increases on the trade balance or imbalance;
– A number of countries like China have been able to cushion the effects of higher prices due to growth in their exports of goods and services not linked to the fuel sector.[34]

As you can see, the IEA's economists have had to give an overview of macroeconomic factors to explain why the world economy is so insensitive to jumps in oil prices. All in all, one thing is clear: the poorest and most heavily indebted countries will suffer the most, while the richest countries or the countries with the greatest energy efficiency will be better cushioned against the vagaries of an evolving and erratic situation. Even so, in the context of high oil prices (for example, $80 a barrel), the world GDP would decrease by almost an entire

---

[28] Chapter 11.
[29] *WEO 2006, op. cit.*, p. 269.
[30] *Ibid.*
[31] *Ibid.*
[32] *WEO 2006, op. cit.,* p. 289.
[33] In particular, higher growth and production rates, paired with a low level of inflation. *WEO 2006, op. cit.*, p. 307.
[34] *Ibid*, pp. 308-309.

percentage point (0.9%).[35] These conclusions confirm those in the previously discussed analyses and reinforce OPEC's projections about what would happen in the event of a significant downturn in the global economy.

The IEA identifies three closely linked components involved in oil price forecasting:

> Economic activity is the primary determinant of energy demand and thereby influences energy prices. Yet, energy prices, in turn, influence energy demand and economic performance. The feedback links between the three variables [energy demand, supply and prices, and economic activity in general] are complex and involve varying time-lags, which can lead to cyclical movements in prices. The economic downturn in the wake of the 1997-1998 Asian financial crisis drove down oil prices, while the economic rebound in 1999-2000 and 2002-2004 pushed them up again. The first oil shock and the second in 1979-1980 led to recessions in the major oil-importing countries.[36]

Oil Crises and Oil Price Shocks

The *World Economic Outlook 2003,* published by the International Monetary Fund (IMF), concluded that a $5 rise in the price of a barrel of oil would translate into a 0.3% drop in world GDP the following year. Two years later, the *World Economic Outlook 2005* returned to this subject, stating that a $10 increase in the price of a barrel of oil[37] would reduce global production of goods and services by only 0.10-0.15%. Another simulation, published by the IEA, predicts that an increase of $10 per barrel[38] would result in a 0.4% reduction in world GDP.[39] According to Kenneth Rogoff of Harvard University, such simulations are based on somewhat outmoded economic models that are likely to be refined in the future, particularly since the impacts of these projections are asymmetrical depending on the region:

---

[35] *Ibid*, p. 304.

[36] *WEO 2006, op. cit.,* p. 270.

[37] In the example cited, the price of a barrel goes from $50 to $55.

[38] In the example cited, the price of a barrel goes from $25 to $35 under a scenario of continued high demand.

[39] All these examples are taken from the study by Harvard professor Kenneth Rogoff, "Oil and the Global Economy", *International Energy Forum*, Riyadh, November 2005, p. 12-14.

> The Impact on Transition and Oil Importing Countries is found to be much larger. The effects on China and India appear to be two or more times that for the world as a whole, whereas the effects on highly indebted poor countries –many of whom face heavy import bills– is four times as large.[40]

In actual fact, multiple disruptions of oil supply resulting from successive international crises tend to have much more significant effects than those predicted by the economists. Although each crisis has differed in scope and duration, with some lasting for several years, they have all had a substantial impact on world production and real GDP growth (see Table 5). Either economists are not measuring the same things or the parameters used vary depending on the crisis.

It is almost impossible to determine whether each crisis was a direct or indirect cause of the accompanying economic decline or whether the situation was simply a coincidence attributable to a conjunction of other macroeconomic factors. For example, according to Jean-Marie Chevalier:

> It was the first oil price shock, occurring at a time when Western economies were sliding into a deep economic crisis, the harbingers of which appeared in the late 1960s. It was the end of the thirty glorious years of growth. In this context and for the first time since the war, world consumption of petroleum products decreased for two consecutive years.[41]

Table 5: International crises and oil supply disruptions

Date	Crisis	Decline in world production	Decline in real GDP in the United States
November 1956	Suez Crisis	10.1%	− 2.5%
October 1973	Arab-Israeli War	7.8%	− 3.2%
November 1979	Iranian Revolution	8.9%	− 0.6%
October 1980	Iran-Iraq War	7.2%	− 0.5%
August 1990	Gulf War	8.8%	− 0.1%
From Hamilton (2003) and Barsky and Killian (2003). For James Hamilton, the work is not cited; for Robert Barksy and Lutz Killian, see "Oil and the Macroeconomy Since the 1970s", *Journal of Economic Perspectives*, Vol. 18, No. 4, pp. 115-134.			

Source: Table taken from Kenneth Rogoff, *op. cit.,* p. 23.

---

[40] Rogoff, *op. cit.*, p. 13.
[41] Jean-Marie Chevalier, *op. cit.,* p. 116.

In terms of plummeting production, the two most severe crises were the Suez Crisis and the Iranian Revolution, with the Gulf War not lagging far behind. On the other hand, the sharpest drop in the U.S. GDP occurred during the 1973 Arab-Israeli (October) War.[42] Although the actual military conflict lasted only a few weeks, the oil embargo persisted for five months, even though its impact (a 5% reduction in deliveries[43]) was more symbolic than anything.[44] In terms of GDP, the second most serious crisis for the United States was the Suez Crisis (1956).

Judging from these figures, increased and more transparent dialogue between oil producing and oil consuming nations is not likely to do away with the intrinsic volatility in oil prices.[45] Prices are not only influenced by crises and political revolutions but also, as Walid Kadduri has pointed out, by long periods of recession or economic growth.[46] Many reports, including that by the WTO, emphasize the fact that the present stability of financial markets has a lot to do with the flexibility that Western economies seem to exhibit in absorbing oil price shocks, which was not the case in the past.[47] We can therefore no longer apply the old rule of thumb that a $5 increase in the price of a barrel of oil spells a 0.5% decline in U.S. economic growth.[48]

To paraphrase an old Chinese proverb, crises are decision-making opportunities. The 1973 oil crisis prompted industrialized countries to establish sizeable oil reserves that would meet their basic needs for 90 days. In the ensuing years, oil investments shifted significantly away from OPEC and to other countries. From 1973 to 1977, OPEC production was around 31 MMb/d but OPEC would have to

---

[42] The 1973 shock "was long lasting, while that of 1979-80 was not", writes Chevalier, *op. cit.*, p. 67.

[43] Jean-Marie Chevalier speaks of "a 5% embargo on oil exports and threats of a further 5% cut each month, as long as the occupied territories were not liberated." Jean-Marie Chevalier, *op. cit*, p. 115.

[44] The embargo was officially announced during a meeting of oil producers on October 17, 1973 (a 5% reduction in deliveries was decided on by the Organization of Arab Petroleum Exporting Countries, or OAPEC). On March 17 and 18, the same countries, except for Syria and Libya, decided to lift the oil embargo against the United States. Therefore, the embargo lasted only five months. During this time, the price of Arabian Light crude quadrupled from $2.32 to $9.00. The embargo resulted in the establishment of oil reserves by Western countries and the creation of the IEA in November 1974.

[45] Professor A. F. Alhajji of Ohio Northern University has published a fascinating map of oil price trends from 1990 to December 2003 which associates price peaks with political crises and a general rise or fall in oil prices with periods of recession or economic crisis. See article entitled "An Overview of Oil Prices between 1990 and 2004", *Oil, Gas & Energy Law Intelligence* (OGEL), Vol. 2, No. 1, February 2004, 7 p.

[46] Walid Kadduri, "Information and Oil Markets", *International Energy Forum*, Riyadh, November 2005, p. 2.

[47] For example, central banks have remained relatively independent of governments in setting interest rates and controlling market liquidity. See *WEO 2006, op. cit.*, p. 311.

[48] Assumption also found in an article in the *New York Times*. See Simon Romero, "Weathering the Rising Prices of Energy", *The New York Times*, March 10, 2004 (Business Section). Although this rule of thumb used to be cited on the U.S. EIA website, this is no longer the case.

wait almost 20 years (until 1998) to reach the same level of production again.[49] In the meantime, non-OPEC countries increasingly invested in and produced oil. In 2005, non-OPEC production was 47.3 MMb/d versus 33.8 MMb/d for OPEC.[50] Time and money can make a difference, as long as there is oil to be found.

The Evolution of Real Crude Prices (1861-2005)

The following graph (Figure 3) gives an overview of crude oil prices from 1861 to 2005.

A few technical explanations are in order here. Although the per-barrel prices shown are based on three different benchmarks, this does not affect the general trends shown, which are expressed in constant dollars. From 1861 to 1944, the average price on the U.S. market was used as the benchmark; during the period 1945-1983, BP switched to Arabian Light, while more recently (1989-2005), the price of North Sea Brent has been used as a benchmark (see Chapter 5).[51]

The topmost line (in green) shows per-barrel oil prices in constant 2005 dollars over time. Despite the steep rise in prices in 2004 and 2005, the peak prices at that time are still much lower than those posted during the 1979 Iranian Revolution but still exceed in real terms those seen during the Arab-Israeli War in October 1973 (also known as the Yom Kippur War). With respect to the Iranian Revolution, however, this event itself was not the only factor influencing prices at the time, since it was immediately followed by the eight-year-long Iran-Iraq War (1980-1988). According to economist Jean-Marie Chevalier, that oil price shock was a product of both the Iranian Revolution and the Iran-Iraq War, resulting in "the doubling of prices in several stages between 1978 and 1982."[52]

In actual fact, daily mean Iraqi production increased steadily during the Iran-Iraq War and then fell dramatically after Iraq invaded Kuwait, while Iranian production

---

[49] See Figure 5 in the article by David Wood and Saeid Mokhatab, "Control and Influence on World Oil Price", 3rd part, *Oil & Gas Financial Journal*, December 2006, pp. 34-37.

[50] This figure includes liquefied natural gas. See *Ibid.*, p. 36.

[51] There is a price differential between Brent and WTI and today IRAC (Imported Refiner Acquisition Cost), the latter representing a weighted mean for all crude imported into the U.S. In June 2004, at the height of the refinery crisis in the United States, the difference was $4.55 a barrel. Since the euro has appreciated in relation to the dollar, the United States is buying its oil with a depreciated currency, which decreases the price differential between WTI and Brent accordingly. See "Herold Oil & Gas Perspectives", *Industry Insights*, John S. Herold Inc., November 12, 2004.

[52] Jean-Marie Chevalier, *op. cit.*, p. 117.

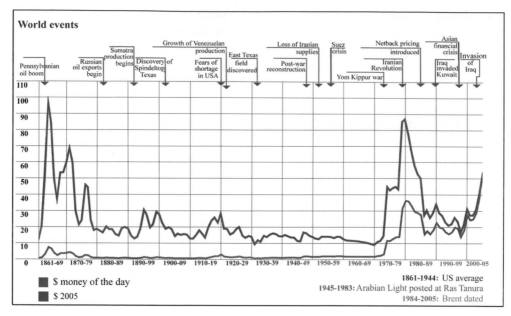

Figure 3: Trends in crude oil prices (1861-2005)
Source: From *BP Statistical Review of World Energy 2006*, p. 16

plummeted in 1981, recovered somewhat in 1982 and then stagnated until 1986.[53] Objectively speaking, Iran suffered more from the war than Iraq, particularly since it was –and still is– a bigger oil producer.

Lastly, readers should note that real prices (in constant dollars) and current prices (in the money of the day) have been virtually the same since roughly 2000. In addition, for the first time since the early 1980s, oil prices in current dollars have exceeded the level of $50 a barrel, a 40% increase over 2004 prices. In 2006, the spot price of Brent (FOB[54]) reached $76.53 in late July and early August and, in September and October of the same year, it fluctuated around $58.[55] In 2007, the short-term outlook for West Texas Intermediate crude is roughly $66 per barrel on average.[56]

---

[53] Iraqi and Iranian production for the years in question can be obtained from OPEC's annual publication *Annual Statistical Bulletin 2005* (*ASB 2005*) available on its web site. BP's report *Statistical Review of World Energy* also provides comparable statistics for the two countries.

[54] Free on Board or FOB: in other words, at the point where the seller's responsibilities end.

[55] See http://tonto.eia.doe.gov/dnav/pet/hist/rbrted.htm.

[56] See http://www.eia.doe.gov/emeu/steo/pub/contents.html.

The Outlook for Oil Prices in 2030

In the *IEO 2006* reference case, the U.S. Department of Energy predicted that oil prices would go from $41 per barrel in 2004 to $57 in 2030,[57] while the Paris-based IEA estimated that the price of a barrel of oil would reach $47 in 2012 and $55 in 2030.[58] No one, however, predicted the spectacular rise in oil prices that began in mid-2004. It is true that hurricanes cannot be predicted, nor can the devastating damage they wreak: if Hurricane Katrina had travelled 20 km farther west or farther east, things would have been much different. Both the Washington-based EIA and Paris-based IEA had to revise their forecasts upwards from their year-earlier ones.

The differences between the *IEO 2005* and *IEO 2006* forecasts are enormous, however. Under the *IEO 2005* reference case, 2025 prices are projected to stand at $35 per barrel.[59] A year later (*IEO 2006*), forecasts are for the price of a barrel to reach $57–admittedly in 2030 this time.[60] Such changes in mid-course do little to improve the credibility of predictive analyses, particularly since price projections affect all the other variables examined.[61] Because oil is expected to be more expensive, the *IEO 2006* predicts that oil's share in primary energy production will decline in relation to other fuels, encouraging coal to make a strong comeback.[62]

Although DOE's analysis model has been the object of criticism on a number of occasions, the most scathing criticism comes from New York University economist Dermot Gately.[63] According to Gately, the DOE's National Energy Modeling System (NEMS) is reductionist to an extreme: calculate world supply, subtract the demand from non-OPEC countries and then ask OPEC countries to make up the difference.[64]

---

[57] All *IEO 2006* forecasts are in 2004 US dollars.

[58] *WEO 2006, op. cit.*, p. 53. Prices are given in real 2005 dollars.

[59] *International Energy Outlook 2005, op. cit.,* pp. 27-28.

[60] *IEO 2005* forecasts stop at 2025.

[61] More than anyone else working in the field, Jean Laherrère has always emphasized the randomness of EIA forecasts. In his article entitled "Énergie et agriculture : Tout a un pic", he lists roughly 15 discrepancies between real oil prices and projected prices (see in particular Figure 17 concerning the period 1982-2001). According to Laherrère, "oil price forecasts are always wrong." It is to be supposed that technology assessors are always wrong. Speech and discussion, April 13, 2005, in Strasbourg, on renewable energies, available at www.hubbertpeak.com/laherrere/Strasbourg.pdf.

[62] Japan's Institute of Energy Economics estimates that oil's share in the primary energy basket will drop to 37% by 2030, or two points less than the *IEO 2005* forecast (see Table 2). See "Japan Long-Term Energy Outlook", available at http://eneken.ieej.or.jp/en.

[63] See Dermot Gately, "How Plausible is the Consensus Projection of Oil Below $25 and Persian Gulf Oil Capacity and Output Doubling by 2025?" *The Energy Journal*, Vol. 22, No. 4, 2001, pp. 1-27. Gately received *The Energy Journal* Outstanding Paper Award from the International Association for Energy Economics (IAEE) for this article published in 2001.

[64] See Glen Sweetnam, "Understanding and Modeling the Effects of High Oil Prices", Oak Ridge National Laboratory (ORNL), April 21, 2006, available at http://cta.ornl.gov/oilTransitions.

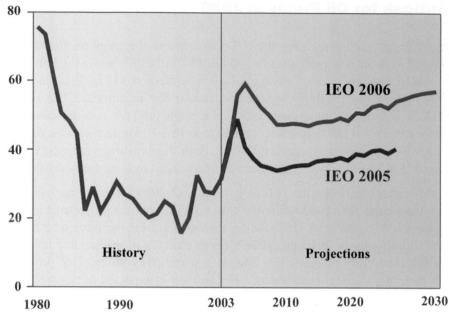

Figure 4: IEO 2005 and IEO 2006: per-barrel oil prices in 2025 and 2030
(in 2004 dollars)
Source: From *IEO 2006*, June 2006, p. 9.

The formula is appealing in its simplicity. It must be said, however, that EIA analysts are very aware of the inadequacies of their models. During a workshop on modelling energy prices, EIA's Glen Sweetnam indicated that there was a great deal of in-depth examination into the following issues:

- OPEC appears less and less willing to increase production rates
- Impediments to investment are more persistent than expected, even after two years of high oil prices
- Exploration and development costs have increased
- This is not a depletion issue, although we continue to follow the "peak oil" issue closely
- How much switching between fuels will occur? What gains in efficiency can be anticipated?
- How much will the development of unconventional resources affect the demand for OPEC conventional oil?
- What will be the impact of non-OPEC liquid supplies on OPEC demand?[65]

---

[65] Sweetnam, *op. cit.*

Most of these questions are addressed in this book. Dermot Gately brings up an important point: it is not in the interest of the OPEC nations to increase production. Instead, OPEC producers should maintain their current rates of production, since a massive increase would result in reduced economic benefits.[66] Furthermore, why should OPEC increase its production at a time when non-OPEC production has peaked; what would be its interest in doing so? Dermot Gately has painted an instructive picture of the contradictions and inconsistencies in OPEC's situation, based on his reading of the four most recent editions of the EIA's *Annual Energy Outlook (AEO)*.

Table 6: Projections from the last four editions
of the Annual Energy Outlook (AEO)[67]

	Real price per barrel	World demand (MMb/d)	Non-OPEC supplies (MMb/d)	Share that OPEC or Gulf countries must supply (MMb/d)
AEO 2003	$26.57	122.9	61.7	61.2
AEO 2004	$27.00	117.5	63.9	53.7
AEO 2005	$30.31	120.2	65.0	55.1
AEO 2006	$47.99	110.6	67.8	42.8
Gately's comments: By 2025, it will no longer be necessary for OPEC or Gulf countries to double their oil production!				

Source: Dermot Gately, ORNL workshop, *op. cit.*, April 2006, slide 5.

OPEC itself is perfectly well aware of the problems looming on the horizon, and in October 2006, it decided to cut back its production by 1.2 MMb/d.[68] The oil minister of the United Arab Emirates (UAE), Mohamed Ben Dhaen Al Hamli, explained that this reduction was calculated based on the actual production of the ten member countries under quota in September (roughly 27.5 MMb/d), rather than on its official production ceiling, which has been set at 28 MMb/d since July 2005. The most fascinating thing about this decision, however, is the motivation behind it. For Algeria's oil minister, Chakib Khelil, a range of $50 to $60 for OPEC's basket price is totally acceptable. Excessively high prices could encourage the development

---

[66] See article by Dermot Gately, "OPEC Incentives for Faster Output Growth", *The Energy Journal*, Vol. 25, No. 2, 2004, pp. 75-96. His basic argument is as follows: "the payoffs to OPEC are relatively insensitive to faster output growth; aggressive output expansion yields slightly lower payoffs than just maintaining current market share."

[67] The domestic equivalent of *International Energy Outlook*. The projections in *Annual Energy Outlook* (AEO) involve the domestic situation and those in *International Energy Outlook* (IEO) involve the international situation.

[68] See "L'OPEP a opté pour une forte baisse de sa production", *Le Monde,* October 20, 2006.

of alternative energies. In addition, as the financial commentator Mike Wittner has suggested, a price of $60 for U.S. oil is considered to be a level that will not affect economic growth, while a price of $70 to $80 would, or would at least raise enough concerns for the central bankers to begin raising their rates.[69] In October 2006, the *Oil & Gas Journal* came to the same conclusion, commenting that prices seemed to be stabilizing, amongst pure conjecture that a peak price of US$60 would trigger a reduction in OPEC production.[70]

All these scenarios are confusing to the extreme. In October 2006, at the same time that OPEC was announcing its production cuts, the Joint Economic Committee (JEC) of the U.S. Congress was accusing OPEC of manipulating prices and being the biggest cause of price instability.[71] In addition, instead of showing leadership and establishing a higher priced reference basket, it adopted a laissez-faire attitude in order to turn the situation to its advantage. [72]

In later chapters, we will take another look at the pressures exerted on demand by the growing energy needs of India and China; on the geopolitical risks caused by various conflicts around the world; and on the role of alternative and unconventional energies in the future. Just after the Second World War, Winston Churchill had a favourite pet phrase for Russia, which was very apt: "a riddle wrapped up in an enigma." This could be applied to oil prices as well.

Regardless of what happens to prices, world demand for oil is not ready to cool down in the future. Even though only 1.4% annual growth in demand is projected for the world as a whole in 2003-2030 (see Table 2), major oil consumers like China and India will continue to influence demand, particularly since their requirements are expected to increase by 3.8% and 2.4% respectively.[73] Among major oil consumers, only Japan will experience negative growth in demand, which is estimated at – 0.9%. The United States will also become less of an oil glutton, with its annual growth in demand (1.2%) remaining below the world average, but above that for OECD countries.[74]

---

[69] Cited in *Le Monde, Ibid.*

[70] See "Crude Prices Test $60/bbl Floor", *Oil & Gas Journal*, October 2, 2006, p. 72.

[71] See Jim Saxton, Chairman, U.S. Congress Joint Economic Committee, Research Report #109-46, October 2006, available at www.house.gov/jec/publications/109/rr109-46.pdf. The *Oil & Gas Journal* also published this report in its November 6, 2006 edition, pp. 29-30.

[72] While pointing out that OPEC's revenues in 2006 should reach $600 billion compared with $200 billion in 2003.

[73] IEO 2006, *op. cit.*, Table 4A.

[74] *Ibid.*

The Outlook for Downstream Prices in 2030

The subject of gasoline prices is beyond the scope of this book. We are happy to leave this issue to the economists given the multiple variables involved. However, gasoline prices should be touched upon briefly in order to address readers' legitimate questions about the spike in oil prices in 2005. As you know, the per-barrel price of oil upstream influences the price of gasoline downstream.

Over time, the major oil firms (also known as the Seven Sisters) formed an oligopolistic cartel allowing them to control prices and markets. This dominance was not broken until OPEC came onto the scene in September 1960. In the meantime, major oil firms worked on the vertically integration of their operations, allowing them to control the entire value chain from oil field to gas pump.

The recent rise in prices is due to a conjunction of two factors. The first is the sustained and growing demand from developing countries, while the second is demand pressures resulting from sudden disruptions to supply in the Gulf of Mexico. When cut off from their supplies, U.S. refineries have been forced to turn to foreign suppliers or draw off large amounts of oil from the strategic reserves (SPR, Strategic Petroleum Reserve) established by the U.S. government.[75] The special nature of the post-Katrina crisis is due to the simultaneous pressure on both ends of the chain, upstream and downstream, which is a typical occurrence in major crises.

The major U.S. oil firms share some responsibility for the crisis since, for several decades, they neglected to invest in the refining sector and no new facilities were built. Global refining capacity increased, however, owing to corporate restructuring and mergers and acquisitions. It took skyrocketing crude prices to get oil companies interested in refining again (see Chapter 5). This neglect is due mainly to the fact that, in relation to the capital invested, upstream profits are much more lucrative than returns from refining. Today, the United States and its consumers are still paying the price,[76] even though the U.S. industry has undertaken to expand its refining capacity by 1.4 MMb/d, or 8%.[77]

Oil companies seem to have learned a lesson and, from 2006 to 2010, they will invest $62 billion a year on average; a little over 60% of this investment is slated for the development of new refineries, mainly in the Middle East and Asia.[78]

---

[75] A total of 20 refineries were shut down by hurricanes Katrina and Rita.

[76] According to the DOE, crude oil's share in the cost at the pump of regular gasoline in 2005 was about 53%, compared with 47% in 2004. See http://www.eia.doe.gov/bookshelf/brochures/gasolinepricesprimer/eia1_2005primerM.html.

[77] *Oil & Gas Journal*, November 13, 2006, p. 29.

[78] IEA, *WEO 2006, op. cit.*, p. 337.

DOE's projections for average gasoline prices at the pump in 2015 and 2030 are $2 and $2.19 a gallon respectively.[79] While waiting to see if these predictions are borne out, consumers may find themselves dreaming of a fairer price than the historic peak of $3.15 reached in September 2005. Do they need to be reminded that, in Europe, automobiles are much less polluting and gasoline prices can be three to seven times higher. This eloquently demonstrates that voluntary policies to improve energy efficiency or encourage consumers to choose less polluting fuels like diesel can have salutary effects.

---

[79] See "Annual Energy Outlook 2006 with Projections to 2030" at http://www.eia.doe.gov/oiaf/aeo/gas.html. One U. S. gallon equals 3.785 litres. According to these projections, the per-litre price of gasoline in the United States will rise from 53 cents in 2015 to 58 cents in 2030. The *International Energy Outlook 2007* (page 30) foresees that oil price will rise to $59 per barrel in 2030 ($95 per barrel on a nominal basis).

8

Global Warming

The Sun's energy drives the Earth's natural systems and largely determines the global temperature. Greenhouse gases (GHGs), which form a thin layer between the sun and our planet, are indispensable to life on earth. Paradoxically, it is these same gases, of which carbon dioxide (CO_2) is a prime example, that are the cause of the global warming that is occurring at present. Rising levels of CO_2 in the atmosphere have come under close scrutiny, particularly because of the emissions from fossil fuel burning, but this gas is also used directly in some industrial applications. Europe now has a CO_2 emissions trading scheme, and although the United States has not followed suit with its own national system, some CO_2 trading is already going on there.

This chapter will describe the key factors that influence the average global temperature, the vital role that greenhouse gases play in maintaining the planet's thermal balance, the lifetime of some of these gases and their contribution to global warming. We will also look at the main legal instruments available to the international community in its efforts to curb GHG emissions and prevent even greater climatic disruption in the future. We will end the chapter by reviewing the technical feasibility of capturing and storing CO_2 over the long term, and then briefly describe the emissions trading system that was implemented in Europe in January 2005.

The Earth's Temperature

Is it possible to determine how the earth's average temperature has evolved over the past two billion years? That is what Christopher R. Scotese has done in Figure 1. The Permian–Triassic transition was likely the hottest period in the earth's history, with high temperatures prevailing even at the poles. Scotese describes the planet as a "hot house" during this period, but as an "ice house" during the Lower Cretaceous. During the Upper Cretaceous, there was no ice at the poles, and the dinosaurs could

163

roam freely between cooler zones and more temperate zones as the seasons changed. This freedom was short-lived, however, as dinosaurs disappeared some 65 million years ago during the fifth largest known mass extinction (see Chapter 1). Interestingly, the five greatest mass extinctions occurred during the hottest periods of the earth's climate,[1] when the average global temperature fluctuated around 22°C.

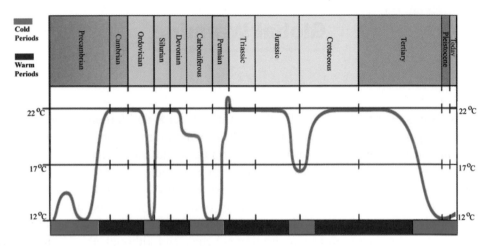

Figure 1: Average global temperature
Source: **C.** R. Scotese, PALEOMAP Project

These figures cannot be checked easily.[2] According to Jean-Marc Jancovici, a leading French expert on climate change, the data covering the last 100,000 years are well-documented, and those for the preceding 300,000 years are "usable."[3] At present, the earth is in a warm, interglacial, period –the Holocene– which began about 10,000 year ago. Paul Crutzen, a winner of the Nobel Prize for Chemistry, once said that the current period should be renamed "the anthropocene" to reflect the impact of human activities on the global climate.[4] The next glaciation could

---

[1] The following information is from the simplified geologic time scale of the Museé cantonal de géologie, Vaud, Switzerland. The duration of each geologic period is indicated in parentheses, followed by the approximate timing of the associated mass extinction. **Paleocene** (– 65-53 Ma) – 65: Fifth mass extinction: disappearance of 65% of species; **Triassic** (– 250-203 Ma) – 215-203: Fourth mass extinction: disappearance of 75% of species; **Permian** (– 295-250 Ma) – 250: Third mass extinction: disappearance of 95% of species; **Devonian** (– 410-355 Ma) – 355: Second mass extinction: disappearance of 75% of species; **Ordovician** (– 500-435 Ma) – 435: First mass extinction: disappearance of 85% of species. See www.unil.ch/Musee/geosciences/profs/Echelle_Dates.pdf.

[2] A history of the glacial and interglacial periods extending as far back as the Cambrian can be found at http://la.climatologie.free.fr/glaciation/glaciation1.htm.

[3] Jean-Marc Janovici, *L'avenir climatique : Quel temps ferons-nous?* Paris, Éditions du Seuil (Collection Science ouverte), 2002.

[4] This idea is supported by Eugene F. Stoermer. See http://www2.mpch-mainz.mpg.de/~air/crutzen

begin in 18,000 years, 41,000 years or 64,000 years, but the timing of this episode cannot be predicted with certainty.[5] We cannot count on a glacial period occurring in time to moderate or reverse the rise in temperatures caused by anthropogenic emissions of greenhouse gases. Atmospheric levels of carbon dioxide and methane are higher now than at any time in the past 650,000 years. The European Project for Ice Coring in Antarctica (EPICA) should provide information that will round out the data derived from the famous Vostock ice core and enable researchers to reconstruct 900,000 years of climatic history.[6] Once the climate record reaches the million-year mark, scientists' extrapolations will become more reliable. A program is being planned in order to obtain an ice core climate record extending back some 1.2 million years.[7]

The Earth's Thermal Balance

At present the earth's mean surface temperature is about 15^0C. This mean equilibrium temperature is dependent on the earth –atmosphere energy balance. More specifically, the energy inputs and outputs of the global system –the atmosphere and the earth's surface (continents and oceans at sea level)– are balanced. The earth's surface reflects or re-emits radiation back to the atmosphere or out into space, and the atmosphere absorbs and re-emits radiation either to the earth or to space.

On average, the atmosphere receives an energy input of 519 W/m^2 every second (see Figure 2) and it radiates some of this energy to the earth (324 W/m^2) and some back to space (195 W/m^2). The earth's energy balance is also in equilibrium: the planet receives a net gain of 492 W/m^2 and has an identical loss of 492 W/m^2. The overall process obeys the laws of thermodynamics. A body that gives off energy cools, and a body that absorbs energy warms.

The situation is actually a little more complex. For now, let us disregard the separate energy budgets of the atmosphere and the earth's surface. Approximately

---

[5]   "In 18,000 years, the earth's orbit is not likely to be elliptical enough to trigger glaciation. In 41,000 years, the ellipticity will be much greater, bringing us closer to the onset of glaciation. But will this actually happen? By 64,000 years from now, the earth's ellipticity will be great enough for a glacial period to begin, or if glaciation began at the + 41,000-year point, glacial conditions will be strengthened at the 64,000 year mark. Pierre Thomas, École Normale Supérieure de Lyon, "Prochaine glaciation ?", at http://www.ens-lyon.fr/Planet-Terre/Infosciences/Climats/Ocean/Articles/prochaineglaciation.html.

[6]   See *Science & Vie*, "Paléoclimatologie", January 2006, p. 29. See also "Deux études pointent la responsabilité de l'homme dans le réchauffement climatique", *Le Monde*, November 25, 2005.

[7]   See "La plus vieille glace exhumée", *Sciences & Vie*, No. 1065, June 2006, p. 19.

342 W/m^2 of solar radiation[8] is received on earth as a whole, averaged over a year. However, only part of this energy goes toward "heating" the earth, since some of it is lost. If these losses are subtracted from the total incoming solar radiation, the **net energy input** to the earth amounts to 235 W/m^2. This incoming radiation is counterbalanced by the 195 W/m^2 re-radiated to space by the atmosphere (see upper left portion of Figure 2) plus the 40 W/m^2 of infrared radiation (abbreviated as IR in the diagram) re-emitted by the earth's surface that escapes directly into space (see the upper right portion of Figure 2).[9]

The situation of energy inputs and outputs can be summarized as follows:

> The earth's surface (oceans plus continents) is in thermal balance: it heats up by absorbing 492 watts per m^2 and it cools by losing an equal amount of energy.
> The earth–atmosphere system is in equilibrium: it is warmed by absorbing 235 watts per m^2, and it loses an equal amount of energy in the form of infrared radiation emitted back to space.[10]

In order to better understand Figure 2, it is necessary to review solar radiation briefly. Only 40% of incoming solar radiation is from the visible wavelengths, that is, the portion visible to the human eye. The rest is distributed in the near infrared (IR)[11] (50%) and ultraviolet wavelengths (10%), which are not visible. The atmosphere protects life on earth by blocking very harmful shortwave radiation from the sun such as X-rays and gamma rays.

The greenhouse effect can be likened to the heat that builds up in a car when the windows are kept shut on a sunny summer afternoon. Solar radiation passes through the windows and heats up the interior of the car, but the heat re-radiated by the interior surfaces is unable to escape. The glass traps the heat in the car. By analogy, the greenhouse gases in the atmosphere act like the glass: they let visible light through but they absorb the infrared radiation re-emitted by the earth. When atmospheric levels of greenhouse gases increase, the earth undergoes warming. It's all relative,

---

[8]   Cited in the text by Marie-Antoinette Mélières, *Laboratoire de glaciologie et géophysique de l'environnement (LGGE)*, "Température moyenne à la surface de la Terre et effet de serre", Grenoble, April 2002, available at http://www.cnrs.fr/cw/dossiers/dosclim/sysfacte/effetserre/index.htm. This is the average value reaching the top of earth's atmosphere (1368/4). This figure is divided by four, "because the surface area of a sphere is four times its cross-sectional area." See Édouard Bard, "Variations climatiques naturelles et anthropiques", *Géosciences* (journal of the BRGM), No. 3, March 2006, p. 30.

[9]   "About 30% of the incoming solar radiation is reflected back to space by clouds, aerosols and the earth's atmosphere and surface. The remaining 70% is absorbed by the atmosphere or by the earth's surface and converted into heat." In Bard, *op. cit.*, p. 31.

[10] Marie-Antoinette Mélières, *op. cit.*

[11] NIR stands for "near infrared."

however. Without the presence of greenhouse gases in the atmosphere, earth's mean temperature would be – 19°C (similar to the surface temperature of the Moon, which has no atmosphere). Conversely, Venus, whose atmosphere is rich in CO_2, has a surface temperature of about 460°C.

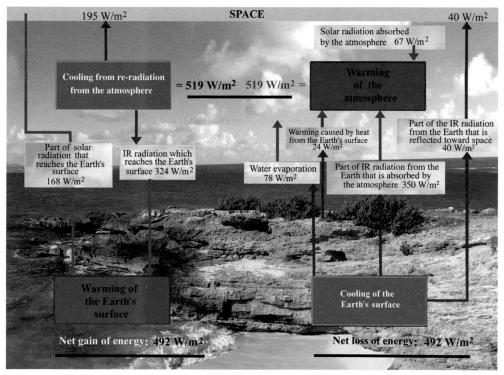

Figure 2: Interactions between space,
the atmosphere and the earth's surface
Source: Study by Marie-Antoinette Mélières, Sagascience

Greenhouse Gases (GHGs)

Although the sun is the primary source of energy for our planet, it is important to understand how energy moves through and is transformed in the earth – atmosphere system. The atmosphere plays an important role in the thermal equilibrium of the overall system through its interactions with the sun and the earth. In a study on global warming, the French climatologist Marie-Antoinette Mélières states:

> Based on an energy loss of 235 W/m^2 to space, the earth's average surface temperature should be − 19°C. The difference between this hypothetical temperature and earth's average temperature can be explained by the global greenhouse effect: 155 W/m^2 of surface heating (about 100 watts due to water vapour and 50 watts due to CO_2) which amounts to about 30°C. This natural greenhouse effect is driven primarily by water vapour and CO_2, with water vapour introducing warming of about 20°C and CO_2, warming of 10°C.

The two main greenhouse gases (GHGs)[12] are water vapour and carbon dioxide. These gases together absorb nearly 75% of the radiation re-emitted by the earth.[13] Water vapour occurs naturally in the form of clouds,[14] which cover 50% of the earth's surface. Clouds absorb infrared energy re-radiated by the earth and have a significant warming effect on the atmosphere like the principal GHGs. Clouds are constantly forming but are short-lived, losing their water content through precipitation.

Although not a greenhouse gas, ozone (O_3) is also a concern because of its tendency to react with certain chemical compounds at low altitudes, forming air pollutants. Ground-level ozone, the primary constituent of smog, can cause respiratory problems in humans. Atmospheric ozone has reached unprecedented levels and, according to a recent study by the National Aeronautics and Space Administration (NASA), ozone in the atmosphere may be to blame for one third to one half of the total temperature rise in the Arctic in the last 100 years.[15] Methane is also a matter of concern because its global warming potential[16] is higher than that of CO_2.

---

[12] There are a number of other GHGs. Some gases, such as nitrous oxide (N_2O) and halocarbons, cause positive radiative forcing of the climate system. Others contribute to negative radiative forcing; this includes aerosol precursors, which are produced primarily by "local" pollution (SO_2 –sulphur dioxide– and dusts) and which have a "cooling" effect, because they give rise to aerosols and thus increase the amount of sunlight reflected to space. The glossary of the Intergovernmental Panel on Climate Change (IPCC) defines radiative forcing as follows: "Radiative forcing is the change in the net vertical irradiance (expressed in Wm^{-2}) at the *tropopause* due to an internal change or a change in the external forcing of the *climate system*, such as, for example, a change in the concentration of *carbon dioxide* or the output of the Sun. Usually radiative forcing is computed after allowing for stratospheric temperatures to readjust to radiative equilibrium, but with all tropospheric properties held fixed at their unperturbed values."

[13] Water vapour absorbs nearly 50% and carbon dioxide almost 25%.

[14] Although it was already known that water vapour plays a role in global warming, recent studies indicate that it probably has a greater influence than previously thought. For example, in Europe, 70% of warming is attributable to water vapour. See *Science & Vie*, January 2006, p. 32.

[15] See "Ozone Major Player in Arctic Warming, NASA Finds", *CBC News*, March 14, 2006, at http://www.cbc.ca/story/science/national/2006/03/14/arctic-ozone060314.html.

[16] "Methane has a global warming potential 20 times greater than that of the main greenhouse gas, carbon dioxide (CO_2), whose atmospheric concentration is nonetheless 300 times higher." Recent studies have confirmed that vegetation, too, gives off a lot of methane. This points up the need to reconsider some of the parameters related to global warming. See the article entitled "La végétation émet de grandes quantités de méthane, puissant gaz à effet de serre", *Le Monde*, January 12, 2006.

What would happen if there were a doubling of CO_2 in the atmosphere (the so-called $2 \times CO_2$ scenario)? Studies have shown that this situation would add about 4 watts per m^2 of energy to the climate system. According to Marie-Antoinette Mélières, "If all the other parameters remained stable, except CO_2 obviously, which would be doubled, this additional warming would lead to an increase of 1°C in the mean global temperature.[17] The atmosphere is like a blanket covering the earth. A change in the composition of the atmosphere, especially GHG levels, can cause an increase or a decrease in the global temperature. It would make more sense to distinguish between warming gases and greenhouse gases, with the first type contributing to the earth's natural thermal balance and the second type to more or less pronounced climatic disturbances. We should keep in mind that at an average global temperature of 15⁰C, we are only five or six degrees Celsius away from a new super hot period.

Figure 3 illustrates the magnitude of the changes associated with the rapid industrialization of the past two centuries or more. The diagram is taken from the *Third Assessment Report* of the Intergovernmental Panel on Climate Change (IPCC), which was released in 2001.[18]

The figure shows a relatively flat curve spanning the centuries from 1000 to 1800, followed by a sharp increase in atmospheric concentrations of greenhouse gases over the past 200 years. According to Environment Canada,[19] the carbon dioxide concentration rose 30%, methane 145% and nitrous oxide 15% during this period.

The figures cited by the IPCC are slightly different since they deal with the period from 1750 to the present.[20] The IPCC has projected a global temperature

---

[17] Marie-Antoinette Mélières stated that "a doubling of CO_2 would not cause a doubling of the 50 watts per m^2 linked to the natural greenhouse effect of CO_2, but rather an increase of about one tenth of this amount (four watts per m^2) because absorption by CO_2 becomes saturated and does not increase linearly with an increase in the quantity of CO_2."

[18] The IPCC was established in 1988 by the World Meteorology Organization (WMO) and the United Nations Environment Programme (UNEP) with the support of the G8. The Intergovernmental Panel on Climate Change (IPCC) has published a series of assessment reports, with the first one appearing in 1990, and the second and third reports in 1995 and 2001. The fourth assessment report was released in February 2007. Each report consists of four documents: "Synthesis Report", "The Scientific Basis", "Impacts, Adaptation and Vulnerability" and "Mitigation." The title of the report referred to here is *Third Assessment Report: Climate Change 2001*.

[19] See the Climate Change section of the Environment Canada Web site.

[20] The nitrous oxide concentration increased by 17%. One third of these emissions are anthropogenic (cropland, livestock feed, chemical industry). The methane concentration rose 151%. A little over half of the emissions are caused by human activities (fossil fuels, cattle, rice crops, dumps). The annual rate of increase in the carbon dioxide concentration has been 0.4 % since 1980. The bulk of the emissions recorded over the past 20 years are attributable to fossil fuels, and the rest (10-30%) to changes in land use patterns, particularly deforestation. The radiative forcing induced by these emissions amounts to 1.46 W/m^2, which represents 60% of the total variation in the concentrations of all persistent greenhouse gases around the world.

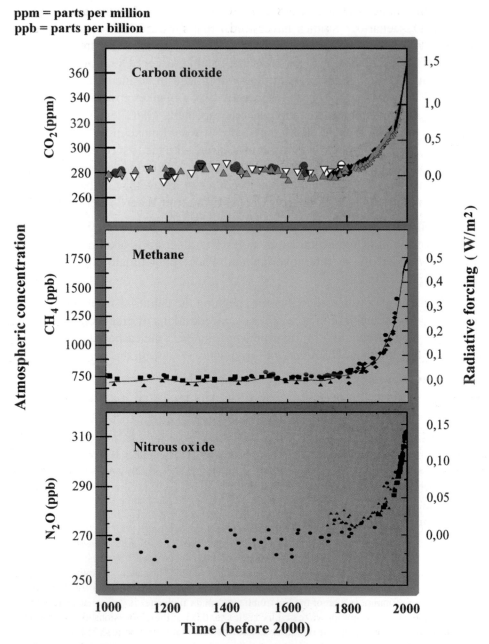

ppm = parts per million
ppb = parts per billion

Figure 3: Global atmospheric concentrations of three well-mixed greenhouse gases

The triangles and other symbols denote ice core data obtained from Antarctica and Greenland. The estimated radiative forcing from these gases is indicated on the right-hand scale.
Source: Climate Change 2001: The Scientific Basis, IPCC 2001

increase in the range of 1.4% to 5.8°C between 1990 and 2100 if anthropogenic greenhouse gas emissions are not reduced. In its Fourth Assessment Report, released in February 2007, the IPCC predicts a global temperature increase of between 1.8% and 4°C. The main conclusions of the report are provided in Table 1.

The Long-Term Effects of GHGs

The build-up of anthropogenic emissions of greenhouse gases[21] changes the atmosphere's composition, increasing its capacity to absorb infrared radiation emitted by the earth. As a result, the planet either has to undergo warming or radiate more energy into space in order to maintain a balance with the incoming solar radiation. This incident solar radiation can be assumed to be constant, in spite of the Sun's 11-year sunspot cycle (the Earth, too, has natural cycles; one example is precession, discussed in Chapter 2). But that is not the issue. Two risks exist, both of which have far-reaching implications. The first is that, although policy makers acknowledge global warming to be real, they may misdiagnose the severity of the problem.

The second risk is that the problem will become irreversible before steps are taken to find a cure. The potential consequences are more drastic. Humans have a tendency to take a "wait and see" approach, which can result in action being put off until it is too late.

The IPCC's predictions related to the long-term effects of GHGs are worrisome. Figure 4 illustrates a situation in which GHG emissions have been reduced to the 1990 level, the target that a number of countries agreed to in signing the Kyoto Protocol (see below). The bottom curve in Figure 4 shows this hypothetical reduction in CO_2 emissions. Despite this stabilization and that of other GHG emissions, "air temperature at the surface should continue to rise by one tenth of a degree per century for at least 100 years, and the sea level rise should continue for hundreds of years."[22] This is because of the inertia of climate systems, which is largely beyond humans' control. There is only one rational way to view the current state of affairs: "it's later than you

---

[21] *Documentation française* defines anthropogenic emissions of GHGs as follows: "The gases responsible for the anthropogenic greenhouse effect are carbon dioxide (CO_2), methane (CH_4), nitrous oxide (N_2O), tropospheric ozone (O_3), CFCs and HCFCs –synthesis gases that are responsible for depleting the ozone layer– as well as replacements for CFCs: HFC, PFC and SF6." Source: http://www.ladocumentationfrancaise.fr/dossiers/changement-climatique/effet-serre.shtml.

[22] "Synthesis Report", *op. cit.*, p. 19. The report makes even more specific statements about the sea level rise: "After 500 years, sea level rise from thermal expansion may have reached only half of its eventual level, which models suggest may lie within a range of 0.5 to 2.0 m and 1 to 4 m for CO_2 levels of twice and four times pre-industrial, respectively. The long time-scale is characteristic of the weak diffusion and slow circulation processes that transport heat into the deep ocean." See "The Scientific Basis", *op. cit.*, p. 72.

Table 1: Main conclusions of the IPCC's Fourth Assessment Report
(February 2, 2007)

Probability	Warming	Projections for the end of the 21st century
Greater than 90% i.e. very probable or very likely	The bulk of the increase in the average global temperature is attributable to human activities (compared with a probability of 66% in the IPCC's Third Assessment Report , 2001).	The temperature rise is projected to be between 1.8°C and 4°C (mean values) relative to the average global temperature during the period 1980-1999. Thermohaline circulation in the North Atlantic will slow during the 21st century (– 25% according to several models); Increase in precipitation at higher latitudes.
Greater than 65% i.e. probable or likely	More frequent tropical cyclones.	Decrease in amount of precipitation (up to 20%) in subtropical land regions.
Lower than 5%	Warming can be explained by natural causes alone.	

Main effects on the oceans
Observations recorded since 1961 show that the mean temperature of the oceans has increased at depths between 0 and 3,000 metres.
The oceans have absorbed more than 80% of the heat added to the climate system; a rise of 1.9°C to 4.6°C in the average global temperature relative to pre-industrial times would virtually eliminate the Greenland ice sheet and drive up sea levels by seven metres.
Arctic and Antarctic
Shrinkage of the polar ice caps
In some projections, Arctic late-summer sea ice disappears almost entirely by the latter part of the 21st century.
GHGs
During the period 2000-2005, emissions of the main greenhouse gas, CO_2, stood at 26.4 GtC. In 2005, the methane concentration in the atmosphere rose to 1,774 parts per billion and the nitrous oxide to 319 parts per billion.

think![23] The situation is less drastic for methane, which has a shorter lifetime than CO_2. However, methane also has a much higher global warming potential. Time is of the essence, because even a reduction in GHG emissions will not lead to a stabilization of atmospheric CO_2 any time soon. In addition, the generalized retreat of glaciers is expected to continue throughout the 21st century.

---

[23] See Juliet Eilperin's article entitled "Debate on Climate Shifts to Issue of Irreparable Change", *The Washington Post*, January 29, 2006, p. A01.

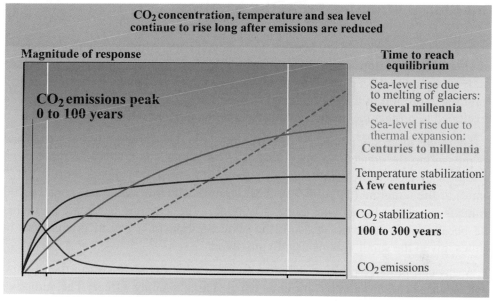

Figure 4: The long-term effects of GHGs

Source: IPCC Third Assessment Report: *Climate Change 2001: Synthesis Report*, p. 18.

Environment Canada has summarized the most likely effects of global climate change as follows:

> – The world's boreal forests are threatened by an increased fire risk because of the drying climate.
> – Water reserves will not be sufficient to meet needs.
> – Severe water loss will occur due to changes in evaporation and precipitation patterns.
> – Flooding will affect low-lying countries and island states, including loss of coastal land to rising sea levels.
> – Tropical diseases, such as malaria, will move northward, where populations have little or no immunity.
> – International trade patterns will be affected.

The main conclusion of the IPCC's Third Assessment Report is as follows: "Many aspects of the earth's climate system are chaotic –its evolution is sensitive to small perturbations in initial condition."

The Global Warming Potential of GHGs

It is not our intention to overwhelm readers with information, but rather to provide a broad picture of greenhouse gases and their impacts on the environment. First, we need to take a closer look at some GHGs. This will make it easier to understand the evolution of the international conventions and instruments that have been developed to protect the quality of the atmosphere and that are discussed below.

There are three key points to keep in mind. First, CO_2 is the reference gas used for measuring the concentrations of GHGs in the atmosphere. GHGs are measured in tonnes of CO_2 equivalent using as a base unit either the gigatonne (Gt = 10^9 tonne) or the teragram (Tg) (10^{12} g). A teragram is one million tonnes, since 1,000 grams is equal to 1 kg and one tonne is 1,000 kg. The teragram has come into wide use because it is easier to measure the concentration of a gas in grams than in tonnes, given the small volume usually involved.

A gas can produce positive radiative forcing, which tends to warm the climate system, or negative radiative forcing, which has a cooling effect. The radiative forcing of a greenhouse gas is measured in W/m^2. The global warming potential (GWP) of a GHG is the ratio of its radiative forcing to that of an equal volume of CO_2. The GWP value depends on the time horizon used in calculating it. In practice, most GWPs are calculated using a time horizon of 100 years. In the IPCC's *Third Assessment Report: Climate Change 2001*, the GWP is defined as follows: "This index approximates the time-integrated warming effect of a unit mass of a given greenhouse gas in today's atmosphere, relative to that of *carbon dioxide*."

According to the authors of the IPCC's *Special Report on Safeguarding the Ozone Layer and the Global Climate System*, the uncertainty surrounding GWPs in terms of direct positive forcing[24] is ±35%.[25] This is a very large range of uncertainty. Furthermore, the method used to calculate the GWP changed between the publication of the second and third IPCC assessment reports. Whereas in the second IPCC report, methane is considered to be 21 times more powerful than CO_2 in terms of positive forcing, a ratio of 23 is used in the IPCC's third report (2001).[26]

---

[24] "*Radiative forcing* is a measure of the influence that a factor has in altering the balance of incoming and outgoing energy in the Earth-atmosphere system and is an index of the importance of the factor as a potential climate change mechanism. It is expressed in watts per square meter (W m^{-2}). A greenhouse gas causes direct radiative forcing through absorption and emission of radiation and may cause indirect radiative forcing through chemical interactions that influence other greenhouse gases or particles. In the *Special Report on Safeguarding the Ozone Layer and the Global Climate System, op. cit.*, IPCC, 2005, p. 18.

[25] See *Special Report on Safeguarding the Ozone Layer and the Global Climate System*, p. 27.

[26] In its document EPA 430-R-05-003, the Environmental Protection Agency (EPA) gives an overview of the main assessment changes between the two reports. See *Inventory of U.S. Greenhouse Gas Emissions and Sinks: 1990-2004*, (Draft Report), February 23, 2006, p. 59.

The second key point relates to the importance of clearly differentiating emissions of CO_2 from those of other GHGs that are equally damaging for the environment. Figure 5 shows the sharp increase in atmospheric carbon dioxide concentrations that occurred over a period of 50 years. There is every indication that this drastic rate of increase will continue in the future. Levels of chlorofluorocarbons (CFC), hydrochlorofluorocarbons (HCFC) and hydrofluorocarbons (HFC) rose rapidly until the end of the 1980s. The Montreal Protocol on Substances that Deplete the Ozone Layer and the United Nations Framework Convention on Climate Change (UNFCCC) have provided the impetus for governments to take action to protect the earth's atmosphere. Most governments have ratified these agreements and sought to meet their commitments. The substantial decrease posted in halocarbon concentrations by 2004, which is shown in Figure 5, underscores the positive results that can be achieved when governments work together. Meanwhile, rapidly increasing emissions of CO_2 have pushed concerns about this greenhouse gas to the fore. Emissions of halocarbons fell from 7.5 Gt CO_2 eq. in 1990 to about 2.5 Gt CO_2 eq. in 2000, when they accounted for nearly 10% of the annual GHG contribution from the combustion of fossil fuels. This is significant progress.

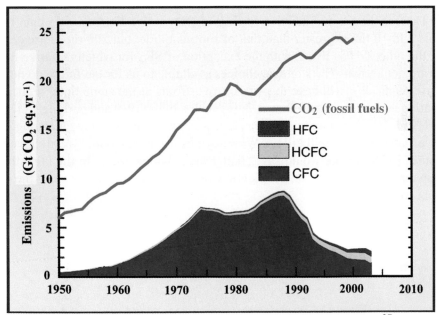

Figure 5: Combined emissions of CO2 and other GHGs[27]

Source: Safeguarding the Ozone Layer and the Global Climate System: Special Report of the Intergovernmental Panel on Climate Change, 2005

---

[27] This graph incorporates direct emissions weighted by the greenhouse effect (horizon = 100 years) of CFCs, HCFCs and HFCs compared with the total emissions of CO_2 caused by the consumption of fossil fuels and cement production. IPCC, *Special Report on Safeguarding the Ozone Layer and the Global Climate System*, 2005, p. 26.

Third, the relationship between the lifetimes of the main GHGs and their global warming potential is important. All six substances listed in the table below are covered in the Kyoto Protocol, but some of them, such as HFCs and PFCs, are also covered in the UNFCCC. CO_2 has a global warming potential of 1, since it is used as the reference gas for determining the GWPs of the other greenhouse gases. Sulphur hexafluoride (SF_6), the greenhouse gas with the highest global warming potential,[28] is emitted primarily by electric power stations and associated transmission and distribution facilities.[29] Another, much smaller, contribution comes from the manufacture of semiconductors and aluminum. Not only is it difficult to measure the quantities of SF_6 that are released, but a great deal of uncertainty surrounds the environmental effects of this gas. It would be helpful to know more about gases like this that have a lifetime of more than 3,000 years. In many cases, perfluorocarbons (PFCs) can be used as replacements for substances targeted by the Montreal Protocol because they do not deplete stratospheric ozone. Nonetheless, PFCs have very high global warming potentials[30] and atmospheric lifetimes of 1,000-50,000 years. In 2005, HFCs, PFCs and SF_6 accounted for 2% of total GHG emissions in the United States.

As Table 2 shows, the radiative forcing of CO_2 is five times greater than that of methane and 10 times greater than that of nitrous oxide, but 200 times greater than that of the other GHGs listed, with the exception of SF_6, for which radiative forcing values are not known. The strategic choices available to us for the future do not look very promising. We will have to work on two fronts at the same time: reducing or eliminating emissions of greenhouse gases with a high GWP and curbing CO_2 emissions. There can be no trade-offs because if we don't reduce all the damaging gases, sooner or later the heat will kill us. While cynics might respond, "we all have to go sometime", most people would say: "better later than sooner." In the meantime, if we keep our heads in the sand, people the world over stand to suffer since the repercussions are global in scale.

---

[28] In 2004 alone, emissions of SF_6 in the United States totalled 15.6 Tg CO_2 eq.

[29] This phenomenon is not limited to the United States. All countries face the same problem.

[30] The 100-year horizon means that an emission of 1 kg of methane to the atmosphere would have the same effect, over a century, as a carbon dioxide emission of 23 kg; a kilo of SF_6 would have the same effect as a CO_2 emission of 22,200 kg. Although the halocarbons together account for 14% of total radiative forcing they make up less than 0.000001% of all GHGs. See http://13millennium.com/encyclo/ency53.htm.

Table 2: GWP, lifetime and radiative forcing of six GHGs

Greenhouse gas	Global warming potential (GWP) (100-year horizon)	Lifetime (Years)	Radiative forcing in W/m2 1970-2000
CO_2 (carbon dioxide)	1	> 100	0.67
CH_4 (methane)	21 or 23	12 (with indirect radiative effects)	0.13
N_2O (nitrous oxide)	310	114 (with indirect radiative effects)	0.068
HFC (hydrofluorocarbons)	From 140 (HFC 152a) to 11,700 (HFC-23)	1 year to two decades	< 0.003
PFC (perfluorohydrocarbons)	6,500 to 9,200 (depending on the molecules considered)	1,000 to 50,000	0.006
SF_6 (sulphur hexafluoride)	23,900 or 22,200	3,200	?

Source: Data compiled based on *Safeguarding the Ozone Layer and the Global Climate System: Special Report of the Intergovernmental Panel on Climate Change*, IPCC, 2005, and the *Inventory of U.S. Greenhouse Gas Emissions and Sinks: 1990-2004.* In the GWP column, the "or" denotes a difference in the estimates used in the IPCC's second and third assessment reports.

Protecting the Ozone Layer and Curbing GHG Emissions: the Montreal and Kyoto Protocols

The first steps toward preserving the quality of the atmosphere date back to the Vienna Convention for the Protection of the Ozone Layer (1985). In September 1987, 24 countries signed the Montreal Protocol[31] on **Substances that Deplete the Ozone Layer**. In this Protocol, which came into force on January 1, 1989, all the parties agreed to meet "near-term targets of freezing consumption of key CFCs and halons[32] at 1986 levels and reducing consumption by 50% within

---

[31] The Montreal Protocol on Substances that Deplete the Ozone Layer was signed by 24 countries on September 16, 1987, ratified by Canada on June 30, 1988 and came into effect on January 1, 1989. The objectives of the Protocol are "to prescribe precautionary measures in order to equitably control and eventually eliminate total global emissions of ozone depleting substances (ODS)."

[32] "Halons are chemical compounds that contain bromine, chlorine, fluorine and carbon; they are used in fire extinguishing equipment, both portable and fixed types. HBFCs are powerful ODS because bromine has a higher ozone depleting potential than chlorine." See Réseau Action climat, France, Fiche Climat no 4, at www.rac-f.org/DocuFixes/ fiches_thema/FicheClimat-ozone.pdf.

10 years."[33] Ratified by more than 175 governments, the Montreal Protocol provides for periodic Meetings of the Parties (MOP) to the Montreal Protocol, a provision that has permitted subsequent amendments to the agreement as well as substantial progress.[34]

> In 1992, hydrobromofluorocarbons and methyl bromide were added to the list of substances subject to control [...] At the Ninth Meeting of the Parties to the Montreal Protocol, held in Montreal in 1997, the Parties decided to accelerate the phase-out of methyl bromide. In 1999, at the Eleventh Meeting of the Parties, held in Beijing, the Parties decided to add bromochloromethane to the list of controlled substances and to ban its production and consumption by 2002.[35]

On the whole, a great deal of progress has been made on the ODS front, and many countries are ahead of schedule in meeting the targets set out in the Montreal Protocol. There is evidence that the concentrations of CFCs in the lower atmosphere have begun to decline. Doubts still persist regarding the future, since China is manufacturing large quantities of air conditioning equipment that use the powerful greenhouse gas HCFC-22 as the primary refrigerant.

The cornerstone of the new environmental protection approach is the United Nations Framework Convention on Climate Change (UNFCCC), which was submitted to participating states for signature at the Earth Summit in Rio de Janeiro in June 1992, and came into force on March 21, 1994.[36] This agreement consists of 26 articles.[37] As specified in Article 2, the objective of the UNFCCC is to achieve "stabilization of greenhouse gas concentrations in the atmosphere at a level that would prevent dangerous anthropogenic interference with the climate system."

The UNFCCC does not really spell out the substances that need to be controlled. In paragraph 2 of Article 4, the Convention talks about "carbon dioxide and other greenhouse gases not controlled by the Montreal Protocol." This deficiency was corrected through the drafting of the Kyoto Protocol, adopted on December 11, 1997, which identifies the following greenhouse gases:

---

[33] See "The Montreal Protocol: History", at http://www.ec.gc.ca/press/001219_b_e.htm.

[34] The principal amendments to the Protocol and their effective date can be found at this Web site: http://www.ec.gc.ca/international/multilat/ozone1_e.htm

[35] *Ibid.*

[36] In March 2006, 189 Parties signed this agreement.

[37] For information about the texts of the Convention and various aspects of global warming, see the "Guide des négociations" prepared under the supervision of professor Philippe Le Prestre, Director of the Institut Hydro-Québec en Environnement, Développement et Société, Université Laval, at www.er.uqam.ca/nobel/oei/ pdf/Guide_IHQEDS_CP-11_CP-RP.pdf.

– Carbon dioxide (CO_2)
– Methane (CH_4)
– Nitrous oxides (N_2O)
– Hydrofluorocarbons (HFC)
– Perfluorocarbons (PFC)
– Sulphur hexafluoride (SF_6)

The Kyoto Protocol did not come into effect until February 16, 2005, four years after it was signed,[38] because governments had to meet some fairly draconian conditions before it could be implemented. For example, Article 25 stipulated that the Protocol could not come into force until it had been ratified by at least 55 countries, including the Parties listed in Annex 1 (see Figure 5), collectively accounting for at least 55% of the total carbon dioxide emissions of industrialized countries in 1990. This condition was met when Japan ratified the Protocol on June 4, 2002. The United States' decision in March 2001 not to ratify the Protocol nonetheless made it essential for the Russian Federation to ratify this instrument, given its 17.4% share of the Annex 1 countries' total GHG emissions in 1990. Since the United States, which accounted for more than 25% of the total, refused to ratify the Kyoto Protocol, the Russian Federation was the only country that could step in and raise the percentage to the 55% level required to bring the Kyoto Protocol into force. On October 22, 2004 Russia's State Duma voted massively in favour (334 votes for, 73 against, and 2 abstentions) of ratifying the Protocol. Russia tabled its ratification instrument on November 18, 2004, and 90 days later the Protocol came into effect.

The Kyoto Protocol is the first legally binding international instrument established to tackle climate change.[39] It calls on industrialized countries to reduce their GHG emissions by 5.2% from 1990 levels between 2008 and 2012, and to help developing countries reduce their own emissions.[40] In addition, the Parties made a commitment to quantify and report their GHG emissions on an annual basis and to forward the results to the UNFCCC Secretariat, which is responsible for implementing the Protocol. The coming into force of the Protocol paved the way for the 11th Conference of the Parties (COP), which was held in Montreal from November 28 to December 9, 2005. In chairing this meeting, Canada's objective was to obtain new commitments extending beyond 2008-2012.

---

[38] According to the information on the UNFCCC Web site, as at February 2006, 161 states representing 61.6% of greenhouse gas emissions had ratified, acceded, accepted or approved the Kyoto Protocol.

[39] Although the Montreal Protocol entailed legal responsibilities, implementation was based on voluntary participation.

[40] In signing the Kyoto Protocol, the European Community made a commitment to reduce its greenhouse gas emissions by 8% during 2008-2012, the United States' commitment was 7%, Japan and Canada both committed to a reduction of 6%, while other countries such as Australia and Iceland made a commitment to keep their emissions in check.

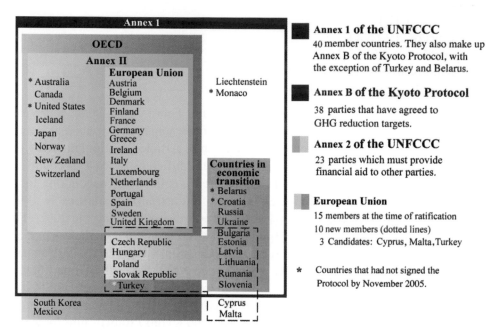

Figure 6: Structural relationships between the UNFCCC and the Kyoto Protocol
Source: "Objectif Terre", OIF, November 2005

The Conference of the Parties event in Montreal produced mixed results. The United States, which still held the view that reduction targets for GHGs must be decided on a voluntary basis, agreed to participate in a dialogue (but not negotiations) on the future of a post-2012 regime, without making any commitments. The Kyoto Protocol is still alive and well and discussions are continuing on what Canada's then-Minister of the Environment, Stéphane Dion, called the three "I's": Implementing, Improving and Innovating.[41] Since May 2006, a working group has been discussing "future commitments for developed countries for the period after 2012."[42] The Montreal Conference also provided the opportunity for the Parties to adopt the rulebook of the 1997 Kyoto Protocol (the Marrakesh Accords), which will permit the establishment of a **global carbon market**. In addition, the procedures related to the Clean Development Mechanism (CDM), which has sparked considerable interest among rich and poor countries alike, were simplified.

---

[41] Speech by the Canadian Minister of the Environment, Stéphane Dion, on December 12, 2005, available at http://www.ec.gc.ca/minister/speeches/2005/051210_s_e.htm.

[42] UNFCCC, *Press Release*, "United Nations Climate Change Conference agrees on future critical steps to tackle climate change."

In November 2006, discussions continued in Nairobi with a view to promoting Phase 2 of the reductions in GHG emissions envisaged by the Parties to the Kyoto Protocol. The next UN Climate Change Conference will take place in Bali, Indonesia in 2007. The aim is to cut GHG emissions by 50% from 2000 levels, a step which should keep global warming below the critical threshold of 2°C. The Nairobi Conference endorsed a finding in Sir Nicholas Stern's economics of climate change report indicating that "deforestation contributes 20-25% of global CO_2 emissions yearly, compared with 14% for the transport sector."[43]

The Kyoto Protocol Six Years Later

What is the state of the atmosphere six years after the signing of the Kyoto Protocol? Are things getting better or worse? The answer depends on one's point of view as well as the time period considered. A few weeks before the Montreal Conference of November/December 2005, the UNFCCC Secretariat published an important statistical study on the progress made by signatory countries in meeting their GHG reduction targets. The statistics cover the year 2003. All the Annex 1 countries of the UNFCCC (see above) have made progress in reducing their GHG emissions relative to the 1990 levels. Overall, the Parties have succeeded in reducing their emission rates by 7.4%. This figure is deceiving, however, because this decrease is due to the low energy consumption of countries whose economies are in transition (CEIT) or rather to their deindustrialization following the break-up of the Soviet Union.[44] These countries have reduced their emission rates by 46.8%, compared with the other Annex 1 countries, which increased their rates by 12.4%.[45] This translates into an increase in the amount of CO_2 emitted by industrialized countries, compared with a decline of 47% (from 5,700 to 3,000 tonnes) for CEITs.[46] This is not a very encouraging picture.

Figure 7 shows that some countries are succeeding better than other countries. In 2004, there was more than a 130-point difference between Turkey and Lithuania. The United States, which turned its back on the Kyoto Protocol, posted a better perform-

---

[43] "La conférence de Nairobi sur le climat n'accouche que de mesures limitées", *Le Monde*, November 17, 2006.

[44] This deindustrialization translated into a decrease of 3.9% in the population and a drop of 9.9% in GDP.

[45] These figures are taken from Secretariat statistics, corrected on January 12, 2006. See *Key GHG Data*, Corrigendum, January 12, 2006.

[46] *Ibid.* Expressed in 1,000 T_g (teragrams) of CO_2 equivalent. A T_g is equal to one million tonnes. The emissions of CEITs went from 5,700 to 3,000 T_g of CO_2 equivalent during the period 1990-2003, a decrease of 47%.

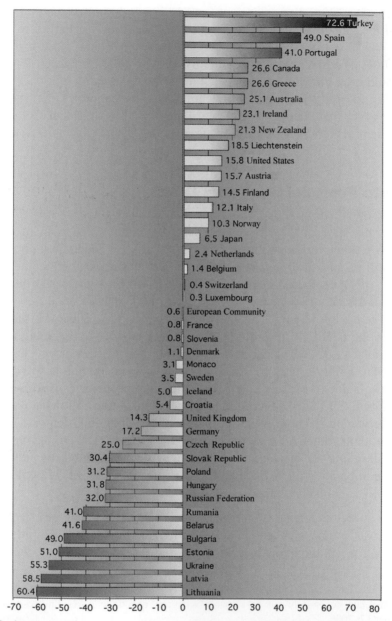

Data are for base year 1990, except in the case of Bulgaria (1988), Hungary (average for 1985-1987), Poland (1988), Romania (1989) and Slovenia (1986). The right-hand scale shows the percentage increase in GHGs in 2004 relative to 1990; the left-hand scale, the reductions in percentage. The emissions data do not include land use, land-use change and forestry (LULUCF).

Figure 7: GHG emissions from Annex 1 countries: percent increase or reduction in emissions in 2004 from 1990 levels

Source: UNFCCC Secretariat, 2006.

ance than Australia, Canada, Greece, Portugal or Spain.[47] Nonetheless, the impressive efforts of Germany and the United Kingdom in acting to protect the environment are noteworthy, as is the contribution of the European Community, which in 2004 reduced its emissions by 0.6% from 1990 levels. In all, 22 countries decreased their emissions rate in 2004 from the 1990 level, whereas 18 countries increased their rates.

In 1994, CO_2, N_2O and CH_4 accounted for 63%, 11% and 25%, respectively, of the GHG emissions of Annex 1 countries. In 2003, carbon dioxide represented 82.7% of GHG emissions, nitrous oxide, 5.6% and methane, 10%. Methane emissions are declining and carbon dioxide emissions are rising, a pattern recorded for many countries. The budget drawn up by the Environmental Protection Agency (EPA) for the United States shows a similar pattern. CO_2 emissions in the United States rose 16.6% in 2003 from the 1990 level; methane declined by 10%; and nitrous oxide decreased by 1.4%. By contrast, emissions of hydrofluorocarbons (HFCs), perfluorocarbons (PFCs) and sulphur hexafluoride (SF_6) rose 50% from the 1990 level.[48] The figures published for 2004 do not augur well. In the United States, CO_2 emissions were up 20% from the 1990 level and HFCs, PFCs and SF_6 were up 57%. The preliminary data for 2005 show that carbon dioxide emissions totalled six billion metric tonnes[49] in the United States.

The UNFCCC Secretariat has reason to be concerned because between now and 2010 there will be an even greater deterioration in the atmosphere. Sergei Kononov of the UNFCCC Secretariat predicts that by 2010 there will be an 11% increase in GHG emissions for the Annex 1 countries as a whole. Industrialized countries will post an increase in total GHG emissions of nearly 20% relative to the 1990 level, whereas CEIT will post a decrease of about 18%.[50] The International Energy Agency (IEA) has sounded the alarm. During the period 2000-2004, China posted a

---

[47] Of all the Annex 1 countries, the United States accounts for just over 38% of the total amount of GHG emissions. From a global standpoint, the United States is clearly the country with the highest GHG emissions, followed by China, which will catch up to the United States by 2010, the Russian Federation, India and Japan. This is the situation that existed in 2002. These statistics are available from the Carbon Dioxide Information Analysis Center, Environmental Sciences Division, Oak Ridge National Laboratory, Tennessee. This organization, like the Point Carbon Web site, presents CO_2 emission statistics for all the countries in the world. See cdiac.esd.ornl.gov/trends/emis_mon/emis_mon_co2.html.

[48] The bulk of this increase is due to the use of replacements for products that deplete the ozone layer. See "The U.S. Inventory of Greenhouse Gas Emissions and Sinks", EPA, Office of Atmospheric Programs, April 2005, at http://yosemite.epa.gov/oar/globalwarming.nsf/content/ResourceCenter PublicationsGHGEmissions.html.

[49] See IEA, *Emissions of Greenhouse Gases in the United States 2005*.

[50] For countries with economies in transition (CEIT), this is a "negative" improvement, since their share went from -39% to -18%. See Sergey Kononov, "Key GHG Data", Bonn, November 2005, Power Point presentation available at http://unfccc.int/essential_background/background_ publications_ htmlpdf/items/ 3604.php.

fourfold increase in its CO_2 emissions. Global emissions are expected to increase to 30.4 billion tonnes in 2010.[51]

And what about in the more distant future? The projections are not very encouraging. According to Claude Mandil, Executive Director of the International Energy Agency (IEA), there will be a 62% increase in global emissions of GHGs by the year 2030.[52] Industrialized countries will produce lower emissions because of an increase in energy intensity (see Chapter 3), but during the 2020s, the bulk of GHG emissions will be linked to the industrialization of developing countries. In the defence of developing countries, it should be pointed out that affluent countries have made every effort to relocate their biggest GHG emitters to developing countries. Note that Canada is not much better since it exports the bulk of its oil derived from bitumen deposits to the United States, thereby boosting its GHG emissions, but also filling its coffers. Whatever the case may be, we cannot expect Saudi Arabia, China or India to foot the bill for cleaning up the planet all by themselves. While China is sensitive to pollution problems, it wants the post-2012 regime envisaged in the Kyoto Protocol to be as "flexible" as possible.

What Can Be Done?

The vast majority of GHG emissions obviously come from fossil fuels. Since the carbon cycle is a natural recycling mechanism (see Chapter 2), the burning of fossil fuels has the effect of removing from storage hydrocarbons that accumulated in the subsurface or in the oceans. As we have seen, most of these hydrocarbons were formed during the Mesozoic Era (see Chapter 2).

Finding alternatives to oil would clearly be beneficial to the future of humankind. The day will come when we are forced to go this route, since oil supplies are shrinking (see Chapter 6). Although there is enough coal to meet global energy requirements for several centuries, switching from oil to coal would be like going from the frying pan into the fire. In the United States, CO_2 makes up 84.6% of GHG emissions.[53] As Figure 8 shows, a large part of the CO_2 emissions come from oil used for transportation, but an even larger proportion of emissions comes from the use of coal to operate U.S. power stations.[54] Globally, in 2005, GHG emissions (see Figure 5) exceeded 25 Gt CO_2 eq.

---

[51] *World Energy Outlook 2006*, IEA, Paris, 2006, p. 80.
[52] See the presentation that Claude Mandil made to the IFP (Institut Français du Pétrole) in September 2005, available at www.co2symposium.com/IFP/en/CO2site/presentations/Colloque CO2_Session1_ 01_Mandil_AIE.pdf.
[53] In 2004, the other main GHGs were as follows: methane 7.9%; nitrous oxide 5.5%; and halogens 2%.
[54] Figure 7 includes emissions of less than one T_g CO_2 equivalent for electricity generation from geothermal energy sources.

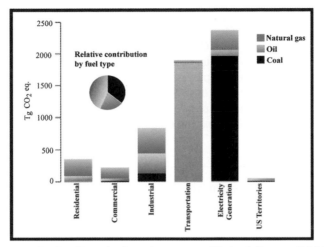

Figure 8: GHG emissions by sector, United States (2005)
Source: IEA, Table ES-6, "Inventory of U.S. Greenhouse Gas Emissions and Sinks", 1990-2005
EPA 430-R-05-003

Carbon Sequestration Methods

To solve the carbon dioxide problem, we need to reduce GHG emissions or find other ways to "put carbon back into storage." A variety of avenues for reducing GHG emissions are being explored today: increasing the efficiency of electric power stations (see Chapter 3); using cogeneration systems; choosing a different mix of fuels, such as switching from coal to natural gas to produce electricity; converting to renewable forms of energy (see Chapter 4); going back to nuclear energy or giving it a more significant role in the future; or developing new energy sources such as fuel cells. Most of these possibilities have been discussed in earlier chapters.

Another potential approach would be to re-sequester hydrocarbons that we have removed from carbon reservoirs. Sequestration or storage of GHGs is a natural process that occurs through photosynthesis. Forests and vegetation act as carbon sinks. In addition, major exchanges of carbon take place between the atmosphere and the oceans.[55] Francis Meunier aptly summarizes the situation:

---

[55] In the UNFCCC, a *source* is defined as "any process or activity that releases a GHG, aerosol, or precursor of a GHG into the atmosphere" (Art 1.9), whereas a *sink* is "Any process, activity or mechanism which removes a greenhouse gas, an aerosol or a precursor of a greenhouse gas from the atmosphere." (Art 1.8). See http://www.ladocumentationfrancaise.fr/dossiers/changement-climatique/glossaire.shtml#p.

> Just as an emission of CO_2 results from a source, the notion of sink is introduced to account for a capture of CO_2. This capture can occur naturally (through photosynthesis, which uses CO_2 to produce plant tissue, or through uptake by the oceans), but it can also be accomplished through human-built systems (for example, CO_2 can be captured in the smokestacks of thermal plants). Added to the chemical concept of capture is the notion of sequestration: CO_2 sequestration involves trapping this gas without altering it. For example, geological caverns can be used for this purpose.[56]

Afforestation is another example of a natural sequestration process since an increase in the carbon pool in the biosphere results in an equivalent decrease in the atmospheric carbon pool. Treatment of agricultural and urban wastes (farming and livestock operations produce large emissions of GHGs, including methane) can also contribute to carbon sequestration as systems can be designed to derive useful biogas from GHGs. It follows that agricultural operations, which are a source of GHGs, can be transformed to create sinks for GHGs.

Before we look at carbon sequestration methods, it will be helpful to review some industrial uses of CO_2. Carbon dioxide is used by oil companies to improve recovery from their oil and gas operations. Carbon dioxide is injected under pressure into oil wells in order to increase recovery rates (see Chapter 6). Today, in the United States, natural gas pipelines extending over more than 2,500 km are used to transport[57] more than 40 Mt of CO_2 annually. This mode of transport is an option when the "sources" are not too far away from the "sinks." CO_2 can also be transported by ship, an approach that is already used for liquefied natural gas (LNG). Both at home and around the world, there is another increasingly popular application for carbon dioxide: it provides the carbonation (fizz) in soft drinks.

There are two basic sequestration options. The IPCC *Special Report on Carbon Dioxide Capture and Storage* provides a concise description:

---

56   Francis Meunier, *op. cit.*, p.99.
57   IPCC, *Special Report on Carbon Dioxide Capture and Storage*, 2005, p 5. Hereafter cited as CDCS.

> Potential technical storage options are: geological storage (in geological formations, such as oil and gas fields, unminable coal beds and deep saline formations[58]), ocean storage (direct release into the ocean water column or onto the deep seafloor) and the industrial fixation of CO_2 into inorganic carbonates.[59]

Three industrial-scale sequestration projects are currently under way. One of them, the Sleipner project initiated by Statoil, Norway's largest oil company, involves injecting CO_2 into an underwater saline formation (Utsira). The other two projects are the CO_2 enhanced oil recovery (EOR) project at the Weyburn oil field in Alberta and the *In Salah* gas development project in Algeria, which includes carbon dioxide storage in a gas reservoir. In all these initiatives, the goal is to trap and store 1-2 million tonnes of CO_2 per year.[60] In the Weyburn project, the aim is to enhance the recovery rate for coal-bed methane deposits.[61] CO_2 is injected into coal-beds where it is adsorbed in the pore matrix of the coal seams, releasing the trapped methane. The methane can be recovered for industrial purposes. The Sleipner project is a gas-producing facility that captures its own CO_2 emissions and re-injects them 1,000 metres under the sea.

What is the global CO_2 storage capacity? The *Special Report on Carbon Dioxide Capture and Storage* (CDCS) identifies a range of capacities.

Table 3: CO2 storage capacity in various geological formations, expressed in Gt CO2

Type of reservoir	Lower estimate of storage capacity	Upper estimate of storage capacity
Oil and gas fields	675	900
Unminable coal seams	3-15	200
Deep saline formations	1,000	Uncertain, but possibly 10,000

Source: CDCS, Table TS.6, *op. cit.*, p. 33

Not all of the options that have been proposed are economically viable at present. Nevertheless, the total carbon dioxide capture and storage capacity is high,

---

[58] This is an excerpt from the IPCC report: "Saline formations are deep sedimentary rocks saturated with formation waters or brines containing high concentrations of dissolved salts. These formations are widespread and contain enormous quantities of water, but are unsuitable for agriculture or human consumption. (...) Because the use of geothermal energy is likely to increase, potential geothermal areas may not be suitable for CO2 storage."

[59] CDCS, *op. cit.*, p. 3.

[60] CDCS, *op. cit.*, p. 18.

[61] See http://carbonsequestration.us/News&Projects/htm/IEAGreen-ecbm.htm.

with the lowest estimate being some 1,685 gigatonnes of CO_2, or 67 times the total CO_2 emissions currently released into the atmosphere on an annual basis.[62] The upper estimate is very high –possibly 10,000 billion tonnes.[63]

It is also important to consider the sequestration capacity of the oceans. The CDSC provides the following summary:

> Ocean storage potentially could be done in two ways: by injecting and dissolving CO_2 into the water column (typically below 1,000 m) via a fixed pipeline or a moving ship, or by depositing it via a fixed pipeline or an offshore platform onto the sea floor at depths below 3,000 m, where CO_2 is denser than water and is expected to form a "lake" that would delay dissolution of CO_2 into the surrounding environment. Ocean storage and its ecological impacts are still in the research phase.[64]

Science and technology promise to perform miracles such as "decarbonizing" our planet as continuing industrialization spurs economic growth. We still have a long way to go, however.

There appear not to be any insurmountable challenges from an engineering standpoint. The proposed approaches are similar to those used by oil companies to bring oil to the surface. Geological formations that are potential candidates for sequestration are those that formerly harboured gas and oil. In other words, depleted deposits would be used for CO_2 storage. Sinks like this with their impermeable cap rock (see Chapter 2) are unlikely to fail. If fissures develop and gas escapes, concrete could be used to seal the cracks. This is similar to the procedure that oil companies follow when they abandon a well. By contrast, the option of using the ocean as a sink is not straightforward at all. Dissolving CO_2 in the water column might increase the acidity of the water, creating a harmful situation for marine fauna. More in-depth study is therefore in order.

Although the real problems related to carbon dioxide storage are economic and legal in nature,[65] we will limit ourselves here to economic issues. With a little encouragement and help from government, energy companies are likely to recognize the potential benefits of this approach. In the electricity sector, for example, a

---

[62] The IPCC report (CDCS) states that it is likely that there is a worldwide technical potential of at least 2,000 Gt CO_2 (545 GtC) of storage capacity in geological formations. CDCS, *op. cit.,* p. 12. Note that carbon makes up only 12/44 of the total molecular weight of CO_2. By definition, it is necessary to multiply Gt CO_2 by 0.2727 to obtain the carbon equivalent.

[63] See also *Science & Vie*, April 2006, p. 98.

[64] CDCS, *op. cit.*, p. 7.

[65] A number of legal studies on the issue can also be found in the Oil, Gas & Energy Law Intelligence (OGEL) Journal, particularly concerning the challenges associated with CO_2 in the oceans.

power station with the capacity to capture and store CO_2 emissions could see its emission rates drop by 80-90%. The problem is the additional energy requirements associated with systems for capturing, transporting and storing CO_2. Initially, in order to maintain a given performance, a power plant would require 10-40% more energy.[66] The flaw of this system is obvious: to curb emissions, it would be necessary to produce higher emissions to start. The company would also have to bear the additional costs associated with carbon capture and storage (CCS) systems.

The estimated costs specified in the CDCS are food for thought: US$0.0-$0.05 per kWh[67]. When the cost of conventional energy sources rises five cents or more per kWh, solar energy, wind power and geothermal energy start to become competitive (see Chapter 4). Energy experts therefore have their work cut out for them. The CDCS estimates that, if all these optimistic forecasts come true, carbon capture and storage could contribute 15-55% to cumulative GHG mitigation activities worldwide by 2100.[68]

Carbon Trading

In small quantities, carbon dioxide is good since it enables the earth to maintain a thermal balance that can sustain life. In large quantities, however, it is harmful. CO_2 trading is aimed at eliminating the harmful portion in a wise manner and at an affordable cost so that everyone benefits.

Carbon capture and storage creates a market for the "black sheep" CO_2. Although this gas is actually colourless, it is sometimes equated with coal. Many people regard CO_2 trading as tantamount to dealing with the devil. However, as is the case for urban waste treatment, it makes sense to try to derive benefit from something by lessening its environmental impact.

Discussions on key environmental issues have gone through a number of phases. Until the UNFCCC came into force, discussion centred on the opportunity to mitigate the risks associated with climate change. With the advent of the Kyoto Protocol, more concrete issues have come into focus and specific sectors have been targeted for action. Since Kyoto, operational issues have emerged and economic aspects have received more attention. How can the Parties be encouraged to co-operate and how can co-operation mechanisms be implemented?

---

[66]   The calculations indicate the following ranges: "For Natural Gas Combined Cycle plants, the range is 11-22%, for Pulverized Coal plants, 24-40% and for Integrated Gasification Combined Cycle plants, 14-25%." See CDCS, *op. cit.*, p. 4.

[67]   Possibly even US$0.02 per kWh, if CCS systems become widespread, permitting economies of scale. *Ibid*, p. 9.

[68]   *Ibid.*, p. 11.

The Kyoto Protocol defines three "flexibility" mechanisms intended to help the Parties reduce their greenhouse gas emissions:
– Emissions Trading (ET)
– Joint Implementation (JI)
– Clean Development Mechanism (CDM)[69]

We will consider each of these mechanisms briefly before we go on to the more fundamental issue of carbon trading.

The three mechanisms share a common denominator: the planet is viewed as a whole. Regardless of the cause of an increase in GHG emissions, the effect of emissions is the same: they contribute to global warming. And whether a reduction in emissions occurs in China, North America or Europe, the result is always the same since we all share the same atmosphere. Global warming is a worldwide phenomenon after all, even if wind circulation in the northern and southern hemispheres causes significant differences in the concentrations of gases that are harmful to human health. Life in Beijing is different from life in Chile or in North America. From the moment that a group of countries make a legally binding commitment to reduce their emissions, they share a common house that they can strive to put in order through collective efforts.

The basic principle behind the flexibility mechanisms is that Kyoto signatory countries are entitled to trade allowances, called Assigned Amount Units (AAUs), or emission reduction credits, which include Emission Reduction Units (ERUs) and Certified Emission Reduction units (CERs).[70] With reference to the reduction targets that governments agreed to under the Kyoto Protocol, emission allowances represent a volume of CO_2 that major industrial emitters are allowed to emit. Any emitter unable to meet its obligations can purchase emission reduction credits from another emitter that has been more successful in reducing its emissions, or it can apply more effective technologies to reduce its emissions. In either case, there is a price to pay. From the standpoint of a major emitter's "balance sheet", an allowance is an asset that can be added to by purchasing emissions credits from another emitter. That is the premise of the first flexibility mechanism–Emissions Trading.

---

[69] Here we are using the terminology of the Government of Canada, which seems more appropriate than that in the Protocol, which talks about Joint Implementation and International Emissions Trading. See http://www.climatechange.gc.ca/cop/cop6_hague/english/kyoto_e.html. The International Emissions Trading Association (IETA) has a comprehensive online document on the CDM instrument: IETA's Guidance Note through the CDM Project Approval Process, May 2005. See www.ieta.org/ieta/www/pages/getfile.php?docID=900.

[70] The Slovak Republic was the first country to avail itself of this provision. In December 2002, it sold 200,000 AAUs to Japan. This allowed Japan to add the AAUs to its own inventory, whereas the Slovak Republic was required to use the proceeds to fund domestic emissions reduction projects. See http://www.evomarkets.com/ ghg/index.php?xp1=aauTchèques First.

The second mechanism, Joint Implementation, is a little more subtle. It arises from Article 6 of the Protocol, which provides that a developed country that funds a GHG reduction project in another developed country can earn emission reduction units (ERUs). ERUs are added to the authorized emission allowance of the investing country and deducted from the allowance of the host country of the project. The investing country therefore gains an additional margin for its own GHG emissions, but it can only use this mechanism to work toward its own reduction targets.

The Clean Development Mechanism (CDM) centres on co-operative undertakings between industrialized countries and developing countries.[71] This mechanism is similar to JI except that investments are made in projects carried out in non-Annex 1 (developing) countries (see Figure 6). In return for providing this type of assistance, a country, or an entity like the World Bank, can earn tradable credits equivalent to the reductions achieved in the host country. These credits can be traded on the international market or the European market. Figure 9 provides an overview of the key mechanisms just described.

Obviously, the flexibility mechanisms set out in the Kyoto Protocol have important economic ramifications. They help to reduce emissions in regions where the cost is lower, achieving the same environmental results at a lower cost. The problem is that the whole debate on climate issues is reduced to monetary considerations through these mechanisms.

This probably was inevitable. The United States has followed suit by participating in the establishment of a Kyoto-type arrangement in July 2005 through the Asia-Pacific Partnership on Clean Development and Climate[72]. This initiative, in which China, India, Australia, Japan, South Korea and the United States are partners, emphasizes technology transfer arrangements, energy security, biotechnologies, nuclear fission and renewable energy sources. Although there are no binding commitments, Washington was quick to depict the initiative as a complement to the UNFCCC. While no one has been fooled by this, the fact remains that this partnership brings together the planet's two biggest GHG emitters.

The European Union's Emissions Trading Scheme (ETS) was launched in January 2005. An ETS emissions credit or allowance equals one tonne of CO_2 equivalent. During the first year of operations, 363 million tonnes of CO_2 were

---

[71] The provisions stem from articles 6, 12 and 17 of the Kyoto Protocol.
[72] See "Vision Statement of Australia, China, India, Japan, the Republic of Korea, and the U.S. for a New Asia-Pacific Partnership on Clean Development and Climate", U.S. Department of State, July 28, 2005, at http://www.state.gov/g/oes/rls/fs/50335.htm.

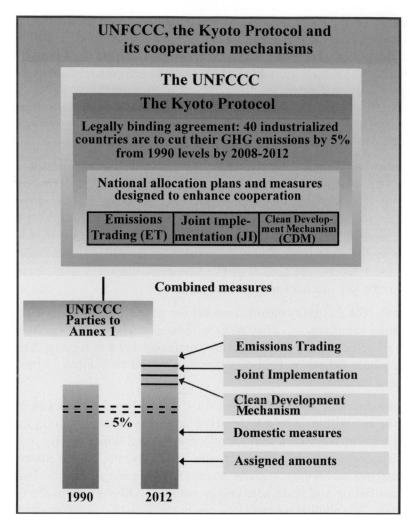

Figure 9: The UNFCCC, the Kyoto Protocol and its main instruments
Source: From Pim Kieskamp, Asian Development Bank (ADB)
www.adb.org/Documents/Events/2002/ RETA5937/Manila/downloads/cw_33_kieskamp.pdf

traded on the market, at prices of up to 30 euros per tonne.[73] The EU ETS covers nearly 12,000 power sector and heavy industry facilities entitled to trade emission

---

[73] See Paula Dittrick, "CO_2 emissions trading grows in Europe, seen likely elsewhere", *Oil & Gas Journal*, March 20, 2006, p. 24. In April 2006 the average transaction was around 25 euros/tonne. See *Science & Vie*, April 2006, p. 97. In November 2006, the price of an emission allowance dropped to 8.5 euros per tonne. See "Bruxelles somme Paris de réduire davantage ses émissions de CO_2", *Le Monde*, November 30, 2006. In April 2007, the price fell sharply to 90 cents per tonne, jeopardizing the very future of the carbon market. See "Le marché des droits d'émission de CO_2 rate son entrée", *Le Monde*, April 6, 2007.

allowances.[74] In addition, under National Allocation Plans, member states will be able to acquire emission credits through JI and CDM.[75] According to the European Commission, which is responsible for approving National Allocation Plans, EU countries should be able to meet their Kyoto targets at an annual cost of 2.9-3.7 billion euros, or a little less than 0.1% of the European Union's GDP.[76] Not everyone shares this optimism, however. Carlo Stagnaro, environment director of the think tank Instituto Bruno Leoni in Turin, Italy, said that for four major EU countries (Italy, the United Kingdom, Spain and Germany), compliance with the Kyoto Protocol will spell a drop in GDP of 2.2%, 1.1%, 3.1% and 0.8%, respectively, in 2010.[77] According to the same author, only through using Russia's emission allowances will the EU be able to save face. Although this is in keeping with national allocation plans, it does not result in a decrease in CO_2 emissions. In addition, according to Point Carbon, a carbon analysis organization, Russia stands to benefit financially, to the tune of $10 billion.[78]

The administration of the ETS entails the use of a Community Independent Transaction Log, providing oversight for the national registries of EU member countries. In March 2005, nine countries had their own registries up and running. Note that the UNFCCC Secretariat also hopes to have an International Transaction Log in place by spring 2007. This log will be instrumental, since it will be able to link the European Union's emissions trading scheme with the international system to be implemented through the UNFCCC Secretariat. In the absence of an effective control mechanism, some countries might be deprived of allowances that they could legitimately claim during the time frame prescribed in the Protocol. The estimated volume of credits that will be generated between now and 2012 has increased, and could reach 2.1 Gt CO_2 eq. by the end of the Kyoto commitment period. Four fifths of this total volume will come from the CDM.[79]

The European emissions trading scheme is a spot market which is open to all interested parties at present, but will in actual fact be used mainly by European players. Market prices for emission credits have been highly volatile in recent years, especially in the United Kingdom, which has its own emissions trading regime.

---

[74] Companies may trade allowances directly with each other, "or they may buy or sell via a broker, bank or other allowance market intermediary." See *Press Release*, European Commission, MEMO/05/84 of March 8, 2005.

[75] This "flexible" program is interpreted by most European countries as a means of selling their solar and wind power technologies to developing countries. Canada, for its part, is interested in environmental and energy technologies.

[76] See *Press Release*, European Commission, *op.cit.*

[77] Carlo Stagnaro, "EU May Miss Kyoto Targets despite EEA Recommendations", *Oil & Gas Journal*, March 13, 2006, p. 26.

[78] Point Carbon, *Carbon Market Analysis*, October 14, 2004, p. 10.

[79] See Point Carbon, *CDM and JI Monitor*, February 7, 2006.

Market prices fluctuated between 2 and just over 12 euros during 2003 and 2004, whereas current ETS prices range from 7 to 20 euros depending on the type of contracts arranged between suppliers and buyers.[80] The carbon market is therefore truly coming to fruition. Denmark has a system, Canada is setting up its own market and Japan is expected to follow suit. Even large oil companies like Shell have begun to set up their own in-house allowance systems which will permit more effective planning on a regional scale. The United States will no doubt establish a national system within a few years. In the absence of an overarching government agreement, some U.S. states are exploring the possibility of participating in the Regional Greenhouse Gas Initiative (RGGI), which is slated to begin in 2009.[81] Similar legislation is being drafted in California.

Analysts' predictions about emissions trading systems are guesses at best. CO_2e talks about a market that could range from \$10 billion to \$1,000 billion in 2010.[82] In a study published in November 2005, the IEA talks about a market of 1 billion tonnes of CO_2 equivalent per year but provides no supporting figures.[83] Claude Mandil, Executive Director of the IEA, believes that the Kyoto Protocol covers only one third of GHG emissions.

The limitations of the Kyoto Protocol are already apparent in that some Parties have failed to meet their commitments. It is clear that no single measure can tackle all of the issues related to global warming. The negotiators of the Protocol were aware of this and emphasized that global synergy must be achieved through a set of measures taken individually, collectively, regionally or globally, in collaboration with industry and the political leaders who establish the framework for commitments. Readers should keep in mind that governments are the true holders of emission allowances.

Debate on this issue will continue. Fluctuations in the prices of emission allowances will depend on the time frame involved, and the United States' decision to reject Kyoto has implications in this regard. Given that energy investors always seek long-term stability, the uncertainty surrounding the post-2012 period does not augur well for the industry. Furthermore, governments and energy equipment

---

[80] See Point Carbon, *CDM and JI Monitor*, March 7, 2006. Between November and mid-December 2006, credits were being bought for 6 to 10 euros. See *CDM and JI Monitor*, December 13, 2006.

[81] The states concerned are Connecticut, Delaware, Maine, New Hampshire, New Jersey, New York and Vermont. The State of Maryland is expected to join the initiative in June 2007. Under this program, the states hope to decrease their CO_2 emissions by 10% between now and 2019. "Coal-fired, oil-fired, and gas-fired electric generating units with a capacity of 25 megawatts or more will be included under RGGI." See Maureen Wren, DEC (Department of Environmental Conservation), New York, August 15, 2006. This initiative launched in 2003 by Governor Pataki was the subject of a memorandum of understanding between the Northeast states signed in December 2005.

[82] See CO_2e.com, *Greenhouse Gas Market Overview*, January 2004.

[83] IEA, "Act Locally, Trade Globally – Emissions Trading for Climate Policy", Paris, 2005.

suppliers have to compete for capital. Is it better to invest in renewable energy sources rather than to capture and store CO_2? And won't the CDM favour countries such as China, India and Brazil that tend to attract the bulk of foreign direct investments (FDI flows)?

Different Types of Environmental Discourse

In general, three different types of environmental discourse can be distinguished. First, there are the environmental sceptics, who listen to concerns raised by much of the scientific community, but refuse to accept certain lines of reasoning that they consider alarmist –either because they believe that the scientific truth is complex and cannot be captured in a single linear system or they feel that, given time and suitable technologies, the planet will be able to pull itself out of the environmental hornet's nest in which it finds itself. Sceptics tend to accept only arguments that bolster their views and reject out of hand anything that does not fit into their conception of reality. This position is more acceptable than attempts by public officials to hide or even twist the truth. For example, White House science advisors have at times suppressed "alarmist" passages in scientific reports about climate change in response to pressure from high-level officials seeking to paint a more positive picture. In addition, some government officials are not allowed to talk about sensitive issues like these outside the halls of government. The case of James E. Hansen, a climate expert with NASA, is a good example of the censorship exercised by the U.S. government to keep its science advisors from disseminating information about the threat of global warming.[84] By following such a policy, government does a disservice to the people. Although it may make a certain degree of sense for a government to exercise this kind of oversight in the area of security, in all other circumstances it is perverse.

Die-hard environmentalists engage in a second type of discourse. Pierre Hassner, a French political thinker, described the peace movements of the 1980s as crying to the West and whispering to the East. Regardless of what some believe, the important split is not between left and right, believers and heretics, or rich and poor, but between those who promote immediate direct action and those who want to avoid action. Although the discourse is not always clear, the message is. For the toughest elements at least, direct political action becomes a right of passage to forcefully highlight their cause. Major divergences of opinion exist within groups that are willing to engage in direct action. Some are not afraid of taking forceful action against genetically modified organisms, seal hunting, the burning of fossil fuels or nuclear power (even if nuclear energy is clean and much less polluting than fossil

---

[84] See "Climate Expert Says NASA Tried to Silence Him", *The New York Times*, January 29, 2006.

fuels). Other, equally dedicated groups will only join in peaceful actions. All these actively engaged people share what Kant called an ethic of conviction: a person is either "in" or "out." Either believe or die. A person like this chooses a path and sticks to it. According to Eugène Enriquez, the problem with this kind of conviction is that it can lead to the best or the worst of outcomes.[85] In many cases, it is only through political arbitration that judicious actions can be recognized and set apart from foolish options. However, if the government lacks a clear vision, the result is often an impasse, which means that it will take longer to find solutions, if any can be found.

The third type of discourse is represented by the efforts of forward-looking environmentalists. Their noble aim is to create a **collective imaginary**. They borrow heavily from the apocalyptic visions of many religions –Humankind is short-sighted and will be punished for failing to heed Nature's warnings. Over the long term, a change of conscience develops, through what can be described as intergenerational education, which encourages humanity to act with a constant concern for protecting the environment and preserving it to meet the needs of future generations.[86] It can always be argued that the tenants of the first two schools of thought are equally forward-looking and that there is no rational criterion that can be used to differentiate the schools of thought. However, the third type of discourse avoids the scepticism associated with the first school and the violent action sometimes advocated by the second. A comment by the French dramatist Albert Guinon aptly summarizes the tensions between the first two schools: "passionate people hold up the world, and sceptics let if fall."

Has the environment become a new religion? Has it become a new industry? It is true that it sells well –the news media run stories on environmental issues every day. The drafting of the most recent IPCC report involved work by 122 co-ordinating lead authors and lead authors, 515 contributing authors, 21 review editors and 420 expert reviewers.[87] These figures do not include the 4,000 some researchers working on associated topics around the world. Grants might dry up if the urgent nature or the legitimate concerns that climate change raises were to disappear. However, this criticism is disingenuous since it could be said to be true of almost any area of endeavour.

There is a saying that "scientists know everything about nothing, and philosophers nothing about everything." History is full of cases of contempt for the truth.

---

[85] Eugène Enriquez, "Les enjeux éthiques dans les organisations modernes", *Sociologie et sociétés*, Vol. XXV, No. 1, spring 1993, p. 25.

[86] Article 1 of the 1997 UNESCO Declaration on the Responsibilities of the Present Generations Towards Future Generations. Articles 5 and 6 of this Declaration concern the preservation of life on earth and the protection of the environment.

[87] "The Scientific Basis", *op. cit.*, p. 3.

Some, such as Galileo, have even lost their lives trying to defend it. Others have simply allowed themselves to be duped, like most scientists in the late 1930s who believed that an atomic bomb could not be created.[88] In the late 1950s, Samuel Glasstone, who at the time served on the United States Atomic Energy Commission, published a manual on the effects of nuclear explosions, which led officials to assume that all the potential effects of nuclear war were known. Some 20 years later, it took the insights of the astronomer Carl Sagan to show us that a nuclear war could have devastating consequences for life on earth, which he termed a "nuclear winter." There are plenty of recent examples of situations in which it was mistakenly believed that a major scientific leap had been made: cold fusion, "cloning" in South Korea and the development of human cells from stem cells. This shows the importance of modesty, of maintaining a critical distance and of avoiding generalizations. However, this does not change the fact that the global climate is changing and all the evidence points to humankind.

It makes sense to treat the atmosphere as a "common good", regardless of the technical meaning ascribed to this term. This collective heritage must be protected from harm. As a minimum, the precautionary principle should be applied to all activities. This principle has already been enshrined in the constitutions of a number of countries as well as in environmental laws.[89] After Galileo publicly confessed that he had erred in saying that the Earth moves around the Sun, he is said to have tapped the floor with his foot and whispered: "And yet, it moves!" We can say: And yet our planet is warming at an accelerating rate!

---

[88] According to a study conducted more than 20 years ago by the Rand Corporation.

[89] In brief, the precautionary principle implies that a company or other entity must always err on the side of caution if there is any chance that its actions will have a deleterious effect on the environment. It can be held responsible for its actions if it is subsequently discovered that it could have foreseen the negative consequences of its actions. This idea is expressed in the wording of Article 3.3 of the United Nations Framework Convention on Climate Change (UNFCCC) states: "The Parties should take precautionary measures to anticipate, prevent or minimize the causes of climate change and mitigate its adverse effects. Where there are threats of serious or irreversible damage, lack of full scientific certainty should not be used as a reason for postponing such measures..."

9

Liquified Natural Gas

In 2005 natural gas made up 21% of world primary energy consumption, compared with 36% for crude oil.[1] Electricity generation accounts for the bulk of the increase in demand (60%) for natural gas. The share of electricity produced by gas-fired power plants is on the rise, a trend that is likely to persist in the coming years. The proof is in the numbers. Thirty per cent of electricity generation in OECD countries comes from gas-fired plants. Between 2000 and 2010, 78% of new capacity built is expected to come from natural gas.[2] Projects under construction in the gas sector amount to some $210 billion during the period 2005-2010, compared with requirements of about $520 billion according to the *World Energy Investment Outlook* (*WEIO*) *2003*. However, many projects are currently planned, and if all of them get the go-ahead, a sum of $300 billion could be added to the capital spending that has already been approved.[3] Despite these large sums, there is still a long way to go. For example, only 6 out of a total of 67 projects for the construction of receiving terminals in the United States have actually gotten under way. The International Energy Agency (IEA) has said that there is a serious risk of underinvestment in the gas sector worldwide.

In 2005 international and intraregional trade in natural gas grew 4.7%, reaching 825 billion cubic metres (Bcm). During the same year, trade in liquefied natural gas (LNG) totalled 192 Bcm, or roughly 23% of the world natural gas market.

---

[1] See *Natural Gas Market Review 2006*, IEA, 2006, p. 33. Hereafter cited as *NGMR 2006.*
[2] *Ibid*, p. 39.
[3] *Ibid*, p. 65.

There has been a spectacular increase in demand for natural gas over the past five years, with even greater demand growth for liquefied natural gas. The IEA provided this summary:

> Over the past five years, trade flows have increased by 29% (up 40 Bcm – billion cubic metres), the liquefaction capacity by 48 Bcm per year (up 35.4 mtpa – million tonnes per annum) and the LNG fleet has grown by 75%. Major new LNG flows are connecting previously distinct regional markets and a global LNG market seems to be emerging.[4]

The LNG Supply Chain

Natural gas liquefaction is a process that uses complex technologies and facilities to convert natural gas into LNG. However, liquefaction is just one of the interconnected segments of the chain of supply that begins with extraction operations in the gas field and ends with regasification and delivery of the LNG to end users. This is called the LNG supply chain.

The first post-extraction segment of the LNG supply chain consists of the facilities and infrastructure required to liquefy the gas, or convert it to a liquid state. At the other end of the chain are the facilities and infrastructure needed to convert the liquefied natural gas back to a gaseous state. Once vaporized, or regasified, the natural gas can be distributed to industrial, commercial and even retail users. LNG shipping, or transport, is a very important part of the supply chain since it links the liquefaction and regasification segments.

Figure 1 illustrates the main segments and processes in the supply chain: photos of the facilities and infrastructure used in the LNG sector in the top panel, a linear depiction of the supply chain components in the middle panel, and a more detailed schematic diagram illustrating the interconnectivity of the different segments in the bottom panel. It is important to emphasize the interdependent nature of the links: all of the facilities shown have to be constructed and brought on stream within the same time period, roughly three or four years.

Table 1 presents a comparative analysis of the costs associated with the different supply chain components and indicates the relative percentage of the overall cost and sometimes the approximate amount involved. The costs are intended solely as examples, since not all of them were calculated on the same basis and year-to-year

---

[4]   *Ibid*, p. 49.

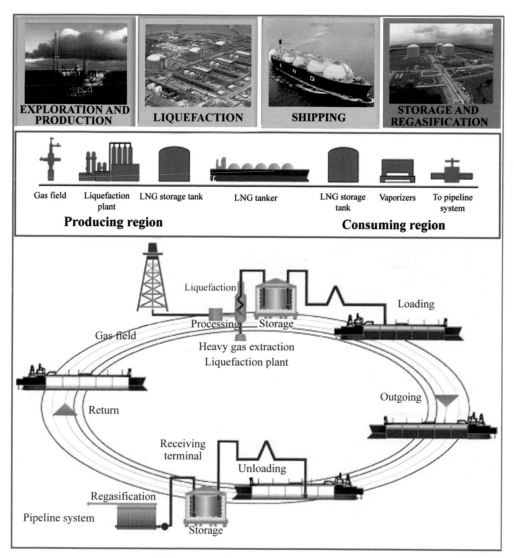

Figure 1: The LNG supply chain

Source: **Upper part**: EXPLORATION PRODUCTION, The Role of LNG in North American Gas
Supply and Demand (Fig. 24), Energy Economics Research, Bureau of Economic Geology, Centre
for Energy Economics, University of Texas, Sept. 2004 (and later editions)/ LIQUEFACTION,
STORAGE AND REGASIFICTION, *Liquefied Natural Gas: Understanding the Basic Facts*, DOE,
August 2005/ SHIPPING Photo courtesy of FERC; **Middle part**: *Liquefied Natural Gas: A Primer*,
Natural Resources Canada, www2.nrcan.gc.ca/es/erb/CMFiles/
LNG_Web_A_Primer_ENGLISH206NDA-04042005-9696.pdf; (image from CSM Energy); **Lower
part**: www.rabaska.net/ page.php?idS=3&idL=fr (Projet Rabaska : L'univers du GNL)

variations play an important role in some cases. For example, increases in gas prices hit consumers especially hard, whereas transportation costs are proportionally less volatile. Although the first two sources cited are authoritative, a wide range of estimates can be found, as evidenced by the figures and percentages obtained from the third and fourth sources listed under the table.

Table 1: Costs associated with the LNG supply chain

Exploration and Production	Liquefaction	Transport	Regasification
Source 1: **15–20%** Costs vary widely with location	**30-45%** US$1.5-2 billion for a plant with a capacity of 8 mtpa	**10-30%** US$155 million per tanker with a capacity of 138,000 m³.	**15-25%** US$400 million to build a terminal with a delivery capacity of 180-360 Bcf per year.
Source 2 $0.50-$1.00 per million BTU	$0.80-$1.20 per million BTU	$0.40-$1.00 per million BTU	$0.30-$0.50 per million BTU
Total cost: US$3.7-$7.8 billion or $2.00-$3.70 per million BTU			
Source 3: **10-20%**	**25-35%**	**15-25%**	**5-15%** Distribution and marketing: 25-35%
Source 4: Total investment in a typical LNG chain: US$3-$3.9 billion	US$1.3-$1.8 billion for 2 LNG trains	Acquisition of 6 carriers with a 127,000 m³ capacity US$1.3-$1.5 billion	US$400-$600 million

Source 1: Liquefied Natural Gas: Understanding the Basic Facts, DOE, August 2005, p. 8. In this DOE study, exploration and production include gas production per se, pre-plant processing and transport to liquefaction plants; liquefaction includes the costs of storage and carrier loading; storage and regasification operations include the cost of building the receiving terminal and the offloading, storage, regasification and delivery infrastructure.

Source 2: The Role of LNG in North American Gas Supply and Demand, (Figure 24), Energy Economics Research, Bureau of Economic Geology, Center for Energy Economics, University of Texas, September 2004.

Source 3: Philip R. Weems, "Overview of Issues Common to Structuring, Negotiating and Documenting LNG Projects", June 2000 (originally published in *International Energy Law and Taxation Review*) available on the web site of King & Spalding, Houston, Texas.

Source 4: TotalFinaElf cited in John L. Keffer and Marisa Reuter, "Gas-To-Energy: Structuring Downstream Projects", 2001, p. 9, available on the web site of King & Spalding.

Total investment in the LNG sector in the period 2006-2010 amounts to $272 billion, of which $148 billion is earmarked for the construction of facilities and another $124 billion for planned or proposed projects.[5]

Liquefaction of Natural Gas

The following diagram, produced by the United States Department of Energy (DOE), provides an overview of the main operations carried out at a liquefaction plant.

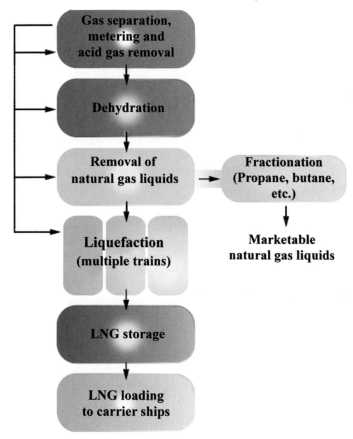

Figure 2: Main steps in the liquefaction process
Source: DOE, *Liquefied Natural Gas: Understanding the Basic Facts*, 2005, p. 11

The diagram covers most of the operations carried out at gas treatment plants, which are described in greater detail in Chapter 5. Since liquefaction is a central concept in the present chapter, we will take a look at this process now. Basically, a gas can be liquefied under pressure or by refrigeration or by both processes (pressure and

---

5   *NGMR 2006, op. cit.*, p. 70.

refrigeration) simultaneously. When gas is held at a constant volume, the pressure of the gas is directly proportional to the temperature. The temperature of a mass of gas therefore increases as the pressure increases. Conversely, the temperature of the gas decreases as the pressure decreases. Under normal atmospheric pressure, natural gas can be liquefied at a temperature of – 167°C (– 260°F). At this temperature, methane is reduced to about 1/600th of its original volume, which can be likened to a soccer ball being reduced to the size of a ping-pong ball. This reduction in volume makes it feasible to store and transport natural gas over considerable distances. If LNG is cooled to a temperature lower than – 186°C, it will turn into a solid.

Liquefaction of natural gas is performed in a succession of stages involving compression, condensation, expansion and evaporation steps, often using more than one cooling gas (refrigerant)."[6] Liquefaction of a gas involves removing heat, or in other words, cooling the gas. The process is similar to that which takes place in a refrigerator.[7]

On average, a liquefaction plant uses 12% of the feed gas it receives for its own operating requirements.[8] This is the most costly component of the LNG supply chain, accounting for about 50% of the overall costs depending on the type of facility. In 2005, there were 30 liquefaction plants in operation around the world, with 15 others under construction, 12 projects under study and 8 projects in an advanced engineering phase.[9] If all these projects are completed, LNG production capacity could reach 571.8 Bcm (420.3 million tonnes) in 2015.[10] All of these facilities are located near the major gas fields of natural gas producing countries.

Regasification of LNG

When transferred to an LNG carrier, LNG is stored in double-walled cryogenic tanks. The space between the two tanks is filled with an insulating material that can retain the gas vapours (the boil-off gas). The inner tank is constructed of an alloy that can withstand the very cold temperatures of the LNG. The outer tank,

---

[6] See Société du Terminal méthanier de Fos-Cavaou at http://www.cavaou-gnl.com/sicsFront/FosCavaou/index.jsp?m0=1&m1=5&m2=2&m3=0. A comprehensive diagram of the liquefaction process can be found in "Projet Rabaska, Étude d'impact sur l'environnement", January 2006, Chapter 2, Présentation du promoteur et du projet, Figure 2.12.

[7] Cited in *Ibid.* "A refrigerant is compressed in a compressor, and then sent to a condenser. Condensation results in heat being conducted to the ambient air in the kitchen (at the back of the refrigerator). The refrigerant then flows through the expansion valve, which causes a quick drop in refrigerant pressure accompanied by a drop in the temperature of the refrigerant. The cooled refrigerant is then channelled to the evaporator: the ensuing evaporation process absorbs a large quantity of heat from the surrounding air (inside the refrigerator)."

[8] *Ibid.*

[9] See IEA, *NGMR 2007*, Appendix 1. pp. 283-285.

[10] *NGMR 2007, op. cit.*, p. 285.

constructed of stainless steel and composite materials, is designed to contain the full contents of the tanks in the event of a leak.

Converting LNG to natural gas involves a process called regasification, or vaporization. LNG has to be heated in order to regasify it, or change it from liquid form to a gaseous state.[11] Several different vaporization processes are currently employed. The two main types of vaporizers are the Open Rack Vaporizer (ORV),[12] which uses heat exchange with seawater to vaporize the LNG, and the Submerged Combustion Vaporizer (SCV).[13]

These two liquefaction processes pose certain environmental problems. In the ORV process, seawater is used as a heating medium and the heated process water is subsequently discharged to the ocean. Some people are worried about the adverse effects that such projects may have on marine life.[14] With respect to the SCV[15] process, the main environmental concerns relate to the NO_x emissions in the exhaust gases. A natural gas cogeneration plant could be operated to harness the residual energy for use in heating the LNG, thereby obviating the need to keep the SCV system running continuously.

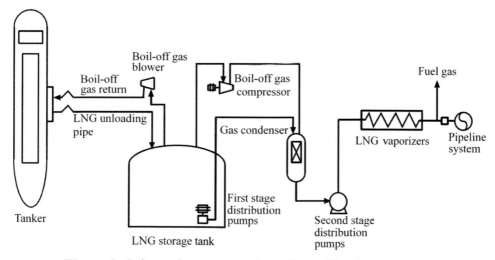

Figure 3: Schematic representation of regasification operations
Source: Cacouna Energy, *Project Notice*, September 2004

---

[11] The opposite process, called "condensation", involves going from a gaseous state to a liquid state.
[12] ORVs are open-loop systems.
[13] SCVs are closed-loop systems.
[14] When the water is returned to the sea, it is about 6°C warmer than the receiving environment.
[15] LNG circulates in a coil which is submerged in a water bath heated using a gas burner.

Other regasification technologies are also under study, such as Ambient Air Vaporizers (AAV) and the Heat Integrated Ambient Air Vaporizer (HIIAV). To date, AAV has been tested on a small scale, but extreme temperature differences in winter are one of the remaining hurdles. While the same problem exists with HIIAV, the designers hope to get around it by using gas turbines and mixing the turbine exhaust gas with ambient air.[16] This would ensure a more uniform temperature and avert frost build-up in gas pipelines.

Another important issue relates to the methane content of regasified LNG. If it is too high,[17] the LNG will have an upper heating value that is too high for conventional gas distribution networks. In some countries, this problem is solved upstream because the propane and butane are extracted from the natural gas before it is liquefied. Upstream removal is done in situations where regional markets exist for these by-products (see Chapter 5). Where this is not done, however, it is necessary to foster interchangeability, or compatibility, between regasified LNG and natural gas distribution networks. In situations where the methane content is too high, the U.S. Energy Information Administration (EIA) proposes the following solutions:[18]

– Dilute the regasified LNG with inert gases such as nitrogen;
– Extract the ethane, propane and butanes at the import terminal prior to delivery of the LNG to the gas pipeline network;
– Extract the heavy fractions at the LNG and export facilities prior to shipping to the United States;
– Blend richer LNG with leaner LNG at the LNG import terminal;
– Blend richer vaporized LNG with leaner pipeline gases downstream of the import terminal (i.e., at a later stage in the distribution chain).

---

[16] See Martin J. Rosetta, Brian C. Price and Lyn Himmelberger, "LNG Vaporization: A Fresh Approach as Ambient Air Vaporization Technology is Integrated with Waste Heat Recovery", *LNG Observer*, September 2005, pp. 25-28.

[17] The content varies with the importing country. The Federal Energy Regulatory Commission (FERC) in the United States defines the acceptable heating value of LNG for distribution networks as being in the range 985-1085 BTU/cf. Most LNG imported from the leading exporting countries (Libya, Oman, Abou Dhabi, Brunei, Australia, Malaysia, Indonesia, Algeria, Qatar and Nigeria) has a heating value greater than 1,100 BTU/cf. See "LNG's Final Hurdle" in *Public Utilities Fortnightly*, March 2006, available at www.fortnightly.com.

[18] See "U.S. Natural Gas Imports and Exports: 2004", DOE, EIA, Office of Oil and Gas, December 2005, p. 9, available at www.eia.doe.gov/pub/oil_gas/natural_gas/feature_articles/ 2005/ ngimpexp/ ngimpexp.pdf.

LNG Shipping

Moss Rosenberg type carriers[19] and membrane-type carriers are the two main carrier systems used by companies involved in the LNG supply chain. The firm Total's web site defines the characteristics of these vessels as follows:

Moss Rosenberg type cargo tanks have a spherical design and are free-standing. Made of thick welded aluminum alloy plates that are insulated, the tanks are supported at their equator by a vertical steel cylindrical skirt, equipped with a special alloy thermal brake; the bottom of the skirt is welded to the structure of the double-hulled ship.

In ships with a **membrane cargo tank** system, the LNG is contained in a thin, dual metallic barrier (membrane), which prevents leakage of the natural gas and maintains the mechanical properties of natural gas at a very low temperature. The ship's hull takes the strain from the cargo load via the protective insulation layer. The tanks conform to the shape of the hull, permitting optimal use of the ship.[20]

In membrane tank systems, the ship's hull constitutes the outer tank wall and the cargo tanks themselves, consisting of a thin membrane, are not very strong; the cargo load acts on the ship structure via the insulation."[21] By contrast, the Moss type tank and the prismatic self-supporting tank design (see Figure 4) both consist of structures that are independent from the hull.

Each of these carriers has its advantages and disadvantages. Tankers with a Moss spherical design maintain an essentially constant draft, and they can make their return voyage with a nearly empty tank. To maintain their stability, they need to keep their double hull filled with the appropriate amount of ballast water."[22] The weight of the ship and its cargo load are much greater than in the case of a membrane tank carrier. Only a few ports can accommodate these ships given their large size.

The main advantage of the membrane tank design is that the internal static or dynamic forces (sloshing of LNG, for example) are transferred from the tank structures to the ship's hull through the insulation material, which acts like a cushion. The other advantage of the design is that it maximizes the available space. Pierre Le

---

[19] They are also called Moss type carriers and are named after the Norwegian company that first introduced them.

[20] See www.total.com/static/fr/medias/topic1492/pdf_GNL_francais11.pdf.

[21] See http://www.mer.equipement.gouv.fr/commerce/02_flotte/02_type_de_navire/ 03_naviresciternes/ navires citernes.htm.

[22] Pierre Le Bris, "Le gaz naturel liquéfié", Groupes professionnels, Conférence Arts et Métiers (April 2002), available at gp34.gadzarts.org/Conf-Le-Bris/GNL_Conf_Le_Bris.PDF.

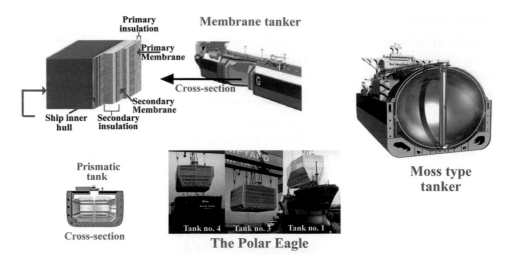

Figure 4. Different types of LNG carriers

Source: **Membrane type** carrier: *The Role of LNG in North American Gas Supply and Demand,* Centre for Energy Economics, University of Texas, Sept. 2004 (and later editions)/**SPB prismatic type**: Seamanhip/Polar Eagle: Ishikawajima-Harima Heavy Industries Co., Ltd. (IHI)/**Moss type** carrier: Moss Maritime.

Bris points out that a membrane design carrier with a capacity of 160,000 m³ "is similar in size to a 135,000 m³ capacity spherical (Moss) vessel."[23]

A third type of tank system, the self-supported prismatic type B design,[24] falls into the free-standing category of tanks (cylindrical, silo and other polyhedral shapes). Since the insulated tanks are independent structures from the ship, their geometry can be fitted to the shape of the vessel. The first prismatic type B carrier dates back to 1993, when the *Polar Eagle* was built by the Japanese firm Ishikawa-jima-Harima Heavy Industries (IHI).

At an international symposium held in 2004 to explore the advantages and disadvantages of the different types of LNG carriers, the principal rapporteur summarized the findings presented in Table 2 below.[25]

---

[23] *Ibid.*

[24] Type B refers to self-supporting tanks used to carry LNG in bulk, as defined in the International Code for the Construction and Equipment of Ships Carrying Liquefied Gases in Bulk (IGC Code), administered by the International Maritime Organization (IMO).

[25] See "Post Conference Report: Operational Strategies for LNG Shipping", 27-28 October 2004, Singapore, *Oil & Gas IQ* (International Quality and Productivity Center, or IQPC), p. 3. One presentation features an interesting comparison of the different LNG tanker propulsion systems, which range from steam and gas turbine machinery through dual-fuel diesel electric (DFDE) systems.

Table 2: Advantages and disadvantages of the different types of LNG carriers

MOSS spherical tank design	Membrane tank design	Prismatic tank design (SPB)
Robust (partial loading) Simple High gross tonnage Easy to inspect Collision protection Superior leak containment Restrictions on berthing, higher berthing costs	Complex Lower costs Low gross tonnage Costly labour force required to build ships Advantages for ship-shore offloading	Robust (partial loading) Simpler Higher costs Effective use of space Easy to inspect Collision protection Superior leak containment

Overall, the cost of building a spherical (Moss) type carrier and a membrane type carrier is comparable. Membrane tank systems may become more costly to build in the future, however, because of the rising cost of the highly skilled labour required. Membrane tank systems do offer an appreciable economic advantage related to their gross registered tonnage (GRT). Overall, the cost of LNG tankers has dropped: whereas the price tag for a 138,000 m³ LNG tanker was $280 million in 2005, these vessels now cost $150 million or $160 million.[26] They are still more than double the price of a large crude oil tanker with a comparable cargo capacity, however.

In 2003, based on the delivery dates for LNG carriers recorded in the order books of the leading shipbuilders, the U.S. DOE predicted that the LNG fleet would consist of at least 206 vessels in 2006.[27] The International Energy Agency (IEA) has predicted that by 2010 the fleet will comprise 326 carriers, with 90 of them belonging to Qatar.[28]

Offshore Platforms and LNG Vessels: Growing Interconnectivity

According to the *LNG Observer*, in summer 2006 there were 204 carriers in service[29] and 139 others on the order books, of which the majority were membrane tank vessels (125 out of 139), and the balance (14 vessels) Moss type designs.[30] The

---

[26] See *Liquefied Natural Gas, Understanding the Basic Facts. op. cit.*, p. 8.

[27] See DOE/EIA, *The Global Liquefied Natural Gas Market: Status and Outlook*, December 2003, p. 71. Hereafter cited as *The Global Liquefied Natural Gas Market.* These numbers are not far off, since according to the Groupe international des importateurs de GNL (GIIGNL), 191 tankers were in service at the end of 2005.

[28] *NGMR 2006, op. cit.*, p. 55.

[29] This total includes 106 membrane design vessels and 92 spherical (Moss) design vessels.

[30] See *LNG Observer*, July-September 2006, Vol. 3, No. 3 (Appendix).

South Korean shipping companies Samsung and Daewoo account for the largest number of ships on order (39 each), and Hyundai has 22. In Japan, Mitsubishi and Kawasaki each plan to build nine LNG carriers. It should be noted, however, that South Korean shipyards receive high national subsidies. China is expected to enter the fray soon, raising concerns that there may be too many LNG vessels in the future. One thing is certain: South Korea will face increasingly fierce competition in this area.

Cargo capacity varies from one ship to another, but the largest vessels can transport between 150,000 m^3 and 160,000 m^3 of LNG. At the end of 2005, the 191 carriers in service[31] had a mean capacity of 126,000 m^3. It is predicted that LNG carriers will have a capacity of 200,000 m^3 by 2010 and 250,000 m^3 by 2015.

Until recently, LNG carriers have played an indispensable role in transporting liquefied natural gas. Although they will continue to perform this role, a much more complex landscape is emerging. With the advent of offshore platforms, which have been likened to floating cathedrals, LNG can now be stored and offloaded far from shore. The offshore platforms include Floating Production Storage and Offloading (FPSO)[32] structures and Floating Storage and Regasification Units (FSRU).[33] All the onshore technology can be extended to the offshore environment but this entails substantial additional construction outlays: projects are in the works to build gravity-based concrete structures[34] for storage and regasification; some LNG carriers have been converted into LNG shuttle vessels;[35] others have their own liquefaction systems; and some are supplied with LNG via offloading buoys connected to risers and subsea pipelines.[36] The growing number of platforms provides increased flexibility in terms of transportation and storage options. Furthermore, with the move toward greater independence of storage, regasification and transfer operations, the market is becoming more diversified and this should help to strengthen the spot market (see below).

---

[31]   According to the GIIGNL (Groupe International des Importateurs de GNL), cited in the *LNG Observer*, July-September 2006, p. 21.

[32]   Concept defined as follows by the United Kingdom Offshore Operators Association (UKOOA): "Floating production, storage and offloading vessel which includes, in addition to its storage and offloading capability, facilities for receiving crude oil from producing wells and processing it for export by separating water and gas." See http://www.ukooa.co.uk/issues/fpso/faq.htm. The facilities will be anchored to the sea bottom for a very long time, and they can be used again elsewhere, should the need arise.

[33]   These units typically consist of converted LNG vessels that have no propulsion system, but feature regasification plants. They are floating storage and regasification units. In the United States, the first floating regasification plant, the Excelerate terminal, received its first cargo in March 2005.

[34]   The platform is held on the sea bottom by the weight of the water in its base.

[35]   A shuttle and regasification vessel (SRV), for example.

[36]   One type is the Submerged Turret Loading (STL) system. It is similar to the systems used to load oil tankers. The buoy is anchored to the sea bottom and connected to the undersea pipeline via a riser. The carrier can even weathervane around the turret system. For more details, go to the APL's web site and click on STL.

Flexible cryogenic hose technology, which includes aerial, floating and submerged hoses, is an important element favouring increased interconnectivity of the different offshore platforms. Flexible cryogenic hoses can now be used to transfer LNG between two vessels either in tandem (bow or stern tandem offloading) or side-by-side, and they can be used to supply both onshore and offshore facilities. This technology is helping to reduce wait times at busy ports. In addition, offshore facilities can be sited away from onshore ones, thereby providing a greater margin of safety since LNG carriers do not need to visit the busy and more populated onshore sites.

Exporting Countries

In 2005 the five main LNG exporting countries were Indonesia, Malaysia, Qatar, Algeria and Australia, in that order (see Table 3). In the same year, the spot market accounted for about 13% of LNG deliveries. Five countries are planning to build an LNG train: Egypt, Nigeria, Qatar, Trinity and Tobago as well as Oman.

Based on the statistics available for the first nine months of 2006, the five leading LNG exporting countries were the same, except that Qatar moved to the head of the pack (179.9 million tonnes); Indonesia was in second place (16.6 million tonnes) and Malaysia was in third place (15.5 million tonnes), followed by Algeria with 13 million tonnes and Australia with 10.1 million tonnes. These five countries alone accounted for 63% of global LNG production, which totalled 116.4 tonnes during the first nine months of 2006.[37]

It is unlikely that these countries will hold the same positions in 2010: Indonesian production is declining and Qatar, with three liquefaction plants under construction,[38] is likely to emerge as the front-runner in LNG production. Nigeria, too, is building some large liquefaction plants, while Russia will be a force to reckon with in 2008 with Sakhalin II; it also has two major projects, Yemal[39] and Chtockman, planned for after 2010. Norway and Australia are not resting on their laurels either. According to Ocean Shipping Consultants, Australia's exporting capacity could increase to 19 Bcm and 38 Bcm in 2010 and 2020, respectively.[40] Several African countries are also expected to play an ever-greater role in the future.

---

[37] See Andy Flower, "Will 2007 dispel disappointment sown by 2006?", *LNG Observer*, Vol. 105, No. 16, April 23, 2007.

[38] Qatargas II, Qatargas II, train 5, and the largest, Rasgas II, with a planned capacity of 15.6 mtpa.

[39] The predictions for Yemal are for 2010, but this project is likely to be delayed until Russia has clarified its legal requirements related to foreign investment.

[40] www.osclimited.com/releases/LNGto2020.pdf.

In summary, according to *LNG One World*, the list of upcoming exporting countries includes Angola, Bolivia, Western Timor, Equatorial Guinea, Iran, Norway, Russia, Venezuela and possibly Yemen.[41]

Table 3: LNG exporting countries

		In millions of tonnes	In billions of cubic metres	As a per cent of the total
Asia/Pacific	Indonesia	23.5	29.3	16.6 (rank 1)
	Malaysia	21.8	26.9	15.3 (rank 2)
	Australia	11.4	13.7	7.9 (rank 5)
	Brunei	6.9	8.5	4.9
		63.6	**78.4**	**44.4**
Middle East	Qatar	20.7	25.6	14.5 (rank 3)
	Oman	6.8	8.1	4.7
	Abu Dhabi	5.6	6.8	3.8
		33.1	**40.5**	**23**
Africa	Nigeria	9.3	11.4	6.5
	Algeria	18.7	23.4	13.1 (rank 4)
	Libya	0.7	0.8	0.5
	Egypt	5	6.8	3.8
		33.7	**42.4**	**24**
Western hemisphere	Trinity and Tobago	9.9	13.3	7.4
	United States	1.3	1.8	1.0
		11.2	**15.1**	**8.5**
Total		**141.7**	**176.76**	**100**

Source: From *LNG Observer*, July-September 2006, p. 22.

Iran and Qatar, with 14.7% and 14.3% of world natural gas reserves, could serve as swing producers in the Middle East in relation to both the United States and Europe.[42] If this happens, OECD countries will become dependent on the Middle East, as is already the case in the oil sector.

---

[41] See http://www.lngoneworld.com/lngv1.nsf/members/index.html.

[42] For comparison, see the DOE, *International Energy Outlook 2006, op. cit.* Cited as *IEO2006*.

Importing Countries

The Pacific Basin market emerged in the 1980s and 1990s to serve Asian countries like Japan and South Korea that were grappling with serious shortages of natural resources. For these countries, LNG represented an alternative to oil, and their goal was to secure supplies even at a fairly high cost. In contrast, the Atlantic Basin market came into being later because until the early 1990s, OECD countries had abundant supplies of natural gas thanks to their own reserves and pipeline imports. This situation explains why imports grew by 4.9% for Pacific Basin countries and 12.5% for Atlantic Basin countries during the period 1995-2003.[43]

In the Pacific Basin region, Japan has posted the lowest rate of increase in gas consumption among OECD countries, with the exception of North America. This situation relates to its declining population and limited economic growth. In all other Pacific Basin countries, gas consumption is expected to increase.[44] Imports by Japan (76.3 Bcm), South Korea (30.4 Bcm) and Taiwan (9.6 Bcm) collectively made up 62% of global LNG imports in 2005. These countries depend on LNG for 90% of their natural gas supplies. Despite the slow rate of increase in Japan's gas consumption, this country, with its 26 terminals (3 more than in 2003),[45] is still the leading importer of LNG worldwide. This fuel, which accounts for 12% of Japan's energy basket, is used primarily to generate electricity.[46] South Korea is the second largest LNG importer in the world.[47]

In the space of a year, from 2004 to 2005, India more than doubled its imports.[48] Because of their limited reserves, India and China will likely have to import 40% of their natural gas requirements in 2030. These two countries are key drivers for economic growth, but the development of an LNG market will be hampered by the high price of this fuel. China, which deals mainly with Australia and Indonesia, is lagging behind, with only two LNG terminals under construction at a time when demand from the United States, India and South Korea is expanding rapidly. Wood Mackenzie has nonetheless predicted that eight additional terminals will be constructed

---

43   See Takeo Suzuki and Tetsuo Morikawa, LNG Supply and Demand in Asia Pacific and Atlantic Markets (2004), IEEJ, Industrial Research Unit, November 2005, p. 3.

44   *IEO 2006, op. cit.*

45   The California Energy Commission drew up a list that showed 24 terminals in operation and 3 under construction in Japan in January 2005, *LNG Regasification-Import Terminals in Japan*, http://www.energy.ca.gov/lng/documents/2005-01_LNG_TERMINALS_JAPAN.PDF# search=%22japan%20lng%20terminals%202006%22

46   EIA/DOE, *The Global Liquefied Natural Gas Market, op. cit.*, p. 19.

47   *BP Statistical Review 2006.*

48   They rose from 2.6 Bcm to 6 Bcm.

in China by 2020,[49] four of which have already been approved by the Chinese government. These new projects will be located on the east coast, where access to coal is limited. In 2015, Chinese LNG imports should range from 21 to 26 mtpa.

The United States straddles the Pacific and Atlantic basins. The supplies that reach the East Coast, which currently takes the lion's share of the country's imports,[50] come from the Atlantic Basin. Those unloaded on the West Coast come from Mexico,[51] Australia and Indonesia, or from Pacific Rim countries.[52] New receiving terminals are being built on the U.S. West Coast, and Mexico has already begun to build regasification facilities. Supplies from the Pacific Basin should therefore represent an increasing share of total imports in the coming years.[53] Another major geopolitical element to consider is the widening of the Panama Canal, recently approved by a 78% majority of Panamanians in a referendum. The enlarged canal will give the United States and the Pacific Basin countries (Japan, South Korea) better access to the LNG supplies of countries bordering the Pacific.[54] The IEA predicts that by 2015, imports in the Atlantic Basin will be equivalent to or exceed the volumes exported to Asia.

Europe's LNG imports jumped 19% in 2004-2005.[55] France, with 5.6 million tonnes (7.7 Bcm), was the largest importer in Europe in 2003, compared with 9.4 million tonnes (12.9 Bcm) in 2005. Today, Spain is the fastest growing market in Europe with imports of 16 million tonnes (22.1 Bcm) in 2005.[56] LNG accounts for 58% of Spanish gas supplies. Turkey,[57] Belgium,[58] Italy,[59] Greece[60] and Portugal[61]

---

[49]   See Catriona Scott and William Durbin, "China's LNG Market Development is at Risk", *LNG Observer,* Oil & Gas Journal (OGJ), March-April 2006, p.17.

[50]   Except for Malaysia (0.25 Bcm).

[51]   "Although Mexico has significant untapped natural gas reserves, the Mexican government does not have the resources needed to develop them. Currently, only the state oil and natural gas company, Petroleos Mexicanos (PEMEX), is allowed to have any ownership interest in Mexico's oil and natural gas reserves. Mexico is expected to be dependent on pipeline imports from the United States and on LNG imports to meet its growing shortfall." *IEO2006, op. cit.*

[52]   David Maul, *LNG Overview,* California Energy Commission, September 3, 2003, http://www.energy.ca.gov/lng/faq.html#200, p. 20.

[53]   OECD/IEA, *Security of Gas Supply on Open Markets: LNG and Power at a Turning Point,* p. 161. Hereafter cited as *Security of Gas Supply.*

[54]   See Agence France Presse (AFP), *Les Panaméens plébiscitent l'élargissement du canal,* October 23, 2006; and Robert Wright, "Bigger Panama Locks the Key to Trade", *The Australian,* October 21, 2006, http://www.theaustralian.news.com.au/story/0,20867,20616263-36375,00.html.

[55]   *BP Statistical Review 2006.*

[56]   *BP Statistical Review 2006.*

[57]   With 3.6 million tonnes or 4.9 Bcm.

[58]   With 2.2 million tonnes or 3 Bcm.

[59]   With 1.8 million tonnes or 2.5 Bcm.

[60]   With 0.3 million tonnes or 0.4 Bcm.

[61]   With 1.1 million tonnes or 1.5 Bcm.

recently jumped on the bandwagon. The first three countries are planning to increase their capacity, whereas the others are just beginning to import LNG. The Netherlands wants to do the same,[62] and Germany, Poland and Croatia are also on the verge of building terminals.[63]

Table 4: The main LNG importing countries

		In millions of tonnes	In billions of cubic metres	As a per cent of the total
Asia/Pacific	Japan	58.1	71.5	40.4 (rank 1)
	South Korea	22.5	27.7	15.7 (rank 2)
	Taiwan	7.2	8.9	5.1
	India	4.6	5.7	3.2
		92.4	**113.8**	**64.4**
Europe	Spain	17.0	21.4	12.1 (rank 3)
	France	9.7	12.2	6.9 (rank 5)
	Turkey	3.4	4.3	2.4
	Belgium	2.0	2.5	1.4
	Italy	1.8	2.3	1.3
	Portugal	1.6	1.6	0.9
	United Kingdom	0.4	0.5	0.3
	Greece	0.3	0.4	0.2
		36.2	**44.8**	**25.4**
Western hemisphere	United States	12.5	16.9	9.4 (rank 4)
	Puerto Rico	0.5	0.6	0.4
	Dominican Republic	0.2	0.3	0.1
		13.2	**17.8**	**10.1**
Total		**141.7**	**176.8**	**100**

Source: *LNG Observer*, July-September 2006, p. 23.

In 2005, the five leading LNG importers (in descending order) were Japan, South Korea, Spain, the United States and France. Asia accounts for nearly 65% of LNG

---

[62] EIA/DOE, *The Global Liquefied Natural Gas Market: Status and Outlook*, Washington, December 2003, http://www.eia.doe.gov/oiaf/analysispaper/global/, p. 17 and pp. 22-24.

[63] *IEO 2006, op. cit.*

imports. OECD countries, which include Japan, dominate the market, importing 93% of global LNG production.[64] It has been forecast that, by 2010, at least 15 other countries will join the list of 15 countries that currently import LNG.[65] *LNG One World* identifies 11 countries as future importers: Brazil, Canada, China, Germany, Hong Kong, Jamaica, the Netherlands, New Zealand, Pakistan, Singapore and Thailand.[66]

Dependence on LNG is unequally distributed, with Japan and Spain being highly dependent, whereas France is less dependent and the United States is even less so.[67] European and North American demand for LNG supplies from non-OPEC countries is expected to be up 10% by 2010.

Emergence of a Spot Market

Until the 1990s, the LNG market was very rigid. Because of their strong dependence on imports, Asian countries had emphasized security of supply by going after sale and purchase agreements (SPAs) with terms of 20 to 25 years. As a rule, facilities were not built until sales contracts were signed to cover the entire capacity. Buyers had to agree to take-or-pay clauses that shifted the volume risk to them. Furthermore, sellers imposed delivery under CIF (cost, insurance and freight) contracts[68] and these contracts contained "destination clauses" that prevented buyers from reselling the cargoes to third parties. That is how "destination contracts" came into being.[69]

In the 1990s, the situation changed with the emergence of new suppliers (Middle East) and new buyers (United States, Europe, India and China). By offering more attractive prices to India and China, producers encouraged all buyers to seek lower

---

[64] *NGMR 2006, op. cit.*, p. 35.

[65] See "New Projects Lead to a Boom in the Global LNG Market: Industry Analysis (2005-2010)", at http://www.researchandmarkets.com/reports/302688/302688.htm. This study refers to 35 LNG importing countries.

[66] See http://www.lngoneworld.com/lngv1.nsf/members/index.html.

[67] *Ibid*, p. 37.

[68] CIF designates a mode of delivery, also called Incoterm, under which the seller bears all costs (including insurance and transport) associated with the cargo. Under an FOB contract, the cargo is delivered directly onto the principal buyer's vessel, and from that point on, the costs fall to the buyer. This gives the buyer less security in terms of transport but more freedom to determine the destination of the cargo, since it is delivered directly onto its ship rather than to the port of destination.

[69] James T. Jensen, "Pacific Rim LNG market to grow but uncertainties loom", *LNG Observer*, April-June 2006, p. 5. See also IEA, *Security of Gas Supply on Open Markets: LNG and Power at a Turning Point*, http://www.eia.doe.gov/cneaf/electricity/chg_stru_update/chapter9.html, p. 115.

prices and more favourable clauses when renegotiating their contracts. To be ready for the expansion and globalization of the market, producers and buyers have sought increased flexibility related to volumes and contract duration. The mode of delivery has also become more flexible. In most new contracts, clients opt for FOB (Free on Board), which enables them to resell part of the cargo if they have a surplus. That is why Europe has put pressure on LNG sellers to remove destination clauses from their contracts.[70]

> When Asian buyers renew their existing contracts, they seek terms of 15 to 20 years rather than 20 to 25 years, greater flexibility to resell volumes and FOB arrangements instead of the CIF provisions that dominated earlier contracts. The contracts signed in February 2002 between Japan and Malaysia were the first signs of a change in LNG marketing in Asia.[71]

The increased flexibility of contracts, along with the surpluses that came onto the market as a result of the Asian financial crisis of 1997-1998,[72] led to the emergence of the short-term market, also called the spot market. On this market, any participant can immediately resell its excess volumes through short-term (spot) transactions, or make spot purchases of LNG as needed and especially to cover seasonal increases in demand.[73] In addition, market arrangements such as swaps and/or self-contracting have developed over time, which enable buyers to make cargo delivery arrangements to cover the operations of their partner terminals or downstream affiliates. By building greater flexibility into destination points encompassing several continents, downstream affiliates allow LNG deliveries to be routed to the most profitable markets.[74]

---

[70] EIA/DOE, *The Global Liquefied Natural Gas Market, op. cit.,* p. 38. See also the article "World LNG Market Structure", http://www.eia.doe.gov/oiaf/analysispaper/global/lngmarket.html and OECD/IEA, *Security of Gas Supply, op. cit.,* p.111.

[71] OECD/IEA, *Security of Gas Supply, op. cit.,* Table p. 164.

[72] Following the Asian financial crisis of 1997-1998, Japan and South Korea ended up with surplus LNG, prompting them to seek greater flexibility in contracts so that the supply system would be less rigid. They wanted to be able to resell part of their cargoes on the spot market. It is for this reason that the South Korean government prohibited Kogas from signing long-term contracts, OECD/IEA, *Security of Gas Supply, op. cit.,* p. 164.

[73] Spot sales give producers an alternative means of selling excess capacity while a project is under construction and they allow buyers to supplement their long-term purchases, *Security of Gas Supply, op. cit.,* p. 41.

[74] Catriona Scott and William Durbin, "China's LNG Market Development is at Risk", *LNG Observer,* March-April 2006, pp. 17-18.

The spot market emerged in the United States and in the United Kingdom during a period of overcapacity, when domestic supply was more than sufficient to meet domestic requirements.[75] If their reserves were depleted, these two countries might opt to enter into long-term contracts with a view to securing their LNG supplies. That is precisely what ConocoPhillips and ExxonMobil have done with Qatar as their supplier. By contrast, European and Asian countries stand to gain from a more flexible LNG marketplace since this will enable them to diversify their sources of supply and reduce their level of dependence.

John Malone of John S. Herold, Inc. has said that, with the emergence of the spot market, U.S. companies now have two different strategies they can adopt. To minimize the cost of their supplies, they can establish an integrated supply chain based on tankers with 40% greater than average loading capacity and company-owned regasification terminals. While this strategy offers obvious financial benefits, it limits flexibility in the choice of suppliers and in the mode of delivery, given that few port facilities can accommodate huge LNG carriers. A problem anywhere along the LNG chain could cause a disruption in supplies. Companies like RDS, Total and BG Group have chosen instead to diversify their portfolios by investing in various liquefaction and regasification projects and focussing on smaller, more mobile carriers so they can take advantage of the arbitrage system[76] linking markets.[77] Companies often adopt a two-pronged approach in making their LNG purchases:

Buyers adopt a portfolio approach to purchasing gas by combining traditional long-term contracts with renegotiated long-term contracts and spot purchases.[78]

Overall, however, long-term contracts are going to dominate the development of LGN facilities, since these facilities call for significant investments that can only be secured through firm purchase arrangements.

---

[75] "It should be noted that in the case of both North America and the UK, this model was developed in markets characterized by overcapacity of domestic supplies." OECD/IEA, *Security of Gas Supply*, p. 86.

[76] We will come back to the topic of arbitrage.

[77] John Malone, "LNG gives multinational companies a competitive hedge", John S. Herold, Inc., March 6, 2006, p. 3.

[78] OECD/IEA, *Security of Gas Supply, op. cit.*, p. 105.

Prices and Arbitrage

There are three different **price systems** for LNG at present. In Asia, LNG prices are linked to crude oil prices. Over the past 10 years, prices have tended to be higher in the Pacific Basin than in the Atlantic Basin. LNG prices are on the rise in the United States since they are indexed to the price of natural gas, creating highly volatile market conditions. In the United States, the benchmark price is either a specific market price for long-term contracts or the Henry Hub price for short-term (spot) sales.[79] In Europe, not including the United Kingdom,[80] LNG prices are related to the price of low-sulphur residual fuel oil, which is used in electricity generation.

The separation of gas supply from terminal operations and the opening up of terminals to third parties (Third Party Access –TPA[81]) has facilitated LNG shipping.[82] Since this mechanism was introduced, gas hubs offering a range of services have sprung up in the United States, Belgium and the United Kingdom:

> At its Zeebrugge LNG terminal, Fluxys offers receiving and offloading services for LNG carriers, regulatory storage for offloaded LNG, regasification and transfer to the Fluxys grid for final delivery.[83]

There are regional (physical) hubs in which transfers are made from specific geographic locations, and virtual hubs which permit trading of gas that has been physically routed to any location on a given grid. One example of a virtual hub is the UK National Balancing Point (NBP). Once gas trading systems are interconnected locally, with storage capacities, transport facilities and arrangements for

---

[79] Spot purchase: "A short-term single shipment sale of a commodity, including electricity or gas, purchased for delivery within one year, generally on an interruptible or best efforts basis. Spot purchases are often made to fulfill a certain portion of energy requirements, to meet unanticipated energy needs, or to take advantage of low prices." Definition from the *Glossary of Terms* on the Duke Energy web site.

[80] A gas market is emerging on the European continent with a new index. In the United Kingdom, sales are already indexed to the price of natural gas, and the price of LNG is indexed to the *National Balancing Point*, OECD/IEA, *Security of Gas Supply, op. cit.*, pp. 192-195.

[81] "TPA –Third-party access: the right or possibility for a third party to make use of the transportation or distribution services of a pipeline company to move its own gas, while paying a set or negotiated charge." OECD/IEA, *Security of Gas Supply, op. cit.*, p. 481.

[82] Miguel Martin, "Shipping Schedules in a Regulated Third Party Access Market", *OGEL*, Vol. 4, No. 1, May 2006.

[83] Fluxys, a natural gas transport company, provides electronic processing of customer requests and delivery services from the Zeebrugge LNG terminal: the Zeebrugge Hub on the Fluxys web site.

dealing with temporary imbalances (*balancing*[84]) and title transfers, the hubs, with their shipping and management tools,[85] become true **markets**.[86]

Through the development of hubs and spot markets, market liberalization has brought greater flexibility and interconnected gas trading and financial platforms.[87] New transportation networks[88] develop, giving rise to new energy and commodities **exchange organizations**. With regard to Europe, we can give the NBP[89] as an example once again, but there are also some more recent exchange facilities such as the Moscow Interbank Currency Exchange (MICEX[90]) and the Russian Trade System (RTS[91]), which were established in Russia in the 1990s. These financial networks are having a unifying effect on the European continent, somewhat like what happened earlier in North America mainly because of the influence of the New York Mercantile Exchange (NYMEX) in the United States and the Natural Gas Exchange (NGX) in Canada.[92]

Hubs and markets can provide opportunities for price arbitrage. **Arbitrage** is defined as follows: "trading the same security, currency or commodity in two or more markets in order to profit from differences in prices."[93] The destination of LNG cargoes is determined by the price on the spot market, which is itself determined in real time. The cargo is sold to the highest bidder in a sort of auction system that plays on differences in price.[94] Arbitrage may give rise over the long term to a convergence of prices between the different basins.

In recent years, an arbitrage market has developed in the Atlantic Basin centring on supplies from Trinidad, Nigeria and Algeria trading off the U.S. terminals

---

[84] *Balancing* is a short-term arrangement that can be used to cover a temporary imbalance. This service is often combined with other delivery arrangements such as parking and loaning. See OECD/IEA, *Security of Gas Supply, op. cit.*, p. 77.

[85] See "Do You Know Your Market Hub?" Uniongas, on the Uniongas Web site.

[86] Spot markets are like auctions, with LNG cargoes going to the highest bidder.

[87] "APX launches gas exchanges for the Zeebrugge Hub and the TTF", February 2005 press release on the Fluxys web site.

[88] The Norwegian pipeline network is a perfect illustration of this phenomenon: http://www.hydro.com/en/our_business/oil_energy/sales_distribution/gas_transport/

[89] OECD/IEA, *Security of Gas Supply, op. cit.*, pp. 79-81.

[90] http://www.micex.com/profile/

[91] http://www.rts.ru/?tid=602 and see the article on the start of trading in oil contracts: http://www.energybulletin.net/16509.html

[92] TSX covers the North American continent, linking Canada and the United States: http://www.tsx.com/en/about_tsx/corporate_information/index.html.

[93] Definition from the *Glossary of Terms* on the Duke Energy web site.

[94] Cargoes follow gas prices. See Figure 5, "Prix du gaz et arbitrages entre marches", (June 2000 to December 2005), Marie-Françoise Chabrelie, Cedigaz, "Le GNL : une commodité en devenir", *Panorama 2006*, Institut français du pétrole (IFP), January 2006, p. 7.

against Spain and Belgium on the European side. LNG cargoes have also been swapped with European cargoes when prices were more favourable on the US market.[95]

There are more arbitrage opportunities for the Atlantic Basin because Middle East countries, capitalizing on their geographic location, can choose to deliver either to the east or to the west. James T. Jensen referred to Qatar as the "Henry Hub of LNG."

The arbitrage system does not work as well in the Pacific Rim because of the distances involved and the absence of arbitraging partners on either side of the ocean, which explains why spot deliveries to South Korea are more stable than those to the United States. In 2004, Korean and Japanese buyers managed to divert LNG cargoes that normally would have gone to the United States.[96]

"Not only did the flow of LNG cargoes into the US from east of Suez entirely stop in August [2004] but a number of cargoes from Atlantic Basin suppliers were sold to Korean and Japanese buyers, who were prepared to offer the producers higher prices than those available in the U.S. market."[97]

In short, when there is a close balance between supply and demand, LNG trade flows tend to switch between markets. According to Andy Flower, we have gone from a buyers' market to a sellers' market, and it is the highest bidder who prevails.[98]

Security and Reliability of LNG Facilities

In the case of nuclear power plants, the security of operations is viewed as being dependent on the reliability of the main facility components. Many different calculation methods are used to predict the probability of accidents (probabilistic risk analysis) and to minimize the consequences of an accident. Even if there is no such thing as zero risk, it is always possible to reduce "residual risk by strengthening the

---

[95] OECD/IEA, *Security of Gas Supply*, *op. cit.*, p. 247.

[96] James T. Jensen said that the Japanese price is higher than the Spanish price and that the United States is an attractive market when prices are high. The United States is more transparent in relation to prices than Spain and South Korea. He also pointed out that it is cheaper to serve the North American west coast by routing supplies from either Sakhalin or Southeast Asia–Australia. James T. Jensen, "Pacific Rim LNG Market to Grow but Uncertainties Loom", *LNG Observer*, Vol. 3, Issue 2, April 3, 2006, pp. 5-8

[97] Andy Flower, "Immediate Future Clouded by Potential Supply Constraints", *LNG Observer*, Vol. 2, Issue 1, January 3, 2005, p. 8.

[98] *Ibid.*

weak links in a facility's design at a given time."[99] The same principle applies to the entire LNG supply chain. Since this fuel is transported by ship for the most part, the concept of maritime security also takes in military or police preventive measures aimed at protecting facilities from terrorist attack.

Security Levels

A study by Michele Michot Foss examines **primary** and **secondary containment** as the two main levels of security for both LNG tanks and double-hull carriers. The third level is based on alarm systems and emergency shutdown systems (ESD), which are designed mainly for fire protection. A fourth level of security seeks to reduce risks by segregating key LNG facilities from residential areas or by enlarging the security zone around tankers in transit, which is the zone that other ships are not allowed to enter.[100]

The Foss study on LNG security mentions some 25 accidents that occurred somewhere along the LNG chain during the period 1944-2002. So far, there have been no major accidents (no loss of life) aboard an LNG carrier. This security record is impressive especially considering the loss of human life (618 crew members) that occurred in connection with the disappearance at sea of 116 bulk carriers during the decade 1991-2001[101]. An accident involving an LNG carrier nonetheless occurred in 1944, when the tank contents spread into the Cleveland sewer system and the ensuing explosion killed 128 people. In 1973, 40 people died when a storage tank exploded on Staten Island, New York. In Skikda, Algeria, an LNG train exploded in January 2004, killing 27 people and injuring 70 others. This disaster followed an accident that occurred in Tiga, Malaysia in August 2003, when a propane compressor exploded, putting the Petronas firm's train 7 out of service.

Maritime Security

Since September 11, 2001, the topic of security has made the headlines almost every day. The main concern in the maritime sector relates to the security of LNG

---

[99] See "La sûreté des centrales nucléaires", Commission Ampère, Belgique, at http://www.ulb.ac.be/sciences/intra/inforsc_archives/nrj/ampere/ampere3.html.

[100] See Michele Michot Foss, Center for Energy Economics (CEE), *LNG Safety and Security*, October 2003, Table 4, p. 77. Hereafter cited as Foss. A January 2005 report prepared by Aspen Environmental Group for the California Energy Commission reviews security issues related to the principal LNG facilities around the world. See "International and National Efforts to Address the Safety and Security Risk of Importing Liquefied Natural Gas: A Compendium", *California Energy Commission* (CEC), January 2005.

[101] Philippe Rocchesani "Les transports maritimes des marchandises en vrac", available at www.cdmt.droit.u-3mrs.fr/memoires/2002/m02roph.html.

carriers, which are attractive targets for a terrorist attack.[102] While some authors such as Andrew Clifton believe that an attack on a tanker would not cause significant mortality,[103] a view also expressed by the OECD Maritime Transport Committee,[104] others are less optimistic.[105]

In order to more effectively "combat illicit and malicious acts and terrorism which threaten the security of ships and their crews and port facilities", the International Maritime Organization (IMO), whose mission is to strengthen maritime security and prevent ship pollution, adopted the International Ship and Port Facility Security Code (ISPS).[106] The ISPS Code is implemented through Chapter XI-2, entitled "Special measures to enhance maritime safety", of the International Convention for the Safety of Life at Sea (SOLAS), as amended in December 2002.[107] "Since July 2004, LNG tankers arriving from a country that has not ensured ship compliance with the ISPS Code are to be refused access to other ports."[108] The ISPS Code applies to Contracting Governments, ships, shipping companies and ports, and sets out documentary and certification requirements. The OECD has estimated that shipping companies will have to spend at least $1.3 billion up front just to implement the new code initially and $730 million per year thereafter. The requirement to designate a security officer within the shipping company entails the largest outlay.[109]

---

[102] "There is no shortage of examples attesting to the relevance of this analysis, including the suicide attack on the American destroyer U.S.S. *Cole* in October 2000; the attack on the French supertanker *Limburg* off the coast of Yemen in October 2002; and even more recently, the attack against the Bassora oil terminal in Iraq in April 2004." See Simon Delfeau, "La sûreté maritime", *Revue Juridique Neptunus,* Centre de droit maritime et océanique (CDMO), Spring 2005, Vol. 11, No. 1, p. 1.

[103] "Contrary to popular belief, a terrorist attack on a LNG tanker is unlikely to produce large-scale loss of life": Andrew Clifton, "LNG on the Boil", *Seaways,* February 2005, p. 4.

[104] According to the committee, LNG tankers are so well protected with their double hull that even incidents such as a fire aboard a vessel and a missile attack have not caused them to explode. See "Security in Maritime Transport: Risk Factors and Economic Impact", OECD, Maritime Transport Committee, July 2003, p. 10.

[105] "Study: LNG – Not in my backyard", Institute for the Analysis of Global Security (IAGS), July 2004, http://www.iags.org/n0121041.htm

[106] "The Code, which came into effect on July 1, 2004, applies to all ships engaged on international voyages: passenger ships, cargo ships of 500 gross tonnage and upwards and mobile offshore drilling units." http://www.mer.equipement.gouv.fr/securite/00_presentation/presentation_securite.htm

[107] "IMO adopts comprehensive maritime security measures", http://www.imo.org/Newsroom/mainframe.asp?topic_id=583&doc_id=2689. See also Marilou Grégoire-Blais, Bulletin n° 71, *Le maintien de la paix*, "Sécurité maritime et terrorisme", available on the web site of the Centre d'études des politiques étrangères et de sécurité (CEPES), Université du Québec à Montréal (UQAM).

[108] "Sécurité Maritime : Des experts américains au port d'Arzew", *HYPROC News*, n°2, September 2004, http://www.hyproc.com/fr/images/hyproc_news01.pdf

[109] This cost does not include the establishment of automated systems, OECD, *Security in Maritime Transport: Risk Factors and Economic Impact*, Maritime Transport Committee, July 2003, p. 29 and pp. 38-39.

The inspection measures put in place by the U.S. Coast Guard to ensure safety and security in connection with LNG carriers that transit through Boston Harbor, specifically around the Everett Terminal, illustrate the tightening of security in the United States in the wake of the events of September 11, 2001: occasional on-board escort; 96 hours' advance notice of the arrival of an LNG tanker; inspection of ship before it enters Boston Harbor; harbour escort by armed patrol vessels; enforcement of a security zone around the tanker; suspension of overflights by commercial aircraft; inspection of adjacent piers for bombs; posting of sharpshooters on nearby rooftops; and additional security measures which cannot be disclosed publicly.[110] These types of strict measures vary from port to port, with mandatory escort being a requirement particularly in strategic regions along the southern portion of the U.S. coasts.

To ensure LNG shipping security, the United States and all other IMO member states will have to strengthen security in their port facilities and along their coast-lines, as well as broaden their control of the seas, in areas often less familiar to them such as the Pacific Basin and the Arctic Ocean. Although ensuring port security is essential, shipping routes are equally vulnerable to incidents and acts of terrorism. If a tanker were to sink or explode in the middle of a strait, this would disrupt LNG supplies and all other flows of trade through the passage.[111] This explains why the United States is stepping up its monitoring and surveillance efforts, particularly in the straits of Hormuz, Malacca and Bab el Mandeb, where the U.S. presence is increasing.[112] The OECD has identified nine vulnerable points on a nautical chart: the Suez and Panama canals, Cape of Good Hope, Bosphorus, the straits of Hormuz, Malacca and Bab el Mandeb, and those of Gibraltar and Magellan.[113]

Security of LNG Facilities

LNG liquefaction and regasification facilities are designed to prevent fires and contain the LNG in the event of one. They therefore have to meet various standards at the regional, national and federal levels.[114]

---

[110] Paul W. Parfomak, *Liquefied Natural Gas (LNG), Infrastructure Security: Issues for Congress*, CRS Report for Congress, March 2005, http://ncseonline.org/nle/crsreports/05mar/RL32073.pdf

[111] OECD, *Security in Maritime Transport: Risk Factors and Economic Impact*, July 2003, *op. cit.* See graph entitled "Terrorist Risk Factors from Shipping", p. 7.

[112] "La lutte contre le terrorisme : des moyens juridico-militaires d'une efficacité variable", *Fiches de l'atelier énergie du Master de Géopolitique 2004-2005*, Université de Paris I, http://www. geostrategie.ens.fr/etudes/hydrocarbures/fiches/1.3.Terrorisme_moyens.html

[113] *Ibid*, p. 13.

[114] EIA/DOE, *The Global Liquefied Natural Gas Market, op. cit.*, p. 3.

Around the world, there are many regulatory requirements pertaining to LNG security and associated environmental issues.[115] In Canada, for example, under the Rabaska project, companies are required to conduct a risk analysis and an environmental assessment to meet government requirements related to safety[116] and the environment.[117] Security requirements for the tabling of the Rabaska file called for descriptions of the following aspects: the project in its entirety, specifically, the terminal, the gas pipeline, the marine jetty and the tankers;[118] potential incidents and the response measures; training for staff; and the emergency response plan and alarm system. Companies that own facilities are required to put in place environmental protection measures: "environmental mitigation measures may be set out in the environmental and socio-economic assessment and then compiled into an environmental protection plan prior to construction."[119] Technical requirements related to LNG, such as the description of the boil-off gas treatment systems, the combustible gas system, pressure vessels and boilers, ventilation equipment, containment measures for LNG leaks and pertinent auxiliary facilities, are also part of this list.

The future of LNG

Demand for Natural Gas

Projections of the share of different fuels in world energy consumption for 2015 and 2030 include both good news and bad news. According to the *International Energy Outlook 2006 (IEO2006)*, oil's share of total world energy use should fall 6% between 2003 and 2030, which is a significant drop, and the share of natural gas should increase by 3% over the same period (see Figure 5). Coal is expected to increase its share by 3%, primarily because of the projected increase in natural gas prices,[120] while the share of renewable energies should rise 1% and nuclear power should lose 1%.

---

[115] For details concerning the decision-making process, see "Liquified Natural Gas Regulatory Requirements", on the web site of *Natural Resources Canada* and "Liquefied Natural Gas: Understanding the Basic Facts", on the web site of *FERC*, August 2005, pp. 16-22.

[116] "Projet Rabaska: la sécurité", at http://www.rabaska.net/page.php?ids=7&idL=fr.

[117] Preliminary Environmental Impact Study, http://www.rabaska.net/page.php?idS=7&idL=en

[118] "Include the volumetric capacity and the flow rates of all project components, that is, the tanker(s), offloading arms, storage tank(s), regasification plant and the connecting pipeline."

[119] Rabaska Project LNG Filing Requirements (October 1, 2004), web site of Natural Resources Canada.

[120] This assumption is especially relevant for the United States. Concerning the projections in the *Annual Energy Outlook 2006*, which deals with domestic U.S. demand, the DOE stated: "The AEO2006 reference case in general projects lower total natural gas consumption than in the other projections, and it is the only one showing a period of decline. The exception is in the early part of the projection period: in 2015, PIRA and Deutsche Bank AG (DB) project lower natural gas consumption than the AEO2006 reference case, but by 2025 the AEO2006 reference case projects lower consumption than any of the others. The primary reason is that AEO2006 expects a stronger demand response to higher natural gas prices, particularly in the electricity generation sector." This document covers projections from eight different sources produced by different organizations. See http://www.eia.doe.gov/oiaf/aeo/forecast.html.

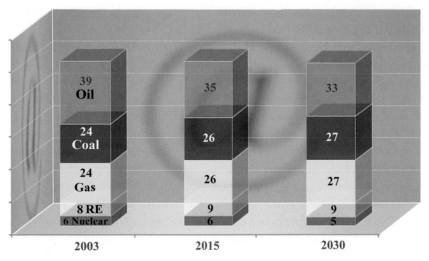

Figure 5: World energy use (2003, 2015 and 2030)
Percent share of different fuels
Source: DOE, *IEO 2006*

The *IEO 2006* forecasts an increase of 2.4% in world gas demand during the period 2003-2030. As already discussed, this demand is driven by the needs of the electricity sector (2.9% per year) and of industry (2.8% per year). The outlook varies from region to region. Since China is expected to post a mean annual increase of 6.7% in its demand during this period, and India, an increase of 4.8%, these two countries will play an enormous role in driving demand. OECD countries (Europe) are expected to maintain an annual demand growth rate of 1.9% compared with 1.2% for North America (United States, Canada and Mexico). Developing countries will account for two thirds, if not more, of the overall increase in demand. Africa is expected to post a mean annual increase of 5.2%, positioning it between India and China. According to IEA projections,[121] annual demand in North America will increase to 140 Bcm by 2030, while the corresponding increase for China and India will be 80 Bcm and annual European demand will amount to some 500 Bcm.

Demand for LNG

The Atlantic and Pacific basins obviously represent the two main importing basins.[122] Qatar will be the driving force for supply growth, and its production is

---

[121] Figures cited in *World Energy in 2006*, published by the World Energy Council, p. 15.

[122] The Asia Pacific Basin encompasses South Asia, India, Russia and Alaska. The Atlantic Basin is comprised of LNG activity in Europe, Western and Northern Africa, the U.S. East Coast and the Gulf of Mexico.

expected to exceed 100 Bcm in 2010, enabling it to supply both basins simultaneously and promote the emergence of a strengthened spot market. According to the IEA, the spot market could represent 20% of all supply contracts in 2010.

According to the IEA, in 2015 LNG could make up 14-16% of the global gas trade. And according to an April 2004 study by Ocean Shipping Consultants (OSC), the international LNG trade, which stood at 153 Bcm in 2003, will expand to 269 Bcm in 2010 and to 429 Bcm in 2020. These figures represent an increase of 70% and 172% in relation to the reference years used.

In 2020, Eastern Asia and Western Europe are each expected to import about 181 Bcm of LNG.[123] The projections for the United States have been revised downwards significantly in relation to those of 2004 and 2005. The *Annual Energy Outlook 2007* (*AEO 2007*) projects annual imports totalling 4.5 Tcf (trillion cubic feet) in 2030.[124] This sharp decrease from previous projections relates to the projected increase in gas prices, on the one hand, and to the use of coal as an alternative fuel for electricity generation, on the other. LNG's share of natural gas imports to the United States was only 2.5% in 2005; however, it should reach 9% in 2010 and 14% in 2020.[125] In 2005, the corresponding share for Europe was 9%. The growth in U.S. demand is due partly to the drop in Canadian gas exports to the United States.

LNG looks like it is headed for a promising future. The tanker fleet is growing rapidly[126] and existing liquefaction and regasification capacities, along with the capacity associated with facilities that are under construction, are enormous. Europe is well endowed in terms of regasification capacity. According to the IEA, LNG capacity will be "more than enough", which means that it will exceed demand.[127]

---

[123] This compares with projected imports of 139 Bcm in 2010.

[124] See *AEO 2007*, p. 94. According to R. Petak, Vice President of Energy and Environmental Analysis Inc. (EEAI), a subsidiary of ICF International, LNG imports to the United States will increase to 13.2 Bcf/d in 2017 and to 18.6 Bcf/d in 2025. *Oil & Gas Journal*, April 9, 2007, p. 31.

[125] *Ibid.*

[126] According to Ocean Shipping Consultants (OSC), from 2010 to 2020, it will increase from 30.4 to 52.4 million m³ (MMcm).

[127] Japan and South Korea have 28 regasification terminals with a total capacity of 290 Bcm (billion cubic metres) per year. In 2005, Europe's total capacity was 76 Bcm, but since it has seven terminals under construction, its capacity could expand to more than 140 Bcm in 2010.

Factors Affecting Demand

Alternative Energy Sources

Many factors may affect these projections. In an editorial in the *LNG Observer*, Warren R. True points out that many other fuels compete with natural gas for electricity generation.[128] Over the next 25 years, natural gas will experience greater growth than the other fuels. However, biomass is making inroads (see Chapter 4) and alternative energy sources are numerous, ranging from biomass sources to thermal power plants combining coal and an integrated gasification system, referred to as Integrated Gasification Coal Combined Cycle, or IGCC.[129] Wind energy is obviously another alternative source of energy that could come into play (see Chapter 4).

Storage Capacities

Following the Arab-Israeli war of 1973 in the Middle East, the fear of a disruption of oil supplies led OECD countries to build and maintain stocks equivalent to a 90-day domestic supply. The United States has a major Strategic Petroleum Reserve (SPR) consisting of about 700 million barrels, a quantity that is to be increased to 1 billion barrels in accordance with the Energy Policy Act (EPAC) of 2005.

Like oil, natural gas can be stored in depleted oil and gas reservoirs (sinks), in deep aquifers or in salt caverns. There is no international legislative framework for the establishment of gas reserves of this sort, but some countries have enacted legislation with the aim of providing a buffer against supply shortages arising from emergency situations such as hurricanes and severe storms and to be able to meet increased consumption requirements associated with cold winters.

In the United States, there are 390 underground storage facilities, most of which are concentrated in the Southeast, including the Gulf of Mexico region.[130] In 2000, the Federal Energy Regulatory Commission (FERC) authorized new storage capacities estimated at 263 Bcf (billion cubic feet) with an estimated delivery capacity of 12.4 Bcf per day. When the seven LNG terminals slated for construction in the

---

[128] See Warren R. True, "Sobering Perspectives", *LNG Observer*, July-September 2006, p. 3.

[129] A combined-cycle plant uses a gas turbine and a steam turbine in combination. Clean coal is used and a synthetic gas is produced in a gasifier. These plants can operate at efficiencies of over 50%. Although in the testing stage at present, these plants are expected to have a promising future. See "Fonctionnement d'une centrale à cycle combiné" on the CD-Rom entitled *L'ère de l'énergie*, Productions COTARDI.

[130] Compared with some 680,000 underground oil storage facilities, most created for the purpose of storing and delivering gasoline within a short time period.

United States are completed, the deliverable volume capacity will reach 19 Bcf per day.[131] In mid-2001, U.S. storage capacity at LNG facilities stood at 86 Bcf.[132]

Storage capacities obviously vary by country. Storage capacity is equivalent to 8% of domestic consumption in Spain, 17% in the United States and 3% in England.[133] While these quantities are too small to permit price manipulation, they can be used to respond to emergency situations and to strengthen the spot market for natural gas. Spanish ports are overwhelmed during the summer, and a number of cargoes have to be re-routed to the United States. In the winter, the United States and Europe compete directly with each another to build up their storage inventories.

France's natural gas storage capacity is equal to 26% of its annual consumption, while Austria, France, Germany and Italy together "hold more than 22% of their annual demand in the form of storage inventories."[134]

All such storage sites are not necessarily located near the regions needing to be supplied in an emergency. The establishment of LNG reserves on the U.S. East Coast would mean that companies would not have to convey gas by pipeline from north to south in an emergency. In addition, the establishment of inventories adds value to the stored quantities, because storing LNG in the summer when demand is weak provides the possibility of reselling it in winter at a higher price, when demand is stronger. Storage policies can help to reduce price volatility and push prices downward. They are therefore a key element in the natural gas supply chain; they constitute an instrument for regulating the gas market. The same is true of refinery stocks.[135] FERC has summarized the advantages of storing LNG as follows: "Shifts supply from when it is not needed to when it is; Shifts supply from when it is not valued to when it is."[136]

National Legislation

An important factor that can contribute to increased natural gas consumption is existing legislation in gas importing countries. An aggressive policy aimed at reducing greenhouse gas (GHG) emissions might boost consumption of natural gas, which is a clean, non-polluting energy source, in contrast with coal and oil.

---

[131] See Federal Energy Regulatory Commission (FERC), *Summer 2006 Storage Overview*, Item No. A-3, June 15, 2006, p. 6. A permanent inventory of cushion (base) gas must be maintained in the storage field to provide the pressure necessary to extract the working gas and ensure deliverability to distribution networks.

[132] See Foss, *op. cit.*

[133] See *Ibid*, p. 8.

[134] See Ministère de l'Économie, des Finances et de l'Industrie, DGEMP, February 14, 2006 at http://www.industrie.gouv.fr/energie/gaz/stockages.htm.

[135] For example, gas prices rise in a situation of excessively low inventories.

[136] *Ibid*, p. 11.

Similarly, policies aimed at encouraging the development of renewable energies can reduce the share of polluting energy sources in a country's energy budget (see Chapter 4). Here again, the issue of the mix of fuels in a country's energy policy needs to be taken into consideration in the overall assessment of natural gas demand.

Final Considerations

Several conclusions can be drawn regarding future trends of LNG consumption per country. First, long-term contracts will continue to set the scene for the development of the LNG market. Secondly, according to the *IEO 2006*, LNG imports will account for more than 20% of domestic consumption in the United States by 2030 and for 78% of net imports of natural gas.[137]

The magnitude of such imports will have very little effect on natural gas prices in the United States, however. This situation is attributable to the size of U.S. industries and the diversity of fuel sources used to generate electricity (and particularly the increased share of electricity produced by combined-cycle thermal power plants). In addition, it is difficult to develop analysis models that incorporate the effects of an internationally traded commodity in a domestic price structure.

Furthermore, the development of major infrastructure will undoubtedly peak around 2015, with growth slowing in later years. This suggests that the industry will reach maturity around that time, with other technologies perhaps playing an increased role subsequently. It is unlikely that the LNG industry will face the same fate as nuclear power, which was viewed as a panacea in the 1960s. Even if the risk of accidents cannot be reduced to zero, it is unlikely that any incident, regardless of magnitude, could have consequences as serious as those of Chernobyl. LNG is not risk-free, but its current safety record is similar to what might be expected of most other types of industrial facilities.

Environmentalists will likely continue to exert pressure on domestic governments to block projects to build new facilities. The gas industry needs to take this into account. Technology and the separation between LNG sites and residential zones are factors that could help to mitigate risks and lessen local, regional and international opposition. In spite of such efforts, a number of projects are bound to be delayed.

---

[137] See Phyllis Martin, "EIA's Current View on LNG Imports into the United States", EIA Energy Outlook and Modeling Conference, March 27, 2006, available at http://www.eia.doe.gov/oiaf/aeo/conf/handouts.html.

Ironically, prices will also have a decisive effect on future energy projects. A return to coal, even clean or refined coal, would not provide the same guarantees as natural gas, at least not with respect to greenhouse gases.

Depending on how markets evolve, we may see the establishment in the future of an international forum for discussion that will seek to monitor and control fluctuations in natural gas prices —or, conversely, to promote a laissez-faire approach to supply and demand and encourage the free circulation of goods and cargoes. This situation applies especially to Europe, which is in the midst of liberalizing its energy market. In Asia, the growing demand in China and India will be a major driver of LNG import and export development.

The advent of new producers and new buyers in the LNG supply chain and markets, the expansion in LNG loading and offloading sites, the emergence of an active spot market and the diversification of sources of supply are all factors that will help to strengthen energy security worldwide over the long term. In this regard, LNG appears to have a promising future ahead of it.

10

The Big Three: Russia, China and the United States

Land, sea and air combat have all had their major strategists: MacKinder, Mahan and Douhet.[1] However, their ideas are probably all neatly contained in the theories of that supreme strategist, Carl von Clausewitz. The development of strategy relies on three main principles: the concentration of forces, control of interior lines and the use of the force multipliers –time and space.

The situation is very similar in the oil and gas field. In a market system, the so-called integrated approach to the resource cycle encompasses all stages from exploration to consumption, including production, processing and transportation –in other words, from the wellhead to the gas pump or the pilot light. Vertical integration is not a new phenomenon. Although the major oil companies (also known as the **supermajors)** may have changed their names over the years, they are the direct heirs of the big oil trusts established in the late 1800s and early 1900s. The firm Total provides a brief history of the oil industry on its web site:

> The two oldest of the major oil companies were created at the end of the 19th century: the U.S. firm Standard Oil belonging to Rockefeller and the Anglo-Dutch firm Royal Dutch/Shell. In 1911, Standard Oil was so powerful that, under the Sherman Antitrust Act of the same year, the U.S. government broke the company up into three pieces: Standard Oil of New Jersey (the future Exxon), Standard Oil of New York (the future Mobil) and Standard Oil of California (Socal). All three would become part of a group later known as the Seven Sisters: Exxon, Socal (later to become Chevron), Mobil, Texaco, Gulf, BP (the heir of AIOC, the Anglo-Iranian Oil Company) and Shell. To these is traditionally added the French company CFP (Compagnie Française des Pétroles, later to become Total) to designate the original eight majors of the petroleum industry.[2]

The wave of mergers and acquisitions that swept through the oil and gas industry during the 1990s is not over yet. It coincides with the liberalization of energy

---

[1]   Halford MacKinder, Alfred Thayer Mahan and Giulio Douhet.
[2]   See http://www.planete-energies.com/content/oil-gas/companies/world/majors.html.

markets and the globalization of trade. Neither Russia nor China has escaped this trend. The recent cooperation between these two countries, once former enemies, is part of a joint strategy to reappropriate their energy resources by establishing strict – some would say too strict– regulations over their oil and gas, a little like the Middle East in the last century. On the opposite side of the globe, Latin American countries are quietly inching towards a more "socialistic" outlook, and some have given in to the temptation of nationalizing their oil and gas sector.

A new fault line is in the process of being created. On one side are the vertically integrated supermajors, otherwise known as the international oil companies (IOCs) –on the other side, the national oil companies (NOCs). Although this division has always existed, it is now reasserting itself with renewed vigour. The NOCs have much greater oil and gas reserves than the IOCs. As full participants in the industry, they are now being called on to play an increased role in setting the rules of the game –to the extent that some commentators have suggested that the IOCs should act as service providers to the NOCs to help the latter develop and exploit their resources.[3] Although this point has not yet been reached, the supermajors have been quick to realize that they can only ignore the NOCs at their own peril.

The Middle East's strategic role in oil and gas has already been discussed in earlier chapters. Here, we would like to focus on the huge strategic energy triangle that is currently forming between Russia, China and the United States. In this triangle, two parties are the buyers –China and the United States (India may soon join this group)– while the third is the seller.[4] And there is no doubt that it is a seller's market. Russia, which is the world's second largest oil producer after Saudi Arabia, is a huge supplier of oil and gas. However, it is not big enough to take on the role of swing producer now assumed by Saudi Arabia. The Arab kingdom is the only producer with sufficient capacity to do so,[5] while Russia is now producing as

---

[3] See Nick Snow, "Big Role Changes seen for Major Oil Companies", *Oil & Gas Journal*, April 3, 2006, p. 28.

[4] The World Energy Council's (WEC) *World Energy in 2006*, p. 13, predicts that Chinese demand will increase to 13.3 MMb/d (million barrels a day) in 2030 and Indian demand to 5.6 MMb/d.

[5] Saudi Arabia has 85 oil fields with 320 reservoirs. To increase its production, the country's major oil company, Saudi Aramco, is banking on five projects: Haradh (300,000 barrels a day, or b/d, in 2006); Khursaniyah (500,000 b/d in 2007); expansion of Nuayyim (100,000 b/d in 2008) and Shayba (250,000 b/d in 2008) and Kurais, or Khoreis (1.2 MMb/d in 2009). The Kurais development includes 2.6 billion barrels from Abu Jifan, an estimated 22.8 billion barrels from Kurais and 1.4 billion barrels from the Mazalij oil field. See "Saudi Aramco Developing Several Fields, Boosting Drilling for Oil and Gas", *Oil & Gas Journal*, May 8, 2006, p. 19. The Kurais megaproject is being undertaken by the U.S. firm Halliburton. See http://www.pipelinedubai.com/press/2006/pr_06_0396.html. John S. Herold, Inc. estimates Saudi Arabia's future production capacity will be 13.5 MMb/d in 2011. See John Malone and Chris Ruppel, "Saudi Arabia's Stated Objective: Increased Production Capacity", *Industry Insights*, November 17, 2006.

much as it can. Moscow will have to develop new deposits to make up for declining production in its traditional fields in western Siberia.

A Question of Resources

China, the United States and Russia all have their strengths and weaknesses in the area of energy security. Before proceeding further, we should provide a more general overview of trade relations between the three points, or poles, in the triangle and the asymmetry characterizing their oil and gas resources and reserves.

Trade Relations

The two big trading nations in the triangle are China and the United States. These two giants together account for 50% of world trade, although Germany is currently the world's largest exporter of goods (9.3% of the total), followed by the United States (8.7%) and China (7.3%). In terms of imports, the United States ranks first (16% of the total), followed by Germany (7.2%) and China (6.1%).[6] Merchandise exports make up 40% of China's gross domestic product (GDP)[7] and 20% of the United States' GDP.[8]

China, with a population 3.3 times greater than that of the United States, has a GDP six times smaller, despite the fact that it has posted annual economic growth rates of close to 10% for at least a decade. At this rate, China, which enjoys a trade surplus and enviable capital flows that make it one of the top-ranking capital recipient countries in the world, should surpass the United States during the first half of the 21st century. The United States' budget deficit and burgeoning external debt are likely to severely hamper its future competitiveness, although it is uncertain whether this will threaten its position as top importer. The size of U.S. imports is due to the offshoring practices of major U.S. companies, which import what they produce abroad. A prime example is Wal-Mart, which in 2004 purchased $18 billion of goods manufactured in China. This single multinational is responsible for more trade volume on its own than that generated by the bilateral trade between China and Australia, China and Canada or China and Russia (in 2002).

---

[6] WTO, *International Trade Statistics 2006*, Table 1.5.

[7] According to Peter Allgeier, U.S. Trade Representative to the WTO in Geneva. See "Trade Policy Review of the People's Republic of China", at http://newsblaze.com/story/20060421085519tsop.nb/newsblaze/TOPSTORY/Top-Story.html.

[8] For 2004, according to World Bank statistics on development indicators athttp://devdata.worldbank.org/external/CPprofile.asp?

Russia's oil and gas sector accounted for 25% of the country's GDP in 2003, but employed less than 1% of the population. If revenues from metals and other raw materials are also taken into account, these sectors together represent over two thirds of the Russian government's revenues.[9] The U.S. Department of Energy's (DOE) Energy Information Administration (EIA) adds:

> Russia is important to world energy markets because it holds the world's largest natural gas reserves, the second largest coal reserves, and the eighth largest oil reserves. Russia is also the world's largest exporter of natural gas, the second largest oil exporter, and the third largest energy consumer.[10]

According to statistics from the World Trade Organization (WTO) for 2005 (*International Trade Statistics 2006)*, Russia is ranked eighth among merchandise-exporting countries (3.1% of world total) and thirteenth among merchandise-importing countries (1.5% of world total). Furthermore, April 2007 data from the same organization suggest that China could surpass the United States in 2007 and Germany in 2008 as the leading merchandise exporter.

Such statistics belie, however, the relative stability of trade between the United States, China and Russia. Table 1 and Figure 1 show the scope of trade relations between China and the U.S. in 2002, 2005 and 2006 (2002 was used as a baseline because it was the year that China became a member of the WTO).

Chinese exports to Russia grew tremendously between 2002 and 2006 – an increase of 882% in four years. During the same period, China increased its exports to the U.S. by 130%, and Russia increased its exports to the U.S. by 191%. Although China recorded substantial growth in its exports to the U.S., the same thing can be said of U.S. exports to China. The 2006 data confirm the trends found in 2002-2005, namely a strong increase in Russian-U.S. and China-U.S. trade. The new element is China's very strong penetration of the Russian market (almost a tenfold increase in four years). China exports mostly manufactured goods to the United States, while Russia exports oil and gas to the Americans. Readers should note that the official statistics do not include the clandestine border trade between China and Russia, which President Putin has estimated at $10 billion, or roughly 30% of formal trade.[11] China and Russia hope to increase the volume of trade between them to $60-80 billion by 2010.

---

9   EIA, http://www.eia.doe.gov/emeu/cabs/Russia/Background.html.
10   *Ibid.*
11   Figures cited in Bobo Lo, *op. cit.*

Table 1: Bilateral trade in 2002, 2005 and 2006
China-Russia, Russia-United States, United States-China
In billions of US$

	2002	2005	2006	Change 2002/2005 (%)	Change 2002/2006 (%)
Russian exports to China	8.4	15.9	17.5	89.3	108.3
Chinese exports to Russia	3.4	13.2	33.4	288.2	882
Russian exports to the U.S.	6.8	15.3	19.8	125	191.2
U.S. exports to Russia	2.4	3.9	4.7	62.5	95.8
Chinese exports to the U.S.	125.2	243.5	287.7	94.5	129.8
U.S. exports to China	22.1	41.8	55.2	89.1	149.7

Source: www.census.gov/foreign-trade/balance/c5700.html#2006
Ministry of Commerce of the People's Republic of China (MOFCOM)

Figure 1 illustrates graphically the asymmetrical nature of trade between Russia, China and the United States.

In 2006, the United States had a $232.5 billion trade deficit with China. Any major disturbance in the trade flow between the two countries could have a profound effect on their bilateral relations as well as on global economic growth as a whole. Interdependency is a desirable status quo. To prevent a devaluation of the yuan, China, like Japan, is reinvesting its monetary surpluses in the United States by purchasing U.S. Treasury Bills. What is most ironic is that the United States is becoming increasingly protectionist, while China more and more favours trade liberalization.

Due to geographical proximity, the two-way trade between Russia and China is greater than that between Russia and the United States. Nevertheless, the geopolitics of three-way relations slightly favours Washington, despite bilateral declarations of Russian-Chinese cooperation.[12] Similarly, there has been much talk about the global role of Moscow and Beijing in countering U.S. economic "hegemony." However, this will not be changed by flowery rhetoric, but rather by changes to the structure of world trade itself.

Petroleum Reserves

In terms of petroleum reserves, at the end of 2005, out of 203 petroleum countries, the ten largest had close to two thirds (64.1%) of global reserves (see Table 2). Six of these ten are multinational firms and four are national (Lukoil, PetroChina, Petroleos Mexicanos and Petrobras). When both oil and gas are taken into account,

---

[12]   For example, 2006 was declared the year of Russia in China and 2007 the year of China in Russia.

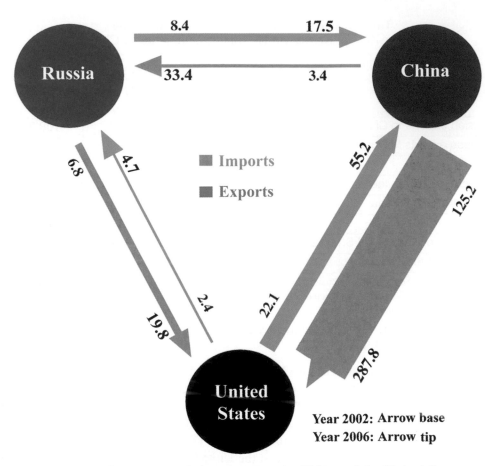

Figure 1: Three-way trade between Russia, China and the United States, 2002, 2005 and 2006

Source: www.census.gov/foreign-trade/balance/c5700.html#2005 (U.S.-China and U.S.-Russia). For Sino-Russian trade, see Ministry of Commerce of the People's Republic of China (MOFCOM)

Lukoil and PetroChina together possess 25% of the reserves owned by the top ten companies. This is a good indication of the oil and gas riches that Russia and China are sitting on. This situation could suggest that it is to firms' advantage to cooperate with one another in developing these resources. The reality is completely different, however. Each multinational jealously guards its resources and tries to maximize its international advantages. Going back to the three main strategic principles, space and time (in other words, investments) play a significant role.

Despite China's and Russia's significant resources, a quick glance at deposits slated for development in 2004-2015 around the world shows that the projects undertaken in the two countries represent only a fraction of those being carried out worldwide by the large Western multinational firms. Barely 5% of ExxonMobil's oil production during this period will come from Russia (2% for gas).[13] The same thing is true for ConocoPhillips (COP), for which Russian and Chinese oil production is projected to be 4% between now and 2015. British Petroleum (BP) is not doing any better, with 5% of its new production coming from Russia. Only Royal Dutch Shell (RDS) stands out, with 14% of its expected future production to come from Russia, 6% from Kazakhstan and 2% from China.[14] RDS is an integrated company with one of the most diversified production portfolios, spread over 17 countries, in the industry. It also has two major projects underway in Russia and China, one with PetroChina to develop the Changbei gas field in the Ordos Basin, and the other in Sakhalin II, whose expected development costs have almost doubled to $20 billion. In December 2006, Gazprom was poised to acquire majority control over the Sakhalin II project.[15]

Table 2: Reserves held by supermajors, NOCsand large Chinese and Russian firms, in barrel of oil equivalents (BOE)

RANK		Reserves as at December 31, 2006 in billions of BOE	% of reserves made up of gas	% of world reserves in BOE held by top ten firms
1	ExxonMobil	22.8	49%	8.69%
2	Lukoil	20.36	22%	7.75%
3	PetroChina	21.09	42%	8.02%
4	BP	17.44	44%	6.63%
5	PEMEX (Petroleos Mexicanos)	15.16	15%	5.77%
6	RDS (Royal Dutch Shell)	12.69	58%	4.83%
7	Chevron	11.62	33%	4.42%
8	Petrobras	11.46	17%	4.36%
9	Total	10.73	40%	4.08%
10	ConocoPhillips	11.41	39%	4.34%
Total		154.76		58.89%

Source: Global Upstream Performance Review 2007, John S. Herold, Inc., p. 26.

---

[13] ExxonMobil Corporation (XOM), *Upstream Profile Supplement: Commercial Development*, John S. Herold, Inc., May 2006.

[14] These figures are taken from the *Strategic Evaluation* of each multinational (calculations by John S. Herold, Inc. Percentages for figures given by Herold are based on barrels of oil equivalent (BOE).

[15] All the details of the transaction are not yet known. In exchange, RDS will acquire an interest in the development of the Zapolyarnoye field (Yemal Peninsula) as well as receiving the sum of $7.45 billion. See "Gazprom 'wins' $22B Shell Gas Plan," *EurasiaNet*, December 11, 2006, and *Herold Oil Headliner*, John S. Herold, Inc., December 22, 2006.

Table 2 also shows the high proportion of gas resources held by RDS (58%), ExxonMobil, BP and PetroChina. This partly accounts for statements in the March 2006 version of the *National Security Strategy* (issued by the Office of the President of the United States) that directly address Chinese energy policy. According to this document, China must not "lock up" energy supplies or "seek to direct markets rather than opening them up" and is reproached for supporting "resource-rich countries without regard to the misrule at home or misbehaviour abroad of these regimes."[16] Although the cornerstone of China's trade policy on natural gas is the signature of long-term contracts with Australia and Indonesia, this also includes other countries such as Iran, Sudan and Myanmar, three nations not exactly viewed positively by Washington. This brings us to the future of natural gas and liquefied natural gas (LNG) production (see Chapter 9). Another issue related to the President's comments is that the long-term contracts favoured by the Chinese interfere with the laws of the marketplace, and in particular may hinder the development of spot markets (and spot contracts) for LNG.[17]

Production Costs

The demand for natural gas will grow exponentially in China and the United States over the next two decades. This is even truer in the U.S., where gas plays a major role in the national energy basket. According to the DOE's *Annual Energy Outlook* 2006 (*AEO 2006*), the U.S. will experience a significant shortfall in natural gas by 2030, which it hopes to remedy by bringing in LNG imports on LNG carriers.[18]

Table 3 shows the same players as the previous table, but ranks them instead according to various categories of production costs per barrel of oil equivalent (BOE), which are averaged over a three-year period (2004-2006). These costs include proved acquisition costs (PAC) –or the costs of acquiring proved reserves (purchased or sold)– finding and development costs (FDC)[19] and total reserve replacement costs (RRC). ExxonMobil ranks third among the firms listed in terms of acquisition costs and well below the 3-year price average for the integrated international firms. In the second category, Lukoil ranks first (26th) among the companies listed, with finding and development costs significantly lower than the other companies and than the mean

---

[16] See *The National Security Strategy of the United States of America,* Office of the President of the United States, March 2006, pp. 41-42.

[17] See Célia DeLalandre, "Le GNL : Instrument de flexibilisation du marché du gaz", Newsletter, *Le maintien de la paix*, No. 80, April 2006, available at http://www.er.uqam.ca/nobel/cepes.

[18] Between 4.4 and 7.4 Tcf depending on the scenario chosen and what happens to gas prices. See *AEO 2006*, p. 89.

[19] Exploration costs, development costs and the costs of acquiring operating licences. Such costs are generally calculated over a three-year period to reduce the effect of appreciation due to the recording of discovered reserves as proved reserves.

for integrated international firms. The most important ranking is obviously reserve replacement costs (oil and gas combined). Again, Lukoil stands out clearly from the rest of the competition, although ExxonMobil and PetroChina come in a strong second and third since they have renewed their resources at a reasonable price. Two of the top four are nationals: Lukoil and Petrochina.

Table 3: Reserve acquisition, development and replacement costs for supermajors, NOCs, Lukoil and PetroChina, per barrel of oil equivalent (BOE) (in US$ and averaged over three years, 2004-2006)

	Proved acquisition costs (per BOE)		Development costs (including research related costs) of reserves (per BOE)		Reserve replacement costs (per BOE)	
		Rank		Rank		Rank
ExxonMobil	$0.56	3	$7.00	21	$6.07	24
Lukoil	$3.47	27	$7.26	26	$6.05	23
BP	n.a.		$7.65	29	$7.16	29
PetroChina	n.a.	n.a.	$6.59	20	$6.59	26
PEMEX (Petroleos Mexicanos)	n.a.	n.a.	n.a.	n.a.	n.a.	n.a
RDS (Royal Dutch Shell)	$6.00	43	$13.28	66	$12.98	87
Petrobras	$3.62	28	$10.27	44	$10.20	60
Chevron	$8.02	61	$29.49	146	$16.37	116
Total S. A.	$4.17	33	$10.64	47	$10.34	62
ConocoPhillips	$8.13	63	$18.94	107	$10.61	65
Mean for integrated international companies	**$3.95**		**$11.41**		**$8.85**	

Source: Global Upstream Performance Review 2007, John S. Herold, Inc., pp. 32-37.

Competition Between China and the United States

In general, three factors account for the fierce competition between the United States and China. First, beginning in the early 1990s, large U.S. oil companies began to concentrate their production abroad, at the same time as domestic production dwindled steadily and U.S. offshore production stalled.[20] The same trends are

---

[20] See *Performance Profiles of Major Energy Producers, 2004*, DOE, EIA, March 2006, Figure 23.

seen in natural gas, although the parameters are slightly different. International production by major U.S. gas companies has increased since 2000, along with onshore domestic production, while offshore production has shrunk considerably.[21] Secondly, oil discoveries (oil reserve additions) in 2004 were negative, while natural gas discoveries increased by 126%. The increase in per-barrel oil prices facilitated these changes.[22] From that point on, NOCs and the major multinationals faced off on the natural gas market. Thirdly, the supermajors are still ahead in deepwater offshore exploitation. In LNG, three major firms stand out, whether in the area of production, liquefaction, regasification or transportation: ExxonMobil, RDS and Total, in that order.[23] The advanced technologies possessed by the IOCs should logically encourage cooperation between China and the multinationals. However, Beijing seems to be experiencing a delay in developing LNG, despite numerous projects currently under study.[24] Rather than confronting the multinationals on their own ground, China has chosen to protect its rear flank by negotiating long-term supply contracts. In one area, however, China is ahead of the pack: investment.

A Battle for Investments?

The importance of this issue has already been discussed in Chapter 6. Readers should keep in mind the IEA's projections. To meet global energy demand by 2030, $3 trillion must be invested in each sector (oil and gas): in other words, a total of $6 trillion, or an annual investment of $210 billion. The required investments can be broken down as follows: for oil, 72% in exploration and development, 13% in refining and 15% in other areas; for gas, 55% in exploration and development, 37% in transmission, distribution and storage, and 8% in LNG.

---

[21] *Ibid*, Figure 24.

[22] *Ibid.* According to the document (page 43): "As a result, foreign oil reserve additions excluding purchases and sales of reserves were a negative 416 million barrels. In the rising price climate of 2004, contracts called production-sharing agreements likely contributed to the negative foreign reserve revisions. These are contracts between foreign governments, which own the reserves, and the oil companies that stipulate the oil company's share of the oil and natural gas produced from any particular project that it has undertaken, based on certain conditions. It is common for these contracts to specify that, as oil prices rise, the share of production that the oil company retains (and thus its implied share of the reserves) decreases."

[23] John Malone, "LNG Gives Multinational Oil Companies a Competitive Edge", *Industry Insights*, John S. Herold, Inc., March 6, 2006.

[24] The main LNG trains will be built in Fujian, Guandong, Shandong, Shangai, Jiangsu and Zhejiang.

Since 2004, China has been the beneficiary of over $60 billion annually in foreign direct investment (FDI). Investment was also high in 2006 and 2007, but these figures must be viewed with caution because they include huge inflows of capital from the banking sector. Table 4 shows FDI in China over the last six years. In 2006, over 38% of FDI in China flowed through Hong Kong and companies registered in the British Virgin Islands.[25] China, and soon India, according to the United Nations Conference on Trade and Development (UNCTAD),[26] should continue to be favoured by investors in the future. In 2004, China was the recipient of roughly 10% of all international FDI and close to 60% of FDI in East Asia.[27] Until recently (except in 2001), China reinvested little abroad. The country's needs for metals, raw materials and hydrocarbon-based fuels are changing the situation, and account for China's growing interest in Latin America and Africa.[28]

Beijing is obviously not short of the money required to ensure the security of its supplies. In terms of the percentage of FDI that goes to energy, the situation is very different from the one in Africa. According to the *World Investment Report 2005* (*WIR 2005*), 93%, 94% and 90% of FDI in Angola, Equatorial Guinea and Nigeria were in the oil and gas sector.[29] The amounts were between $1 billion and $2 billion annually for Equatorial Guinea (2003-2004) and over $2 billion for Nigeria. As a comparison, the three largest Chinese petroleum companies (PetroChina, SINOPEC and CNOOC) invested $50.3 billion upstream over five years (2000-2004), and $34.6 billion during the last three years of the period in question.[30] These are capital expenditures slated for exploration and development. China is a country seeking production and acquisition opportunities; it is not looking for international hand-outs. On the other hand, although Chinese petroleum companies may have plenty of

---

[25] Other countries investing in China (ranked according to US$ investments) are Japan ($6.5 billion), South Korea ($5.2 billion), the United States ($3.1 billion), Singapore ($2.2 billion), Taiwan ($2.1 billion) and Germany ($1.5 billion). See *China's Trade with the United States and the World*, August 18, 2006, Congressional Research Service Report to Congress, p. 38.

[26] See *Prospects for FDI Flows, TMNC Strategies and Promotion Policies: 2004-2007*, report published by UNCTAD in 2004.

[27] This concentration of investments in China does not seem to have had an appreciable effect on investment in other Asian countries. See Benoît Mercereau, "FDI Flows to Asia: Did the Dragon Crowd Out the Tigers?", *IMF Survey*, Working Paper 05/189.

[28] In November 2005, China signed a free-trade agreement with Chile. Chinese trade with Latin America is expanding quickly. See "China Doubles Latin FDI", Special Report, *Latin Business Chronicle*, April 24, 2006. Two oil-producing countries, Brazil and Venezuela, are also being courted by China. In Ecuador, China has bought the assets of the large Canadian gas firm EnCana for over $2 billion.

[29] *World Investment Report 2005*, UNCTAD, p. 42. Hereafter cited as *WIR 2005*.

[30] Figures taken from *Company Insights* (John S. Herold, Inc.) for each firm. For PetroChina: $4.67, $4.8, $5.6, $6.7 and $7.5 billion for the years 2000, 2001, 2002, 2003 and 2004. For SINOPEC (same years): $2.2, $2.9, $3.3, $3.5 and $9.8 billion. CNOOC: $578 million, $599 million, $1.5 billion, $1.3 billion and $2.1 billion.

cash to invest, they have to rely on available oil and gas reserves. Projections are for a 2.4% annual decrease in production for PetroChina over the period 2005-2007, which explains Beijing's buying spree abroad.[31]

Table 4: Foreign direct investment (FDI) in China (2000-2006)
(in billions of $)

	2000	2001	2002	2003	2004	2005	2006
Inward FDI flows	40.8	46.8	52.7	53.5	60.6	72.4	70.0
Outward FDI flows	n.a.	6.8	2.5	− 0.15	1.8	11.3	16.1

Source: UNCTAD, *World Investment Report 2002, 2005* and *2006* for 2002-2005;
for 2006, U.S.-China Business Council at www.uschina.org.

Table 5: Foreign direct investment (FDI) in Russia (2000-2006)
(in billions of $)

	2000	2001	2002	2003	2004	2005	2006
Inward FDI flows	2.7	2.5	3.5	7.9	11.7	14.6	28.4
Outward FDI flows	n.a.	2.5	3.5	9.7	9.6	13.1.	< 12.9

Source: UNCTAD, *World Investment Report 2002, 2005* and *2006* for 2002-2005; for 2006, see
UNCTAD Press Office, January 9, 2007, and Columbia Program on International Investment at
www.epii.columbia.edu/pubs.

The situation is much less clear for Russia (Table 5). Foreign direct investment in that country has had its ups and downs, with capital usually going out of the country almost as soon as it enters.[32] For the period 2001-2004, Russia was just breaking even, with inflows equalling outflows until 2003. Beginning in 2003, capital outflows exceeded inflows, but the reverse situation was seen as of 2004. In 2006, there was a spectacular jump in foreign direct investment in Russia; a third of investment inflows were in the energy sector.

Owing to the reorganization of Russia's oil and gas sector, the dismantling of Yukos, and Rosneft's acquisition of Yuganskneftegaz, there are no definitive figures on individual exploration and development costs for all the Russian oil

---

[31] "PetroChina Company Ltd. (PTR)", *Herold Comparative Appraisal Report*, December 1, 2005.

[32] For example, Cyprus was the recipient of massive outflows of Russian capital at a time when the brutal privatization of state-owned enterprises was at its peak. The year 2003 was also disastrous for Russia.

companies. There are statistics for Lukoil, Sibneft and Rosneft[33] but little information on Surgutneftegaz.[34] Among Russian transnational corporations (TNC) not associated with finance or banking, Lukoil ranks first with assets of $7.2 billion in 2003.[35] In September 2004, Moscow sold off some of Lukoil's assets (7.59%) to ConocoPhillips for $2 billion, making Lukoil one of the few companies over which the Russian government does not have direct control. However, Moscow still controls fiscal policies and petroleum royalties.

Despite the limited availability of statistics on the main Russian and Chinese oil and gas companies, the little information that does exist on their financial situation allows some interesting comparisons to be drawn (see Table 6).

Table 6: Net and gross revenues of Russian and Chinese oil and gas companies (in billions of US$)

	Gross revenues (A)		Operating expenses and costs (B)		Net pre-tax revenues (A-B)		2005 ranking (based on net pre-tax revenues)
	2005	2006	2005	2006	2005	2006	2005
Gazprom	50.0	79.1	34.3	?	15.7	?	2
Lukoil	55.7	67.7	47.2	58.0	8.9	10.3	3
Rosneft	25.5	?	19.8	?	5.7	?	5
PetroChina CNPC	67.4	86.4	45.0	62.9	22.9	24.1	1
SINOPEC	101.7	135.1	94.4	125.4	7.4	9.7	4
CNOOC	8.6	11.5	4.2	5.9	1.9	5.6	6

Source: Herold Financial Summary, Company Insights, 2005 and 2006.

Gazprom owns 60% of natural gas reserves in the country, handles 90% of production and its economic activities represent 8% of Russia's GDP. The two petroleum giants Gazprom and Lukoil dominate the oil and gas market in the

---

33 For the years 2001, 2002, 2003 and 2004, exploration and development expenditures were as follows: Lukoil, $2.6, $1.6, $2.8 and $2.7 billion, for Sibneft, $399, $638, $738 and $804 million. Figures taken from the *Operational Summary* for the firms in question, John S. Herold, Inc. In terms of operations and operating costs, Sibneft is doing much better than Lukoil. Sibneft is generating net revenues of $9.49 per BOE produced (ranked 88th), compared with $6.73 for Lukoil (ranked 142nd). These figures are taken from the *Global Upstream Performance Review 2005, op. cit.*, pp. 44-45.

34 During the first six months of 2006, Surgutneftegaz produced 32.4 million tonnes of oil and its capital expenditures (one billion dollars) increased by 30% over 2005. See *Russian Petroleum Investor,* September 2006, p. 33.

35 The *World Investment Report* follows the UNCTAD tradition in that service firms (banks, insurance and finance) are treated separately from other TNCs. See *WIR 2005, op. cit.*

country, with net revenues close to $25 billion in 2005. On the Chinese side, PetroChina towers above all the other players, although SINOPEC is breaking all the records in terms of gross revenues ($135.1 billion in 2006). For 2000-2004, Russia and China had the best returns on upstream capital investment, with rates of 36% and 33% per annum respectively.[36]

In 2005, the two hundred and some oil and gas companies analyzed by John S. Herold, Inc. invested $195 billion in exploration and development, with 57% of this amount coming from vertically integrated companies.[37] Some companies' buybacks of their own stocks in 2004 exceeded their operating expenses by 20%.[38] Together, these indicators show that there is no shortage of cash in the industry and oil companies are doing well. The IEA therefore has good reason to believe that the industry will be able to finance its own oil and gas development activities.

Two major sources of concern cloud the investment picture: political instability and competition. Up to now, the risks of political instability in various parts of the world have been largely ignored. The choice of regions for investment often has geopolitical consequences that are difficult to foresee. In terms of competition, as we have seen, capital is not a problem, since China and the large multinationals have plenty of money; however, securing reserve leases and long-term operating licences abroad can be difficult.

As was the case for oil several times in the last century, the problem of finding new domestic resources to tap, along with the need to develop foreign resources, is at the heart of the triangle. Around it revolve the different poles and power relationships, with a new element being the oil companies' growing interest in natural gas.

The Russian Pole

Hydrocarbon fuels have both advantages and disadvantages for the Russian economy, owing to several factors. First, most Russian oil and gas facilities have become severely dilapidated or obsolete, particularly since the dismantling of the former U.S.S.R., although some improvements have since been made. In addition, the country's economy is in thrall to oil market volatility. In 2005, according to the U.S. Department of Energy (DOE), a $1 increase in the barrel price (Urals crude) translated into $3.4 billion in additional revenues for the Russian government.[39]

---

[36] *Ibid.*, p. 13. Return calculated by dividing net upstream revenue by cumulative capital costs.

[37] See *Global Upstream Performance Review 2006*, John S. Herold, Inc., pp. 19-24.

[38] *Global Upstream Performance Review 2005, op. cit.,* p. 7.

[39] DOE, EIA, *Country Analysis Briefs,* "Russia."

Although Russia has created a stabilization fund[40] to insulate the economy from price volatility, it would like to dissociate its economic growth from the energy sector, which will not be easy. Another factor is Moscow's takeover of Yukos (including the imprisonment of its executives), which led to an internal power struggle, essentially allowing the Russian government to reap the benefits of nationalization without having to do it officially. This occurred at a time when Europe and the United States were asking Russia to liberalize its energy market and become a signatory to the Energy Charter.[41] Russia agreed to open up its market but still refuses to sign the Charter. Therefore, there is a major imbalance between market laws, openness to competition (the purpose of which is to encourage competitiveness rather than strengthen monopolies) and the need to protect investors' interests over the long term. Lastly, Moscow is becoming increasingly greedy to collect taxes and other proceeds from its energy resources. This is not unusual and the same tendency is still seen in Latin America, China and even the industrialized world. This represents a legitimate government desire to maximize revenues when oil prices reach unequalled heights, such as in 2006, although the industry is quick to denounce such practices.

The break-up of the Soviet empire plunged Russia into an unprecedented economic crisis. Similarly, most countries that now make up the Community of Independent States (CIS) suffered economically from the ensuing upheaval and involuntarily became victims of Russia's trade practices. Before Russia's "gas war" with Ukraine and Belarus, landlocked states like Turkmenistan and Kazakhstan had to pay dearly for Russia's economic collapse, since their oil and gas exports had to go through Russian territory. On an annual basis, the Russian Federation exports a little over 6 MMb/d; this is still a far cry from Russia's best years (1988 in particular) when it produced 12 MMb/d, compared to a little over 9 MMb/d in early 2005. The reason is simple. Most of Russia's production comes from mature fields.[42] In addition, some but not all pipelines are operating at full capacity. Oil pipelines still remain under the control of Transneft, which has a monopoly on the network and can impose its own conditions. Consequently,

---

[40] According to Trade Minister German Gref, Russia hopes to increase this fund to 3,000 billion rubles (US$112 billion) or 13% of its GDP by the end of 2007, and stabilize it by the end of 2006 at 2,300 billion rubles (8.5% of Russia's GDP). See *The MoscowTimes.Com*, October 2, 2006, p.6.

[41] The Energy Charter aims to liberalize the energy sector and guarantee the continuity of investments. T. W. Walde, "Energy Charter Treaty-based Investment Arbitration –Controversial Issues", *Oil, Gas and Energy Law Intelligence*, Vol. 2, No. 5, December 2004, pp.1-64.

[42] See Julien Vercueil, "Les hydrocarbures en Russie, entre promesses et blocages", *Géoconfluences*, http://geoconfluences.ens-lsh.fr/doc/etpays/Russie/RussieScient3.htm. In 1995, Russia exported roughly 2.6 MMb/d. See Eugene Khartukov and Ellen Starostina, "Russian Oil Exports", (Part 1), *Oil & Gas Journal*, March 27, 2006, pp. 57-60.

Russia has launched a number of projects to build petroleum terminals and port facilities.[43]

To increase production and build more oil and gas pipelines, Russia must collect more revenues from its exports, which is the one of the reasons for its battle with Ukraine and Belarus. Moscow has a valid argument: because it has not yet joined the WTO and because of the policies to liberalize Europe's energy sector, it has to use world market prices for oil and gas in trading with its partners. Be that as it may, Russia still has a dual price policy: a domestic price (which is far below the market price) and a price for exports, which enables it to fill its coffers with oil and gas revenues.

The Giant with Blocked Nostrils

When Winston Churchill referred to Russia as a giant with two blocked nostrils over 50 years ago, he was alluding to the fact that the country is constrained geographically. The only exit it has in the south runs from the Black Sea, through the Bosporus Straits (the narrow straits bordered on either side by Turkey), to the Mediterranean and the Strait of Gibraltar (between the U.K. and Spain) while, in the north, it faces considerable geographic hurdles in reaching the Atlantic from the Baltic Sea. The situation has changed little since then, except that Russia is now lured by sirens in the Atlantic and the Pacific. In the future, it will find it easier to reach these oceans due to global warming and technological advances in navigation. Furthermore, the world demand for oil and gas is expanding steadily. The geographically blessed United States still rules the waves and intends to capitalize on its position to meet its domestic demand.

To transform crude oil into useful products, it must be processed in a refinery, while gas must be transported over distances of thousands of kilometres to the points of consumption. Gas and oil pipelines are therefore essential. Over a distance of 1,000 or 2,000 km, pipeline transportation is competitive with shipping of natural gas. It is only at a distance of 3,000 km or more that liquefied natural gas (LNG) carriers start to become more competitive than pipelines. Russia's oil and distribution capacity is largely dependent on its transportation networks.

Table 7 gives a good idea of the main changes that have occurred in Russia's petroleum distribution infrastructure along with projected capacity and use in 2012.

---

[43] See Laurent Rucker, "Le pétrole russe", *Synthèse n° 97*, at http://www.robert-schuman.org/ Synth97.htm.

In 2002, the most important regions in terms of handling capacity were the Black Sea and the Baltic, followed by Eastern Europe; in terms of use, however, the Eastern European pipelines ranked first. Similarly, in 2012, it is expected that the Russian Far East (RFE) oil pipelines will see the heaviest use, even though the Black Sea and Baltic ports will have a greater handling capacity.[44] This shows that the Russian Far East is a key priority for Moscow, although many other political and economic factors also come into play.

Table 7: Main export routes for Russian oil in MMb/d

	Capacity in 2002	Use in 2002 (note 1)	Capacity in 2012	Use in 2012
Eastern Europe	1.38	1.22	1.98	1.56
Black Sea	2.23	1.02	2.95	1.66
Baltic ports	1.71	1.00	2.06	1.78
Russian Far East	0.08	0.04	2.04	1.84
Barents Sea (Murmansk)	0.07	0.01	0.60	0.54
Total	**5.47**	**3.29**	**10.23** (with Kazakhstan-China pipeline)	**7.68** (with Kazakhstan-China pipeline)
Note 1 Does not include possible deliveries via Croatia's Adria pipeline and the reversal of the flow through the Odessa-Brody pipeline.				

Source: Khartukov and Starostina, *Oil, Gas & Energy Law Intelligence*, June 2005.

The annual report of the *Oil & Gas Journal* on current pipeline construction is unfortunately only available by region and not by country. Nonetheless, the figures do show the significant and growing need for natural gas infrastructures. In terms of oil and gas pipelines, projects underway in 2006 or scheduled for completion in 2006 or 2007 are expected to add nearly 100,000 km of pipeline to the existing networks, including 62,719 km of gas pipeline, 12,500 km of oil pipeline and 5,500 km for the transport of petroleum products.[45] A total of $116 billion is slated for this construction. The biggest projects are in the Asia Pacific region (31,000 km), the United States (19,136 km) and Europe (14,726 km).

---

[44] Figures taken from the article by Eugene Khartukov and Ellen Starostina, "Ex-Soviet Oil Exports: Constraints, Outlook and Global Impact", *Oil, Gas & Energy Law Intelligence*, Vol. 3, No. 2, June 2005.

[45] *Oil & Gas Journal*, February 13, 2006, pp. 57-68 (62).

Russian Oil Deliveries to Europe

To show the importance of Russian oil deliveries to Europe, we will take a look at Moscow's production and distribution structure for oil and gas.[46] Moscow is undeniably a world player on oil and gas markets, but only a regional player in terms of its distribution networks. Figures 2, 3 and 4 show the extent of resources in western Siberia, and the degree of European dependence on oil and natural gas imports from Russia. At present, Europe depends on foreign sources for over 50% of its oil and gas, and imports may make up 70% of its supply in 2030.[47]

The Druzhba Pipeline

In delivering oil to Europe, Russia can use several distribution networks, the main one being the **Druzhba** ("Friendship") **pipeline** running from Samara[48] to Belarus. It is divided into a **northern branch (Druzhba North)** (route 1) and a **southern branch (Druzhba South)** (route 2). The pipeline has a capacity of 1.3 MMb/d (900,000 b/d for the northern branch and 400,000 b/d for the southern branch). The northern branch[49] goes through Belarus, Poland and Germany, while the southern one goes through Belarus, Ukraine, Slovakia and the Czech Republic, ending in Hungary. Two projects to extend the pipeline are underway. The first would extend the northern branch to the German port of Wilhelmshaven, which would reduce oil tanker traffic in the Baltic Sea and facilitate Russian exports to the United States through Germany. The second project, the Adria-Druzhba Extension, under discussion since the 1990s and launched in 2004, will reverse the flow of Croatia's **Adria pipeline** to connect it with the southern branch (route 3). Originally, the Adria pipeline was designed to bring oil from the Middle East to the former Yugoslavia and Hungary. Reversing the flow of the Adria pipeline will provide Russia with an outlet to the Adriatic Sea, thus reducing oil tanker traffic in the Black Sea, which has been the focus of increasingly stringent environmental and security regulations. (Currently, Croatia appears to be worried about the potential environmental impacts of increased tanker traffic from Omisalj [see Figure 2], a deepwater port able to accommodate large tankers.) This extension could allow Russia to increase its export shipping capacity by roughly 100,000 b/d during the

---

[46] In March 2005, BP (British Petroleum) published a groundbreaking study on the range of options for energy corridors to supply Europe with gas from Russia, Central Asia and the Middle East. See T.M. Quigley, "Gas by Pipeline from the Caspian and Gulf to Europe: Pre-Requisites for a Commercially Viable Project", available on the BP web site.

[47] "Quelles stratégies énergétiques pour l'Europe", Green Paper presentation to the European Parliament by Energy Commissioner Andris Piebalgs, Brussels, March 28, 2006.

[48] A favoured route for oil from the Urals, Western Siberia and the Caspian Sea.

[49] The handling capacity of the Belarussian–Polish section will also be increased.

first year of reversed flow and perhaps by 300,000 b/d in subsequent years.[50] The costs of reversing the flow are around $20-30 million, and $320 million has been budgeted for the extension.[51]

The Baltic Pipeline System (BPS)

The second major pipeline is the **Baltic Pipeline System (BPS),** phase I of which was completed in December 2001. The main terminal is in Primorsk (route 4) in the Gulf of Finland. Phase II, which is currently being constructed, will add a second pipeline from Palkino (near Yaroslavl) at a cost of $1.4 billion, and a second terminal may be built at Vyborg. The total capacity of the BPS is currently over 1.2 MMb/d. This system gives Russia direct access to the western and northern European markets while bypassing the three Baltic States. As a result, the amount of oil sent through Ventspils, Latvia has decreased by 30% since 2000. This illustrates Russia's determination to favour its own ports over foreign ones and thus avoid paying high transit dues. In the event of severe winter conditions in the port of Primorsk, Transneft is thinking of using the Lithuanian port of Butinge instead or constructing an additional pipeline from Primorsk to the more clement port of Porvoo in Finland.

Farther south, Russia often uses the **Odessa-Brody-Plock pipeline** (route 6) to export oil by sea (in the opposite direction from the original plan). This line's purpose is to facilitate the transport of oil from Siberia or the Caspian Pipeline Consortium (CPC) to Northern Europe. Upstream, it is clearly intended primarily for Kazakhstan and Russia. In terms of downstream routing, everything will depend on the arrangements that can be made with Ukraine. Kazakhstan has floated the possibility of using the Pivdenny terminal near Odessa to transport its oil as far as Plock. The expansion of the Brody-Plock section will cost between $300 million and $500 million, not counting the $160 million already invested in the Odessa-Brody section. The project will require two to three years to complete. Ukraine, Poland, Germany, Lithuania and the European Union (EU) are supporting it. Ultimately, the whole undertaking depends on the long term guarantee of supplies from Azerbaijan and perhaps Kazakhstan. It has recently been agreed to build the Plock-Gdansk section.[52]

---

[50] See Bernard A. Gelb, "Russia Oil and Gas Challenges", *CRS Report to Congress*, January 2006, p. 8, available online.

[51] See Eugene Khartukov and Ellen Starostina, "Projects Focus on Pipeline Terminal Expansion", *Oil & Gas Journal*, March 27, 2006, p. 57.

[52] O&GJ, October 15, 2007, p. 10.

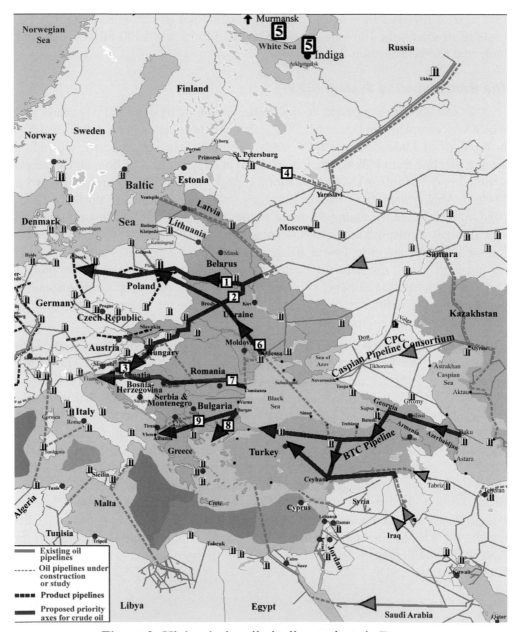

Figure 2: High-priority oil pipeline projects in Europe
Source: From Inogate (Interstate Oil and Gas Transport to Europe)
http://www.inogate.org/inogate/en/resources/maps

These options must be examined in conjunction with other routes to the Adriatic and the Atlantic that allow a detour of the Black Sea. The **South East European Line (SEEL)**[53] –which extends 1,000 km from Constanta to Trieste (route 7), with an alternative route to Ingolstadt in Bavaria– has a projected capacity of 0.5 MMb/d. It could come on stream as early as 2007. Another possibility is the 300-km-long **Burgas-Alexandropolis pipeline** (route 8), the capacity of which could be increased to 0.3, 0.5 or 0.7 MMb/d in coming years. This project is supported by Russia, Bulgaria and Greece, which signed a memorandum of understanding in April 2005. Chevron could become a partner in the project[54]. The pipeline is expected to go into operation in 2009. A third route through the Balkans is the 0.7-MMb/d **Albania-Macedonia-Bulgaria Oil (AMBO) pipeline**, which runs 950 km from Burgas through Macedonia to the port of Vlore in Albania (route 9). This pipeline, which will cost over $1.2 billion, is the subject of an agreement between the three governments and should begin operating in 2008. It follows the route of a former secondary pipeline. Routes 8 and 9 will compete with each other, one supported by Russia and the other by the AMBO pipeline consortium (AMBO Pipeline Corporation), which is under U.S. control. Oil transported to the port of Vlore is probably destined for the Atlantic market.

Murmansk or Indiga?

In the north, until very recently Russia was contemplating sending its oil from the Timan-Pechora basin and Western Siberia to Murmansk and then over water through the Barents Sea to the United States. This option (route 5) would allow Russia to export 1.6-2.4 MMb/d by tanker. The project is supported by Gazprom and Rosneft, particularly since the two firms are planning to build a major natural gas liquefaction facility in Murmansk or Arkhangelsk, farther south on the White Sea.[55] Transneft is not enthusiastic about this project, deeming it not profitable enough. Instead it suggests that this oil be shipped out of the port of Indiga (route 5); however, Indiga, unlike Murmansk, is not ice-free in winter. The future of the project supported by Gazprom and Rosneft appears to be in limbo, given the past battles between Yukos and Transneft. Transneft's reasoning seems to be just as political as economic: it claims that there are insufficient resources to warrant the construction of two major pipelines, one to Murmansk and the second (the Taishet-Nakhodka pipeline, or the Eastern Siberia/Pacific Ocean Pipeline) to the Pacific. We will return to this subject later. It is certain that, although neither Murmansk nor Indiga represents Russia's long-dreamed-of warmwater port, either site would

---

[53] This project was formerly known as the Constanta-Omisalj-Trieste pipeline

[54] See "Chevron May Expand Cooperation with Russian Company", *The Mercury News,* June 30, 2006.

[55] Project costs are estimated to be between $10 billion and $15 billion. See Igor Yegorov, "Gazprom Projects in Northwest Russia, 2005 Update", at http://www.bisnis.doc.gov/bisnis/bisdoc/0501NWRusGazpromProj.htm.

provide direct access to the Atlantic through the Barents Sea. Alternatively, Russia could simply abandon the Atlantic option and export its oil to Europe rather than to the United States.

The CPC Versus the BTC

The geopolitical stakes are highest in the south, where there are two competing pipeline networks. The first is Russian, the **Caspian Pipeline Consortium (CPC)**, in the northern Caucasus, which is an important thoroughfare for oil from Central Asia to the Black Sea and on to Europe. This is the first private pipeline to be built in the former U.S.S.R. The second is the 1,768-km-long **Baku-Tbilisi-Ceyhan (BTC)** pipeline, inaugurated in May 2005.[56] With a projected capacity of 1 MMb/d beginning in 2008, the BTC will enable the former Transcaucasian Republics (Central Asia) to send their oil to the West without having to go through Russia. Even Kazakhstan has signed an agreement with the BTC consortium, giving it a right of transit for its oil to be shipped by tanker to Baku. Up to now, Kazakhstan has sent its oil over the CPC instead (25 million tonnes in 2005).[57] The Russians claim that the CPC route is underused and that there is enough capacity for Kazakhstan to increase the amount of oil transported through this line. In April 2006, Russia and Kazakhstan signed an agreement to increase the capacity of the CPC to 67 million tonnes a year.[58] The agreement between the BTC and Kazakhstan is therefore likely to come under a great deal of pressure, particularly if Russia goes ahead with its project to create a "common economic space" between Belarus, Russia and Kazakhstan.[59] Furthermore, Moscow does not view kindly the agreement between Kazakhstan and Azerbaijan, nor the latter's increased naval presence in the Caspian Sea, which is being encouraged by Washington. Under the policy of ambiguity skilfully wielded by Moscow, discussions are underway (or, more accurately, were restarted in July 2005) to link Novorossiysk with the Georgian section of the BTC.[60] In other words, despite Russian reluctance, possibilities of cooperation with the West in the area of oil distribution networks have not been ruled out

---

56 The primary shareholders in BTC are BP (30.1%); Azerbaijan BTC (25.00%); Unocal (8.90%); Statoil (8.71%); TPAO (Turkish Petroleum Corporation) (6.53%); ENI (5.00%); Total (5.00%), Itochu (3.40%); INPEX (2.50%), ConocoPhillips (2.50%) and Amerada Hess (2.36%).

57 See Sergei Blagov, "Russia Tries to Scuttle Proposed Trans-Caspian Pipeline", *EurasiaNet*, March 28, 2006, at http://www.eurasianet.org/departments/insight/articles/eav032806.shtml.

58 See "Moscou et Astana souhaitent que le réseau d'oléoducs de la Caspienne fonctionne à plein rendement", *Novosti*, at http://fr.rian.ru/business/20060404/45185308.html.

59 See Sergei Blagov, "Russia Registers Significant Victory in Caspian Basin Energy Context", at www.eurasianet.org/departments/ business/articles/eav040506.shtml.

60 This issue has been under discussion for a number of years, but the idea seems to have been taken up again by Rosneftegazstroy. See Khartukov and Tarostina, *op. cit.*, p. 60.

altogether,[61] particularly since Kazakhstan must find a commercial outlet for the oil from its offshore Kashagan field, which is of great interest to BTC shareholders.[62] In June 2006, the Kazakh president agreed to send 25 million tonnes a year through the BTC pipeline.[63] Bets are still off on the final outcome.

Table 8 provides a summary of the high-priority oil pipeline projects in Europe.

Table 8: High-priority European oil pipeline projects

	Capacity	Route	Costs in US$
Druzhba North (route 1)	900,000 b/d Capacity may be increased to 1.3 MMb/d by late 2006.	Belarus/Poland/ Germany	
Druzhba South (route 2)	400,000 b/d	Belarus/Ukraine/ Czech Republic/ Slovakia/Hungary	
Adria (route 3) 750 km	100,000-300,000 b/d when completed	Link with Druzhba South through Slovakia and Hungary to Croatian port of Omisalj on the Adriatic	Flow reversal: $20-30 million Increased capacity: $320 million
BPS (Baltic Pipeline System) (route 4) 2,560 km	> 1.2 MMb/d	From Primorsk, under the Baltic, to Germany with extension possible in the future; Possible construction of a second terminal at Vyborg	$1.4 billion

---

61 According to the *Russian Petroleum Investor,* June-July 2006, p. 35, the purpose of expanding the CPC's capacity is to increase oil tanker deliveries from Novorossiysk to Bulgaria, to meet the needs of the Burgas-Alexandropoulis pipeline, another project favoured by Moscow.

62 Production from this oil field, estimated to have reserves of 2 billion barrels and 1 Bcm of natural gas, is expected to begin in 2008. Two terminals will be built on either end of the Caspian Sea on Azerbaijani and Kazakh soil. Tankers will be used to export the petroleum. The entire project is estimated to cost $4 billion. See *Herold Oil Headliner*, John S. Herold, Inc., June 9, 2006.

63 See "BTC: Kazakhstan Finally Commits to the Pipeline", *Eurasia Insight*, (Business & Economics), June 27, 2006.

Table 8: High-priority European oil pipeline projects

	Odessa-Brody 180,000 b/d Brody-Plock line will soon be increased to 500,000 b/d and later to 900,000 b/d	Ukraine/Belarus/ Poland	Odesssa-Brody: $160 million Brody to Plock: $300-500 million
Odessa-Brody-Plock (route 6)			
SEEL (South East European Line) (route 7)	500,000 b/d	From Constanta (Romania) to Trieste	
Burgas-Alexandropoulis (Route 8)	0.3-0.7 MMb/d	Burgas (Bulgaria) to Greece	$924 million
AMBO pipeline (Albania/Macedonia/ Bulgaria) (route 9)	0.7 MMb/d	Burgas to port of Vlore (Albania)	> $1.2 billion
Murmansk/ Indiga (route 5)	1.6-2.4 MMb/d	From the White Sea to the Atlantic via Barents Sea	Between $10 billion and $15 billion

Russian Supplies of Natural Gas to Europe

As we have seen, Russia has a number of irons in the fire. However, it must first find the necessary financial resources if it wants to develop its Chtokman and Yamal natural gas fields. The former is located 650 km northeast of Murmansk; Yamal, which means "the end of the world" in the Ostyak Samoyed language, is a peninsula that juts into the Kara Sea. Both have significant natural gas potential.[64]

North European Gas Pipeline (NEGP) and Yamal-Europe II pipeline

In Figure 3, the most northern route shown in blue (**route 1**) is the **North European Gas Pipeline (NEGP),** often abbreviated as **NEG.**[65] It has since been renamed the **North Stream** pipeline. From its source field of Chtokman, it is slated to run to Finland, underneath the Baltic Sea to northern Germany and then through

---

[64] 3,200 billion m³ (Bcm) for Chtokman alone. See Élisabeth Studer, "La Russie se renforce sur l'échiquier du gaz", January 26, 2004, *Le BlogFinance*, at www.leblogfinance.com/2006/01/gaz_de_sakhalin.html.

[65] Project partners include Gazprom (51%), E. ON (24.5%) and BASF (24.5%).

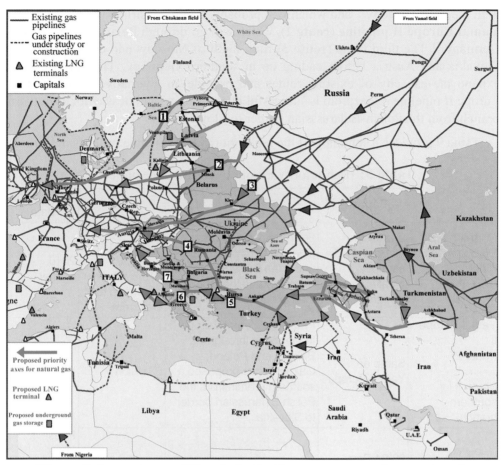

Figure 3: Importance of Russia in the European natural gas network

Source: From Inogate (Interstate Oil and Gas Transport to Europe)
http://www.inogate.org/inogate/en/resources/maps

the Netherlands to the United Kingdom.[66] This route would allow Russia to avoid paying transit dues to its former partners in the Soviet Union. The pipeline, with a capacity[67] of 27.5 billion m^3 (Bcm), was originally slated for completion in 2007 but will not be up and running until at least 2010. The DOE has estimated the cost at $5.7 billion,[68] while Gazprom puts the cost at $10.5 billion.[69] A second pipeline

---

[66] 1,120 km (700 miles) of the 3,200 km (2,000 miles) pipeline will run under the Baltic Sea. Another will go through Finland. A branch to Sweden is also planned.

[67] According to the *Oil & Gas Journal* of February 13, 2006, p. 66, Gazprom already had plans for a second parallel pipeline. The combined capacity of NEGP 1 and II would be 55 Bcm.

[68] See DOE, EIA, "Major Russian Oil and Natural Gas Pipeline Projects", March 2005.

[69] See *Global Pipeline Monthly*, Vol. 2, No. 4, April 2006. Other sources (*Agence France Presse*, December 9, 2005) mention a total cost of $4.7 billion.

with the same capacity[70] and which will probably begin construction in 2012, is the **Yamal-Europe II pipeline (route 2)**, which will go through Belarus and Poland to Germany.[71] The third route **(route 3)** runs south of Moscow and crosses Ukraine, Slovakia and Austria before ending up in southern Germany. The purpose is to expand the capacity of existing routes and provide an alternative to the Yamal-Europe II pipeline if Gazprom is successful in securing a right of way for a southern branch from the Polish-Belarusssian border to Slovakia.

Table 9 provides a summary of the high-priority gas pipeline projects in Europe.

Table 9: High-priority European gas pipeline projects

	Capacity	Route	Cost	Completion date
Northern European Gas Pipeline **(NEGP)** (route 1)	27.5 Bcm; 55 Bcm annually, if parallel pipeline constructed	From Shtokman (gas pipeline) to Finland then under the Baltic Sea to Germany and then through the Netherlands to the U.K.	$6.7 billion according to the DOE; $10.5 billion according to Gazprom	2010 or later
Yamal-Europe II (route 2) (route 3 for southern branch)	Same as Yamal-Europe I	Parallel to Yamal-Europe I; to Germany through Belarus and Poland; Gazprom has proposed a southern branch from the Polish-Belarussian border to Slovakia	$2 billion	
Nabucco pipeline (Corridor 4) (route 4)	23-31 Bcm when completed		4.5 billion euros	Phase 1: 2010 Phase II: 2012 Operational in 2015
SEEGR (South-East European Gas Ring) (routes 5 and 6)	8-10 Bcm between Greece and Italy	Reversible flow between Greece and Italy and between Greece and Turkey	350 million euros for Italy-Greece section; 650 million euros for the Greece-Turkey section	2010

---

[70] Possibly 30 Bcm or 1,060 cubic feet per year. See DOE, EIA, "Major Russian Oil and Natural Gas Pipeline Projects", March 2005.

[71] From its origin, the Yamal II pipeline will run parallel to the Yamal I (see Figure 2) to a point northwest of Moscow.

SEGR (South European Gas Ring) (route 7)		From Turkey to Slovenia (also maybe to Austria), through Greece, Macedonia, Serbia, Bosnia-Herzegovina and Croatia	2010	
ITC (Turkey-Greece Interconnector)	11.4 Bcm	Karacabey (near Bursa) to Komotini (near Alexandropoulis) under the Sea of Marmara		

Source: *Oil & Gas Journal*, February 13, 2006 and March 27, 2006, and
DOE, EIA, *Country Analysis Briefs*, "Russia", January 2006.

Black Sea, Caspian Sea and Middle East

Again, note Turkey's important role as a transit zone for natural gas from the Caspian Sea countries (Azerbaijan and Iran) and from Turkmenistan and Kazakhstan. The same is true of Romania (**route 4**), through which a 500-km section of the **Nabucco pipeline** runs.[72] This pipeline route, also known as Corridor 4, goes from Erzurum, Turkey through Bulgaria, Romania and Hungary to Baumgarten, Austria.[73] In January 2006, the Austrian press described the situation as follows:

Readers should note that the Nabucco project is being undertaken by the Austrian company OMV and specialized gas transmission firms in Turkey, Bulgaria, Romania and Hungary. The Nabucco is the largest pipeline project in recent years. Its purpose is to supply natural gas from the Caspian Sea region and the Middle East to the European market and provide an alternative to natural gas from Russia and Norway. At a length of 3,300 km, it is expected to cost 4.6 billion euros. The first 2,000-km section, between Ankara and the Erdgas Baumgarten hub at the Austrian-Hungarian border, will be completed in 2010. It will then be extended to Iran's border region, Turkey and Georgia.[74]

Recently, Gaz de France became a partner in the pipeline, which may help the project stay on schedule. The first section (2,000 km) is expected to be completed in 2010 and the second (1,300 km), in 2012, and the pipeline should be up and running

---

[72] This project is part of the TransEuropean Network (TEN) supported by the EU.

[73] Corridor 4 includes the Gulf region and the Caspian Sea. Other corridors comprise LNG, North Africa, North Sea and Norway and Russia. See presentation by Valentin Kunev, "Balkan Region Oil and Gas Supplies and Diversification Prospects", BBSPA (Balkan and Black Sea Petroleum Association), Sofia, September 2005, available at www.bbspetroleum.com/files/Presentations/BBSPA_Sofia_Presentation.ppt.

[74] Review of Austria's business press, January 17, 2006, at http://www.missioneco.org/statique/autriche/rp/RP%2017%2001%2006.htm.

by 2015. Once commissioned, the pipeline will have a capacity of 23 Bcm, and when fully completed, 31 Bcm.[75] According to other sources, the 3,300-km pipeline could be finished as early as 2010 or 2011, at a cost of $5.5 billion, provided that construction begins in 2008, which would mean that the final decision would have to be made in 2007.[76] This ambitious project could threaten the primacy of Russian gas in Europe and meet 8% of Europe's gas needs. However, the **Nabucco** project was dealt a severe blow in May 2007, when an agreement was signed between Turkmenistan and Russia whereby Turmenistan agreed to increase its gas exports to Russia. This may substantially strain the Turkoman capacity to supply both Europe and Russia at the same time.

Southeastern Europe is seeing an increasing number of pipeline projects. A cooperative arrangement was signed between Greece and Turkey in 2001, followed by a memorandum of understanding (MOU) in March 2002 and an intergovern-mental agreement in February 2003. These agreements support two major undertak-ings. The most ambitious is the construction of the **South-East European Gas Ring (SEEGR) (routes 5 and 6)**, which will primarily benefit Turkey, Greece and Italy[77]. Gas flow will be reversible between Greece and Turkey and Greece and Italy[78], with the two latter countries linked by a submerged pipeline with a capacity of 253 billion cubic feet (Bcf[79]). It should be completed in 2010. An alternative route is the **South European Gas Ring (SEGR) (route 7)** extending from Turkey to Slovenia, through Macedonia, Serbia, Bosnia-Herzegovina and Croatia. Informa-tion about this project is scarce, although, according to the International Gas Union, the pipeline could be extended to Austria.[80] The alternative route 7, supported by the European Commission, does not serve many major natural gas consumers, with the possible exception of Croatia. It is difficult to know whether one or both projects will be implemented; in any case, neither can go ahead without Turkey's consent.[81]

---

[75] See "Gaz de France prévoit d'investir 1,5 milliard dans les gazoducs européens", *La Tribune.fr* at http://www.latribune.fr/Dossiers/energie.nsf/DocsWeb IDC1256F480049C237C125713200713019?OpenDocument.

[76] A. F. Alhajji, "The Politics of Pipelines", *Oil, Gas & Energy Law Intelligence* (OGEL), Vol. 4, No. 1, May 2006 (online edition, unpaginated).

[77] See "Turkey-Greece Natural Gas Pipeline Project", at http://www.botas.gov.tr/eng/projects/allprojects/greece.asp.

[78] This initiative is also known as the Poseidon project, from the name of the Greek and Italian consortium (DEPA and Edison).

[79] Or 7 Bcm.

[80] See www.igu.org/database/2004/ Gas04_belgrade/speechBelgradePanman.pdf.

[81] John Roberts of the Centre for European Policy Studies in Brussels has published an impressive study on Turkey and these issues, although it goes back a few years. See "The Turkish Gate: Energy Transit and Security Issues", October 2004, available in a pdf file at http://shop.ceps.be/BookDetail.php?item_id=1166.

A prerequisite for both projects is the construction, now under way, of the **Turkey-Greece Interconnector (ITC),** which links Karacabey (a little west of Bursa, Turkey) to Komotini (west of Alexandropoulis in Thrace), through a pipeline running under the Sea of Marmara.[82] When completed, the pipeline's capacity will be 11.4 Bcm annually. It is now considered essential to the construction of the Turkey-Greece-Italy gas pipeline.[83] Turkey also plays a key role as a transit zone for gas sent from Central Asia and Iran through the South Caspian Pipeline, also known as the **Baku-Tbilisi-Erzurum (BTE)** pipeline.[84] Turkey is becoming a major strategic east-west artery.

Two projects are also under study with a view to transporting oil and gas through Turkey via a submerged oil pipeline between Aktau (Kazakhstan) and Baku,[85] and a submerged gas pipeline between Azerbaijan and Turkmenistan. Both initiatives are part of a planned trans-Caspian bridge that Russia believes is premature as long as the boundary issues involving the Caspian Sea seabed and territorial waters have not been resolved. One thing is certain: neither Iran nor Russia will support these projects if they do not see them as being in their interest.[86]

This mushrooming of energy networks warrants three observations. First, countries used as oil and gas transit zones are in an unenviable position, often becoming pawns in a larger geopolitical game. For example, there are very few interconnections between southeastern Europe and Belarus, Ukraine, the Baltic States and Poland, although these states serve as transit zones from the oil and gas fields to markets elsewhere. The liberalization of markets and the deregulation of the electric power sector should result in a greater interdependence between nations and better interconnectivity. These trends should also result in a wave of mergers and acquisitions in which the small players are bought out by the bigger ones. The process is no doubt already underway and Gazprom's intention to acquire Bieltransgaz is a sure sign of things to come[87].

Secondly, as the crisis with Ukraine has recently demonstrated, Europe must decrease its energy dependency on Russia and diversify its energy sources. Russia could decide to turn off the taps at any time, which would deprive transit-zone countries of both the revenues and energy supplies required for their economic develop-

---

[82] See "Transit Development in Turkey: Current Situation and Prospective", at www.iea.org/ Textbase/work/2002/seegas/NMCACY.PDF.

[83] See "East-West Corridor", *Global Agenda*, at www.globalagendamagazine.com/2006/ Erdogan.asp.

[84] The project is slated for completion in 2006 at a cost of $1 billion. Its initial capacity of 1.5 Bcm will be doubled in 2007. See *Oil & Gas Journal*, February 13, 2006, p. 67.

[85] By 2012-2013, it should transport oil from the large Kashagan field, which could make up for the future shortfall in Azerbaijani production.

[86] See Taleh Ziyadov, "Europe Hopes to Revive Trans-Caspian Energy Pipelines", *Eurasia Daily Monitor*, Vol. 3, No. 38, February 24, 2006.

ment. Although Finland has been able to resist pressure from Russia, Belarus and Ukraine remain under Moscow's thumb. A similar scenario is currently being played out in Armenia, Georgia and elsewhere in Central Asia. Russia's monopoly over transport and distribution networks nips in the bud any possibility of healthy competition. If Russia does not eventually sign the Energy Charter and open itself up to competition, the future of Russian-EU dialogue is dark indeed. This opinion is shared by Françoise Thom:

> The prospect of the EU widening its membership has accelerated Russia's efforts to get its hands on the energy infrastructures of prospective members. Lukoil and Gazprom are the most active in this area. In the CCEE (Countries of Central and Eastern Europe), major Russian companies are systematically acquiring refineries, distribution networks, pipelines and port infrastructures. In this context, it is easy to understand why Russia stubbornly refuses to acquiesce to EU demands that all hydrocarbon fuel transport within the EU be considered as "internal" and not as "in transit": this would deprive Russia of an important tool for exerting pressure on the CCEE, to which it is linked through bilateral agreements. It is also one of the reasons why Russia refuses to ratify the European Energy Charter.[89]

Thirdly, Turkey has a major role to play on the east-west axis, since it is becoming an essential partner in the transport of oil and gas from the Black Sea, the Caspian Sea and even the Middle East. Based on this notion of a strategic crossroads, new models of cooperation between Russia and Europe could be developed. At present, the northern and southern pipelines running through the Caucasus (CPC and BTC) tend to compete with each other rather than complement one another. This situation could worsen if Moscow brings its iron fist down harder on Kazakhstan (particularly since Russia still has friendly relations with Iran). The die has not yet been cast. But a win-win situation for both parties is still far off.

---

[87] The first pipeline built before the fall of the U.S.S.R. now belongs to Belarus, but the Yamal-Europe pipeline belongs to Moscow. The land on which it was constructed is used by Russia under a long-term lease. Moscow wishes to purchase this servitude, which Beltransgaz is dependent. According to Russia, the pipeline is only worth $500-$600 million, while, according to Belarus, it is worth five times more. See Peter Lavalle, *Weekly Analysis & Commentary*, at http://www.untimely-thoughts.com. See also Marie Jégo, "Moscou presse Minsk de lui céder ses gazoducs", *Le Monde*, April 2, 2006. At present, roughly 20% of Russian gas goes through Belarus. See Marie Jégo, "La Russie menace de relancer la guerre du gaz avec son voisin biélorusse", *Le Monde*, December 16, 2006.

[88] Françoise Thom, "La Russie, la France et l'Europe", Géopolitique de l'Union européenne, available at http://www.diploweb.com/forum/thom2.htm.

Russian Supplies of Oil and Gas to China

The second largest oil importer in the world in 2005, China has accounted for much of the growth in the world demand for crude.[89] It practices a wide-ranging policy to secure its long-term supplies. China's main suppliers of oil in 2006 were the Middle East (Saudi Arabia and Iran) and Africa (Angola is China's biggest supplier of crude), with Russia in fourth place.[90] Chinese dependency on the Middle East has been reduced somewhat but can only increase in the future.[91] Beijing is one of the major competitors in the race for crude oil, vying with the United States, Japan, India and Europe.

Figure 4 shows the extent of Russian gas production in western Siberia. Russian resources in eastern Siberia are sizeable, though lightly exploited at present. According to the U.S. Congressional Research Service (CRS), roughly 25% of Russia's total oil reserves and 6% of its gas reserves are on Sakhalin Island.[92] Eastern Siberia (including the Sakha Republic region and Sakhalin Island and its continental shelf) probably accounts for 20% of all Russian gas reserves.[93] Just as Murmansk is the jump-off point for the Atlantic Basin market, Sakhalin Island could supply oil to Japan, several countries in Northeast Asia and eventually the United States. Major LNG facilities being constructed on the island's southern tip (Prigorodnoye) could serve Asian and American markets.[94]

In 1997, the United States Geological Survey (USGS) estimated that 70% of Russia's oil production and 90% of its natural gas production came from western Siberia.[95] In August, an interagency task force created by Moscow estimated gas reserves in eastern Siberia and the Russian Far East to be 45 trillion cubic metres (Tcm), 70% of which is in eastern Siberia.[96] These estimates appear excessive given

---

[89] David Zweig and Bi Jianhai, in "China's Hunt for Energy", *Foreign Affairs*, Vol. 84, No. 5, September-October 2005, speak of over 30%, while others like the DOE estimate that China was responsible for 40% of the growth in demand in 2000-2004, and still others put its share at over 50% depending on the time frame. For the period 1995-2004, the DOE estimates that China accounted for 25% of the growth in world oil demand. See "Performance Profiles of Major Energy Producers, 2004", March 2006, p. 34. Hereafter cited as *Profile 2004*.

[90] See DOE, EIA, *Country Analysis Briefs*, "Russia", August 2006.

[91] 70% in 2030 according to Pablo Bustelo, "China and the Geopolitics of Oil in the Asian Pacific Region", November 2005, English-language translation from the original Spanish, available at http://www.realinstitutoelcano.org/documentos/226.asp.

[92] See Bernard A. Gelb, *op. cit.*, p.1.

[93] See Igor Tomberg, RIA Novosti, "Future Oil and Gas Development in Siberia and the Russian Far East", at www.pacificenvironment.org/article.php?id=893&printsafe=1.

[94] With a capacity of 9.6 million tonnes per year. The project could be completed as early as 2008.

[95] *Oil and Gas Resources of the West Siberian Basin, Russia*, DOE/EIA-0617, November 1997.

[96] See Roman Kupchinsky, "Russia: Moscow Mulls its China Energy Strategy", September 8, 2006 at http://www.rferl.org/featuresarticle/2006/09/93a2db5a-9043-4482-bb4b-681a2be6f40a.html

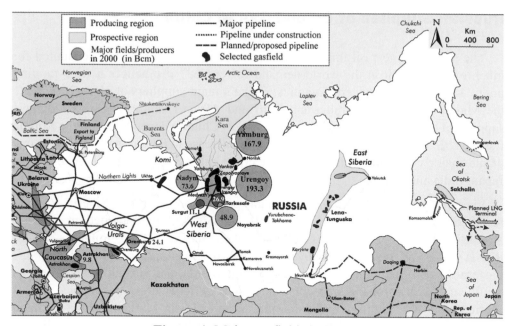

Figure 4: Main gas fields in Russia
Source: IEA, "Security of Gas Supply in Open Markets", 2004, Figure 7.14
iea.org/textbase/nppdf/free/2004/**security**.pdf

that Russia's total gas reserves have been estimated at 47.6 Tcm, according to the *British Petroleum Statistical Review of World Energy 2007*. Nevertheless, the development of eastern Siberia, which suffered greatly after the collapse of the Soviet Union in the 1990s, is one of Moscow's priorities, along with maintaining national unity and the integrity of Russian territory. Illegal Chinese labour is abundant in the Transbaikal, Khabarovsk and Primorye regions, which prompted a remark by the former deputy chief of the Russian general staff, General Valerii Manilov, that in 10 or 15 years China could find itself in a "serious demographic and energy crisis."[97] Although these concerns are not universally shared, they do

---

[97] Cited in Mark Kramer, "Civil-Military Relations in Russia and the Chechnya Conflict", in PONARS (Program on New Approaches to Russian Security), *Policy Memo*, No. 99, Harvard University, December 1999. Manilov's complete statement was as follows: "...in 10-15 years China can find itself on the brink of a serious demographic and energy crisis. As a result China's interest in the energy reserves of Siberia and Russian Far East is growing. Even now illegal immigration is growing (*narastaet*) from China into the strategically important regions of Transbaikal, Kahbarovsk Krai, and Primorye. In some border districts of Primorye, Chinese outnumber Russians by one and one-half to two times. As the migration stream intensifies and broad areas of compact Chinese settlement form in the Russian Far East, the territorial problem between the two states can assume particular sharpness and become highly explosive (*vzrivopasnii*)."

illustrate the thinking in some quarters and particularly the ambiguities inherent in Sino-Russian relations.[98]

The Atasu-Alashankou Oil Pipeline

In 2006, there was still no operational oil pipeline to transport oil from Russia to China. All Russian crude that is currently exported to China goes by rail, tank truck, cargo ship or by seaport.[99] The sole exception is Kazakhstan's **Atasu-Alashankou pipeline** (998 km), which was inaugurated in December 2005 with a capacity of 100,000 to 200,000 b/d.[100] The pipeline's capacity is expected to double in 2011 to 20 million tonnes a year, or 10% of China's imports.[101] Given the connections between Atasu and western Siberian oil, Russia will benefit greatly from the pipeline since part of the oil will be Russian.

This is undoubtedly the price that Kazakhstan has to pay to free itself from the Transneft monopoly's control over its distribution networks. It provides Kazakhstan with an escape route similar to the one Azerbaijan enjoys with the BTC. From Alashankou, Kazakh oil will be shipped by train to the main Xinjiang refineries. Oil deliveries began in May 2006 and should reach 10 million tonnes a year. At a cost of $2.7 billion, Kazakhstan and China have already begun to extend the pipeline upstream to Atyrau, thanks to a link added between Kumkol and Kenkiyak (see Figure 5), which will also give China access to Caspian Sea oil.[102] Furthermore, China plans to double the capacity of the Atasu-Alashankou route by constructing a parallel pipeline that could go into service by 2008-2010. A gas pipeline along the same route is also envisaged to transport gas from Turkmenistan.

---

[98] For Bobo Lo, a combination of the "Mongol complex" and "historical black spots" is largely responsible, for example, for the "hoary myth of millions of Chinese flooding into the sparsely populated spaces of the Russian Far East (RFE) and the reluctance by many to credit Beijing's assurances that it has given up any irredentist claims. Despite the formal demarcation of the frontier, there is a lingering suspicion in Moscow that, when the opportunity presents itself, Beijing will look to recover lost lands by one means or another—if not militarily, then through a 'creeping' expansion that exploits the huge (and growing) demographic imbalance on either side of the border." See Bobo Lo, "A Fine Balance—The Strange Case of Sino-Russian Relations", *Russie.Cei.Visions*, No. 1, April 2005, p. 4.

[99] In 2006 alone, Russia agreed to deliver by rail 15 million tonnes of oil to China. See *Rising Energy Competition and Energy Security in NorthEast Asia*, CRS Report to Congress, RL32466, January 20, 2006, p. 12.

[100] The pipeline was built at a cost of $850 million. See *China Brief*, Vol. 6, No. 3, February 1, 2006, available at the Jamestown Foundation web site: http://www.jamestown.org/publications_details. php?volume_id=415&issue_id=3605&article_id=2370732.

[101] Annie Jafalian, "Équilibres géopolitiques en Asie centrale : La montée en puissance de la Chine", CHEM-CEREMS 2005, available at www.ihedn.fr/portail/cerems/cerems_0510enrgie_dossier.pdf.

[102] See Eugene Khartukov and Ellen Starostina, "Russian Oil Exports, Conclusions", *Oil & Gas Journal*, April 3, 2006, pp. 64-66.

The East Siberia/Pacific Ocean (ESPO) Oil Pipeline

The largest Sino-Russian project is the **East Siberia/Pacific Ocean (ESPO)** oil pipeline. Bilateral discussions between Beijing and Moscow, on one hand, and Moscow and Tokyo, on the other, have been going on for years, with the two Asian countries vying for Moscow's favours. This 4,000-km-long pipeline, with a capacity of 1.6 MMb/d, will cost between $6.5 billion and $11.5 billion (or much more according to the DOE).[103] The Russian Minister of Industry and Trade, Viktor Khristenko, considers the project a "window on Asia." The route of the pipeline has changed significantly over the years, with proposed routes disappearing and reappearing on Chinese maps.[104] Throughout the project's history, Russia has always tried to run with the hare and hunt with the hounds, but the real question is whether the Kovykta field has enough oil to supply both China and Japan.[105] In addition, the proposed route of the Angarsk-Nakhodka pipeline would take it through part of a UNESCO World Heritage Area.[106] As a result, the route was altered slightly and renamed the Taishet-Nakhodka pipeline (the town Taishet is farther northwest of Irkutsk). Although the decision to build the pipeline was originally made late in 2004, Moscow announced in September 2005 that it would be carrying out the project in two phases: first the completion of the Taishet-Skovorodino section, which should be achieved by mid-2008,[107] and then its extension to Nakhodka. Two thirds of the oil would be sent to Daqing over the pipeline, which has a total capacity of 30 million tonnes a year, and the other third to Nakhodka by rail until the Skovorodino-Nakhodka section is completed in 2010. There is no news yet of when the Chinese portion of the ESPO will be constructed. Moscow has thus succeeded in killing two birds with one stone: pleasing both China and Japan without making either country officially loose face.[108] Moscow's procrastination

---

[103] Transport costs will be $38 per tonne, which is 40% lower than current rail costs to China. See Eric Watkins, "Russian Pipeline Challenges Europe", *Oil & Gas Journal*, May 8, 2006, p. 29. The U.S. Department of Energy estimates the pipeline will cost US$16-18 billion in 2005 dollars. See DOE, EIA, *Country Analysis Briefs,* "Russia", January 2006.

[104] See www.chinapage.com/map/russsian-pipeline.html.

[105] To do so, the Kovykta field would have to contain over 2 billion barrels, according to a 2003 statement by *Interfax* cited in the June 9, 2003 issue of the *Oil & Gas Journal*, p. 8. Natural gas reserves in the basin are estimated at over 2 Tcm. Even according to the most optimistic forecasts, the region's production would not exceed 1.6 MMb/d in 2020. See "Russia Energy Summit Executive Seminar", Baker Institute Study, October 2003, at bakerinstitute.org/Pubs/study_23.pdf.

[106] The entire Lake Baikal region in actual fact. See whc.unesco.org/archive/2005/whc05-29com-07Brevf.pdf. On December 31, 2004, the Russian prime minister signed government resolution No. 1737-r defining the final itinerary of the pipeline: Taishet (Irkutsk region) –Skovorodino (Amur region)– Perevoznaya (Primorye region).

[107] *Oil & Gas Journal*, February 13, 2006, p. 66.

[108] Russia probably had no alternative since Japan agreed to fund this pipeline up to an amount of $7 billion. Costs estimated by Moscow range between $15 billion and $18 billion for the 4,130-km oil pipeline.

over building the ESPO has revived tensions between China and Japan. As Catherine Locatelli and Jean-Marie Martin-Amouroux comment:

> Chinese interests run counter to those of a certain number of major powers, which could be a source of significant uncertainties. The rivalry between China, Japan and India for access to hydrocarbon resources is becoming increasingly apparent. The issue of the first Russian oil pipeline to Asia illustrates the conflicting interests of China and Japan over hydrocarbon resources in eastern Siberia, while clashes between these two countries over who owns oil and gas resources in the China Sea will not go away. Similarly, Chinese petroleum companies and the Indian national oil company have found themselves competing over numerous projects, including the acquisition of PetroKazakhstan and Slavneft, the Sakhalin projects and the development of fields in Angola and Libya.[109]

One thing is certain, Moscow's about-turn regarding the ESPO pipeline demonstrates the ambiguity of the Russian government's position.[110]

Russian Gas Exports to China

In March 2006, during President Putin's fifth visit in a year to China, Russia simply reiterated its commitment to the ESPO pipeline and its firm intention to supply China with energy ahead of Japan. To lessen Chinese discontent with the slow progress of these supplies, Moscow promised to provide Beijing with 60-80 Bcm of natural gas per year by 2011, which is double its 2004 consumption.[111] No information was provided on the location of the two promised pipelines, except that China would get gas from eastern and western Siberia.

As Figure 5 shows, there are many possible routes for gas pipelines to China. The first would transport western Siberian gas from Tomsk to Shanshan in Xinjiang. A second route, the long-time favourite of Moscow, goes from Irkutsk to Beijing through Mongolia. China, however, prefers the route from Irkutsk and Chita to Daqing in the southern province of Heilongjiang. A fourth route would bring gas exports from northern Sakhalin Island to Shenyang through Harbin.

According to a *Reuters* dispatch dated March 22, 2006, an agreement was reached on the provision of 30-40 Bcm of natural gas for each of the two proposed

---

[109] Catherine Locatelli and Jean-Marie Martin-Amouroux, "L'intégration internationale des industries chinoises de l'énergie et ses conséquences géopolitiques", LEPII (Laboratoire d'économie de la production et de l'intégration internationales), Grenoble, October 2005, p. 19. Available at http://web.upmf-grenoble.fr/iepe/Publications/publicRech2.html.

[110] *Ibid.*

[111] As of late 2004, Chinese natural gas consumption was estimated to be 39 Bcm, according to the *BP Statistical Review of World Energy 2005*.

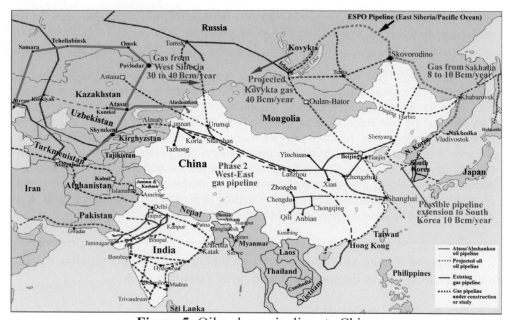

Figure 5: Oil and gas pipelines to China

Source: IEA, "China and India's Energy Development in Global Perspective"
Presentation by Yo Osumi, Beijing, March 2006

routes. If this is correct, the gas from Sakhalin Island is not enough. The main exploitable fields in eastern and western Siberia include Kovykta (Irkutsk), Chaya-dinsk (Yakutsk), Sobinsk-Paiginsk (Krasnoyarsk) and the Sakhalin Island fields, whose size is not yet known. Based on this, gas from both Sakhalin Island and Kovykta would be needed to meet the demand for the first route, while the fields in western Siberia would supply the second route. According to some experts, Moscow's promises are exaggerated,[112] particularly since the Institute of Energy Policy in Moscow predicts that, by 2010, Russia will have an annual shortfall of 100 Bcm annually.[113] It will therefore not be able to meet all its obligations.

Deliveries of Gas from Turkmenistan

A dozen days after President Putin's trip to Beijing, the Forbidden City also hosted Turkmenistan's President Separmourad Nyazov. After the building of the Atasu-Alashankou pipeline with oil-rich Kazakhstan, China is now turning to

---

[112] See R. Kupchinsky, *op. cit.*

[113] See "Russia's Natural Gas in Trouble", *Energy Tribune*, December 13, 2006, available at www.energytribune.com. Production in 2010 is projected to be 732 Bcm, compared with expected demand of 828 Bcm.

Turkmenistan, which has large gas fields. The two countries used the visit to sign a framework agreement on oil and gas. Under Article 2 of the agreement, Turkmenistan promised to provide China with 30 Bcm of natural gas annually for 30 years when the pipeline is commissioned in 2009. Both sides also pledged to jointly explore and develop gas fields on the right bank of the Amu Darya River, the border between Turkmenistan and Uzbekistan. Lastly, under Article 4, the two countries also vowed to set fair and reasonable gas prices by December 2006, based on the prevailing international market price.[114]

Some observers are wondering if Turkmenistan will be able to deliver the goods, particularly since it has already made a commitment to supply 100 Bcm of natural gas annually to Moscow over 25 years, beginning in 2010. It has also made a similar promise to Iran: 8-10 Bcm annually, which will no doubt be increased in 2007.[115] The purpose of this strategy is undoubtedly to get Russia to acquiesce to Turkmenistan's pricing demands.[116] The agreement between Turkmenistan and China specifies that it will not affect in any way the rights and obligations of other parties already bound by international agreements. To meet all these needs, Turkmenistan will have to at least double its current production. Furthermore, relations between it and Uzbekistan are not going smoothly and the route of the gas pipeline to China must pass through Uzbekistan and Kazakhstan. The pipeline will take six years to build at a cost of some $10 billion.[117]

Closer to home, China is planning to modernize its own oil and gas transportation networks. The largest of the proposed projects will double the capacity of the west-east gas pipeline, with a second phase in the works soon (see Figure 5). This 4,000-km-long pipeline, which cost $17 billion, has been up and running since 2004. The construction of the second parallel pipeline will be carried out in two phases. The first phase, to be completed in 2009, will bring the pipeline's capacity to 10 Bcm; in the second phase, to be completed in 2012, capacity will be increased to 40 Bcm.[118] This project illustrates the importance China puts on developing its northwest territories, the home of the Uighur minority which is demanding, in part, the independence of the Xinjiang Uighur Autonomous Region. It also demonstrates China's determination to diversify its sources of supply from Central Asia, which would help to protect it from unexpected disruptions in supplies passing through the Strait of Malacca. Lastly, the Sichuan-to-East China gas project was officially

---

[114] See Sergei Blagov, "Turkmenistan Seeks to Strengthen Energy Ties with China", *Eurasia Daily Monitor*, April 10, 2006, available at www.jamestown.org/edm/article.php?article_id=2370963.

[115] See "Turkmenbashi Pipes Gas to China", *Kommersant*, Russia Daily Online, April 12, 2006.

[116] In September 2006, Turkmenistan got its way. The price of gas delivered to Moscow went from $65 to $100 per 1,000 m³. See Sergei Blagov, "Russia Bows to Turkmenistan's Gas Pricing Demand", *EuraAsiaNet*, September 6, 2006, available at www.eurasianet.org/departments/business/articles/eav090606.shtml

[117] *Oil & Gas Journal*, March 13, 2006, p. 40.

[118] *Oil & Gas Journal*, April 16, 2007, p. 10.

aproved by the state Council on 9 april 2007. The 1,700-km pipeline is expected to channel 12 billion cubic meters of natural gas annually from the Puguang field in Sichuan Province to the central and eastern regions that cover Hubei, Anhui, Jiangxi, Jiangsu, Zhejiang provinces and Shanghai. The pipeline is scheduled to be completed by late 2010 at a cost of US$8.25 billion.

Issues Involving Central Asian Resources

The scope of the parallel agreements concluded one after another between Russia and China and China and Turkmenistan surprised the world and are particularly worrisome to Western nations. The close game being fought between Moscow and Beijing over the exploitation and distribution of petroleum resources in Central Asia could endanger Western interests in the region.[119] Both exploration and development on one hand, and distribution on the other could be affected, and European and East Asian markets could find themselves in a highly competitive situation. Although Sino-Russian relations have been friendly as of late, the two countries have not held back from exercising their pre-emptive rights in the area of oil and gas acquisitions. For example, the Chinese purchase of PetroKazakhstan precipitated Lukoil's acquisition of Nelson Resources Ltd.[120] Although there is cooperation between the two countries, tension also seems to be rising despite a series of high-sounding declarations of friendship issued successively by Moscow and Beijing.

For the time being, the danger is that Moscow is embarking willy-nilly on a frenzy of acquisitions, and neglecting the rebuilding of its infrastructures. This lack of investment concerns the head of the IEA, Claude Mandil, who, in an article in the *Financial Times* stated that Moscow would be unable to meet its obligations to European consumers if it did not concentrate its investments on its domestic infrastructures.[121] Russia is currently investing barely two thirds of the $10 billion it should be spending annually on equipment modernization. The country's stranglehold on the resources of Central Asia and its former satellites in Eastern Europe allows it to delay investing in the development of its new fields at home (Shtokman, Sakhalin and Yamal). Lastly, even though small independent Russian firms are now free to compete with the major state-owned enterprises like Gazprom and Lukoil, it is still a very unequal playing field, since the latter are monopolies that control almost all the distribution networks and set the prices.

---

[119] See the two articles by Andrew Neff, "China Competing with Russia for Central Asian Investments" and "Russian-Chinese Competition may Marginalize US, European Influence" in the March 6 and 13, 2006 issues of the *Oil & Gas Journal*, pp. 41-46 and 39-42.

[120] A small Kazakh producer headquartered in Bermuda. Neff, *op. cit.,* p. 40. Furthermore, Western countries have also exercised pre-emptive rights against China when it expressed its desire to acquire a piece of the pie of the huge Kashagan field north of the Caspian Sea.

[121] Cited on EurActiv.com, April 18, 2006. See www.euractiv.com/Article?_lang=FR&tcmuri=tcm: 28-153594-16&type=News.

As for China, recent experience suggests that it has the necessary funds to meet its oil and gas needs.[122] According to Pablo Bustelo, professor of applied economics at the University of Madrid, China began (1992-1995) by making a few experimental acquisitions in Thailand, Canada, Peru and Indonesia. During a second stage (1997-2002), it became actively involved in acquisitions involving oil and gas in 18 countries. Lastly, during a third stage (mainly since the war in Iraq), it accelerated its acquisitions in Algeria, Gabon, Egypt, Brazil, Argentina, Iran, Venezuela and Canada.[123] The battle with Moscow, despite the high-sounding declarations of solidarity, is far from over. China is thirsty for energy. In 2006, under the auspices of the Shanghai Cooperation Organisation (SCO), it formalized the creation of a working group on energy, in accordance with a proposal Russia made to Beijing during a SCO summit.[124] This was a smart move in the sense that it gives the Central Asian Republics a broader forum for discussion, so that they do not have to deal one-on-one with Moscow. Moscow would like to make Central Asia into an energy-producing region firmly under its control, while China would like to transform the region into an economic zone favourable to Chinese trade and investments. Although the Central Asian countries agree on what they do not want –a U.S. presence in Central Asia– they do not hesitate to take on new petroleum customers when it serves their interests.

Sino-Soviet Energy Relations

China and Russia have sometimes been allies, sometimes enemies. By 2006, Moscow and Beijing were no longer talking about their common struggle against capitalism, but rather about building a multipolar world that left as little room as possible for the United States. In the 1950s, Stalin was not far off the mark when he compared China to a radish: red on the outside and white on the inside. In the 1960s, Raymond Aron wrote that two major powers sharing a common border were more likely to take offence than if they did not share a border. What is the situation today with China and Russia?

---

[122] According to the World Bank's office in Beijing, in June 2005, China had US$711 billion in foreign currency reserves. According to the IMF's *World Economic Outlook 2005,* this amount will increase to $1.0 trillion and $1.3 trillion in 2006 and 2007. See Table 35 in the *World Economic Outlook,* Statistical Appendix.

[123] Bustelo, *op. cit.*

[124] Created in June 2001, the SCO includes Russia, China, Kazakhstan, Kyrgyzstan, Tadjikistan and Uzbekistan. Mongolia has had observer status since 2004, and India, Iran and Pakistan since 2005. Discussions are underway with Afghanistan. Originally established to fight terrorism, separatism and extremism, the organization now has economic and energy objectives.

Table 10: Major Russian and Chinese oil and gas companies, 2004
The figures in parentheses show the firm's ranking among the world's top 130 oil and gas companies according to Petroleum Intelligence Weekly[125]

Russian firms	Oil reserves in millions of barrels (MMb) (1)	Gas reserves in billions of cubic feet (Bcf)	Oil production in thousands of barrels a day	Gas production in millions of cubic feet a day (MMcf/d)	Assets in millions of US dollars	Number of employees
Lukoil	15,972 (9)	24,598 (20)	1,735 (12)	475 (65)	29,761 (23)	150,000 (4)
Gazprom	14,372 (11)	1,140,000 (11)	240 (50)	52,574 1	115,441 (4)	332,800 (3)
Surgutneftegaz	7,211 (21)	15,359 (28)	1,197 (19)	1,385 (29)	22,389 (30)	82,717 (13)
Yukos	12,581 (12)	4,490 (50)	1,714 (13)	331 (71)	?	?
Rosneft (see Note 1)	4,745 (26)	137,670 (7)	433 (36)	887 (43)	25,987 (26)	50,200 (22)
Chinese firms						
PetroChina	11,019 (14)	44,645 (27)	2,124 (9)	2,786 (19)	73,605 (10)	424,175 (1)
Sinopec	3,267 (32)	3,033 (60)	749 (25)	566 (56)	52,273 (13)	389,451 (2)
CNOOC	1,455 (?)	4,646 (?)	380 (?)	110 (E)	11,366	2,696 in Dec. 2005

Note 1: Since Yukos was dismantled, Rosneft has become, after Lukoil, the second largest Russian oil producer. This is due essentially to Rosneft's acquisition of Yuganskneftegaz, which does not appear in the table. Rosneft's gross revenues in 2005 are estimated at $25.5 billion.

Source: Petroleum Intelligence Weekly, Special Supplement, December 12, 2005 and for CNOOC (China National Offshore Oil Corporation), John S. Herold, Inc., Company Insights, June 22, 2005 and CNOOC's 2005 annual report.

---

[125] The ranking by *Petroleum Intelligence Weekly* is based on six criteria: oil reserves and production, gas reserves and production, refining capacity and sales revenues, all with equal weighting. The final ranking is based on the mean cumulative total of the rankings obtained.

China has been a net importer of oil since 1993 and its dependence on foreign supplies is increasing as time goes on. It does not lack resources, however. In terms of reserves, PetroChina ranks 14th among major oil firms, compared with 9th and 11th for Lukoil and Gazprom.[126] There is not a large gap between major Russian and Chinese firms. When cumulative reserves are taken into account, however, PetroChina's holdings pale beside those of the Russians. In 2005, Gazprom, the world's largest gas producer, had 1,140 trillion cubic feet[127] (Tcf) of gas reserves (or over two thirds of all the country's reserves), compared with PetroChina's 45.6 Tcf (25 times less than Gazprom). On the other hand, PetroChina produces more oil than Lukoil and ranked first among the 130 firms surveyed by *Petroleum Intelligence Weekly* (PIW) for number of employees (425,000 versus 333,000 for Gazprom). As readers can see, the relations between the two countries are asymmetrical. The same is true for assets: PetroChina and SINOPEC together form a larger economic unit than the largest Russian firm, Gazprom.

In Russia, two firms dominate the scene: Gazprom and Rosneft, both state owned.[128] As part of the massive restructuring that occurred in the Russian oil and gas industry, Gazprom acquired Sibneft for $13 billion and Rosneft acquired Yuganskneftegaz for $9.4 billion.[129] This gave Gazprom additional production capacity of 660,000 b/d and Rosneft, over 1 million b/d.[130] Both firms are headed by close associates of President Putin: Gazprom by Dmitri Medvedev, who is also first deputy prime minister of Russia, and Rosneft by Igor Sechin, Deputy Chief of Staff. Moscow has its energy destiny well in hand. By opening up these firms to the West, Moscow intends to allow them to tap into Western capital and technologies. The big multinationals must come to terms with these new realities.

---

[126] According to the ranking by *Petroleum Intelligence Weekly, Special Supplement,* December 12, 2005. See also the footnote accompanying Table 10.

[127] 1.140 Tcf = 1,140 Bcf.

[128] Rosneftegaz, which not only controls Rosneft but also 10% of Gazprom's shares, could become the number three company in the public oil and gas sector. "The question is how Rosneftegaz will pay back its debts: by refinancing or an IPO for Rosneft. The second seems more probable", commented Alexandre Razouvaiev, head of the analysis department of the financial company Megatrustoil. See Gazeta.Ru, "L'État entre Gazprom et Rosneft", at http://fr.rian.ru/analysis/20060517/48241808.html.

[129] *Ibid.*

[130] Locatelli and Martin-Amouroux, *op. cit.*, p. 12.

On the Chinese side, three major players dominate the oil and gas sector, each with different roles: CNPC and Sinopec, which are responsible for onshore production, and CNOOC, for offshore production. They also differ in other respects:

> CNPC is in charge of production mainly in northern and western China, and Sinopec in the south and east Refining facilities are divided among Sinopec (56%), CNPC (42%) and CNOOC (9%); and distribution assets between Sinopec (41%) and CNPC (20%). These firms have been transformed into joint stock companies under a "corporatization" process that is typical in former planned economies when there is a need to partially open the economy up to new capital. CNPC is 90% state run, and Sinopec, 56%, which allows the government to have a firm hand in guiding corporate strategy.[132]

In actual fact, economic relations between the two countries have always centred on energy and the arms trade. In 1993-2003, Russia sold $13 billion worth of arms to its eastern neighbour. For the last few years, according to a report submitted to Congress by the U.S. Defense Department (*China Military Power 2005*), China has continued to buy Russian arms at a rate of $3 billion a year. All observers are well aware of the seemingly close relations between Moscow and Beijing, but according to Bobo Lo, this cooperation "is accompanied by a palpable and pervasive sense of unease." The author adds:

> On the other hand, the drawbacks to expanded economic cooperation with China are by no means negligible. Oil and gas exports to China help drive the furious pace of modernization in that country, a modernization fundamental to its transformation into a global power. Similarly, the transfer of arms and weapons technology enhances Chinese military capabilities, with potential consequences not only for regional stability, but also for Russia's own long-term security (including the possibility that such hardware and know-how could one day be used against it). Such fears, exaggerated though they may be, have considerable resonance across the Russian political spectrum, from westernizing liberals to 'great power' nationalists (***derzhavniki***).[133]

For Russia, a partnership with China is mandatory. And China needs Moscow, since the former cannot carry out its penetration of Central Asia without Russia's tacit support. In oil and gas production, refining and distribution, the two countries are pursuing the same strategies, objectives and ends: to go global and compete

---

[131] Bobo Lo, *op. cit.*

[132] Thanks to, it appears, a Chinese loan of $6 billion. China will be well placed to make a minority buyout offer for Yuganskneftegaz, which India is also interested in. See Gabe Collins, "With Oil Companies, Russia Seeking Control Plus Capital", *Oil & Gas Journal*, May 15, 2006, pp.18-22.

successfully in the international arena. Moscow intends to maintain control over its gas and oil fields, which contain over a billion barrels in oil reserves and 1,000 Bcm in gas. This market remains largely closed to foreign capital. On the other hand, Russia is ready to open its doors to foreign investment in remote regions or fields where foreign technology is essential to exploit the resources. The United States is impatiently waiting for Russia to clarify its regulations on subsurface rights.[133] Moscow's decision to review the Sakhalin II project, on the pretext that it does not meet the government's environmental objectives, and to exclude Western firms from equity investment in the Shtokman project augur poorly for future relations between Russia and multinational oil companies. China is also keeping careful control over its own oil and gas companies. Under a deliberate strategy formulated by former leader Deng Xiaoping and at a faster pace than Russia did, Beijing has been able to form contacts with the major Western firms and secure cooperative or joint venture agreements.[134]

Towards a Pan-Asian Pole?

Describing in depth all the factors that could affect the stability of oil and gas markets would take too much time here. In large measure, geopolitics is a product of geographic constraints: concentration of resources, essential means of transport and routes, disruptions in supplies and energy security. These elements of a classic analysis should be expanded to include areas of regional instability and bilateral conflicts, as well as countries at risk of civil war. The list is long and going through it in detail would be too time consuming.

The Middle East is not the only major area of political instability in the world, although it has been torn by many conflicts, including several wars between Israel and the Arab states and involving the United States and the United Nations. Other unstable regions where events are affecting oil and gas production include Africa (particularly Nigeria), Latin America (the wave of nationalization), Central Asia and Indonesia (the irredentism of the Aceh separatist movement). However, most well informed observers agree that, by 2030, the Middle East will regain the dominance over world markets that it enjoyed during the 1973 oil crisis.

---

[133] See "Bush Asks Russia to Clarify New Mineral Plan", *Reuters* and *Washington Post*, October 24, 2005.

[134] Locatelli and Martin-Amouroux found 18 upstream agreements between Chinese petroleum companies and foreign interests. See *op. cit.*, 2005, p. 14.

How about Iran? Some observers, such as Michael Klare,[135] are convinced that the United States wants to seize control of Iran's resources. However, it is highly implausible that Washington would venture into such a morass, particularly after the setbacks it has experienced in Iraq. As for Iran's rapidly evolving nuclear capabilities, they go beyond the framework of this study.

Instead, we would like to focus on the situation in Asia: the confrontation between China and Japan, the apparent rapprochement between China and India and recent events in Central Asia that could have an enormous impact on the outlook for oil and gas production.

The enmity between China and Japan has a long history. Japan's imperialist past is a fixture of Chinese textbooks and the former Japanese Prime Minister Junichiro Koizumi fanned the flames by making repeated visits to the Yasukuni Shrine[136]. Certain contested territories and islands in the East China Sea are also grist for conflict. Ownership of the Diaoyutai Islands (which the Japanese call the Senkaku Islands) would allow Tokyo to extend its exclusive economic zone to a portion of the East China Sea, where major exploration activities by CNOOC are underway[137]. Japan has accused China of "siphoning off" its gas, baptized Chinese exploration blocks with Japanese names, passed laws authorizing Japanese companies to prospect in the same region and occasionally sent air patrols to monitor Chinese activities. In certain right-wing quarters of Japan's Liberal Democratic Party, people have been saying that the time for talking is over and Japan should just go ahead and drill in the region.

Although the dispute may get ugly from time to time, a major showdown is unlikely as long as Japan and China are bound by close economic ties. In oil and mining (coal) exploration, the Japan Bank for International Cooperation (JBIC) gave China loans totalling $140 billion during the period 1979-1997.[138] The conflict between Beijing and Tokyo eloquently illustrates the principle that one party's

---

[135] Michael Klare, "Oil, Geopolitics, and the Coming War with Iran", at http://www.commondreams. org/views05/0411-21.htm.

[136] Actions declared unconstitutional by the Osaka High Court. Koizumi repeated the offence on August 15, 2006, to the great displeasure of China, which accused the outgoing Prime Minister of tarnishing Japan's international image. The temple was built to honour the memory of the victims of the Second World War, but also honours convicted Japanese war criminals.

[137] There are also territorial disputes between South Korea and Japan over the rocky islets variously called the Liancourt Rocks, the Dokdo Rocks (by the Koreans) and the Takeshima Rocks (by the Japanese). Each country wants to use the islets to extend its territorial waters and hence its fishing zones. See Peter Beck, "East Asia's Troubled Waters" at http://www.crisisgroup.org/home/ index.cfm?id=4086&l=1.

[138] See Tsutomu Toichi, "Energy Cooperation and Competition Between Japan, China and the U.S.", IEEJ (Institute of Energy Economy Japan), Ninth Meeting of China-Japan-U.S. Trilateral Dialogue, Beijing, March 20-21, 2006, p. 3.

search for energy security is a source of insecurity for the other party. Cooperation between the two countries is fraught with difficulties, but still exists. No bilateral negotiations have been successfully completed up to now, although both parties have spoken now and then of "joint exploration", but each interprets the term differently.[139]

Major changes are afoot in Southwest Asia. In the best tradition of "offensive realism" advocated by political scientist John J. Mearsheimer—who has claimed that the United States cannot impose its hegemony on the entire planet but rather only on specific regions at a time thanks to support from allies or nations that side with it—the Bush administration is pressuring Japan to assume more military responsibilities in the region. Washington has signed a strategic partnership agreement (which remains yet to be implemented) with India in the nuclear and space fields. Is Washington's purpose to prevent India from going ahead with its Iran-India gas pipeline to Pakistan? Some people think so, but India has much bigger projects in mind: some quarters are toying with the idea of building a pan-Asian oil and gas network.

New Delhi has a 2.5 MMb/d shortfall of oil and the U.S. Energy Information Administration (EIA) forecasts that the country will have a mean annual economic growth rate of 3.5% between now and 2025.[140] Oil makes up 34% of India's energy basket, and the annual growth in its gas demand has been estimated at 5.1%.[141] In 2015, annual demand for gas should reach 1.8 Bcf. As for oil, in 2025, imports should reach 7.4 MMb/d. Therefore, India has a pressing need for hydrocarbon fuels and competes directly with China to secure supplies. The Oil and Natural Gas Corporation (ONGC), the largest Indian oil company, is carrying out prospecting and exploration in Cuba, Vietnam, Russia (Sakhalin I), Sudan and Myanmar.[142] It is also actively seeking operatorships in Brazil (ExxonMobil's interests in the Campos Basin), Syria (acquisition of Petro-Canada's interest in the al-Furat deposit), Libya

---

[139] See Wenran Jiang, "East Asia's Troubled Waters –Part I", *YaleGlobal Online, www.yaleglobal.yale.edu.*, April 25, 2006. "To Japan, it means that China must stop current projects, turn over all geological data to Tokyo before both sides can share the potential resources of the region, including the gas fields developed by CNOOC on the Chinese side of Japan's own declared median line. The Chinese find such demands unacceptable, with Beijing interpreting "joint-exploration" as Japan not interfering with any current Chinese development on the Chinese side, even according to Japan's median line. Instead, China agrees to share resources found in the disputed area between the two median lines claimed by Tokyo and Beijing."

[140] The country's annual growth rate in 2005 was 6.9% and should be similar in 2006 (6.7%). See EIA, *Country Analysis Briefs,* "India", December 2005.

[141] *International Energy Outlook 2006.*

[142] Negotiations are underway between India and Myanmar on importing gas via Bangladesh, a country that is also well endowed with gas reserves. The construction of a gas pipeline between Myanmar and India could restart discussions on the possibility of Indian imports of Bangladeshi gas.

(Gulf of Sidra), Angola and Nigeria.[143] China is obviously not blind to India's needs and the two countries' major national oil companies, CNPC and ONGC, have signed the Memorandum for Enhancing Cooperation in the Field of Oil and Natural Gas.[144] Indeed, China and India can be found operating side by side in Sudan or Syria. Sino-Indian cooperation has not, however, prevented PetroChina from acquiring, at the last minute and to India's great displeasure, PetroKazakhstan at a cost of $4.1 billion. A few months earlier, CNOOC lost its bid to acquire UNOCAL, now owned by its U.S. competitor Chevron.

Despite the fierce competition among them, Asian countries also have an interest in cooperating with one another. Several times in the past, during summits of Asian gas producers and consumers or round tables of Northern and Central Asian energy ministers, India has proposed the establishment of a pan-Asian energy network, which would cost $22.4 billion. According to *Hindu Times* correspondent Siddharth Varadarajan, the project would have four phases:

> The first would extend the existing Baku-Tbilisi-Ceyhan pipeline system –originally conceived by the US as a means of shipping central Asian hydrocarbons westwards– down to the Red Sea via Syria, Jordan, and Saudi Arabia, allowing Caspian crude to be exported easily to the Indian Ocean littoral. Second is the famous Iran-Pakistan-India pipeline, with the possibility of two additional sourcing spurs, one from the Caspian-Turkmenistan region to Iran, the other from Turkmenistan via Afghanistan. The third element would be a pipeline system connecting eastern India to Myanmar and southwestern China with one connection running from Sittwe on the Burmese Bay of Bengal coast to Mizoram, Manipur, and Assam into China, eventually connecting up to the West-East China gas pipeline near Shaanxi, the other from Yangon to Kunming. The fourth element would involve the laying of pipelines that would connect the Sakhalin deposits in Russia to Japan, China, and South Korea.[145]

Several comments are in order here. First and foremost, India intends to adopt a well-defined Asian vocation. After founding the Non-Aligned Movement in the 1950s, today it is eyeing Asian governments, which it believes must escape the "Western world's wretched domination", in the words of Indian cabinet minister Shankar Aiyar. After the peaceful emergence of China and the somewhat more brutal awakening of Iran, are we in the process of witnessing the political and

---

[143] In Nigeria, the $6 billion project extends to refining and electricity production. See *Country Brief, India*, John S, Herold, Inc.

[144] Signed January 12, 2006 by the Indian Petroleum and Natural Gas Minister, Mani Shankar Aiyar, and the Minister in Charge of the Chinese National Development and Reform Commission, Ma Kai.

[145] Siddharth Varadarajan, "Energy Key in the New Asian Architecture", at http://www.thehindu.com/2006/01/25/stories/2006012506601300.htm.

economic rebirth of India, or even the emergence of a strengthened Asian identity in the broader sense? Although opinions are divided over the former, there is even less agreement on the pan-Asian energy network, even within the Indian government itself. Indian Prime Minister Manmohan Singh ventured as far as saying that his government must first feed its people before making energy a priority. Furthermore, India is being courted by Russia, which puts it in a better negotiating position over oil and gas supplies. However, it is universally acknowledged that additional Russian supplies will have to come mainly from Central Asia. Under the current conditions, it is difficult to know whether China will invite India to become a member of the Shanghai Cooperation Organisation (SCO).

Secondly, despite the prospect of various pipelines from Myanmar possibly supplying India with natural gas in the future, there is actually nothing new on offer. The proposed route from Myanmar studiously avoids Bangladesh (see Figure 5); therefore, this project was probably intended to supply China rather than India. Most of the pieces of the pan-Asian network described earlier are already under construction, although there was no conscious intention in the past to create such a network. In fact, it seems a bit grandiose to speak of it. Furthermore, India has already embarked on the LNG route and Oman and Qatar would be only too happy to supply the west coast of India and Australia, to supply the east coast. Iran's commitment to provide 5 million tonnes of LNG to India over a 25-year period is being held up by a dispute over prices that has been going on for several years. The original contract stipulated a price of $3.25 per million BTUs, but Iran is now asking for $5.10.[146] Owing to the recent thaw in India's relations with Pakistan, the United States and China, New Delhi probably has more room to manoeuvre now than it did in the past.

Thirdly, either out of a fit of pique or lassitude, Iran recently signed a gas supply contract with Pakistan. The volume to be supplied will increase from 2.2 to 2.8 Bcf/d, a rise of 33%. The agreement on constructing the gas pipeline is supposed to be formalized at a cost of $2.5 billion. India is not excluded from the project, however, since Iran is thinking about constructing a second pipeline from the North Pars field with Indian consent. The first pipeline would run from the South Pars field to Bhong, in the Rahimyar Khan region of Pakistan. However, for the first time, Iranian authorities recently referred to this project as the Iran-Pakistan (IP) pipeline, while its former name, the Iran-Pakistan-India (IPI) pipeline, has suddenly disappeared from the Iranian lexicon.[147] All bets are off on the completion of the IPI pipeline, therefore. There are also projects in the works to ship gas from Turkmenistan to Pakistan.

---

[146] See RFE/RL *Iran Report*, Vol. 9, No. 28, August 1, 2006.

[147] See Khaleeq Kiani, "Pakistan to get 33 Per Cent more Gas: India almost Out of Iran Pipeline Project", May 1, 2006, at http://www.dawn.com/2006/05/01/top1.htm.

The Geopolitics of Oil and Gas

When it comes to oil and gas, there are a thousand and one factors that could influence the way a country chooses to play its cards. By way of a conclusion, we will summarize some of the most important ones:

There are three main global centres (or heartlands) of oil and gas production: the Middle East, Russia and Central Asia. The first will grow in importance in the future, while Russia's and Asia's reserves will continue to decline despite temporary increases in production.

The vertical integration of major petroleum companies allows them to play a dominant role in the production, transport and distribution of oil and gas. Russia has taken advantage of its state-owned firms' monopoly to regain control of oil and gas infrastructures in Central Asia, the Caucasus and Eastern Europe. To make its former partners bow to its demands, Moscow has gone so far as to cut off supplies or has simply acquired their oil and gas facilities.

Geography is a determining factor in Russia's desire to circumvent transit zones that decrease its profits. The NEGP gas pipeline was constructed for this very reason. In addition, Russia is seeking outlets to the Atlantic and Pacific oceans, either by exploiting its fields in Eastern Siberia and the Russian Far East or by constructing LNG facilities.

In the short term, Russia remains a regional producer, with most of its deliveries going to Europe. Given Transneft's monopoly over distribution networks, Central Asia cannot exploit its reserves without Russia's support. Increased production in Central Asia will result in fierce competition between Russia, which controls the major infrastructures in the region, and China, which has abundant capital that could lure the Central Asian Republics away from Moscow.

Over the longer term, Sino-Russian trade in oil and gas will increase, as will supplies of Russian energy to China. Russian national interests are at stake in the Russian Far East. In addition, Russia will increasingly seek to use energy as a lever for advancing the most important elements of its foreign policy.

On the same subject, Moscow will no doubt continue to maintain its skilful balancing act in granting favours to Tokyo and Beijing. Similarly, by diversifying its deliveries to Asia, Russia will not call into question the security of European supplies, which are guaranteed under long-term agreements. However, the process will still be subject to a differential in oil and gas prices for the two regions in question. This method of doing things will increase the flexibility of Moscow's tariff policies and consequently its room for manoeuvre in economic development.

Sooner or later, Russia will have to choose between cultivating its oil nationalism and opening itself up to Europe. The second option will require Russia to sign the European Energy Charter. This issue is currently hampering the dialogue between Europe and Russia. The globalization of the LNG market will no doubt force Moscow to make concessions in this area, since sales of LNG and natural gas in Europe must meet the same requirements for a liberalized market as those in the Charter.

The globalization of trade and liberalization of energy markets contain their own solutions. Since oil and gas are becoming increasingly rare, major national oil companies (NOC), though less efficient than major multinationals (IOC), will play an increasingly important rule in determining the rules of the game in the future. Supported by their respective governments, they already have a clear advantage over the IOCs in acquiring foreign reserves. The process will result in overbidding, keeping crude prices high.

Despite the concerns of the IEA, the capital required for oil and gas development between now and 2030 will not be lacking. The oil and gas industry will obtain the necessary funds from its own revenues. Exceptionally high crude prices will no doubt facilitate the multinationals' task, but will also serve producing countries' interests. On the other hand, resource development projects in Central Asia will delay major investments by Russia in more remote regions.

Located halfway between the Middle East and Asia, India's geographical situation is much more favourable than China's. Its territory is one third the size of China and its west and east coasts give New Delhi more choices in importing oil and gas. Gas and oil pipelines are one thing; regasification plants are another. Economic choices are a third.

Although China has been accused of "locking up" energy supplies to keep out foreign interests, the overheating of demand that has occurred is simply a manifestation of its dazzling economic growth. China's search in all directions for new energy sources only belies its insecurity regarding supplies. It considers oil and gas pipelines more secure than shipping by tanker through the narrow straits that the country is forced to use as its transit zones. Although China's official line on this matter no doubt suits Beijing ideologically, it is difficult to reconcile with the increased LNG imports the country is counting on in the future.

China likes to insist on its "peaceful emergence" as a nation, which is a work in progress. This desire to keep a low profile, however, is at odds with the country's need to assert its broader economic interests and it does not hesitate to prospect for oil and gas in many countries where human rights are completely ignored. China is not the only country to practice a double standard in this area, however.

Index of names

A

Ahlbrandt, Thomas, 128
Aiyar, Mani Shankar, 278
Al Husseini, Sadad , 120
Alhajji, A. F., 154, 260
Allgeier, Peter , 235

B

Babajan, S.A.W., 108
Ball, Allison, 131
Bard, Édouard, 166
Bardinko, Mohammed S., 148
Baudouin, Colin, 107, 142
Beck, Peter, 276
Becquerel, Antoine, 75
Becquerel, Edmond, 75
Bedard, Roger, 88
Belson, Ken, 120
Benchrifa, Rachid, 92
Bennouna, Abdelaziz, 92
Bentley, Roger, 123
Bertani, Ruggero, 80
Bettayeb, Kheira, 7
Betz, Albert, 74
Blagov, Sergei, 254, 269
Blum, Justin, 70
Blyth, William, 64
Bois, C., 35
Bouche, P., 35

C

Cacchione, David, 36
Campbell, Colin, 123-124
Chabrelie, Marie-Françoise, 220
Chapin, Daryl, 75
Chevalier, Jean-Marie, 141, 153-155
Churchill, Winston, 160, 248
Cincotta , Richard P., 142
Clifton, Andrew, 223
Collins, Gabe, 274
Criqui, Patrick, 116
Crutzen, Paul, 164
Cuchet, Isabelle, 7
Cushman, J.H., 70

Bourdaire, JM, 55-57
Bourque, Pierre-André, 8, 12, 23, 26-27, 36-37, 48
Bustelo, Pablo, 263, 271

D

Dalziel, W. D., 10
Dees, Stephane, 150
DeLalandre, Célia, XI, 240
Delfeau, Simon, 223
Deng, Xiaoping, 275
Desouki, A.H., 108
Dickson, Mary H., 79-80
Dion, Stéphane, 180